✔ KU-185-386

Philip Norman has an international reputation as a chronicler of pop music and culture. *Shout!*, his groundbreaking biography of the Beatles, first published in 1981, has been continuously in print ever since. He went on to write definitive biographies of the Rolling Stones, Elton John, Buddy Holly, John Lennon, Mick Jagger, Sir Paul McCartney, Eric Clapton and Jimi Hendrix. Also an award-winning writer of fiction, he was one of the first authors named in *Granta*'s Best of Young British Novelists. His comedic talents were recently on show in *We Danced On Our Desks: Brilliance and Backstabbing at the Sixties' Most Influential Magazine*.

Praise for *George Harrison*

'Norman has fashioned an authoritative portrait of Harrison that leaves you liking and feeling sympathy for his subject while being fully aware of the tetchiness ... that was never far away'
Will Hodgkinson, *The Times*

'(A) fleet and confident new biography... Norman is hardly the first writer to unspool Harrison's life ... but his status as a respected chronicler of The Beatles, and 1960s culture more broadly, makes this biography a significant addition'
Telegraph

'A deep dive by the acclaimed Beatles biographer paints a revealing portrait of perhaps the most undervalued band member ... A fascinating story about a man of contrasts, and a must-read for fans of the Fab Four'
Woman & Home

'A fully realised portrait of a complex man: spiritual but peevish, brilliantly talented, but for ever shadowed by the Lennon/McCartney axis'
The Times, **Books of the Year**

'Beatles chronicler Philip Norman turns his attention to the shadowy George Harrison ... Norman sheds light on his poor but happy childhood in Wavertree, Liverpool, and traces the path to The Beatles with assurance'
Daily Express

'[A] partial re-evaluation of the most underrated Beatle [which] contains valuable input from Harrison's second wife Olivia and their son Dhani'
Uncut

'You've got him'
Pattie Boyd

'You have taken your readers right down the steps and into the Cavern as it really was'
Bill Harry, editor of *Mersey Beat*

'Norman captures the creativity, the humanity, and the great humour of the man in this keen and lovely tribute'
Booklist, **Starred Review**

GEORGE HARRISON

THE RELUCTANT BEATLE

PHILIP NORMAN

**SIMON &
SCHUSTER**

London · New York · Sydney · Toronto · New Delhi

First published in Great Britain by Simon & Schuster UK Ltd, 2023
This edition published in Great Britain by Simon & Schuster UK Ltd, 2024

1 3 5 7 9 10 8 6 4 2

Simon & Schuster UK Ltd
1st Floor
222 Gray's Inn Road
London WC1X 8HB

Simon & Schuster: Celebrating 100 Years of Publishing in 2024

www.simonandschuster.co.uk
www.simonandschuster.com.au
www.simonandschuster.co.in

Simon & Schuster Australia, Sydney
Simon & Schuster India, New Delhi

A CIP catalogue record for this book is available from the British Library

Paperback ISBN: 978-1-3985-1343-3
eBook ISBN: 978-1-3985-1342-6

Typeset in Bembo by M Rules

Printed and Bound in the UK using 100% Renewable Electricity
at CPI Group (UK) Ltd

CONTENTS

PROLOGUE: AN UNEXTINGUISHABLE
LAST LAUGH

On 29 November 2001, George Harrison dies after a four-year battle with cancer, aged fifty-eight. The 9/11 atrocities were only two months earlier, but despite the continual grim tidings from the still smouldering wreckage of New York's World Trade Center and President George W. Bush's purblind 'War on Terror', his passing leads the television news bulletins and leaps into banner headlines worldwide.

Even at such a time there are no complaints of trivialisation; the Beatles long ago ceased to be just a pop group and became almost a worldwide religion. And, sombre though the coverage, it includes generous helpings of music that, thirty years after their breakup, still has undiminished power to charm and comfort.

Inevitably, it also unlocks memories of John Lennon's assassination in 1980 – but the two tragedies differ in more than their circumstances. That horrifically sudden obliteration of John seemed to have half the human race in tears at what felt like the loss of a wayward but still cherished old friend. With George, struck down by a quieter killer, millions can mourn the musician but there's much less to go on in mourning the man. For no more private person can ever have trodden a stage more mercilessly public.

In later years, he took to calling himself 'the economy-class Beatle', not quite joking about his subordinate status from the day he joined John and Paul McCartney in the Quarrymen skiffle group until almost the end of their time together. Yet by sheer dogged persistence, he made it into the First Class cabin with songs equalling the best if never the vast quantity of Lennon and McCartney's: 'While My Guitar Gently Weeps', 'Here Comes The Sun', 'Something', 'My Sweet Lord'.

As a guitarist, he indisputably belongs in the Sixties' pantheon of six-string superheroes alongside Eric Clapton, Jimi Hendrix, Keith Richards, Jeff Beck and Jimmy Page, though he never considered himself more than 'an okay player'. Alone in that company, he had a serious turn of mind; the Beatles, then commercial pop as a whole, radically changed direction after his discovery of the sitar and embracing of Indian religion and philosophy. Better, rather, to call him the Beatles' Great Minority.

Back in the Beatle madness of the early Sixties, no one would have taken him for an underdog. In live shows, he was adored almost as much as Paul with his fine-boned face, beetling brows and hair so thick and pliant that – as a Liverpool schoolfriend once enviously said – it was 'like a fuckin' te-erban'. But the fine-boned face could be noticeably economical with the cheery grin his fans expected at all times; indeed, it first planted the amazing thought that being a Beatle might not be undiluted bliss.

This was the endlessly self-contradictory 'Quiet One', actually as verbally quick on the draw as John at press conferences; who accepted the workhorse role of lead guitarist, poring dutifully over his fretboard while John and Paul competed for the spotlight, yet offstage was the most touchy and temperamental of the four; who railed against 'the material world', yet wrote the first pop song complaining about income tax; who spent years lovingly restoring Friar Park, his thirty-room Gothic mansion, yet mortgaged it in a heartbeat to finance his friends the Monty Python team's *Life of Brian* film; who, paradoxically, became more uptight and moody *after* he learned to meditate; who could touch both the height of nobility with his Concert For Bangladesh and the depths of disloyalty in his casual seduction of Ringo's wife.

His obituaries agree his finest post-Beatles achievement to have been *All Things Must Pass*, the 1970 triple album largely consisting of songs that John and Paul had rejected for the band or that he hadn't submitted, anticipating their indifference. A blend of his Indian influences and high-octane pop, 'World Music' before the term existed, it far outsold their respective solo debuts and has done ever since: an unextinguishable last laugh.

'My Sweet Lord', the defining track, was an anthem for any creed a year ahead of John's 'Imagine', with a slide guitar motif like a tremulous human voice that would become a signature as personal and inimitable as Jerry Lee Lewis's slashing piano arpeggios or Stevie Wonder's harmonica.

But, as Sir Bob Geldof observes, almost every George Harrison solo or riff planted itself in the mind's ear for evermore ... the pauses as eloquent as words in his masterpiece, 'Something' ... the downward carillon, so full of optimism he wasn't feeling, in 'Here Comes The Sun' ... the 'backwards' solo compounding the euphoric haze of John's 'I'm Only Sleeping' ... the drawn-out jangling coda to 'A Hard Day's Night' ... the jazzy acoustic ripple lending a touch of sophistication to Paul's Cavern show tune 'Till There Was You' ... the languid chords reining back the frenzy of 'She Loves You' ... the Duane Eddying bass notes on 'I Saw Her Standing There' that still exhale the smoky, beery, randy air of Hamburg's Reeperbahn.

The tributes from fellow megastars were numerous and usually heartfelt, albeit sometimes generously sprinkled with amnesia. 'He was a lovely guy and a very brave man – really just my baby brother,' says Sir Paul McCartney, though even royal brothers might not have matched their sniping at each other during the immediate post-Beatle years. 'I feel strongly there was a beautiful soul in him,' says his sitar master and surrogate father Ravi Shankar. 'His life was magical and we all felt we shared a little bit of it,' says Yoko Ono Lennon, about whom George was so horrible during the *Get Back* album sessions that John physically attacked him. 'He found something worth more than fame, more than fortune, more than anything,' says Sir Elton John. 'It takes courage to be gentle,' says Brian May from Queen. 'He was an inspiration.'

His second wife, Olivia – an inconspicuous figure throughout their twenty seven years together until the night in 1999 when she saved his life – issues a statement on behalf of herself and their twenty-three-year-old son and only child, Dhani. His mourners should try to be as positive as he managed to be, Olivia says, for the Hindu precepts he lived by had banished all fear of death. 'He gave his life to God a long time ago. George said you can't just discover God when you're dying ... you have to practise. He went with what was happening to him.'

Still, across every culture and in every language, the same

chill thought occurs, often to somebody born after – in many cases, long after – the Beatles broke up:

Only two of them left.

The first anniversary of George's death is marked by a concert at London's Royal Albert Hall, organised by Olivia and Dhani with support from many prominent figures in the music business. The proceeds will go to the Material World charitable foundation, set up by him in 1974 to support a range of causes and nurtured by a share in his song copyrights, of which the general public has been largely unaware.

The Albert Hall is a red plush-lined Colosseum facing Kensington Gardens, commissioned by Queen Victoria as a young widow to memorialise her adored Prince Consort. It is London's most celebrated classical music venue, principally for the summer Promenade Concerts, or 'Proms', on whose ritualistic last night the audience still sing of Britain as a 'Land Of Hope And Glory'.

It permits rock recitals, too, as a rule as apprehensively as a Victorian dowager would sip Jack Daniel's. But with the Concert for George, there's no cause for concern. Rock is on its best behaviour tonight, banked with flowers, perfumed with incense, and about nothing but love and respect.

There cannot but be poignant reminders of New York's Madison Square Garden thirty-one years ago when George summoned his superstar friends to perform gratis in aid of the victims of famine, floods and genocide in newly created Bangladesh. It was the first significant stirring of social conscience in a music business that until then had seemed only about greed and egotism. And George himself was never more impressive as East and West seemed to meet in his narrow beard and dandyish white suit with an OM badge, marking an advanced meditator – or was it a rose? – in his lapel.

Several of those appearing in the Concert for George also did in the Concerts for Bangdalesh, like Ravi Shankar, who'd turned to his devoted sitar student for help after his own family became caught up in the country's agonies; like Ringo Starr, whose friendship with George survived even being cuckolded by him; like bass-player Klaus Voormann, who befriended him when he arrived in Hamburg aged seventeen in 1960; like Billy Preston, whom he brought into the Beatles' acrimonious *Get Back* album sessions, hoping Preston's keyboard genius and abounding good nature might lighten the combative atmosphere.

The years have taken their toll on these revenants, except for the one least expected to survive them. This is Eric Clapton, both George's best friend and his rival in rock's strangest love triangle, who wooed away his first wife with a song but whom he not only forgave but became even closer to afterwards.

Only it's a very different Clapton than showed up in New York in 1971 so palsied by heroin that George had to dose him with methadone to get him onstage and keep another lead guitarist on standby lest the man his followers called 'God' should keel over where he stood.

Now, long weaned off smack and recovered from eighteen years of alcoholism, he is the Concert for George's musical director. The former pampered, passive deity once incapable of doing anything for himself let alone anyone else, is responsible for keeping the outsize cast in order and on cue as well as filling multiple slots as a soloist or sideman.

Others taking part represent milestones in George's happier post-Beatle musical journey, such as Jeff Lynne and Tom Petty from the Traveling Wilburys who rekindled his enthusiasm for playing in a band during the 1980s. What he would surely think the best milestone, onstage almost throughout, wearing an Indian kurta and playing rhythm guitar, is his son, Dhani, with the same good bone-structure and luxuriant hair as his father but, also, an air of repose possibly owing more to his mother.

There also are random George buddies such as Gary Brooker from Procol Harum and Andy Fairweather Low, formerly of Amen Corner, plus various guest stars' backing groups, all told mustering nine guitarists, two keyboard-players and six drummers, not counting the master percussionist Ray Cooper, a pink, hairless dynamo in granny-glasses who packs the power of at least three more. There are both Indian and Western string orchestras, three female backing singers and two choirs. It looks like a formula for chaos but, thanks to the high calibre of everyone involved and sedulous rehearsals under the clean, new Clapton, the two-and-a-half-hours go without a hiccup.

Just as George decreed at the Concerts for Bangladesh, they begin with a substantial acknowledgement of his Indian influences: a Sanskrit prayer and dedication by Ravi Shankar, a performance of 'Your Eyes' on sitar by his daughter, Anoushka, then of George's own 'The Inner Light' with Jeff Lynne on lead vocal, wearing a contender for Most Annoying Rock Star Hat, then a piece specially written by Shankar entitled 'Arpan', the Sanskrit for 'to give'.

Western audiences today are better informed about Indian music than when Shankar's ensemble at the two Concerts for

Bangladesh were solemnly applauded after their extended tune-up. Nor, this time around, does he need to ask people to show respect by not smoking.

From the sublime to the super-ridiculous, as George was never averse to going, there's a comedy interlude with Michael Palin, Eric Idle, Terry Gilliam and Terry Jones from the Monty Python team whose television show, he always said, kept him sane during the Beatles' breakup and who later prompted his unintended transition into film producer.

Palin does the 'Lumberjack Song', backed by a chorus of Royal Canadian Mounted Police growing increasingly dubious about the tree-chopper's leisure activities. Co-opted as special constables are Neil Innes, creator of the Rutles, the Beatles parody which this ex-Beatle, at least, thought hilarious, and Tom Hanks.

For love of George, Hollywood's biggest male star has crossed the Atlantic to put on a Mountie's red tunic and Boy Scout hat and join in a song that a few years from now will risk being called 'transphobic'.

The concert's Western segment begins with Jeff Lynne, still in That Hat, singing 'I Want To Tell You' from *Revolver*, where for the first time George was allowed *three* songs on a Beatles album.

Then, thanks to John's visionary 'Tomorrow Never Knows', its inventiveness went largely unnoticed – the stuttering tempo like a car engine misfiring, the repetitive atonal piano chord foreshadowing ragas soon to come. And along with its abstract musings about communication, the personal message almost as startling and mystifying as John's 'Help!':

'I feel hung up and I don't know why.'

The focus briefly switches to keyboards and Gary Brooker, the voice of Procol Harum's 'A Whiter Shade Of Pale' doing 'Old Brown Shoe' with Clapton, Fairweather Low, Albert Lee and other noted soloists willingly playing back-up and seemingly stretching to infinity.

The privilege of performing George's best-known works has been allocated with the care of a Nobel Prize committee and there's some surprise when the first, 'Here Comes The Sun' (the most streamed of all Beatles songs) goes to Joe Brown, one of the late-Fifties British popsters they made instantly redundant. Not to George, though, since Brown had played lead guitar for some of his greatest American rock 'n' roll idols, like Eddie Cochran and Gene Vincent, and shared his un-rock 'n' roll passion for the ukulele.

George had continued to make music almost until the end, collaborating with Dhani on an album called *Brainwashed*, a typically blunt reference to his terrible illness, which Dhani would have to finish without him. His last time in a recording studio had been with their jointly written 'Horse To The Water' when the backing track was recorded by Jools Holland's Rhythm and Blues Orchestra. It was only eight weeks before George's death and, too weak to hold a guitar any more, he could only join in the backing vocals.

Tonight, 'Horse To The Water' is sung by Joe Brown's ebullient daughter, Sam, with Holland on piano: the next generation, as it were, showing that all this isn't just about Golden Oldies with their stubbornly ungreying hair. For all its inherent sadness, it's perhaps the show's most exhilarating moment with its vaguely gospel messaging subverted by a sexy fizz of brass.

Tom Petty, George's other ex-'Wilbury', does 'Taxman', that

deeply-felt hymn of hate, then 'I Need You' from *Help!*, his shark face and scary long blond hair so at odds with its mood of adolescent hypersensitivity that when he asks, 'How was I to know you would upset me?' he might be about to pull a switchblade from his boot.

Then Billy Preston at his keyboard lights up the dim plush vault, as expected, wearing a sumptuous checked suit with waistcoat rather than mourning designer-black and the gap-toothed smile that Queen Victoria herself in her bleakest widow's weeds would have found impossible not to reciprocate. His version of 'Isn't It A Pity' beautifully articulates George's sorrow at humanity's inhumanity, none present guessing how grievously the title applies to Preston himself.

Over the years, he's struggled with drugs, alcohol and a homosexuality his strict church upbringing forbade him to acknowledge, been arrested for drunk-driving, assault with a deadly weapon, child-molestation and possessing pornography, and served time for insurance fraud after torching his own house. Three years from now, he too will be gone, having spent a year in a coma after an unsuccessful kidney transplant.

There's a quickening excitement as the climactic time of ex-Beatle participation approaches. Ringo is first with 'Photograph', co-written with George, the best-selling single of his solo career, then Carl Perkins's 'Honey Don't' from *Beatles For Sale* when they were still partly a covers band. That featured yet another solo destined to lodge in the memory, cued by Ringo's faux-Country 'Aw, rock on, George, one time for me . . .'

That Sir Paul McCartney will be up next comes as no surprise. Although the film clip of him and George locking horns at the *Get Back* sessions has always epitomised the Beatles' breakup and they stayed on bad terms until the late Eighties, they'd made up long before George fell ill.

But few people realise the extent of the reconciliation. The final blow for George was being unable to spend his last days at Friar Park for fear of voyeuristic media camped outside its gates, waiting for him to die. So Paul lent him a house in Los Angeles as a refuge that was never discovered.

Nowadays, Paul's stage show includes songs identified with both John and George; hence some slight friction over the generally ego-free setlist. Originally, Eric Clapton had seemed the natural choice for 'Something', which George wrote about his wife, Pattie, when Clapton was already in hot pursuit of her. Paul was to have been allotted 'For You Blue', from *Let It Be*, and 'All Things Must Pass'. But he, too, lobbied for 'Something' on the grounds of having performed it numerous times onstage with a ukulele George had given him.

The diplomatic solution is a shared vocal; Paul starts 'Something in the way she moves . . .' on ukulele at a slightly accelerated, loping pace, then Clapton comes in on guitar at the familiar one. The same happens with 'While My Guitar Gently Weeps', Paul playing the piano intro more dramatic than the most lachrymose guitar, Clapton adding the searing riffs he improvised for it as a supernumerary on the White Album. And Paul still gets 'For You Blue' and 'All Things Must Pass', the latter giving no hint of how little he once thought of it.

If George, somewhere, is tutting a bit about this, Billy Preston will surely restore his smile with a version of 'My Sweet Lord' he'll happily concede to be far superior to his. And he'll be grimly amused that the show's finale is an ensemble version of

'Wah-Wah', written later in the day he walked out of the *Get Back* sessions with no intention of returning, although he did reluctantly the following week.

So the last words from George at the Concert for George commemorate the moment when the economy-class Beatle had finally had enough: ' You made me such a big star, being there at the right time/And I know how sweet life can be/If I keep myself free.'

But they aren't quite its last words. In a surprise coda, Joe Brown comes back out with a ukulele so small that he has to strum it violin-fashion almost under his chin. No rock classic nor cosmic valediction this, but Isham Jones and Gus Kahn's 'I'll See You In My Dreams', dating from 1924: a Cockney-sparrow version, one might say, of 'Goodnight, sweet Prince'.

As the uke's plinkety-plonk echoes cheekily around a space built for great orchestras and choirs, everyone somehow knows this is the part of the evening its dedicatee would have liked best.

PART ONE

1

'TAKE CARE OF HIM BECAUSE HE'S GOING TO BE SPECIAL'

The modest childhood homes of John and Paul in the Liverpool suburbs long ago joined the medieval castles, great country houses and historic monuments preserved for posterity by Britain's National Trust – although each is less a monument than a shrine.

No such honour has been given to George's beyond-modest birthplace in Wavertree, a couple of miles from the Lennon and McCartney properties. Number 12 Arnold Grove remains in private ownership, inexplicably denied even a commemorative plaque. It is a monument without an ID; a shrine without a Beatle-fringed saint; nonetheless, multitudes of his fans from all over the world have found their way to it and worshipped remotely from the pavement.

George's parents, Harold and Louise (née French), moved into 12 Arnold Grove directly after their marriage in 1931, for a weekly rent of ten old shillings (about 50p in today's money). Louise gave birth to a daughter also named Louise there a few months later, then to two sons, Harry and Peter, in 1934 and 1940.

George was born on 25 February 1943 in the same room – and

same bed – as his three siblings had been. The Second World War still had two years left but the tide had well and truly turned against Nazi Germany, and the blitz on Liverpool's docks and naval installations unleashed in 1940 had long since ended. There were no more wailing air-raid sirens at dusk, no more terrified nights in flimsy Anderson shelters or under tables.

His eleven-year-old sister, Louise, held him in her arms when he was only eight hours old. She would always remember their mother's words: 'Take care of him because he's going to be special.'

His father registered his birth, naming him just George without consulting his mother. 'If it's good enough for the King [George VI],' Harold declared, 'it's good enough for him.'

Ironically for someone so obsessively private, we owe the most intimate view of his earliest years to George himself.

In 1995 the Beatles made the comeback that had been awaited for more for than a quarter of a century with their multimedia *Anthology*, a set of double albums of studio out-takes and rarities and a film documentary with all three survivors taking part, their old animosities laid to rest at last.

Released at the same time was a large-format book in which they told their own story in words and pictures; the words in John's case necessarily compiled from past interviews and quotes but the others' in newly recorded first-person mono-logues. George's 'pieces-to-camera' for the documentary have his usual wary reserve and occasional bitter moments, but his recollections of his childhood for the book are unexpectedly detailed and warm.

They begin in a setting that feels more late nineteenth than mid-twentieth century: the Harrison family's tiny mid-terrace house, indistinguishable from ten thousand others throughout Liverpool with its two cramped rooms downstairs and two upstairs. You walked through its street door into the front room which, despite the drastic shortage of space, was kept as the 'best' parlour and used only on special occasions. 'It had the posh lino and a three-piece suite [matching sofa and armchairs], was freezing cold and nobody ever went in it.'

Family life was squeezed into the back kitchen/living room where two adults and four children coexisted in a space no more than ten feet by ten. The small coal fire in its iron grate provided the house's only heating and there was neither a bathroom nor indoor toilet. On the wall outside the back door hung a tin bath which, on strictly scheduled bath-nights, would be put in front of the fire and filled with kettles and saucepans of water warmed on the gas stove.

The backyard containing the outside toilet was mostly paved but had one narrow strip of flowerbed and a well-populated chicken coop. A gate – always left unlocked – gave onto a 'jigger', or alley, and 'down a little cobbled lane was the slaughterhouse, where they used to shoot horses.'

Like countless other Liverpool men, Harold Hargreaves Harrison had answered the call of the sea, joining the White Star Line, whose most famous ship was the *Titanic*, and rising to First Class steward. With the birth of his eldest son, Harry, he'd come ashore for good and, after eighteen months on the dole – this was at the height of the Depression – found employment on Liverpool's dark green double-decker buses, initially as a conductor, then a driver.

Harold stayed on the buses for the rest of his working life, never making more than around £7.10s per week. Yet George had no sense of being poor or deprived; nor – unlike all his future fellow Beatles – was his childhood marred by any trauma or instability in the family. Harold and Louise stayed happily married; his older sister and brothers all got on well with their parents and one another and were equally kind to him. Louise's numerous relatives meant he was well provided with uncles, aunts and cousins, and her mother, who'd worked as a street-lamplighter during the Great War, lived in Albert Grove, just around the corner.

He came to full awareness in the bleak post-war years, when supposedly victorious Britain remained in the grip of food shortages and rationing long after the Continental countries that had suffered invasion and occupation, to say nothing of Germany itself; when men still wore their khaki army great-coats back in civilian life and women in headscarves or turbans queued stoically outside butcher or fishmonger; when new cars were a rarity, and then still only black or beige; when winters somehow seemed harsher than they'd ever been before 1939 and the very summer sun felt 'on the ration'.

Liverpool presented a scene of devastation rivalling London's East End; even strategically insignificant suburbs like Wavertree had been left cratered by bomb sites, known in Liverpool patois as 'bombies', often with unexploded parachute mines buried in their rubble. Many bombies would still be there when George left the city for ever in Beatlemaniacal 1963.

His mother and father materialised as utterly different characters, Harold calm and methodical as bus drivers must be; Louise with the vivacity and romanticism of her Irish ancestry, always ready for a laugh, a song or a party. In an age when most women in hard-drinking Liverpool chose gin or sherry, her favourite tipple was Drambuie, a gold-coloured liqueur whose blend of Scotch whisky, honey and herbs was like her personality in a bottle.

Her namesake daughter – known as 'Lou' to avoid confusion – was by now already in her teens when George was a toddler, so expected to take a turn at looking after him. But for Lou, it was never a chore. She loved dressing him, taking him for walks and bathing him when his turn came in the tin bath in front of the fire. It was Lou who showed him how to prise new-laid eggs from beneath the hens in the coop without alarming them, and laughed away his fears of the cold, shadowy outhouse. Her ambition was to become a schoolteacher and she rehearsed for it by teaching George his first words.

'I remember looking at him,' she would say in later life, 'and thinking, "I'll always be there for you."'

His earliest aesthetic awakening was not to music but architecture. It can be said to have run in the family since his paternal grandfather was a builder who'd helped put up several of the grand Edwardian houses in Princes Road, Toxteth, then an enclave of Liverpool's wealthiest merchants. Even as a small boy, George felt an appreciation for 'a nice building' that he couldn't express to grown-ups, still less the vague feeling of aspiration it awoke in him.

'I always thought that life was to go through and grow and make opportunities, make things happen,' he was to recall. 'I never felt that because I was from Liverpool, I shouldn't live in a big mansion house myself one day.'

Just around the corner from Arnold Grove was Wavertree's ornate centrepiece, the tower-mounted, four-faced Picton Clock, erected in 1884 by the architect/philanthropist Sir James

Picton and known affectionately as 'Clockie'. With its Gothic flourishes and wonderfully irrelevant spire, it might have been an offcut of that very 'big mansion house' far in his inconceivable future.

Out shopping with Louise, he would often see showmanship flourishing in the most unlikely surroundings. 'There would be crowds of people on one or other bomb site, watching a bloke in handcuffs and chains inside a sack, trying to escape,' he says in *The Beatles Anthology*. That shrouded, struggling figure might have been acting out the age-old belief that, despite the city's unique character and vibrant culture, it was a place from which anyone with a grain of talent or ambition had to break free.

Just as essential was to lose the pungent native accent which to the rest of Britain had always represented the furthest one could get from glamour or romance. Liverpool had produced many famous entertainers, comedians especially, but for all of them – even Tommy Handley, the war years' most popular funny man – the essential first step to national success had been to wipe away any clue as to their origin and speak with the same artificial nasal twang.

True to her Irish heritage, Louise was Roman Catholic, albeit observant only of the major festivals and holy days. Harold was 'nothing', as the British define agnosticism, but had no objection to their children being baptised Catholics, George in his turn. To begin with, his mother's faith appealed strongly to his senses, the smell of incense, flickering candles and multi-coloured, bearded saints not a million miles from the Hinduism he would one day embrace so full-heartedly.

But for George as a small boy there was to be very little getting up at ungodly hours to go to Mass or making confession and doing penance. His attendance at Louise's church, St Anthony of Padua, was mainly as a member of its Cub Scout troop and when he started school, it was at the Anglican Dovedale Road Infants in Mossley Hill, close to a then-unremarkable, winding thoroughfare named Penny Lane.

He was a sociable and sporty boy – although prone, as he always would be, to recurrent, sometimes alarming illness – who joined happily in the playtime rough-and tumble. At Dovedale, he expressed only one concern when Louise took him there each morning, and it had nothing to do with the teachers or his schoolfellows. He asked her not to come right up to the school gate for fear that she'd get involved with other children's 'nosy mothers' and be inveigled into gossiping about him.

At the age of eight, he progressed from the mixed-sex infants to the all-boys primary school. His first year there coincided with the final one of a hilarious class clown and chronic rule-breaker named John Lennon but as John was two years older, their paths never crossed.

He became friendly with a classmate named Iain Taylor, in later life, a distinguished academic and geographer. 'I remember him as a nice guy,' Taylor says. 'He came from a fairly tough area, but never tried to throw his weight around, although if anyone threatened him he knew how to take care of himself.'

As at most British boys' schools in that era, corporal punishment was a normal and recurrent part of everyday life, here up to six strokes of a cane or wooden ruler on the wrongdoer's outstretched palm. One day, when a teacher named Mr Lyons was administering it to George, the ruler accidentally whacked down on the tender underside of his wrist instead, causing him extreme agony and leaving a nasty contusion.

Nine-year-olds then were supposed to take their punishments without complaint so at first George tried to hide his swollen wrist from his father, but inevitably Harold noticed it and demanded an explanation. Most fathers would have let the incident pass – saying the same thing had happened to them at school and never done *them* any harm – but not this one. 'Next morning while we were in class, there was a tap on the window,' Iain Taylor recalls. 'It was Mr Harrison. He called the teacher out and smacked him one. Knocked him over in fact.'

The Harrisons had waited years to be rehoused on one of the local authority-built estates in outer Liverpool that symbolised the promised good times to come after the War. In 1950, they'd finally left 12 Arnold Grove for 25 Upton Green, Speke, a modern mid-terrace house with three bedrooms, a bathroom and indoor toilet. It seemed the more spacious as Lou, now seventeen, had gone away to teacher-training college in Newcastle upon Tyne, never to live at home again.

The estate was supposed to be a haven of luxury and modernity after places like Arnold Grove with their outhouses, tin baths and jiggers. Yet it had none of the community spirit which had allowed people in those old 'bad' areas to leave their front doors permanently open. Under-provided with shops and services, its only lifeline the number 86 bus into central Liverpool – which Harold Harrison often drove – it engendered a feeling of isolation, often expressed through drunkenness, domestic violence and antisocial behaviour.

As George would recall, walking down an avenue of neat council houses in Speke held more risks than Wavertree's murkiest jigger, for the slightest 'funny' look at some local tough, or suspicion of it, could earn him a beating. One day, a noisy, helpless drunk careened off the pavement into the Harrisons' front door – which had the further refinement of a glassed-in porch – but was seen off by the doughty Louise with a saucepan full of cold water.

Living in Speke also turned George away from the faith into which he'd been baptised and in which his mother fully expected him to be confirmed. For Catholic priests always seemed to be calling to solicit donations for a new church they wanted to build on the estate. Louise and some Catholic neighbours kept a small boy on watch at likely visitation times to raise the alarm, but generally the black cassock was inescapable. If Harold was home, despite not being Catholic, he'd generously donate five shillings he could ill afford.

By the age of eleven, George recalls in his *Anthology* testament, he'd decided there was 'some hypocrisy going on' in the ease with which the estate's most antisocial Catholics could be excused their bad behaviour. 'Everyone's out there getting pissed, then go to the church and say three Hail Marys and an Our Father and stick a fiver in the [collection] plate ... It all seemed so alien to me.' As would any form of worship for many years to come.

A special niche in Liverpool's maritime history is reserved for its 'Cunard Yanks', the seamen and stewards on the luxury liners plying to and from New York. These hugely glamorous figures wore American clothes, smoked American cigarettes, used American slang and brought back new American records long before they were available in Britain, if ever.

Harold Harrison had been a typical example, albeit with the White Star rather than Cunard line: among the trophies of his many transatlantic trips before he came home for good in the 1930s were a wind-up gramophone in a wooden cabinet and a pile of big old-fashioned wax discs that Louise never tired of playing and replaying.

As a result, 25 Upton Green might echo to 'Waitin' For a Train' by Jimmie Rodgers, 'the Singing Brakeman', or 'One Meatball' by the pioneering African/American folk singer Josh White, each accompanying himself on an instrument which as yet meant nothing to George. The first vocalist with a guitar he became aware of was the Country singer Slim Whitman, whose eerie falsetto voice scored its biggest hit with theme song of the operetta *Rose Marie*.

Britain's pop music charts, of which the first had appeared in 1952, mostly featured big American stars like Eddie Fisher, Frankie Laine, Nat King Cole and Patti Paige, cover-versions by Dickie Valentine or (secretly Liverpudlian) Lita Roza and songs from Walt Disney films or Broadway shows. Home-grown smashes tended to wackiness, like 'The Railroad Runs Through The Middle Of The House' by Alma Cogan, 'the girl with the giggle in her voice', and Max Bygraves's 'You're A Pink Toothbrush'.

'All that is still in me,' the most earnest of rock musicians concedes in *The Beatles Anthology*, 'and is capable of coming out at any time.' To his parents' surprise, he also liked George Formby, a superstar of the Thirties and war years who sang songs of innocent double-entendre like 'When I'm Cleaning Windows' and 'With My Little Stick of Blackpool Rock' in a squeaky Lancashire voice, grinning toothily and strumming a banjolele, a hybrid with a banjo's body and the neck of a ukelele.

In 1954, aged eleven, he won a scholarship to the Liverpool Institute High School for Boys in the hilly quarter dominated by the Anglican Cathedral. Its rather convoluted name – inevitably shortened to 'the Inny' – derived from having been founded, in the 1830s, as an adult-education 'institute' which had later been split into two to form the school and Liverpool College of Art.

Although part of the state system, the Inny boasted the same refinements as a public school like Eton or Harrow: a uniform of black and green blazers, ties and caps, and 'masters' rather than teachers in scholarly gowns, licensed to administer public chastisement with a cane.

Behind its heavy wrought-iron gates was an interior scarcely changed since Victorian times save that the ornate gas lamps were no longer lit on winter afternoons. An ethos of public service was reflected in its roll of distinguished alumnae in politics, science and academia and its Latin motto '*Non nobis solum sed toti mundo nati*': not for ourselves only but for the whole world were we born. And George – who was to help to give new meaning to those words – hated the place from the beginning.

Iain Taylor, who'd also come from Dovedale but been put into the class above him, noticed an immediate change for the worse. 'He'd always been a bit of a happy-go-lucky character; now he'd become quiet and resentful.'

As winning the scholarship had shown, he was intelligent and perceptive, while his excellent memory should have enabled him to sail through exams. But he couldn't bear authority or compulsion in any form and, almost on principle, did poorly in every subject except art. Even by the time of *The Beatles*

Anthology, when so many other old resentments have softened, his comments about the Inny are still vitriolic. 'That was where the darkness came in,' he says. '[imitating teacher commands] "Be here, stand there shut up, sit down ..." It was the worst time of my life.'

Music had no attraction since the only instruments for which tuition was available were the violin or the recorder. His one form of exertion was in avoiding school rituals and routines he considered pointless; for instance, despite having mentally rejected his mother's Catholicism, he used it as an excuse to get out of morning assembly because Anglican hymns and prayers were included.

Next to him in class sat a boy named Arthur Kelly from Edge Hill who'd become his best friend on their very first day as they'd griped about the feeling of regimentation after the informality of their primary schools, and the black and green uniforms that symbolised it.

At the Inny, Arthur became his partner in inertia. 'We never bothered to do our homework. Every morning, we'd go to the class swot and copy out his, making it just different enough for the teacher not to notice. Our school reports always used to say how strange it was, considering the high standard of our homework, that we always did so badly in exams.'

The one subject that caught his interest was architecture. Teacherly praise must surely have been given to his draughtsman-like diagrams of three tall Gothic windows illustrating 'Development of Tracery in the Early English. Period. Stage 1, Lancet Window, Stage 2, Plate Tracery, Stage 3, Geometrical Tracery.' So when he came to live in a house bristling with such windows, he'd able to categorise each one.

He was never openly rebellious, but always to be found hanging out with the skivers and wastrels in the secluded alley off the playground known as Smokers' Corner. Although far below the legal age for smoking, he was soon getting through so many unfiltered cigarettes each day that the nicotine stained his fingers bright yellow. 'Been smoking again, Harrison,' a teacher commented sarcastically one day as he returned to class. 'Your fingers are like Belisha beacons.'

When rock 'n' roll music arrived from America in 1955, George was twelve. In its homeland, although scandalous, it was recognisably part of the national culture, a fusion of black R&B and white country music, but to staid, sleepy post-war Britain, it seemed to come horrifically out of nowhere.

In London and several provincial cities simultaneously, showings of an American film named *Blackboard Jungle* moved its youthful audiences to tear the cinemas to pieces. Its subject was juvenile delinquency in an inner-city high school, but what caused the mayhem was the record played over its opening credits, 'Rock Around The Clock' by Bill Haley and the Comets.

Those first infected by the madness were somewhat older than George, but as 'Rock Around The Clock' streaked up the bland British pop charts and the tally of wrecked cinemas mounted, his curiosity was sufficiently aroused to spend his pocket-money on a copy. He asked his eldest brother, Harry, to get it for him but the shop had sold out and, thinking any American group would do, Harry brought back a single by the gospel-singing Deep River Boys.

Bill Haley-mania stalled when Haley visited Britain and proved to be a chubby, amiable man of thirty with a kiss-curl like a query-mark on his forehead as if himself questioning his own suitability to be the figurehead for a youth uprising. And once he'd used the 'rock' tag in every possible song-title, even the Scottish anthem 'Comin' [now Rockin'] Through The Rye,' he sank from the charts. Rock 'n' roll seemingly had been just another short-lived craze from the States like cocktail-shakers, crewcuts and the Black Bottom.

Arthur Kelly's sister, Barbara, was engaged to an officer in the American Merchant Navy, nicknamed Red for his shock of ginger hair, who was liberal with gifts from his unrationed homeland to the whole Kelly family. 'One time, Red brought back a box of records for George and me,' Kelly recalls. 'They were in the new small vinyl format and when he found out we didn't have a record-player that was compatible with them, he very generously went into town and bought one for us.

'Among the records were some by Elvis Presley. We both said, "What a silly name . . . it can't possibly be his real one."'

It was. And to Britain's newly inflamed youth it brought sounds which, after Bill Haley and the Comets, were as bootleg gin to orange Fanta.

Presley's 'Heartbreak Hotel', released in January 1956, was the voice of rock 'n' roll – immaturely masculine, moody, randy and angst-ridden – and changed its key instrument from wailing saxophone to stabbing electric guitar. At the same time, reports were crossing the Atlantic of Presley concerts in which his uninhibited body language – long natural to black R&B vocalists but shocking in this white one – goaded young women to extremes of hysteria far beyond any seen with Frank Sinatra and the bobby-soxers of the 1940s.

The British Broadcasting Corporation, which held a

monopoly on the nation's radio, banned Presley and all rock 'n' roll with him as a corrupter of youthful innocence. It was unanimously condemned by newspapers, politicians, school-teachers, the clergy and pretty much everyone else over the age of twenty-five, its lyrics derided as both nonsensical and obscene. Much of the attack centred on the guitar Presley wore in performance but seldom found time to finger. From that it was inferred that he couldn't play it, so was a con artist along with everything else.

Until the mid-1950s, most young British men had passed straight from childhood to middle age, donning the same grey suits and dowdy tweed jackets as their fathers. Now, the first specifically 'young' look arrived with the Teddy Boys, so named because their long velvet-collared jackets and bootlace ties had a touch of Edwardiana. They had in fact, slightly pre-dated rock 'n' roll but claimed it as their own and, abetted by their less dressy Teddy Girls, had been in the vanguard of its signature cinema-smashing.

Thirteen-year-old Inny pupils like George and Arthur Kelly had no means of acquiring authentic 'Ted gear' which, unavailable in normal menswear shops, had to be expensively tailor-made. But they tried to give their school uniforms a suggestion of it, in defiance of the dress code strictly enforced by the headmaster, J. R. Edwards, nicknamed 'the Baz' (short for bastard) or 'the Stump'. 'We'd turn our school ties around so the thin bit showed instead of the thick bit,' Kelly says. 'And we'd make our blazers look like plain black jackets by cutting the badges off the breast-pockets, then when we got near school we'd fasten them on again with pins.'

In a world where manliness was defined by army-style short

back and sides, the Teds' most outrageous feature were their top-pling quiffs and long sideburns, known in Liverpool as 'sidies' or 'bugger-grippers'. Almost as deplorable were the Edwardian-style 'drainpipe' trousers they favoured in place of the baggy kind worn by men and boys alike since the 1920s.

George's thick, pliant hair – 'like a fuckin' te-erban', as the envious Arthur said – was easily sculpted into an impressive cockade and swept past his ears to interleave in a DA (duck's arse) at the back. But even his usually tolerant parents shared the adult dislike of 'drainies', so he had to taper his school trousers surreptitiously on his mother's sewing-machine to glorious, ankle hugging sixteen-inch bottoms.

One morning, Kelly recalls, coming to school didn't seem the usual penance to George. For the first time since they'd started there, he was actually excited. '"There's something called skif-fle," he told me, "and we've got to get a record called "Rock Island Line."'"

Skiffle had its origins during America's Great Depression of the 1930s when people whom poverty and hardship could not rob of the impulse to make music would blow melodies into kazoos and jugs, scraping the ridges of a kitchen-washboard with thimble-capped fingers for the rhythm. But it was a wholly British variant, drawn from every genre of American music, blues, folk, jazz and gospel, which appeared at the same moment as rock 'n' roll rather like a pilot-fish swimming along-side a shark.

Its most notable practitioner – and only enduring star – was a jazz banjo-player named Lonnie Donegan who, in 1956, recorded Huddie (Lead Belly) Ledbetter's 'Rock Island

Line', backed by a 'skiffle group' with the simplicity of those Depression-era plunkers and thumpers. The title merely referenced a Chicago railroad in a craggy locale, but the word 'rock' was enough to slingshot it to the top of the British charts. It even reached the US Top 10, an unheard-of instance of British musicians selling Americana back to America, not to be repeated until well into the next decade.

Its effect was galvanic on boys like George who'd been slightly too young for the full Haley and Presley experience. Through its multiple ancestry, skiffle offered everything about America most romantic to British adolescents – freight trains, chain gangs, New Orleans – with a frantic beat as heady as rock 'n' roll's but untainted by riot and vandalism. Reassured by its connection with jazz and folk, the BBC happily granted it airtime.

What was more, anybody could start a skiffle group like Donegan's by borrowing their mother's washboard and fitting a wooden crate, a broom handle and a length of string together to make a rudimentary 'bass'. Hundreds were formed all over the country with rugged-sounding names like the Wreckers, the Nomads or the Cherokees. Buttoned-up British youths who once would rather have committed hara-kiri than sing in public discovered the narcotic of performing and the nectar of applause.

In most skiffle groups, the only real musical instrument was the guitar, that immemorial companion of blues, folk and country singers, invested with a glamour it had never known before. Skiffle's songbook was almost entirely based on the three simple chords of 12-bar blues, some needing only one finger, so anyone could strum something within minutes. And, thanks to Elvis

Presley, guitars had taken on a magnetic attraction for girls. The rush to buy them temporarily created a national guitar shortage, like the still-lingering ones of meat and sugar.

George with his always delicate health was in Alder Hey children's hospital, suffering from nephritis, a potentially dangerous kidney infection. It was while lying in bed for six weeks, on a dreary non-protein diet heavily featuring spinach, that he decided he, too, had to have a guitar. Harold Harrison had owned and played one during his seafaring days, but it had long since disappeared, along with any expertise he'd ever possessed. Equable as always, he was quite happy for George to pick up where he'd left off and Louise, as always, found it impossible to say 'No' to him.

There were in fact plenty of second-hand guitars in Liverpool, taken up and then abandoned by seafarers like Harold, and a boy named Raymond Hughes, whom George knew from Dovedale Primary, currently had one for sale. Made by the Dutch Egmond company, it was a small Spanish-style model, strung with steel rather than gut, which, when new, was the cheapest in the Egmond range. But it was a *guitar*. Raymond wanted £3.10s for it, the equivalent of a week's housekeeping money, but Louise unhesitatingly gave George what he needed.

The relationship with this first manifestation of the love of his life didn't begin well. At the back of the Egmond, where the body met the neck, was a large bolt. Practically minded George couldn't resist unscrewing it, and the guitar fell into two pieces. Guiltily he hid them in a cupboard, where they stayed until his brother, Peter, found them and screwed them back together.

With the Egmond made whole again in his hands, George, as they say in Liverpool, was 'lost'. A family snapshot of the time shows him flourishing its puny silhouette, a wishful mini-Elvis against a background of flowery living-room curtains, a look of something near rapture on his serious little face.

Arthur Kelly also had managed to get a guitar out of his parents, a rather more expensive one than George's, and Harold arranged for the two of them to have lessons from a friend named Len Houghton who played semi-professionally with local dance bands. 'We used to go to a room he'd rented above a pub called The Cat on Wavertree Road,' Kelly recalls. 'He didn't really understand our kind of music, but he taught us the basic chords like C, D and G7.'

To supplement Len Houghton's lessons, they pored over a guitar-tuition manual alluringly titled *Play in A Day*. Its author was Bert Weedon, then seemingly the only man in Britain who could play electric guitar, an instrument so unfamiliar that it was banned from television shows as a fire risk. Almost all early British rock 'n' roll records featured Weedon, trying to forget his orchestral and jazz milieu and sound young and raw.

His photograph on the cover of *Play in A Day* showed him already to be nudging middle-aged, sober-suited with old-fashioned crinkly hair and an ingratiating smile. But his book was eventually to sell in millions, and George and every other British guitar giant of the Sixties acknowledge their debt to 'dear old Bert'.

Having learned about seven songs from the meagre skiffle hit-parade, George and Arthur decided they were ready to launch their own group. Rather than cast around for other members, which might well not have produced any results, George persuaded his brother, Peter, to join them on box 'bass', a role calling for no musical ability whatsoever.

They called themselves the Rebels and their first – and, it would prove, only – gig was arranged by Harold at Speke's British Legion Club where he sometimes went for a drink. 'It was on an evening when only about a dozen people were there,' Kelly recalls, 'none of them under about sixty. George and I shared the vocals and Peter plucked his single bass string until his finger was red-raw.

'We did Johnny Duncan's "Last Train to San Fernando" ... Chas McDevitt's "Freight Train" ... the Vipers' "It Takes A Worried Man" ... and "Maggie May." I'd describe the applause as polite. Afterwards the club secretary told us, "I'm sorry we can't pay you lads, but there's a couple of pints each for you at the bar."'

George's first girlfriend, Iris Caldwell from Wavertree, was only twelve to his fourteen when they started dating and the dates could not have been more innocent. 'We'd walk down Lily Lane, which was like a lovers' lane, and have a kiss and cuddle,' she remembers. 'George was the best kisser ever. I can still feel it down in my tummy.'

Iris was tiny and fragile-looking but forceful and eloquent as only Liverpool girls can be, and with a career ahead of her as astonishing in its way as George's. Later – after dating another Liverpool Institute boy who doesn't come into this story yet – she was to run away from home, join a circus and became a trapeze-artist.

Her mother, Vi, a warm-hearted, young-spirited woman, rather in the Louise Harrison mould, kept open house for her children's friends at the Caldwells' comfortable house in Broad Green Road. Part of its attraction for George was that Iris's brother, Alan, led a popular skiffle group called the Ravin'

Texans in the intervals of training for a local running club, the Pembroke Harriers. 'George wanted to be in Alan's group but my brother thought he was a bit young.'

She remembers him mainly as being sweet, shy and polite, but tact was not one of his virtues – and never would be. Grown-up though Iris felt with a fourteen-year-old boyfriend, her birthday parties, organised by her mother, were still firmly child-oriented, with jellies and trifle and games that included a variant of Postman's Knock called Shop. The boys would go out of the room while the girls were allocated the names of different fruit. When each boy came back in, he had to choose between two of them for the ritual kiss.

In one game, George was offered either 'Grapes' or 'Strawberries', neither of whose personifications appealed to him. 'I'm not hungry,' he replied, going too far even for sharp-tongued Liverpool. 'I wouldn't speak to him for hurting my friends,' Iris recalls.

As well as being a bit young, the obstacle to his joining the Ravin' Texans or any other serious skiffle group was his puny Egmond guitar and he was looking around, albeit without much hope, for something bigger and better.

He even tried to build an acoustic model in the Inny's wood-work class, carefully cutting out its f-holes and varnishing its body to give a 'sunburst' finish. But the first time he tautened its strings with the tuning-pegs, 'it ripped itself apart'.

In those days, restrictive import controls prevented American guitars from being sold in Britain and the most desired makes came from what was then West Germany, particularly the Höfner company in Bubenreuth, Bavaria. Höfner also made violins, cellos and double basses; their guitars had similarly lustrous woodwork and stately American-sounding names like the Congress, the Senator and the President. To guitar-mad British boys, Höfner's catalogue seemed almost erotic with its page after page of curvaceous shapes, its promise of 'blonde or brunette finishes' and 'warm responses'.

George had known Tony Bramwell since they were seven-year-olds, playing together on the various 'bombies' in the Speke area. Bramwell still bore on his neck the mark of an arrow George had shot at him during a game of Robin Hood – a fore-taste of his future as one of the Beatles' key employees.

His interest for George in their teens was that he had a munif-icent mum who'd bought him not one but two Höfner guitars, a Senator and a Club 40, an early attempt at an American-style solid body. 'He was always coming to our house in Hunts Cross to play them,' Bramwell recalls. 'I was stuck at being a rubbish player but he seemed to get a little better every time.'

George was not by any means the best guitarist at his school. That distinction belonged to a boy named Colin Manley in the class above his, who could play finger-style like the Country virtuoso Chet Atkins.

George was no flashy virtuoso like Colin Manley, but he had a keen musical ear that allowed him to reproduce the riffs and solos of the latest skiffle hit after only a couple of hearings. And the guitar awoke the student in him that the Inny never had or would. The margins of his exercise books teemed with draw-ings of guitars of every size and wavy shape; the attention he denied to geometry or algebra was lavished on page after page of chord shapes, the little latticed squares with dots representing the fingers.

By now, skiffle was becoming something more than simple

strumming. Lonnie Donegan had exchanged his plaid shirt for a black tie and augmented his backing group with an electrified jazz guitarist named Denny Wright, who took the ragged-arsed Depression-era ballads on all kinds of lyrical flights with his own scat-singing descant. Wright had since moved on to Johnny Duncan's Bluegrass Boys, whose big summer 1957 hit, 'Last Train to San Fernando', featured a Wright solo in rumba time.

'When we played "Last Train to San Fernando" at Speke British Legion Club, George couldn't play the solo,' Arthur Kelly recalls. 'But a couple of weeks later, he could.'

It surprised no one that Harold and Louise Harrison should buy their adored youngest son a new guitar, despite his poor record at school. But what a guitar! It was a Höfner, his dream make, no mere Congress or Senator but a President, playable either acoustically or electrically, with a single cutaway, inlaid fret-markers and a garnish of impressive-looking knobs and switches. The price was £30, equal to around £500 today.

It was purchased from Hessy's music store in central Liverpool, which no guitar shortage seemed to have affected. The assistant manager, Jim Gretty, was himself an accomplished player of the old school who appeared around the clubs performing Country & Western music. With every guitar he sold, the brawny, good-natured Gretty offered free lessons in the store after hours, where his class of learners could number as many as a dozen. 'George couldn't get enough lessons,' he later recalled. 'But I was telling him to be Hank Williams when he wanted to be Chet Atkins.'

He preferred to teach himself by the method he knew, listening to the same record time and again, duplicating what he heard by trial and error, with a concentration and patience never given to his schoolwork. Louise would sometimes sit up with him into the small hours, taking care not to distract him but inwardly cheering him on as his fingers searched among the President's inlaid fret-markers until the right note rang true.

2

'HE WAS SO MUCH IN THE BACKGROUND HE WAS LIKE THE INVISIBLE MAN'

In the class above George's at the Inny was a conscientious, well-behaved boy named Paul McCartney with soulful brown eyes, a pleasant manner and the lightest of Scouse accents. He too lived on the Speke estate, where his mother, Mary, worked as a domiciliary midwife, so every morning, he and George travelled into central Liverpool by the same number 86 bus (often driven by Harold Harrison and then free of charge to them both). At school, the difference of a year in their ages barred them from socialising but on these nearly hour-long journeys they could talk as equals.

They immediately bonded over music, George with a guitar of implausible magnificence for so small and shy a boy, Paul with nothing half as glamorous. On his recent thirteenth birthday, his father, Jim, a former amateur dance-band leader, had given him a trumpet. He was practising on it dutifully – as he did everything – but increasingly felt he'd rather be strumming than blowing.

The two also had in common a deep loathing of the compulsory Inny uniform that seemed even more dull and restrictive with Teddy Boys and their glorious sartorial revolution now in riot everywhere. But whereas Paul dared to deviate from the dress code in only small, marginal ways, George had put together a 'Ted' version of the uniform, using cast-offs from his older brothers, which his interview for *The Beatles Anthology* book in the 1990s could still reassemble to the last detail.

'[I had] a dog-tooth check-patterned sports coat I'd dyed black to use as my school blazer. It hadn't quite taken, so it still had a slight check in it. [And] a shirt I'd bought in Lime Street that I thought was so cool. It was white with pleats down the front and it had black embroidery along the corners of the pleats ... Powder-blue drainpipes with turn-ups I had dyed black as well ... and I had black suede shoes from my brother. That outfit was very risky and it felt like all day, every day I was going to get busted.'

This greatly impressed Paul – no easy thing to do – and as time passed, the two schoolbound Inny boys found more and more common ground. They talked about their mothers, both of Irish descent who'd had them baptised as Catholics but never insisted they went to Mass or Confession. They talked about life on the wild frontier of the Speke estate: Mary McCartney's position as a much-loved midwife and nurse saved her family from the worst of it – but still didn't qualify for an indoor toilet.

Above all, they talked about rock 'n' roll, still the outlaw music, incessantly attacked and derided by the grown-up world. Primarily about 'Elvis' in all his glamour and mystery, but also those who'd had the nerve to follow him: Little Richard, whose scalded Banshee scream could rattle window-frames, and Jerry Lee Lewis, who'd added a piano explosively to the equation, and the wheedly-voiced Gene Vincent with his backing group the Blue Caps and sublimely nonsensical hit single, 'Be-Bop-a-Lula'.

Early in 1956 the McCartney family moved from Speke to 20 Forthlin Road, Allerton. Again, they were living on a council estate, but one far less isolated and better situated; the green, affluent suburb of Woolton was barely a mile away. Paul and George no longer shared a long morning bus ride but their out-of-school friendship continued.

Paul by now had managed to part company with his trumpet because he wanted to sing, an impossibility with a 'horn' unless you were Louis 'Satchmo' Armstrong. With his father's permission he took it back to the shop and exchanged it for a Zenith guitar. Because he was left-handed, its neck pointed the opposite way from those of other guitarists when he played; an oddity then but in the future a silhouette marking out genius.

In October 1956, when he was fourteen, his mother died from breast cancer, aged only forty-seven. British boys in those days didn't show their emotions, this boy least of all, nor was there any of the modern apparatus of bereavement counselling and therapy. For Paul, the only therapy to hand wore a shiny suit and played an electric guitar, the only words of any real comfort were 'Be-Bop-a-Lula'. Being around George therefore became an essential part of the healing.

By the summer of 1957 he had pretty much mastered the Zenith, like the trumpet, piano and drums before it, and was regularly practising with George, though without any particular object in view. His singing voice, with its range from choirboy-pure to Little Richard-rowdy, made him a prize to any skiffle group, but so far he'd made no move to join even the one under his nose. For two of his Inny classmates, Len Garry and Ivan

Vaughan, shared the role of box bass-player in a group from Woolton named the Quarrymen. Ivan was a friend of Paul's and also of the Quarrymen's leader John Lennon, whose garden backed onto the Vaughans'.

Hoping to pique Paul's interest in the Quarrymen, Ivan offered to introduce him to this 'great fellow', and he consented. A perfect opportunity would be on 6 July when the Quarrymen were to play at a summer fete in the grounds of Woolton's parish church, St Peter's.

Lennon and McCartney's discovery of each other, in a pastoral setting of home-made cake stalls, hissing tea-urns and hoopla games, has been so often told and retold, one hardly needs to reprise Paul's first sight of John with his Quarrymen on the little outdoor stage, wearing a checked shirt and making up his own words to the Del Vikings' 'Come Go With Me', or the rather awkward introductions later in the adjacent church hall when Paul broke the ice by singing Eddie Cochran's 'Twenty Flight Rock' while impressively playing a right-handed guitar left-handedly.

They seemed the unlikeliest of soulmates, one with his deferential charm, the other a aspirant Teddy Boy whose scabrous wit concealed depths of anger and insecurity that, in the future, the whole world's adoration would be unable to assuage.

Rock 'n' roll and guitar-worship drew many disparate characters together, but between these two there was an instant additional bond. Soon after meeting, each admitted to the other that he 'tried to write songs'. As they well knew, writing songs was something done by old men with names like Cole Porter and Irving Berlin seated at grand pianos among the New York skyscrapers, not schoolboys in exercise books in the utter obscurity of Liverpool. Still, they decided to persist with it, together now.

Paul's recruitment to the Quarrymen had an immediate effect on what had essentially been a gang of John's mates, in it for the laughs and the beer. Now, thanks to the smiley adjutant figure he'd brought in, they found themselves expected to dress alike, turn up punctually for gigs and be more professional altogether.

In the floating membership of up to eight, Paul soon identified those who were there only because they were John's friends and secure in the knowledge he'd never get rid of them. However, by the autumn of 1957, the unwieldy line-up was contracting of its own accord as various members went away to college or began trade apprenticeships. John himself had left Quarry Bank High School – an establishment as first-rate as the Inny where he'd been a notorious disruption – to enrol at Liverpool College of Art, though keeping the group going, still under its same name.

John had been inching it away from skiffle to rock 'n' roll, as with its washboard version of a New York doo-wop song at Woolton church fete. Paul now persuaded him that it needed a dedicated lead guitarist like Scotty Moore in Presley's backing trio or Cliff Gallup in Gene Vincent's Blue Caps. 'John and I were okay on the guitar,' the present-day Sir Paul remembers, 'but we couldn't solo. So I said, "Oh, I know this feller ..."'

Actually, getting George into the Quarrymen was a tricky operation requiring all of Paul's already well-developed diplomatic skills. Firstly, it meant dropping the group's existing third rhythm guitarist, a pleasant boy named Eric Griffiths who'd been one of the Quarrymen's founder members and was not without ability.

Secondly and trickier, George was two-and-a-half years younger than John, something that was likely to matter even more from the heights of the Liverpool College of Art. At four-teen, he was undersized for his age; indeed, still looked more child than teenager, never more so than when hefting his bulky Höfner President.

Paul had already started bringing him into the Quarrymen's orbit to get John used to the sight of him, but so far the results hadn't been encouraging, After registering George's serious face and opulent upswept hair at the forefront of several successive audiences, John had irritably demanded, 'Who's that bloody kid who's always hanging around?'

According to the Quarrymen's drummer, Colin Hanton, the scene of their formal introduction to George was carefully chosen to show him at his best. Iris Caldwell's brother Alan, helped by their dynamic mother, Vi, had started a skiffle club named the Morgue (skiffle iconography always tended to the macabre) in the cellar of a large Victorian house in Oakhill Park. Although it was mainly an arena for Alan's group, the Ravin' Texans, George was allowed the occasional solo spot in return for helping Iris with the coats.

The audition that would lead him to fame and frustration on an equally massive scale is remembered in none of the vivid detail of Lennon-meets-McCartney. Official Beatles history has it that he won John over by playing 'Raunchy', an instrumental written and recorded by Bill Justis, the in-house arranger at Sun Records in Memphis (where Elvis had been discovered) and released to an innocent Britain that had no idea that 'raunchy' meant sexy.

In fact, 'Raunchy' consists of one simple five-note riff that

John himself, or any beginner, could easily have managed. It's likely that George played something more ambitious but likelier that John regarded his Höfner President as the real acquisition.

So Eric Griffiths was out of the band – by no means the last to suffer that sudden shock – and George donned the Quarrymen's post-Paul stage outfit of white cowboy shirts with black shoulders to make his debut as their lead guitar with a borrowed amplifier at the New Clubmoor Hall Conservative Club in Norris Green on 10 January 1958, still a month shy of his fifteenth birthday.

The 'bloody kid' effect was soon apparent. Three gigs later, the Quarrymen appeared at the Cavern club in Mathew Street, near the docks, a traditional jazz stronghold that was one of rock 'n' roll's bitterest foes. When the group had played there just before Paul's arrival, John had slipped in Elvis's 'Don't Be Cruel' and been handed a stern note from the management, ordering him to desist.

Since then, the Cavern seemed to have softened its anti-rock policy – though it was still far from what it would become partly thanks to that 'bloody kid'. Situated underneath a fruit warehouse, it consisted of three brick tunnels with low barrelled ceilings; its makeshift stage was in the middle tunnel and the audience sat on kindergarten-size wooden chairs. When a jazz band played, which was the usual thing, nobody stirred from their seat.

That night, Colin Hanton remembers, the Quarrymen paid lip-service to some skiffle but gave their all to 'Be-Bop-a-Lula', 'Twenty Flight Rock', Elvis's 'All Shook Up' and Jerry Lee Lewis's 'Whole Lotta Shakin' Goin' On'. To their dismay, while they were playing members of the audience began to disappear, more and more seemingly leaving in disgust until the rows of kiddy chairs were almost empty.

Only when they came offstage, even John thoroughly deflated, did they learn what had really been happening. Their audience hadn't walked out, but simply moved into the two flanking tunnels out of their sightline, to dance.

'We thought we'd given the worst show of our career,' Hanton says. 'But we'd given our best one.'

In the Britain of the 1950s, class distinction and snobbery were all-powerful and omnipresent. In Liverpool, they were supplemented by the age-old snobberies of the sea; no greater social gulf existed than between a ship's captain and a pilot, or a Chief Steward and a plain steward. It was said that if you looked up at the Cunard company's monolithic headquarters at the Pier Head, you could be sure that behind every one of its flotillas of windows someone would be feeling superior to someone else.

Only the city's land-based working class took no part in the game thanks to their traditional hard-left politics and consequent fierce egalitarianism.

This was where George belonged, and throughout primary school, even amid the unashamed elitism of the Inny, he'd never had cause to feel insecure about it. His first experience of discrimination because of where he lived and how he spoke came from knowing John Lennon.

It was a surprise to him to discover that the reckless, sometimes lawless Teddy Boy lived on Woolton's Menlove Avenue, a leafy enclave of Liverpool's professional class, in a substantial semi-detached house named 'Mendips', with faux-Tudor embellishments, a 'morning room' such as normally existed only in

Noël Coward plays, and a kitchen with a row of bells to call the servants employed there within living memory.

John's father, a ship's steward, had disappeared from his life just after the end of the war and his mother, Julia, had handed him over to her older sister, Mary, known as Mimi, to raise at 'Mendips'. Mimi was an admirable woman in many ways but a snob from the lower middle class, always the fiercest kind. Since being widowed when John was fourteen, she had dedicated herself to protecting him from undesirable influences, meaning the proletariat of his native city, their penchant for drinking and fighting and their uniquely coarse and nerve-jangling accent.

To Mimi, John's playing rock 'n' roll had opened the door to these forces of barbarism and she was striving with all her considerable might to slam it shut again. 'The guitar's all very well,' she told him, logic overwhelmingly on her side, 'but you'll never make a living from it.'

She refused to allow the Quarrymen to practise in her spotless home, banishing them instead to its glassed-in front porch where they would be inaudible. On these trying occasions, she had regarded even Paul's perfect manners with suspicion, thinking him 'a snake-charmer'. However, although he lived in working-class Allerton, he passed her social X-ray because his mother had been a nurse (as had Mimi herself), which counted as honorary middle class.

George was a walking catalogue of her worst nightmares. Not only did he have the abhorrent Scouse accent at full strength and dress like a Teddy Boy but he lived in Speke, a place Mimi equated with Dante's seventh circle of Hell. 'She didn't like me at all, she was really sharp,' he would recall in the 1990s, with no glimmer of amusement even after so long. 'She'd be "Who is this boy . . . he looks terrible" and John would just say, "Oh shuddup, Mary."'

As John would confess, the problem for him was not George's accent but the baby face and sticky-out ears that went with the outrageous wardrobe. 'I didn't want to know him at first [i.e., socially]. He was too young. He came round to Mendips one day and asked me to go to the pictures with him, but I pretended I was too busy.'

Altogether different was the welcome from John's mother, Julia, who lived only a short way from her older sister. Since turning John over to Mimi, Julia had acquired a boyfriend with whom she'd had two daughters, yet she remained a constant presence in John's life and an antidote to Mimi's authoritarianism. Easygoing, vivacious and music-mad, she seemed more like his mischievous older sister than his mother. Coming from the utterly conventional, stable family that George did, the whole set-up must have seemed bizarre to him, not least in that John called both his mother and aunt by their Christian names. But here there were no sarcastic remarks about his accent nor slighting references to Speke.

Julia could play the banjo and had taught John the four-string chords he continued to use on the guitar she'd bought him – until 'that bloody kid' rose considerably in his estimation by showing him their six-string fingering. She loved having the Quarrymen practise at her house, even let them play standing in the bath because the echo in the bathroom was almost as good as an amp.

At Paul's home in Forthlin Road, rehearsing was never any problem. His widowed father had once led the locally popular

Jim Mac Jazz Band and still played the piano by ear at family gatherings where he'd once hoped Paul would similarly entertain on trumpet. He didn't understand the new music, but was glad to hear any kind being made under his roof. And the Quarrymen were quite willing to make the trek out to Upton Green, where Louise Harrison was always welcoming.

Louise's attitude towards John contrasted with that of the usually mild and tolerant Jim McCartney, who'd warned Paul, 'He'll get you into trouble, son.' Nothing that he said could ever shock her and deep down she seemed to feel a responsive flicker of devilment. She used to give him tots of whisky and say George and John were 'just a pair of fools'.

John's Aunt Mimi had hoped his transformation into an art student would put an end to this rock 'n' roll nonsense. So it might have but for the fact that between the College of Art in Hope Street and the Inny in Mount Street there was a connecting door, a last residue of their once having been a single educational establishment. In rock 'n' roll mythology, it was to rank with the door into the Secret Garden or Narnia.

John would bring his guitar into college each day and at lunchtime Paul and George would remove all incriminating insignia of their school uniforms, slip through the door unseen and join him for fish and chips in the student canteen, followed by a practice session in an empty lecture-room.

George felt uncomfortable at these illicit rendezvous, since John always seemed nervous that his obviously pre-college age would give the game away. And, despite the freedom to smoke ad lib and the abundance of 'chicks', the girls he met touched the newly exposed nerve of his class. Rock 'n' roll then was considered exclusively blue-collar music and the most fetching of the chicks were bound to share the student preference for intellectually superior jazz.

At art college, John acquired a steady girlfriend, a mild young woman named Cynthia Powell from Hoylake on the Cheshire Wirral, Liverpool's genteel commuter belt. He asked his mates for their opinion of 'Cyn' – who was, indeed, a surprising choice for him – and they expressed the requisite approval, all but for George, who said bluntly that she had 'teeth like a horse'.

Among John's new art college friends were two who held neither George's youth nor rock 'n' roll against him. The first was Stuart Sutcliffe, a precociously talented painter and a cult figure somewhat resembling James Dean (with a similarly tragic early death ahead of him) who was awakening John's interest in his Art and Design course as no tutor had been able.

The second was a diminutive, curly-haired boy named Bill Harry, unequivocally from George's side of the tracks. Raised in dire poverty in Parliament Street near the docks, bullied by bigger boys and tyrannised by Catholic priests, he'd escaped by winning a scholarship to the junior art college, educating himself in modern American culture to a formidable degree and becoming a prolific writer, often in newspapers, magazines and fanzines of his own creation.

'Paul was always the most pleasant to chat to, but with George you'd get virtually nothing going on between you,' Harry recalls. 'He was so much in the background in those days, he was almost like the Invisible Man.'

Yet in his quiet way, George became so absorbed into the college's social life that he scarcely felt his alien class and background. He attended student parties that went on all night; everyone had to bring a bottle and an egg for their breakfast

the next morning. At such times, when he relaxed, an innocent charm shone out of him which more than made up for his
occasional jarring gaucheries.

John's girlfriend, Cynthia, had heard about his comment that
she had 'teeth like a horse' and hadn't known whether to laugh
or cry. But all was forgiven when he sat beside her, looking
about eleven and said wistfully, 'I wish I had a nice girl like you.'

He almost became a student himself on the college's 'Panto
Day', a parade with fancy dress and decorated floats through
the centre of Liverpool collecting money for charity. George
would be in John's contingent, rattling a collection tin; afterwards, John would break open the tins and shamelessly divide
up their contents.

One condemnation of rock 'n' roll at least – that Elvis Presley
and his ilk were con-artists just using their guitars as props –
could by now be thoroughly refuted, although its critics
remained just as vituperative.

Eddie Cochran, who'd appeared at Liverpool's Empire theatre
during a British tour, had shown real brilliance on his cherry-red
Gretsch with an enraptured George in the audience. Carl Perkins,
Sun Records' main attraction since Elvis's departure, who'd
written and first recorded 'Blue Suede Shoes', proved to have
been equally maligned when he appeared in the film *Disc Jockey
Jamboree*. Even Tommy Steele, Britain's 'answer' to Elvis, designed
solely to make little girls shriek, could sometimes be caught shap-
ing complex six-string chords on his big white Höfner.

The charge was most preposterous in the case of Buddy Holly,
a twenty-one-year-old Texan who played virtuoso electric lead
as well as singing in an intriguing, hiccuppy voice in a trio called

the Crickets. Their September 1957 hit 'That'll Be The Day' featured a dazzling Holly intro, reprised in the solo: a backward tumble of treble notes that practically set the blood of Britain's L-plate pickers alight.

Holly was a 'buddy' indeed to skifflers in the throes of trying to rock 'n' roll-ise themselves (who were not only future Beatles but future Rolling Stones, future Who, future everyone-who-would-be-anyone in the Sixties beat boom) for his songs, while wholly original and more exciting every time, were constructed from the simple chords they already knew.

He handed the Quarrymen a ready-made repertoire to which, every few months, he added a further title that was just a touch more complicated as if to bring them on another step. And, like 'That'll Be The Day', many were written or part-written by him. He showed John and Paul that songwriters need not be remote sophisticates with names like Cole Porter but that they were just as entitled to have a crack at it.

Even the few pictures of Holly to appear in the British press brought his young British disciples comfort and encouragement, for here was no pouting deity like Elvis but an amiable-looking beanpole in glasses, hitherto the stigmata of school swots and nerds. The short-sighted John had so hated his that, rather than suffer the shame of being a 'four-eyes', he'd gone around half-blind. Now he could look like his hiccupping hero and see the world.

George studied Buddy Holly and the Crickets as he never had any subject at school. To pay his parents back for his guitar, he'd taken a Saturday job delivering meat for the butchers E. R. Hughes, much to the further social agony of John's Aunt Mimi.

His round included the Hunts Cross home of his childhood friend, Tony Bramwell, who owned a copy of the Crickets' first album, *The Chirping Crickets*. Hughes's big iron delivery bike would be parked outside for long periods with people's week-end steaks and chops spoiling in its front pannier as Bramwell good-naturedly played George the twelve magic tracks, not only original rock 'n' roll but country and R&B covers, over and over.

Holly came to Britain with the Crickets on what would be his only visit early in March 1958, performing in theatres and cinemas throughout the country – dedicated rock 'n' roll venues then being limited to coffee bars – and reaching Liverpool's Philharmonic Hall on the twentieth. George couldn't get a ticket and was consumed with envy that his friend Tony Bramwell had won a newspaper competition to see the show and meet Holly afterwards.

He himself had to be content with the Crickets' fleeting appearance, dinner-jacketed, on the television variety show *Sunday Night at the London Palladium*. The flickery black and white screen showed Holly playing a two-horned shape, flat against his side, that looked less like a guitar than a spaceship fitted with a strap. It was the first Fender Stratocaster ever to cross the Atlantic.

One improvement for the Quarrymen that Paul particularly urged on John was to make recordings of their performances to let them hear how they sounded and also circulate among prospective bookers rather than have to do a live audition every time. Other groups possessed reel-to-reel tape-recorders but in 1958 these were horribly expensive and far beyond their means.

Then a fellow guitarist at the Morgue named Johnny Byrne

told George about a studio in Liverpool where people could simply walk in and record their voices just as Elvis Presley had walked into Sun Records that world-altering day in 1954. It even had the same surname as the man lucky enough to have discovered Elvis: the Phillips Recording Service. An appointment for the Quarrymen was booked with its owner, Percy Phillips, for a fee of 17 shillings and sixpence (about 75p today) between them.

By now their personnel had shrunk to John, Paul, George, Colin Hanton and an occasional pianist named John Lowe. They were to record two songs of which only one had so far been decided, the Crickets' 'That'll Be The Day'. Many other groups covered it but few, if any, could aspire to Buddy Holly's wondrous lead riff. 'George told me he was going to learn it,' his schoolfriend Arthur Kelly recalls. 'And a couple of days later, he had.'

The experience of making a record proved sadly lacking in Presley-esque romance. The Phillips Recording Service was located at its owner's home, 38 Kensington, one of Liverpool's many thoroughfares with London names. A shabby terrace house, its bay window contained a selection of electrical goods for sale. Above the front door was an enormous sign, BATTERY CHARGING DEPOT EST. 25 YEARS, and a sign in an adjacent window offered LOANS £5 TO £500 WITHOUT SECURITY.

Percy Phillips – who, Colin Hanton says, 'looked like anyone's dad' – was not expected to have any affinity with rock 'n' roll but treated the Quarrymen politely enough, even if his most pressing concern was that they had the money to pay for his time. Like his usual clientele of amateur opera singers and children reciting party-pieces, they recorded at a single microphone in the middle of what must once been the Phillips family's dining-room.

The session, preserved for posterity on YouTube, seems to

come from the same remote past as some Victorian music-hall turn captured on wax cylinders. First, 'That'll Be The Day' with John's rather acid lead voice and George note-perfect throughout the Holly solo, sharing the handful of watts from Paul's little Elpico amp. Then a pastiche country song, 'In Spite Of All The Danger', written by Paul before he met John. George is well to the fore, not only in framing riffs but ah-ah-ing a counterpoint to their harmony that just about manages to stay on-key.

Editing was not included in Percy Phillips' fee and after a few minutes' wait he handed over a single small shellac disc with the song-titles handwritten on its yellow 'Kensington' label. Thanks to George's riffs, 'In Spite Of All The Danger' was credited to 'McCartney-Harrison', his first – and last – experience of being Paul's musical equal in the band.

The plaque that eventually replaced BATTERY CHARGING DEPOT outside 38 Kensington gives the date of the recording as 14 July 1958, but Colin Hanton is certain it took place on the twelfth. This would mean that only three days after John casually sang 'that'll be the day when I die' and harmonised about 'all the danger', his mother, Julia, was knocked down and killed by a speeding motorist a few yards from his Aunt Mimi's front gate.

The five Quarrymen had agreed to share the Percy Phillips disc on a rota of a week each. After the pianist, John Lowe, had his week, he failed to pass it on; no one else claimed their turn and Lowe drifted away from the group soon afterwards with it still in his possession.

It would lie forgotten in his attic for twenty-three years, then resurface to be rated by a long way the world's most valuable record.

3

'Playing just chords was better than not playing at all'

George was still much more Paul's friend than John's, especially during school holidays which fell at the same time for them both and shrank their age difference to nothing.

During one long summer break, they went hitchhiking to the alien land known as 'Down South', taking only a small backpack each, the most basic of tents and a tiny portable stove. They lived on tinned food, which they heated by holding the tins against the stove's feeble glimmer. 'We'd buy Smedley's spaghetti Bolognese or Milanese,' George recalls with his meticulous memory in the *Anthology* interview. 'They were in striped tins, Milanese was red stripes, Bolognese was dark blue stripes.'

They got as far south as Paignton in Devon, which George knew from family holidays, half-froze by sleeping rough on the beach, then thumbed their way back up through South Wales, hoping to make contact with a cousin of Paul's on the entertainments staff at the Butlin's holiday camp in Pwllheli (pronounced Puth–welli).

One lorry that stopped for them had no passenger seat, so

George had to perch on the gearbox cover while Paul sat on the exposed battery. They hadn't gone far when Paul let out a yell of agony. The battery had connected with the metal zips on his jeans' back-pockets, searing two zipper-shaped scorch marks into his buttocks.

The Butlin's at Pwllheli turned out to be protected against non-campers by barbed-wire fences, 'like Stalag 17', George later recalled, so they had to reverse every prison-camp escape film they'd ever seen by breaking *in*.

They moved on to Chepstow, so broke and weather-blown that they asked the police if they could spend the night in a cell, but were turned away and ended up on a wooden bench at the town's football ground.

In the seaside town of Harlech, they got talking to a boy around their age named John Brierley, who fixed for them to pitch their 'crappy' tent in the field behind his parents' bungalow. It poured with rain on their first night and the next day Brierley's mother took pity on them and invited them into the house.

As they undressed in the spare room, two large spiders ran across the wall, which they made haste to flatten with rolled-up newspapers. 'Did you meet Jimmy and Jemima?' their hostess enquired the next morning. The slain arachnids were evidently family pets.

They spent a week at the Brierleys', sharing a double bed – normality for schoolfriends in that era – and being served three generous meals a day. They sat in with John Brierley's skiffle group, the Vikings, at the local pub and Paul used the family piano to practise the bass-note solo to Buddy Holly's 'Think It Over'.

From first to last, they had no idea they were staying in a B&B and the Brierleys were too nice to mention it.

By 1959, the cavilling chorus of broadcasters, parents, teachers, clergy and 'professional' musicians were congratulating themselves on their prescience: rock 'n' roll had blown over or, more accurately, blown itself up.

Elvis was no more; at least, not as an incarnation of raw sex on rubber-soled shoes. He had been drafted into the US Army in a cynical managerial ploy to rebrand him as a respectful, dutiful all-American boy and move him into the ballad market. To underline the point, cinema newsreels showed him receiving his first army haircut; a meek Samson, shorn of his dyed-black locks.

America's other biggest rock 'n' roll names showed similar lack of staying-power. Little Richard renounced his screaming high camp to become a minister, singing only gospel. Jerry Lee Lewis's career evaporated after he was found to be bigamously married to his thirteen-year-old cousin. On 3 February 1959, Buddy Holly was killed in a plane crash along with fellow tour artistes Ritchie Valens and J. P. 'The Big Bopper' Richardson: 'The Day the Music Died', as the Canadian folk singer Don McLean would later eulogise it without any accusations of hyperbole.

Compounding the funeral rites, American music radio was convulsed by an exposé of payola, the bribes paid by record companies to deejays to give their product preferential airtime. Part of their public penance was to cleanse their catalogues of anything grubbily rock 'n' roll and substitute a race of boy crooners all as edgy as cotton buds and nearly all named Bobby.

In Britain, the music's only acceptable face was Cliff Richard, a sawn-off Elvis whose 'Move It' in 1958 had been the first authentic home-grown rock 'n' roll record but who was now following the industry's sage advice to get into ballads or cabaret or films as soon as possible. Rock had been sanded down to less threatening beat music and Richard, at least, maintained a backing beat group, the Shadows, whose lead guitarist, Hank B. Marvin, wore Buddy Holly-style glasses and played his much-envied red Fender Stratocaster.

Otherwise, the singing cotton buds now in favour diminished the guitar's importance and for George, any conspicuous soloist was someone to latch on to in hopes of learning something new; the legendarily young James Burton, for instance, whose elegant country breaks lit up the otherwise bland pop singles of Ricky Nelson, or Duane Eddy, whose 'twangy' guitar, mostly employing the bass strings, resembled a hugely amplified dog-bark. Even Bert (*Play In A Day*) Weedon merited a listen, cashing in on the bass-string boom with a polite version of Arthur Smith's 'Guitar Boogie Shuffle'.

George was especially drawn to Carl Perkins, writer of the immortal 'Blue Suede Shoes' even though he already seemed a little old for his milieu with his lantern jaw, receding hairline and strangely effete flourishes of an undersized guitar. The songs he wrote for himself, like 'Glad All Over', 'Matchbox' and 'Honey Don't', were quite unlike the usual sweltering Sun Records sound, playful rather than provocative and full of off-beat imagery ('Well, I'm sitting here wondering will a matchbox hold my clothes').

Though enticingly simple in construction, they often included a curve-ball of a chord, some obscure nineteenth or sixth that neither John nor Paul had ever encountered before but George could be relied upon to pick up pretty much instantaneously.

Rock 'n' roll might have blown over elsewhere but in Liverpool it had stuck fast among the docks and warehouses and cobbled streets and imperial monuments and palatial bank buildings and elegant Georgian terraces and lofty sandstone churches and lingering 'bombies' and splendiferous Victorian pubs, and soon would become mixed in with the muddy Mersey itself.

Dozens of yesterday's just-for-fun skiffle groups had metamorphosed into semi-professional rock 'n' roll bands without a trace of their former homespun simplicity. Almost all owed a debt to Cliff Richard and the Shadows in their matching shiny suits, frilled shirtfronts and blobby bow ties. Their names celebrated an America most of them had only ever seen on the films – Karl Terry and the Cruisers, Johnny Sandon and the Searchers, Kingsize Taylor and the Dominoes – with the occasional exotic touch like Cass and the Cassanovas, Faron and his Flamingoes or the Remo Four, featuring the Inny's star guitarist, Colin Manley.

They still called it 'rock 'n' roll' even though their repertoire extended beyond the limited legacy of Little Richard and Jerry Lee Lewis, into R&B country and blues, usually brought home in the holdall of some Cunard Yank. And in place of the Shadows' polite little dance routines was very Liverpudlian exuberance, not infrequently stoked up beforehand in one or several of those splendiferous Victorian pubs.

For onstage showmanship, none could equal Alan Caldwell, the brother of George's old flame Iris, now renamed Rory Storm as his former Ravin' Texans were the Hurricanes. Blond and statuesque, Rory possessed athletic prowess that gave him a unique edge; his performance might include scaling a wall or putting on gold lamé briefs to dive from the top board at one of the public swimming pools that doubled as music venues, perform a triple somersault, then surface for a bravura finish to 'Whole Lotta Shakin' Goin' On.'

Two other new identities were created along with Rory's. His adoring mum, Vi, named the family home 'Stormsville'. And the Hurricanes' drummer Ritchie Starkey, a sad-faced boy from the tough Dingle area whose twin passions were flashy rings and Western movies, decided henceforward to be known as Ringo Starr.

Of least significance in this blow-waved, box-jacketed multitude was the quartet still known as the Quarrymen, comprising John, Paul, George and the drummer, Colin Hanton, the last survivor from John's original line-up. Groups higher up the picking-order could afford cars to transport their drumkits to gigs but the Quarrymen had to lug Hanton's kit around by bus, stowing it in the luggage compartment under the stairs.

Hanton looked even younger than George, so much so that he carried his birth certificate around to pubs to prove that he was old enough to drink. But alone of the Quarrymen he was already a working man, with all the middle-aged seriousness that went it. He felt excluded from the other's practice sessions at the art college and resented Paul, who was more than competent on drums as well as guitar and piano, for continually finding fault with his performances.

Matters came to a head when Harold Harrison secured the Quarrymen a Saturday night booking at the busmen's social club in Finch Lane, where he was chairman of the entertainments committee and Louise ran a ballroom-dancing class. Harold had also persuaded a local cinema manager to be present with a view to offering them further work.

The first of their two sets went over well, but at the interval, the fatal words were uttered: 'There's a pint for each of you lads at the bar.' That pint led to others and as a result their second set was an incoherent muddle. George's parents were publicly embarrassed and after recriminations on the homeward bus ride, Colin Hanton disembarked with his drums one stop early, never to return.

A drummer, even one as average as Hanton, was the mark of any true rock 'n' roll band, and replacing him seemed an impossibility. None other 'worth a carrot', in the Liverpool saying, was likely to join up with an art student and two schoolboys, nor would any booker of worthwhile gigs be interested in a line-up consisting of three guitarists only. John and Paul would try to brazen it out when the inevitable question of their non-percussivity was raised by declaring brightly: 'The rhythm's in the guitars.'

An almost equal handicap was their name: 'the Quarrymen' seemed set in stone when all self-respecting bands these days were such-and-such-and-the-so-and-so's. They tried out various alternatives on the rare occasions when a gig was imminent. One was an amalgam of their Christian names, Jopage 3, quickly dropped when people said it sounded like a cleaning-fluid. Another night, when they happened to be wearing different brightly coloured shirts, they called themselves the Rainbows.

Despite the busmen's social club fiasco, George's family did their best to encourage the once-more-nameless trio. When his eldest brother, Harry, got married, he was told he could bring John and Paul to the reception 'to practise on the guests', as Harry put it. A famous snapshot shows the three of them in performance, John unusually dressy in a jacket and waistcoat, Paul with the camera not loving him quite as much as usual, and George, although now sixteen, still a bit undersized for the Höfner President.

The other entertainment came from one of the guests, an elderly woman who was 'a real pub pianist', Harry was to recall. 'While she was playing, John emptied his pint [of beer] over her head and said, "I anoint thee, David."

'What amazed me was that she just smiled and went away to get dry again. After every Liverpool wedding, people always ask, "How many fights were there?" At mine, the only almost-fight was because of John.'

By now, George was feeling some of Colin Hanton's frustration at the doldrums in which John, Paul and himself seemed permanently marooned; some of the same exclusion, too, since they had taken to spending long hours together at Paul's house, writing songs.

In his part-time job delivering meat for the butcher's E. R. Hughes, George had become friendly with one of the shop's permanent staff, a boy named Ray Skinner who played drums in a foursome called the Les Stewart Quartet, mainly working in and around the quiet suburb of West Derby. One Saturday as George was complaining about the Quarrymen, Skinner mentioned that the Stewart Quartet was currently a guitarist light. Without formally casting off from John and Paul, George auditioned for Les Stewart who, like John, was two years older but showed no sign of regarding him as a 'bloody kid'.

The Stewart Quartet's regular venue was the Pillar Club,

open on Sunday nights only in the basement of Lowlands, an imposing Victorian mansion on Hayman's Green. Stewart was its main attraction, playing banjo and mandolin as well as guitar, and handling all the vocals in a mainly blues repertoire. George stayed on the sidelines with a third guitarist, Ken Brown. But playing just chords was better than not playing at all.

Not fifty yards away, in another of the Green's rambling Victorian properties, a vivacious Anglo-Indian woman named Mona Best, recently separated from Liverpool boxing promoter Johnny Best, lived with her teenage sons, Peter and Rory. The long school summer holidays were at hand and to keep the boys amused, she decided to open a 'coffee club' for them and their friends in her capacious cellar, very much as Vi Caldwell had started the Morgue.

Mrs Best named it the Casbah and mustered a group of its prospective members to help her decorate it in a semblance of an exotic Eastern market, among them George's current girlfriend, Ruth Morrison. Like the Morgue, it was to have live music, so through George the Les Stewart Quartet was booked to launch it on 29 August.

George's next appearance with the quartet was to have been at West Derby British Legion club on 22 August. That day found him heading back from another hitch-hiking trip with Paul, including a stop-off to see the Brierley family in Harlech, and he reached Liverpool too late for the evening's gig. His fellow guitarist Ken Brown also failed to show and in pique both Les Stewart and drummer Ray Skinner pulled out of the Casbah opening.

George didn't want to disappoint the formidable Mona Best but realised that half a quartet wasn't much of an opening-night attraction so he enlisted Paul and John to join Brown and himself the following weekend. Since none of the trio's new names had brought them any luck, they decided to fall back on their shabby but comfortable original one.

Bill Harry, John's fellow art student – later the supreme authority on everything that came after – has no doubt about the importance of this moment.

'The Quarrymen had broken up, John and Paul were writing songs, it was all finished,' Harry says. 'Then George re-formed them to play at the Casbah ... and that really was where the Beatles began.'

4

'FROM THEN, NINE-TO-FIVE NEVER CAME BACK INTO MY THINKING'

George spent his final term at the Inny that summer like a convict waiting out the end of a sentence. His friend and fellow malingerer, Arthur Kelly, had been expelled for cheating in an exam, leaving him an isolated figure in the school uniform that by now could be recognised only with the help of a magnifying glass.

'He seemed to have reached a tacit agreement with the teachers – they didn't bother him and he wouldn't bother them,' says Iain Taylor, who'd been sorted into a higher class when they both arrived from Dovedale Primary. 'I remember seeing him sitting at the back of the room during a lesson, hanging his head, completely cut off from what was going on around him.'

So private was he about his extra-school life that even the sympathetic Taylor hadn't realised how it was largely spent. 'Every term there was a day when we were allowed to bring our hobbies into school and during one of those I saw George sitting out in the playground with a guitar and a crowd of people around him. That was the first I knew about his music.'

At a time when just 3 per cent of British school-leavers went on to university, the academic finale for the other 97 per cent was the

General Certificate of Education O- (for ordinary) Level examination, which dictated what kind of ordinary jobs they could expect. At the Inny, this was preceded by 'mock' O-Levels where one had to pass in three subjects to qualify for the real thing.

George passed in only one subject, Art, thanks mainly to a sympathetic teacher named Stan Reid. In English Language, dealing with grammar and comprehension, he got only 2 per cent, which he assumed was for spelling his name correctly at the top of the paper.

He agreed to spend an extra year with the next crop of O-Level hopefuls, before trying again. But it was demeaning to be taught alongside younger boys and the second time around, the work seemed even more paralysingly dull. 'After an hour,' he was to recall, 'I went over the [school] railings to the movies and didn't come back.'

The final report from his headmaster – crucial in future job-seeking – was a comprehensively damning document, evidently taking many past sartorial offences into consideration and ending: 'He has taken no part in any school activities whatever.' George was too ashamed to show it to his family and secretly burnt it.

Like most British boys leaving school at the end of the 1950s, he had dreaded the subsequent two years' compulsory military service, most likely into the vast regular army the country still maintained a decade and a half after the Second World War. Although most of those conscripts accepted the inevitable, George felt a deep revulsion at the idea of being a soldier and had been determined to get out of it somehow. Fortunately, by 1959 the draft had been limited to those born before October 1939, so even John escaped it.

Harold Harrison had always impressed on his sons the value of having 'a trade' rather than just an occupation like his own bus-driving. Both Harry and Peter had heeded his advice, one becoming a mechanic, the other a panel-beater and welder, and Harold's dearest wish was that George would become an electrician and the three start their own garage. His last Christmas present from his father had been a set of screwdrivers and assorted tools as a first step towards 'Harrison Brothers – Motor Engineers – Sales & Service'.

When George showed no interest in the screwdrivers, Harold hid his disappointment and, instead, arranged for him to take the entrance examination for Liverpool Corporation – of which he himself had been an exemplary employee since the mid-1930s – which might have led to some white-collar position in the street-lighting or sanitation department. To please his father, he really tried this time, but still did no better than in his mock GCEs.

After that, his only option was the government Labour Exchange where as a rule the kinds of labour on offer were uniformly depressing. Surprisingly, the first vacancy offered to him was for a trainee window-dresser at Blacklers, one of the three substantial department stores in central Liverpool. What he'd seen of window-dressing made it seem undemanding, even prestigious; standing there in one's stockinged feet, arranging houseware or slipping dresses around nude female mannequin, studiously ignoring the stares of passers-by.

By the time he got to Blacklers for his interview, the window-dressing vacancy had been filled, but there happened to be one still open for an apprentice electrician. So George gave in to what he hadn't yet learned to call Karma. 'With winter coming on, it was nice to be in a big, warm store,' he would recall. 'And at least it wasn't school.'

The Casbah Club underneath Mona Best's rambling old house on Hayman's Green was never simply to be the holiday den she'd intended for her sons, Pete and Rory. On its opening night, 300 local teenagers queued for admission; the succeeding weeks and a 'puff' in the local paper brought so many more that Mrs Best had to hire a doorman–cum security guard. And the revival George had engineered for the Quarrymen there turned naturally into a residency.

They became the Casbah's main attraction every Saturday night, their only rival the first espresso coffee machine to be installed in a Liverpool club. Mrs Best paid £3 for the four of them, John, Paul, George and Ken Brown, his fellow defector from the Les Stewart Quartet.

George always thought of it as 'our club' for they'd put their stamp on it during the pre-opening decorations, John painting Aztec-like figures and hieroglyphics on one ceiling, Paul rainbow stripes on another. Half a century later, these and other mementoes of their presence would bring the cellar a year-round flow of paying pilgrims, a Grade II listing from English Heritage and one of the blue plaques that were always to elude George's birthplace.

By the time he left school, his once-cherished Höfner President had come to feel old-fashioned and he'd changed it for a semi-solid Club 40 in a straight swap with Ray Ennis of the Bluegenes, later the Swinging Blue Jeans. John had also acquired a Club 40, with his Aunt Mimi's reluctant financial aid, but neither he nor George could yet run to an amplifier.

'That's where Ken Brown came in,' recalls Arthur Kelly,

who turned up every week to support George. 'They both plugged into Ken's amp and in return he was allowed to sing one song a night.'

Everything went swimmingly until the eighth Saturday, when Brown was suffering from a heavy cold. Mrs Best, with whom he'd become rather a favourite, decided he wasn't well enough to perform but at the end of the evening, she still gave him his fifteen-shilling (about 75p today) quarter-share of the Quarrymen's fee. This so incensed John, Paul and George that they quit their residency on the spot.

In any case, they had larger aspirations than being the toast of West Derby. Back then, before television talent shows manufactured stars by the hundred, the sole beacon of hope for any amateur entertainer was to be a Carroll Levis 'Discovery'. Levis, an oleaginous Canadian, toured the country with his *Star Search* show, offering a first dip in the limelight not only to singers and musicians but jugglers, contortionists and players of musical saws.

The Quarrymen had already competed in one *Star Search* on the hallowed stage of the Liverpool Empire in 1957, shortly before Paul joined them: not winning or even being placed but receiving a special word of praise from 'Mister Starmaker' Levis himself. When the show next returned in November 1959, John, Paul and George entered under the name of Johnny and the Moondogs. 'Moondog' was the nickname of the American disc jockey Alan Freed, who claimed to have invented the term 'rock 'n' roll'.

Despite lacking the drummer they'd had as the Quarrymen two years earlier, they got through to the finals at the Hippodrome theatre in Ardwick, Manchester. That night, even 'the rhythm in the guitars' was deficient since John, for some reason, was without his new Club 40. Their adroit solution was to perform Buddy Holly's 'Think It Over' standing in a row with John in the middle, resting one hand on Paul's shoulder and the other on George's, and the necks of their left-hand and right-hand instruments jutting out in opposite directions somewhat like a pair of wings.

The winners were chosen in a grand finale when the applause for each contestant was measured on a giant dial known as the Clapometer. At the Hippodrome, this didn't come until late in the evening; Johnny and the Moondogs couldn't afford an overnight hotel stay, so they had to leave to catch the last train back to Liverpool before learning how they'd fared. The only gain, Sir Paul McCartney recalls, was that 'someone else on the bill was relieved of his guitar by John.'

Otherwise, it was an Icarus plunge from guitars like spread wings to even lower than they'd been before the Levis show. For there could be no going back to the Casbah: since their haughty exit, other groups had been taking turns in their former exclusive slot, one with Ken Brown and Mona Best's oldest son, Pete, on drums.

Almost their only remaining source of gigs for the group was the Art College where they still had loyal friends and supporters in Bill Harry and Stuart Sutcliffe. Both sat on the college entertainments committee and would book them to play at student dances, regardless of the jazz lobby. After bringing them no luck on *Star Search*, 'Johnny and the Moondogs' was dropped but no other name took its place except the unofficial one of 'the College Band'. So much a part of the college did they seem that Sutcliffe and Harry persuaded its Entertainments Committee to buy an amplifier for them to use on condition that it would stay on the premises.

These largely gig-free weeks reopened the class divide within the trio, for while John was hanging out with his Art College friends and Paul revising for his Advanced-Level GCE at the Inny, George was already a working man, 'clocking in' each day to Blacklers department store.

Apprentices traditionally start with the most menial jobs and for him learning the mysteries of electricianship often meant being up a stepladder, cleaning out fluorescent light-tubes with a bucket of water and a sponge. In addition, the fashion-conscious, uniform-averse sixteen-year-old had to spend eight hours a day wearing an anonymous grey boiler suit.

Yet it was a far from miserable experience. The camaraderie among the store's many apprentices was a pleasant change from George's complex relationships with his bandmates, and he made some good friends, among them Peter Cottenden, who'd beaten him to the window-dressing job. 'Occasionally we broke the lifts so we could have a skive in the lift shafts,' George was to recall. 'I learned to play darts ... and to drink fourteen pints of beer and three rum and blackcurrants ... all in one session.'

Blacklers was celebrated for the magnificence of its Christmas grotto, to which George and all the other future Beatles had been taken as children to meet Santa Claus and ride the outsize rocking horse known as 'Blackie' (nothing to do with its colour; merely an abbreviation of the store's name).

During that one Christmas season George spent at Blacklers, he was part of the grotto's maintenance team, and somehow managed to fuse all its lights. The labyrinth of cotton-wool snow and fairy bulbs plunged into darkness ... Santa cut off mid-'Ho ho ho!' ... the queue for Blackie became immobilised ... the uproar of disappointed children and outraged parents ... The worst of his future nightmares as a Beatle can hardly have compared with that moment.

Saving the Quarrymen from extinction still hadn't made George an equal partner creatively speaking, for John and Paul still spent hours closeted together turning out songs to which, unusually, each contributed both words and music. During this time, Paul wrote to a local journalist for an article which never ran that they'd amassed 'more than 50 numbers, among them Looking Glass, Thinking of Linking, Winston's Walk and The One After 909'.

But in spite of his friendship with George, there had been no development of the McCartney–Harrison credit for 'In Spite Of All The Danger' on the Percy Phillips disc that had long since disappeared from their lives.

That friendship, too, had been usurped in the form in which it used to be closest. As a Blacklers employee, George had only limited time off while John and Paul still enjoyed the long vacations of college and school. So, in the spring break of 1960, it was they who went hitch-hiking down to Caversham, Berkshire, where Paul's cousin, Bett Robbins, and her husband, Mike, ran the Fox and Hounds pub. They spent a week there, sharing a bedroom without built-in spiders, helping behind the bar and performing to its customers under the ad-hoc name of the Nurk Twins.

Even Paul was pushed from the foreground of John's attention by Stu Sutcliffe, not only a brilliant painter but an intellectual omnivore who was awakening John's torpid senses to art in all its forms, literature and even philosophy. The two now lived in a large mixed-gender flat where a 'college band' rehearsal would often turn into one of John's informal tutorials from Stu on anything from Van Gogh and Benvenuto Cellini to Jack Kerouac, James Joyce, Kierkegaard or Sartre, and George, with his abhorrence of book-learning, would feel himself excluded in yet another way.

Since the search for a drummer seemed hopeless, they decided the only means of strengthening the rhythm in their guitars was one of the new electric basses. 'George asked me if I could get a bass and join them,' Arthur Kelly recalls. 'I said, "How much are they?" "Sixty quid," he said. I was earning four pounds ten shillings a week with the Cunard company at the time, so I missed my chance.'

John was determined Stu Sutcliffe should join the band on bass guitar, deaf to all objections, largely from Stu himself, that he hadn't the first idea how to play the instrument. Then he happened to sell one of his paintings for the remarkable sum of £65 just when a Höfner President bass appeared at Hessy's music store. John talked him into buying it even though, small and slender as he was, it looked as cumbersome on him as the President guitar had on fourteen-year-old George.

All this was very different from George's struggle to get into the Quarrymen two years earlier, but he bore Stu no ill will and was quietly amused that for both of them, a Höfner President had been the real entrance ticket. As he rationalised it later, 'Having a bass-player who couldn't play was better than not having a bass-player at all.'

Stu further took on the role of manager, which primarily meant finding bookings outside the art college precincts. The long indecision about what to call themselves therefore needed resolving, and seemed to be in a brainstorming session between himself and John.

Its starting point was Buddy Holly's Crickets, the prototypical rock group; pursuing that entomological theme, the obvious choice was 'the Beetles' which John, unable to resist a pun, spelt with an 'ea' as in beat music – by now, the generic term for watered-down rock 'n' roll – or beat writing, as in Jack Kerouac, or beatnik. Pun begetting pun, it became 'the Beatals', as in beating all competition.

Paul and George, to whom it was presented as a fait accompli, accepted it without demur. But from everyone else, particularly members of rival bands, it provoked the same disbelieving laughter. Putting aside the second 'a', how could they think of calling themselves beetles (actually what Buddy Holly's band had contemplated before thinking of 'crickets')?

Brian Cassar, the charismatic frontman for Cass and the Cassanovas, said they were mad to depart from the tried and tested formula of so-and-so and the such-and-such with a similarly distinctive persona; they should use their leader's first name to create a Treasure Island effect and become something like Long John and the Silver Men.

John flatly refused to identify with the one-legged villain of Robert Louis Stevenson's seafaring classic but the surname Silver became coupled with Beatles, making them sound more like scarab jewellery in some mystery story by Sax Rohmer or E. Phillips Oppenheim.

It's revealing of the dynamic among the four that in this whole beetle-like crawl towards the name that would eventually consume George's existence, he never once seems to have expressed an opinion on the subject.

In Britain thus far, pop management had scarcely existed as a business, let alone a profession. When the demise of rock 'n' roll was expected at any moment, what would have been the point? But by the threshold to the 1960s, entrepreneurs of every calibre – none particularly high – had realised it wasn't going away as predicted and there could be big money in it.

These pioneer managers were exclusively male, some a bit older than their protégés, so ignorant of and indifferent to the music itself, and usually with only tenuous connections to show business. Liverpool's most visible specimen of the breed was a chunky black-bearded Welshman named Allan Williams who operated a small coffee bar named the Jacaranda in Slater Street.

Since 'the Jac' stayed open late and had no objection to rowdy behaviour, it was a popular meeting place for bands like Rory Storm and the Hurricanes and Cass and the Cassanovas after their various night's gigs. Williams therefore could hardly fail to notice a commodity with rather more potential than coffee and 'jam butties'.

At the time, the only nationally known pop manager was Larry Parnes, a former dress-shop owner who'd discovered 'Britain's First Rock 'n' Roller', Tommy Steele, singing in a Soho coffee bar. Parnes had gone on to create a 'stable' of young performers whose mundanity he camouflaged with stage names designed to press every button in the adolescent female psyche as well as his own as a secretly gay man: Billy Fury, Marty Wilde, Vince Eager, Duffy Power, Dickie Pride.

He'd also developed a profitable sideline in touring American rock 'n' rollers eclipsed by the singing cotton buds in their homeland but with their British following still fanatical. In March 1960, he brought two of the biggest, Eddie Cochran and Gene Vincent, to the Liverpool Empire for six consecutive nights that still didn't satisfy the demand for tickets.

Parnes himself was along, as usual, to watch over the receipts, and Allan Williams was able to connect with him and negotiate a joint promotion bringing back Cochran and Vincent to appear at Liverpool's boxing stadium on 3 May after their present theatre tour ended.

On 17 April, as the two Americans were returning to London from a show in Bath, their taxi skidded off the road into a concrete lamp post and Eddie Cochran was fatally injured. Although Gene Vincent suffered a broken collarbone – plus further trauma to a left leg that was already in a metal brace, the result of a previous car crash that had almost led to its amputation – he was passed fit for the boxing stadium show. To compensate for Cochran's absence, Allan Williams had to fill out its programme with some of the hometown bands who were his customers at the Jacaranda.

What was to have been a rock 'n' roll nostalgia show thus became the first-ever manifestation of a specific 'Liverpool' or 'Mersey' sound, with acts including Rory Storm and the Hurricanes (Ringo Starr on drums), Cass and the Casanovas, Bob Evans and the Five Shillings and the former Gerry Marsden Skiffle Group, lately renamed Gerry and the Pacemakers.

Yet the band destined in its final form to take Liverpool and the Mersey halfway to the Moon was merely part of the huge crowd standing around the boxing ring which deputised as a stage. 'We weren't big enough to play because we didn't have a drummer,' George was to recall. '[I thought] how we'd got to get ourselves together because the Hurricanes all had suits, and dance-steps.'

Allan Williams had been aware of the Silver Beatles only as the 'gang of right layabouts' who haunted the Jacaranda, making four coffees last as many hours and whose only talent between them, in his eyes, was Stu Sutcliffe's painting. But with Williams's emergence as a major concert promoter and associate of the great Larry Parnes, John nagged him into 'doing something for us.'

What Williams immediately did was fill the void that had bedevilled them under all their names for almost three years by finding them a drummer.

His name was Tommy Moore, his day-job was driving a forklift truck at the bottle-making factory in Garston and at twenty-eight he was virtually an old-age pensioner to his teen-aged bandmates. Nonetheless, he could hammer out a serviceable rock beat on a kit of spectacular dimensions, although the bass drum had an insecure mount from which it sometimes broke free and rolled away.

The quality and variety of the Liverpool bands Williams had rounded up for the boxing stadium show soon brought him further prestigious dealings with Larry Parnes. For in them the thrifty Parnes had seen an alternative to sending expensive London backing musicians with his vocalists on northern tours. A week later, he asked Williams to arrange a mass audition to choose possible sidemen for the leading stud in his stable, Billy Fury.

Fury was himself a Liverpudlian, born Ronald Wycherley and a Mersey tugboat hand until Parnes had discovered him, rebaptised him and, in a long-familiar syndrome, wiped away all traces of his origin as being too impossibly unglamorous for a pop idol. Originally just an Elvis copy, he'd shown unexpected depth by writing his own songs; not just the odd one, like some other British vocalists, but a whole album-full entitled *The Sound of Fury.*

The audition created huge excitement among the city's musicians, for Fury was to be present in person with his manager.

And as the Silver Beatles with Tommy Moore now had much more rhythm than in their guitars, Allan Williams allowed them to take part.

It took place on 10 May at the Wyvern, a run-down working men's club in Seel Street that Williams planned to turn into an upscale nightclub called the Blue Angel. Here the Silver Beatles found all the usual crushing, sensibly named competition: Rory Storm and the … Cass and the … Gerry and the … etc. etc.

While their chances against such titans were negligible, there was the thrill of being at close quarters to Billy Fury. He was in every way the antithesis of his name, a shy young man from the Dingle who cared less for the girls who swooned over him than for his pet tortoise and already suffered from the heart trouble that would kill him at forty-one.

From then on, George would recall, 'it was a bit of a shambles'. Their new drummer, Tommy Moore, had arranged to meet them at the Wyvern after rounding up some stray pieces of his kit but when their turn came in the audition, he still hadn't arrived. Williams had to arrange the loan of Cass and the Cassanovas' drummer, Johnny Hutchinson, a famously tough and aggressive character of whom even John was terrified.

The celebrated action shot by Liverpool photographer Cheniston Roland shows the Silver Beatles, in dark short-sleeve shirts, matching jeans and cheap Italian two-tone shoes, seemingly blowing their big moment. John and Paul cavort like a pair of urchin Elvises in a too-obvious effort to get Larry Parnes's attention. Stu Sutcliffe, painfully self-conscious about his lack of expertise on his unwieldy President bass, plays with his back turned. The stand-in, 'Johnny Hutch', does the union minimum on drums, clearly bored to death. George alone is utterly invested in the music, a look of such tender care on his face that he seems afraid he'll spill it.

Predictably, the honour of backing Billy Fury went to Cass and the Cassanovas, yet, despite their shambolic audition, the Silver Beatles ended up with a consolation prize. Larry Parnes also happened to need musicians for a lesser stallion in his stable named Johnny Gentle, who was about to go on tour in Scotland. They were the only band Allan Williams knew whose diary on the relevant dates was completely blank.

For John, Paul and Stu, the stakes were not so very high; each could easily 'sag off' school or college for a week with no lasting harm. But since George had no holidays owing from Blacklers and was refused any leave of absence, he'd have to resign his apprenticeship, sacrificing the lifelong security of a trade.

Before taking such a step, he sought the advice of his oldest brother, Harry, to whom he'd always deferred as much as to their father. Instead of the discouraging lecture he expected, Harry told him: 'You may as well ... you never know what might happen.'

'So I packed in my job and joined the band full-time,' he would recall, 'and from then, nine-to-five never came back into my thinking.'

5

'WE WERE LIKE ORPHANS'

That Scottish tour seriously dented George's illusions about going on the road with a band – although at its worst it didn't compare with roads he would have to travel in the future.

Billed as 'The Beat and Ballad Show', it consisted of seven consecutive one-nighters in small towns up and down Scotland's bleak north-east coast and into the Highlands. The wage was £18 each, from which the five had to pay their own train fares from Liverpool and back.

There was a feeling that as Larry Parnes protégés, however temporary, they should give themselves the kind of exotic stage names that adorned his 'stable'. Paul exchanged McCartney for Ramon, thinking it had a sultry Latin feel, Stu became Stuart de Stael after the Russian abstract painter Nicolas de Staël and George became Carl Harrison after Carl Perkins. The only dissenters were John, still embarrassed by his brief transformation into Treasure Island's Long John Silver, and their new, rather old drummer, Tommy Moore, who seemed beyond any glamorising.

Time having been too short for rehearsals, they didn't meet their star vocalist, Johnny Gentle, until half an hour before first going onstage with him in Alloa, Clackmannanshire. He turned out to be another undercover Liverpudlian, born John Askew and a ship's carpenter before Larry Parnes had discovered and renamed him as a less frenetic alternative to Fury, Wilde, Eager and Co.

Their performance that night at the town hall in nearby March Hill was so ragged that Parnes's Scottish co-promoter, a pig farmer named Duncan (aka 'Drunken') Mackinnon, wanted to put them straight onto a train back to Lime Street. But Gentle liked them and persuaded Mackinnon that they'd improve with practice.

The venues that followed were mostly town halls or ballrooms – actually a cut above what they'd been used to in Liverpool – with Gentle heading a bill of local singers and groups at each stop. The long journeys in between were in a single small van driven by a Mackinnon employee named Gerry Scott.

While Gentle, as the star, was accommodated in hotels, the others shared rooms in spartan boarding houses, eating in cheap 'caffs' or getting takeaway fish and chips. As it turned out, few Scottish teenagers were ever aware of watching Paul Ramon, Stuart de Stael or Carl Harrison, never mind the Silver Beatles, since the press advertisements and posters along the way were merely for 'Johnny Gentle and His Group'.

The twenty-four-year-old star proved to be a regular Scouser whose intensive grooming (in the equine sense) by Larry Parnes had not made him in the least big-headed. Despite his soft-pop milieu, he'd become part of rock 'n' roll history after appearing with Eddie Cochran and Gene Vincent on the show in Bristol that preceded their car crash. They'd asked him for a lift to

London afterwards, but as all the seats in his car were already promised, they'd taken their doomed taxi instead.

So His Group put themselves out to burnish Gentle's repertoire of Ricky Nelson, Elvis Presley and Buddy Holly ballads. He, in turn, did what he could to improve their meagre wardrobe. 'They'd come without any stage clothes,' he recalls. 'George had a black shirt and I had one, too, that I didn't wear. So I let them have that and we scraped up the money between us to buy another one so that at least their three frontmen looked the same.'

George was playing a new guitar for which his mother had signed the hire-purchase agreement: a solid-body Höfner Futurama with the same horned shape and triple pickups as a Fender Strat. But, as he would recall, the tour hardly seemed worthy of it.

'We were playing to nobody in little halls, until the pubs cleared out and about five Scottish Teds would come in and look at us. It was sad because we were like orphans. Our shoes were full of holes and our trousers were a mess, while Johnny Gentle had a posh suit. I remember trying to play … Elvis's "Teddy Bear" and we were crummy.'

That may have been pitching it a little strong: the only known photograph of the Silver Beatles in action on the tour shows him beside Gentle with his new Futurama in all its two-horned, three-pickup glory, and a stage-front packed with shining young female faces.

Usually at the end of a show it would be Gentle whom the shining-faced girls surrounded, sometimes with a little overspill for 'Paul Ramon'. But one night, as the band slipped out of a hall by the back door, a group of five mobbed George so enthusiastically that they ripped his black shirt. He wasn't in the least thrilled, only resentful of the damage to the precious shirt.

If Gentle was the frontman, John was still their leader, or ringleader, and the long intervals of boredom and discomfort gave extra edge to his sarcastic tongue and a sense of humour that had never known any brakes. The new recruit, Tommy Moore, was a favourite target of his practical jokes: while Moore was asleep John would stealthily open the door of his room, lasso one of his bedposts with a towel and by infinitesimal degrees drag the bed into the corridor.

Moore got off lightly in comparison with Stu Sutcliffe, whom John almost hero-worshipped at art college but now mercilessly teased and tormented for his ineptitude on bass guitar. Paul and George went along with it, baiting Stu not only for his fretboard fumbles but his smallness and poetic pallor, deliberately overflowing their allotted places in the back of the van so he'd have nowhere to sit but on the metal rim over a wheel-arch. 'We were terrible,' John would admit. 'We'd tell him he couldn't sit with us or eat with us. We'd tell him to go away, and he did.'

En route from Inverness to Fraserburgh, the tour came horribly close to replicating the Eddie Cochran/Gene Vincent tragedy when the van driver Gerry Scott was feeling hungover, so Johnny Gentle took over behind the wheel. Near the town of Banff, at a confusing road-fork, Gentle turned the wrong way and hit an approaching car head-on. The impact hurled a sleeping John from the back of the van to the front and a flying guitar case struck Tommy Moore in the mouth, loosening two of his front teeth.

Luckily, no police were involved but Moore had to be taken

to the nearest hospital suffering from concussion. Even so, there was no question of his missing that night's show at Fraserburgh's Dalrymple Hall. While he was in the casualty department, John arrived with the promoter and all but frogmarched him off to play, and try to control his freewheeling bass drum, with a bandage around his head.

A Fraserburgh schoolgirl named Margaret Caul had special cause to remember their visit. The day after the accident, Margaret and a friend were on the town's expansive beach when they met a group of dejected-looking young Liverpudlians wandering among the dunes. The one who said his name was John asked if there was a café anywhere near because they were all starving.

The girls told them not to go away, then ran to Margaret's house and returned with a picnic of 'baker's softies', fresh bread rolls thickly spread with jam. Margaret, who'd noticed George's torn shirt, even brought a needle and thread to mend it.

The tour struggled onward with its drummer on painkillers and its barely functional bass guitarist all but shunned by his bandmates, trying to bring bring beat and ballad to places that showed an increasing preference for heel and toe. At one hall, the promoter, who was also the town baker, nicknamed 'Bert the Bapper', shut them down after a couple of songs to announce a ballroom dancing competition. At another, they found they'd been bumped from the stage by a traditional ceilidh band and were expected to perform in a small upstairs room.

With only five of the seven dates behind them, their subsistence allowance from Larry Parnes was all spent and no more seemed to be forthcoming. At Forres in Morayshire, near where Shakespeare's Macbeth met the Three Witches, they had to do a runner from the Royal Station Hotel to escape a collective bill of just over £9.

None of these indignities was known about in Liverpool, where the mere fact of having been on a Larry Parnes tour incalculably raised the prestige of a band previously thought 'not worth a carrot'. A few day after their return, they found themselves on a dance poster as 'The Fabulous Silver Beetles', with nary a snigger to be heard.

Indeed, they'd done better than the audition winners, Cass and the Cassanovas, for whom touring with Billy Fury hadn't led to the predicted fame and fortune. But Johnny Gentle had ended up loving His Group and urged Larry Parnes to sign them up permanently. Parnes, however, felt he already had his hands full with solo singers – like Dickie Pride, the so-called 'Sheik of Shake', who was prone to drunkenness, drug-taking and car-theft – and preferred not to risk such problems multiplied by five.

In any case, they already had a manager-cum-agent in Allan Williams, albeit one who would always regard the office as more burden than privilege. Williams began handling their bookings under the same loose arrangement he had with Rory Storm and the Hurricanes and Derry and the Seniors, alongside what he considered more serious enterprises like his Jacaranda coffee bar and Blue Angel nightclub.

Williams's clout as an impresario brought them an instant upgrade in venues from parish halls and social clubs to ballrooms – although in Liverpool these were seldom devoted to 'balls'. The Grosvenor, for instance, across the Mersey in Wallasey, may have sounded like a haunt of Mayfair debutantes but was notorious for violence, especially between local Teddy Boys and invading ones from next-door Birkenhead.

The sartorial revolutionaries of 1955 had become ultra-conservative: nothing offended a Ted's aesthetic sensibilities more, especially with ten pints of Tetley's bitter inside him, than the new Italian-influenced Mod style that George was now heavily into. Every time he played the Grosvenor in a high-buttoning jacket, 'winklepicker' shoes and horizontal-striped, square-ended tie, it felt like taking his life in his bands.

Williams also gave the band a residency of sorts in the music venue under the Jacaranda, playing – for free – on Mondays when its usual attraction, a West Indian steel band, had the night off. Their name remained fluid – sometimes Silver Beetles, sometimes Silver Beatles, sometimes truncated to Silver Beats or backtracked to Beatals – and their cultural geiger-counter swung from one extreme to the other, from battling Teds at the Grosvenor to cutting-edge culture.

The latter crossed their path in June of 1960 when the celebrated young poet Royston Ellis came to Liverpool to appear in an arts festival at the university. Nineteen-year-old Ellis was a beat poet in the literal sense, the first to have fused highbrow spoken verse with low-brow or, rather, no-brow live rock 'n' roll. Apart from John Betjeman, he was the only British poet regularly seen on primetime television, where he would read his work backed by, among others, Cliff Richard's Shadows and the future Led Zeppelin guitarist Jimmy Page.

After his Liverpool University event, the by no means secretly gay Ellis gravitated to the Jacaranda, where he fell into conversation with 'a dishy-looking boy' whose name turned out to be Stuart Sutcliffe. Stu introduced Ellis to John, with whom he got on so well that he was invited to stay at their flat in Gambier Terrace.

During his visit, Ellis taught his new friends an inexpensive method of staying awake all night that was to prove useful sooner than they knew. Ordinary nasal inhalers, sold over the counter at every chemist's, had wicks impregnated with Benzedrine. One had only to break the plastic tube and chew the wick to keep going until dawn.

Ellis also sat in on another of their debates over whether they were Silver Beetles, Silver Beatles, Silver Beats or Beatals. With all the authority of a published and televised poet, he said they should be unadorned Beatles as a double play on beat music and beat poetry, and that finally settled the matter.

To round off his visit, Ellis gave a poetry reading at the Jacaranda, with John, Paul, George, Stu and Tommy Moore providing background music. It was such a success that he urged them to come down to London and join him on the avant-garde poetry circuit. Had they done so, it's safe to say that George wouldn't have gone with them.

They had scarcely become Beatles when they became beatless once again for the Scottish tour had left Tommy Moore feeling more battered than his drums and he'd decided to return to his far more profitable occupation of driving a forklift truck at the Garston bottle factory. The others showed up there and followed his forklift around the factory yard pleading with him to reconsider but to no avail; he thus became the only person ever to resign from the Beatles.

The void was temporarily filled by a picture-framer named Norman Chapman, an accomplished spare-time percussionist whom they happened to overhear practising alone in an office building directly opposite the Jacaranda. Chapman was amenable to becoming a Beatle and fitted in well enough but after appearing with them only three times, he was one of the last to be called up for National Service.

Since they were unlikely to be so lucky again, it was decided that Paul should take over as drummer – a role in which he'd always been at least as good as the official ones – using the various odds and ends of equipment they'd left behind. His debut with the sticks took place in surroundings which, like Royston Ellis's tip about how to stay awake all night, were strangely prophetic.

Allan Williams had recently expanded his entertainment empire with a strip joint in Kimberley Street, grandiosely styled the New Cabaret Artists Club. Here, as elsewhere, the Beatles were Williams's all-purpose workhorses: having recently played incidental music for Ellis's poetry, they now found themselves doing the same for a stripper named Janice.

They tried their best to enhance Janice's disrobing for the small audience of covert masturbators. With unintended appropriateness, George played 'Ramrod', the Duane Eddy instrumental he'd just learned, and Paul indulged his fondness for Latin rhythms in 'The Gipsy Fire Dance'. They evidently pleased Janice, for after shedding her last garment she turned round and gave them a 'flash'.

'We were just young lads,' Sir Paul McCartney recalls. 'We'd never seen anything like it and we all blushed. Five red-faced lads . . .' But they hadn't seen anything yet.

6

'MY FIRST SHAG ... WITH JOHN AND PAUL AND PETE BEST ALL WATCHING'

The Beatles' first stay in Hamburg, between August and November 1960, is the most romanticised episode in their career. Irresistible that vision of brash boy troubadours in their cracked black leathers, blasting out raw rock 'n' roll among the strip clubs and sex shows ... fumbling amateurs forging themselves into hardened profession-als ... the apprenticeship in the underworld without which their later flight through the Heavens could never have been.

From a twenty-first-century perspective of health and safety and employee-protection, it reads more like people-trafficking, with guitars.

Hamburg had a historic affinity with Liverpool, both located in the far north-west of their respective countries and both seaports, thronging with each other's shipping like neighbours who could walk in without knocking. The difference was that Hamburg had a red light district called the Reeperbahn whose name even the bawdiest Liverpool sailors spoke with awe.

A large part of the Reeperbahn's business came from West Germany's military bases, both American and British, on standby to counter the expected nuclear attack from the Communist East. The clientele were mostly young men whose idea of a good time, as much as getting drunk and laid, was live rock 'n' roll. Hamburg's porn merchants therefore began importing music groups from its mercantile soulmate, and for a time the sole exporter was Allan Williams.

Earlier in 1960, Williams had contracted to supply one of the bands he – sort of – managed to a Reeperbahn club-owner named Bruno Koschmider. He sent Derry and the Seniors, acknowledged to be Liverpool's most dynamic live act with their Afro-Caribbean vocalist Derry Wilkie.

They went down so well at Koschmider's Kaiserkeller club that he requested another band exactly like them. Williams's first choice, Rory Storm and the Hurricanes, were already committed to a residency at a Butlin's holiday camp; his second, Gerry and the Pacemakers, turned him down flat, so in desperation he turned to the Beatles. When the news reached Derry and the Seniors in Hamburg, their sax-player, Howie Casey, wrote to Williams, protesting that such a 'bum group' would be a severe embarrassment to them.

But the Beatles couldn't take the job without a drummer, nor could Paul continue in the role since Koschmider wanted a five-piece line-up like the Seniors. John briefly considered making Royston Ellis the fifth member as a 'poet-compere' as if he expected their Hamburg audience to resemble some earnestly attentive students' debating society.

This time, no long, dispiriting search was necessary, for the ideal candidate materialised at Mona Best's Casbah Club in West Derby, where George had saved the Quarrymen from disintegrating a year earlier.

It was during their Casbah residency that Mrs Best's good-looking son, Pete, had first become interested in rock 'n' roll, and after their petulant exit he'd formed a group named the Blackjacks, with himself on drums, to fill the gap they'd left. Now John, Paul and George came back looking for a drummer just when Pete's adoring mum had bought him a sumptuous new kit in a blue mother-of-pearl finish from Blacklers department store.

So one could say that George and his old-apprentice-masters were jointly responsible for Pete Best becoming a Beatle – an experience that was to leave Pete with the saddest eyes in rock.

Allan Williams smuggled the new quintet into West Germany by road, without work-permits or any kind of official documentation but their passports. If challenged, Williams said, they were to pretend to be students on vacation. To compound the illegality, George was seven months shy of eighteen, the minimum age for entry to the Hamburg clubs where they'd be performing,. And alone among the five traffickees, and constantly teased about it, he was still a virgin.

The city's St Pauli district, of which the Reeperbahn is the main thoroughfare, came as a profound shock after Liverpool's general nocturnal blackout and quiet. Continuous neon lights shimmered and winked in gold, silver and every suggestive colour of the rainbow, their voluptuous script – Bar Monika, Mambo Schankey, Gretel & Alphons, Roxy Bar – making the entertainments on offer seem even more untranslatably wicked. This was a place with no distinction between day and night which would turn the Beatles' body-clocks upside down for ever.

Their new employer, Bruno Koschmider, proved to be a tiny man of indeterminate age with the face of a carved wooden puppet, a femininely frothy coiffure and a limp supposedly acquired during wartime service with Hitler's Wehrmacht. But if Koschmider seemed to have stepped straight out of a Grimms' fairy tale, his Kaiserkeller club was spectacular, a subterranean barn decorated on a nautical theme with booths shaped like rowing-boats, lifebelts, brass binnacles and ornamental rope-work.

Only now did they learn they weren't to play here at the heart of the Reeperbahn but in a run-down strip club called the Indra that Koschmider owned in Grosse Freiheit, meaning 'Great Freedom', a much less buzzy side-street. Their job was to turn the Indra into as big a crowd-puller as Derry and the Seniors had made the Kaiserkeller.

Worse was to follow when Koschmider took them to the living quarters he was contracted to provide. Around the corner in Paul Roosen Strasse, he owned a small cinema called the Bambi, showing a mixture of porn flicks and old Hollywood gangster movies and Westerns. The Beatles' quarters were behind its screen; one dingy concrete room and two glorified broom-cupboards with camp-beds and naked overhead light-bulbs, exactly the kind of hell-hole regularly uncovered nowadays, packed with desperate illegal immigrants.

The only washing facilities were the adjacent cinema toilets. George would later say this hadn't been as hard on him as on the others 'because I used to live in a house without a toilet'.

In all its various incarnations back in Liverpool, the band had never been on any stage for longer than about twenty minutes. At the Indra Club, they found they were expected to play for four and a half hours each weeknight in sets of an hour and a half with only three thirty-minute breaks. On Saturdays and Sundays, it increased to six hours.

Unlike the Kaiserkeller, the Indra wasn't a dance-hall; its few customers sat at tables and watched an act, previously a stripper named Conchita. And on the Beatles' opening night, in matching lavender-coloured jackets tailored by Paul's next-door neighbour, it was made plain that they had to do more than just stand there.

Bruno Koschmider and Allan Williams acted as warm-up men, in this case to warm up the performers rather than the audience. '*Mach schau!*' Koschmider shouted in peremptory German fashion, clapping his hands. 'Come on, lads, make it show!' Williams translated.

In Liverpool, to 'make a show' of someone means to mock or humiliate them. John, characteristically, took it that way with a take-off of Gene Vincent as he'd appeared at Liverpool's boxing stadium only days after the Eddie Cochran death-crash, stumping around the stage and rolling on the floor in heartless mimicry of Vincent's calipered left leg. One night, he appeared onstage in shorts and, half-way through a song, pulled them down and showed the audience his bare bottom; not just in a 'flash' but an extended view. Blissfully unaware they were being made a show of, the audience loved it.

To fill the daunting ninety-minute sets, George recalled, they needed 'millions of songs', going far outside rock 'n' roll to country, folk, blues, even Broadway show-tunes and the current pop hits. Every one would be padded out to around twenty minutes and have about four instrumental breaks, either by him or Paul on the house piano; Ray Charles's 'What'd I

Say' could be stretched like a piece of chewing-gum to almost an hour in itself.

Their great standby was the prolific Chuck Berry whose elegies to American high school life seemed not in the least weird from a beady-eyed man with a golf-club moustache in his mid-thirties, and whose framing guitar riffs were the most seductive since Buddy Holly's. George could soon reproduce them all, even the finger-tangling solos like two players duelling in 'Johnny B. Goode'.

During the few hungover hours between shows, they'd try to grab some sleep in their ratty beds at the Bambi Kino or wash their clothes in the toilets they shared with a constant stream of cinema patrons. Even the fastidious George soon gave up the struggle to keep clean. 'I never used to shower,' he remembered. 'There was a washbasin in the lavatory . . . but there was a limit to how much of yourself you could wash in it. We could clean our teeth or have a shave. I remember once going to the public baths, but they were quite a long way away.'

There were already tensions within the band, magnified by the stress of being in a strange country and worked half to death. John's leadership remained unchallenged but Paul was ever his zealous adjutant; convinced that they could be spotted by some talent scout at any moment, he called for maximum effort, however late the hour or sparse the audience. And Stu Sutcliffe's bass playing, though now reasonably competent, was clearly never going to satisfy Paul.

Then, Pete Best was no longer regarded as the eleventh-hour lucky break without whose sparkly blue drums they wouldn't be here at all. Pete was a thoroughly amiable character who endured the hours he had to work and the conditions at the

Bambi Kino with unfailing cheerfulness – yet something about him somehow didn't fit. The problem would later be said to be his playing, but he produced a pounding rock beat more than adequate for a noisy club and a solid underlay to George's lead guitar. Only recently, George had written to a friend in Liverpool that 'Pete is drumming good.'

More tellingly, he was the best-looking member of the group, his crisp-cut hair and brooding expression giving him a look of the Hollywood matinee idol Jeff Chandler. He was the only one to have a stripper as a girlfriend, so spent most of the band's meagre time off with her instead of sharing in their adventures and misadventures. The German word for him was '*reserviert*' and it had already started to be his undoing.

The most famous Reeperbahn story, told and retold in Liverpool dockside pubs, was of women being mounted by donkeys with washers around their penises to limit penetration. Although this new definition of donkey-work proved a myth, there were other sights to awe a seventeen-year-old whose experience of erotica had been limited to British 'tit' magazines like *Razzle* with all the nipples blacked out.

In some clubs, George could see men and women of every race and colour have sex in twos, threes or even fours, in every possible and improbable configuration; in others, he could watch nude women wrestling in a pit of mud, cheered on by plump businessmen tied into a communal bib to protect their suits from the splashes. At Bar Monika or the Roxy Bar, he could meet trans men as beautiful and elegant as Parisian models; around the corner in the Herbertstrasse, he could find shop windows displaying sex workers as living merchandise complete with price tickets.

Sex was the Reeperbahn's main recreation as well as business and to its female population, jaded by years of drunken sailors and furtive businessmen, a young and relatively inexperienced young Liverpool rocker was the tastiest of novelties. As the Beatles built a following at the Indra Club, they found themselves repeatedly propositioned both by women customers and their fellow employees.

It was done in a forthright manner that might be said to have antedated Women's Lib by a decade. Someone who fancied a bit of boy Liverpudlian would make her choice while the band were playing either by pointing him out like a restaurant customer selecting a live lobster or, if stage-side, reaching up to fondle his leg. Many dispensed with even these slight formalities, going straight to their slum quarters at the Bambi Kino and waiting in one or other bed until their entrée arrived.

There, George finally lost his virginity, the total lack of privacy turning it into a formal initiation. 'My first shag was ... with Paul and John and Pete Best all watching,' he would recall. 'We were in bunk beds. They couldn't really see anything because I was under the covers but after I'd finished they applauded and cheered. At least they kept quiet while I was doing it.'

The Beatles' mission to wake up the Indra Club had succeeded only too well. Above the club lived an elderly war widow who complained incessantly to Bruno Koschmider about the noise. Fearing more serious comebacks from the police, Koschmider closed it down only seven weeks into their residency and moved them to his Kaiserkeller as support to Derry and the Seniors, where they'd wanted to be in the first place. Their original three-month contract was extended to 31 December, but with no improvement in their living conditions.

At the Kaiserkeller, their work schedule was even more punitive: five-and-a-half hours per night with only three half-hour breaks. The clientele were mostly sailors from a dock area as extensive as Liverpool's and there were frequent explosions of violence far surpassing anything seen at Wallasey's Grosvenor Ballroom.

To contain it, Koschmider employed a team of waiters mostly recruited from local boxing and bodybuilding gyms and renowned for the ruthless speed with which they quelled any disturbance. Especially fractious customers weren't simply thrown into the street but taken to the boss's office, where Koschmider would work them over with an antique wooden chair-leg he kept hidden down his trousers.

Unlike in Liverpool, musicians were not regarded as legitimate targets for attack, yet still faced hazards from the mass brawls at their feet. Along with flick-knives, coshes and brass knuckledusters, a popular accessory with Reeperbahn revellers and waiters alike were pistols firing tear-gas shells that could be bought over the counter at a nearby store. Certain numbers in the Beatles' repertoire were guaranteed to bring out this particular weaponry, especially the Olympics' 'Hully Gully', intended to be a line-dance promoting togetherness. 'By the end,' George recalled, 'we'd have to stop playing because of the gas.'

Also unlike in Liverpool, they were bought drinks by appreciative customers while they played; so many that by the end of their set, the stage-front would be crowded with empty bottles and glasses. Generally it was beer but now and again, someone in one of the rowboat-shaped side-booths, traditionally reserved for St Pauli's top gangsters, racketeers and porn merchants, would send a tray of Schnapps or a magnum of domestic champagne that it would have been highly inadvisable not to drain to the last drop.

The free-flowing fizz spurred John to a type of mockery that might have been expected to get him lynched in a city which had suffered wartime bombing even worse than Liverpool's. He'd goose-step around the stage, taunting the already bellicose crowd as 'fuckin' Nazis' and press a black comb to his top lip like a Hitler moustache. But the Germans still didn't get it or found it hilarious.

The Kaiserkeller's Liverpool headliners, Derry and the Seniors, had revised their opinion of the Beatles as 'a bum group' who would only bring discredit on them and their home city. But the partnership was not to last. They, too, had been sent into West Germany without permits to work as musicians; if challenged, Allan Williams had told them to say they were plumbers who'd brought their instruments along to entertain themselves between jobs.

In October of 1960, they were finally found out and ordered to leave the country. Despite many months as darlings of the Reeperbahn, they'd saved no money, and spent their last days in Hamburg living rough before the British Consulate could be persuaded to pay their airfares home.

As replacements Williams sent out Rory Storm and the Hurricanes, fresh from their season at Butlin's holiday camp in Skegness. On arrival, they found they were expected to take over Derry and the Seniors' old quarters above the Kaiserkeller, sleeping in beds covered with threadbare flags instead of blankets. They declined, opting instead for the comparative luxury of one room between five of them at the British-run Seamen's Mission down at the docks.

Rory was a long-time friend of the Beatles and the brother of George's first girlfiend, Iris Caldwell. Although he and his 'Hurikan Von Liverpool' outranked them on Kaiserkeller posters, there now was little difference in the two bands' musical ability apart from athletic Rory's penchant for dancing on piano-tops and shinning up walls.

Yet they were still only slightly acquainted with the Hurricanes' doleful-looking, bearded drummer. Back in Liverpool, Ringo Starr had seemed an intimidatingly adult figure – although he was only four months older than John – as well as hugely sophisticated with the chunky rings that clotted his fingers like a Reeperbahn waiter's knuckledusters, his taste for imported American Lark cigarettes and his impressive Ford Zephyr car.

Now they discovered he was more a fan of their music than they'd ever realised. While they were winding up a long night at the Kaiserkeller, he'd come in, sit drinking by himself, and sooner or later send up a request for George to play the Duane Eddy instrumental 'Three-30 Blues'. "He looked like a grown-up,' George would recall, 'with this grey streak in his hair and half a grey eyebrow and that big nose.'

Rory Storm and the Beatles together at the Kaiserkeller were an incendiary combination. They competed with each other in outrageousness onstage, even in pushing the boundaries of their chain-gang working-hours, once keeping going in alternation with only minimal breaks for an astonishing twelve hours.

They also vied with each other in baiting Bruno Koschmider, rather as British POWs had done with their guards at Colditz Castle – a place with rather better accommodation than the Bambi Kino.

After the Beatles' already huge mileage on the Kaiserkeller's stage, they knew its planks to be half-rotten and its supporting timbers in an equally decayed state. This inspired a nightly competition between the Hurricanes and themselves to be the first to stomp a hole in it. Rory took the prize during 'Whole Lotta Shakin' Goin' On' with a leap onto the piano that caved in the fragile floor underneath and he sank from view still astride the piano like a rodeo-rider on a bucking bronco.

During these weeks, Ringo increasingly took to hanging out with the Beatles rather than his own band. He came from the Dingle, Liverpool's poorest quarter, and, due to prolonged childhood illness, had received next to no formal education. Yet he had a natural perceptiveness and articulacy together with a deadpan wit that was a match even for John's. His Liverpool accent was broader and deeper by far than George's, but no one had ever found fault with it, nor ever would.

It seemed natural that he should sit in with the Beatles during Pete Best's frequent absences, still more natural that his drumming style instantly fitted them like a broken-in pair of the best jeans. 'When there were the four of us with Ringo,' George would remember, 'it always felt rockin'.'

They also palled around with the Hurricanes' bass-player Lu Walters, known as Wally, who had ambitions to escape from Rory's antic shadow and become a vocalist in his own right. Wally had heard about a walk-in recording studio named Akustik at Hamburg's main railway station and was bursting with eagerness to make a demo there. He recruited the Beatles as sidemen, Allan Williams agreed to pay the minimal cost and, with Pete Best not being around yet again, it seemed only natural to ask Ringo to take Pete's place.

So, in a cramped booth only just insulated from train noises and station announcements, backing their temporary vocalist through a set of standards like 'Summertime' and 'Fever' and afterwards to be billed on the flimsy little Akustik disc as 'The Beatles mit Wally', the right four recorded together for the first time.

Hamburg differed from Liverpool most in being a media and publishing centre whose many first-class art, design and photography schools had nurtured the most distinctive student population in post-war Europe.

They called themselves 'existentialists' after the French literary school led by Jean-Paul Sartre and Albert Camus which preached the supremacy of the individual will over society's rules and conventions. It was an idea with special appeal to young Germans after the terrible mass conformism of the Nazi era, and found expression in radical stylishness that often blurred the line between male and female. Most radically, an essential part of an 'exi's' costume was the black leather that had formerly symbolised Hitler's Gestapo and SS: in a small way, an exorcism of that infinite tyranny and brutality.

At the same time, they were middle-class and respectable and had always avoided the Reeperbahn until an evening in the autumn of 1960 when one of their leading figures, a design student named Klaus Voormann had a tiff with his girlfriend and went off there on his own for a bit of mutinous slumming.

The first bar he visited happened to be the Kaiserkeller where that night, as every night, the Beatles were working.

Voormann has never forgotten that first sight and sound of them. 'It was like hearing every great rock 'n' roll tune there had ever been, sung by the greatest singers. They were like chameleons. John would be Gene Vincent, then he'd be Chuck Berry. Paul would do Elvis, then he'd do Fats Domino, then he'd do Carl Perkins. And in between, the two of them would argue, "I want to do Be-Bop-A Lula." "No, I want to do it."'

Two magnetic front men couldn't hog absolutely all Voormann's attention. 'George was a catalyst. He brought a certain calm between those two great characters. You noticed him because he *wasn't* showing off. When he played a solo, it wasn't saying "Look at me"; it was an organic part of the song.

'Offstage, he was a fresh, cocky kid but he was calm, he was funny and he always seemed to have his feet firmly planted on the ground. Something about him told you that he came from a good home with good parents and that he'd grown up loved.'

The girlfriend with whom Voormann had fallen out that evening was twenty-two-year-old Astrid Kirchherr, a talented photographer who worked as an assistant to the great photo-journalist Reinhart Wolf. She was herself a perfect subject for the camera, beautiful in a way not yet called 'androg-ynous', her creamy pallor and close-cropped blonde hair setting off an all-black wardrobe that soon would seem like mourning-in-waiting.

Astrid was rather disgusted to hear of Voormann's adventure on the grubby Reeperbahn and only with the greatest reluc-tance agreed to accompany him back there to see the Beatles for herself. She, too, loved them at first sight but also fell *in* love:

not with reckless John or adorable Paul but the least assertive one, Stu Sutcliffe.

At first she hid her feelings behind a professional interest in the group, photographing them in what would become an historic session in Hamburg's Dom fairground, posing them with their instruments perched on traction-engines or standing moodily around silent calliopes, trying to prevent her lens from lingering overlong on Stu's James Dean looks and unwieldy Höfner President bass.

Discovering, to her horror, the conditions in which they were living, she took them back to the comfortable house in the Altona district she shared with her mother, so they could have long-overdue baths, and served them the English food they'd been longing for in all these months of bratwurst and sauerkraut.

She instantly warmed to George, whom she thought 'just a baby boy with his piled-up hair and his ears sticking out. He was so sweet when I gave them ham sandwiches. He said he didn't know we had ham sarnies in Germany.'

The visit included a peep into Astrid's bedroom-cum-studio, which was decorated entirely in black, with silver-painted tree-branches hanging from its ceiling. 'I believe George thought I was a bit mad. It was Paul who asked all the questions . . . who painted this picture? . . . who wrote that book? George was just as inquisitive, but quieter.'

Where Astrid and Klaus led, their exi set obediently followed and soon the Beatles found themselves playing to a foreground of black leather and pale, solemn faces. 'We could only look on these Liverpool people as fantastic creatures because they were open, they were friendly, they were quick, very, very quick humour,' Voormann says. 'We knew how stiff we were, how hard we found it to let go. They had no problem, they talked about anything, they took the mickey out of themselves all the time. And we had to learn that. To laugh about our own hang-ups.'

While John and Paul claimed most of their attention, a small cohort, led by Astrid's friend and fellow photographer Jürgen Vollmer, appreciated George's musicianship and refused to let him be eclipsed. 'We made ourselves a fan club for him,' Vollmer says. 'We'd shout out, "We want George."'

Astrid's undisguised adoration had a transformative effect on the shy, self-conscious Stu – and not only that. Since he had started thumbing a bass guitar to please John, he'd all but abandoned his true talent. Now, the nightly company of art and design students spurred him to start painting again, inspired anew by the Reeperbahn's frenetic colour and motion.

At the insistence of Astrid's mother, he left the Beatles' horrible quarters behind the Bambi Kino and moved into the Kirchherr home, where an attic room was converted into a studio for him. In late November of 1960, only a month after first meeting, he and Astrid announced their engagement.

George, too, had acquired a German girlfriend as opposed to the one-night stands the Kaiserkeller provided so liberally. Seventeen-year-old Monika Pricken had been among the Beatles' earliest fans at the Indra Club; she and George had been dating ever since in the brief spells between his time onstage, and with a chasteness he may by then have found restful. 'He was unbelievably funny and open,' she would recall,' but our friendship was totally platonic.'

Monika's family owned a well-known clock and watch shop in the city centre, and were highly dubious about her seeing a

Reeperbahn musician until she brought all the Beatles home for a meal. Afterwards, they thanked her parents politely, 'with a bow and a handshake', and John gave an impromptu performance on his guitar, singing in a mixture of English and cod-German.

They had been longing to find a way out of Bruno Koschmider's clutches and, as Christmas approached, they seemed to have succeeded. A few doors away from the Kaiserkeller, a rival club called the Top Ten was about to open on the site of an indoor circus whose female bareback riders also used to be bare. The owner, Peter Eckhorn, was a new kind of St Pauli showman, young, go-getting and a genuine rock 'n' roll fan rather than just a reluctant exploiter.

Eckhorn lost no time in poaching Koschmider's star attraction to headline at the Top Ten Club. The hours wouldn't be much less punishing than the Kaiskerkeller's but at least they'd be treated like human beings, living above the club in a flat with an actual bathroom.

For more than three months, the fact that George was only seventeen and so too young to be in the Kaiserkeller after 10 p.m., let alone play music there, had seemed to bother no one. Each night at curfew hour, in a sudden gust of morality, the official *Ausweiskontrolle*, or youth-protection squad, would arrive, harsh overhead lights would go on, passports and IDs be inspected and all illegal juveniles escorted from the premises.

Now at last George was found out, not by the *Ausweiskontrolle* but through a tip-off to the police, most likely from Bruno Koschmider in revenge for the Beatles' defection. While the band were in the act of moving into their new quarters at the Top Ten, George found himself ordered to leave the country immediately.

Stu and Astrid took him to the train station, still in shock, with his guitar and new Gibson amplifier and his single little suitcase overflowing into miscellaneous boxes and paper bags. Monika Pricken was there, too, with her friend, Helga, 'to give him a bag of sandwiches and fruit for the journey,' she would recall, 'and wave him off with tears.'

His journey home took twenty-four hours, first by rail to the Hook of Holland, then by ferry across the North Sea to Harwich, then another train to London's Liverpool Street station, where he had just enough money left for the cross-town taxi to Euston station and the train to Liverpool.

Back in Speke, he imagined the Beatles playing at the Top Ten Club without him, presumably for keeps. He had no idea that his brush with the West German authorities had had a far more dramatic sequel.

When Paul and Pete Best were collecting the last of their belongings from the Bambi Kino, they'd said goodbye to their slum quarters with the not inappropriate gesture of setting light to a condom. Bruno Koschmider retaliated by having them arrested for attempted arson. They spent a night in a police cell before being deported back to Britain by air. Meanwhile, Stu Sutcliffe had gone to ground at Astrid's house and John, with no band left, had returned home by train in a journey as fraught and demoralised as George's had been.

Straight after reaching home, George had a mission to perform indicative of his closeness to Stu Sutcliffe. Even this distance from the war, it was no small thing for a British boy to want to marry a German girl, especially if he came from bomb-quarried Liverpool. Stu had written to his parents about getting engaged to Astrid and he'd asked George to suss out their reaction.

'Your dad seems OK about the idea,' George wrote to Stu, 'but your mum seems a little "disappointed" in you (that is as far as I can make out.)'

He's clearly over his train and boat nightmare and three months-worth of accumulated fatigue, and back in training for whatever his Höfner Futurama may hold. He tells Stu he's hoping to get an echo-chamber for his amp ('£34 or £6 down'). And he's bought 'Eddie [Cochran]'s "Singin' To My Baby" LP, "Man of Mystery", "Lucille", "Only The Lonely", "Like Strangers" (Everlys' new one), "Perfidia" (Ventures' new one) and an instrumental called "Chariots".

'I am learning everything I can get my hands on now.'

7

'The first rock 'n' dole group'

George didn't make contact with John and Paul until some days after their respective ignominious homecomings, and then it was only to sit around and bemoan what little good those three and a half sweated months in Hamburg seemed to have done them.

In a world without social media and mobile phones, there had been no way of keeping Liverpool informed of their exploits but the occasional postcard home, scrawled in the Bambi Kino's grim twilight. Their latter quasi-criminal status hadn't generated a single newspaper story that might have lent them a touch of glamour. And as far as Merseyside's music promoters were concerned, they'd gone back to the bottom of the heap.

The penniless, half-starved state in which they returned had redoubled parental pressure to forget this rock 'n' roll nonsense once and for all. John was facing a recriminatory onslaught from his Aunt Mimi who, in memory of Dickens's Ebenezer Scrooge in this Christmas season, deliberately mispronounced 'Hamburg' as 'Humbug'. Even Paul's father, Jim, had insisted he find 'a proper job' and he'd become a temporary employee of the Speedy Prompt Delivery Company, dropping off parcels around the docks by truck.

George had been spared any such inquisition, his parents and brothers remaining as supportive and sympathetic as ever. Still, as Harold and Louise Christmas-shopped at Blacklers department store, whose Santa's grotto this year was as spectacular as ever, the thought of a thrown-away electrical apprenticeship and 'job for life' must surely have crossed their minds.

To add to the general gloom, Allan Williams's career as Liverpool's Mister Rock 'n' Roll now lay in smouldering ruins. His latest enterprise had been a music club on the same pack-'em-in-and-rip-'em-off lines as the Reeperbahn's. Like the one for which the Beatles had been bound before their expulsion, it was to be named the Top Ten and he'd promised them regular work there as its house band.

But they'd never even set eyes on the place. Six days after opening on 1 December, it mysteriously burnt to the ground out of hours when no one was on the premises. That, added to Williams's well-known talent for offending people, suggested a 'torch job'.

The single booking on offer, Mona Best's Casbah Club, heightened the feeling of having come full-circle, but the vivacious Mrs Best made it a gala night for Pete's band, as she now thought of them, with welcome-home posters for 'THE FABULOUS BEATLES'.

With Stu Sutcliffe still in Hamburg, they were without a bass guitarist, so Pete brought in an old schoolfriend of his named Chas Newby who'd played guitar in his previous band, the Blackjacks. Earlier, Pete had approached Newby to replace George after his deportation – just as George had feared somebody might. But Newby had been unwilling to interrupt his study of Chemistry and Chemical Engineering at St Helens College and, anyway, the Beatles were already fragmenting amid charges of illegal immigration and attempted arson. Now was college vacation-time, however, and Newby agreed to switch instruments and temporarily join them as their first, but not last, left-handed bass-player.

Newby had known John, Paul and George since they were Quarrymen, and was amazed by the change in them, in George especially. 'During their residency at the Casbah, he'd just been an average guitarist, not much above the level of the other two. Now he was the best I'd ever seen.'

Newby seemed to bring them luck, for one day at the Jacaranda coffee bar they got talking to an older man with a pink, pixie-ish face and somewhat the air of a pedantic school-master, though one to whom even George gave full attention.

His name was Bob Wooler and he worked as a part-time compère and deejay at dances throughout Liverpool, combining a voice as rich as a Merseyside Moondog with an encyclopaedic musical knowledge. Not long previously, he'd left his steady job as a British Railways clerk briefly to preside over Allan Williams's ill-fated Top Ten Club.

Wooler listened sympathetically as they complained about their lack of work, then went to the phone and got them a booking at a dance he was to emcee at Litherland Town Hall, a gloomy municipal building in the north of the city, on 27 December. The fee was £6 between them.

Among those making the trek to Litherland that snowy night in the post-Christmas hangover was George's child-hood friend Tony Bramwell, who never missed seeing live music anywhere if he could help it. 'I went on the number 81 bus, which was the one George's dad usually drove, though he wasn't on that night,' Bramwell recalls. 'On the top deck George was sitting with his guitar case, on his way to the gig. I asked him if I could carry his guitar in for him because that way I'd get in free.'

The small coterie of Beatles supporters also included Pete Best's younger brother, Rory, and his friend, Neil Aspinall, a trainee accountant with the Prudential insurance company who'd lately become a lodger in the Bests' home. Aspinall had been at the Inny in the year above George, but they'd often met on equal, unhealthy terms at the break-time Smokers' Corner.

Otherwise, the crowd in the 1,500-capacity hall were there to dance the newfangled Shake or old-fashioned jive to three familiar bands, the Deltones, the Delrenas and the Searchers. Bob Wooler had billed this last-minute addition as 'the Beatles – direct from Hamburg'; they were thus assumed to be a German group unconscious of the absurdity of their name to British ears.

As the stage-curtains parted, there was palpable surprise and – just for a moment – disappointment. For here was not the expected line of ersatz Cliff Richard's Shadows, dancing the neat, synchronised two-step which, until then, had been the height of performing cool. Here were defiantly asymmetric figures, dressed all in black like their Hamburg exi friends but with none of black's usual neatness or sleekness, pitching into Little Richard's 'Long Tall Sally' with the *mach schau* that had become second nature.

According to official Beatles history, their stunned audience spontaneously surged forward in the first-ever outbreak of Beatlemania. According to their temporary bass-player, Chas Newby, the response was less extreme but no less extraordinary. 'Everyone just stopped dancing and watched them. I'd never seen any crowd do that with a band before. A couple of the bouncers even thought there must be a fight going on and went around looking for it.'

Later came another 'first' in the annals of Liverpool bands: when the promoter, Brian Kelly, block-booked the Beatles for dates far into the future, he posted a guard outside the door to prevent any rival from outbidding him.

That night, they acquired two followers, both destined to be important future allies for George. The first was Tony Bramwell, who would carry George's guitar into so many gigs to gain free entry that the others would eventually say he might as well carry theirs in, too.

The second was the Bests' lodger, Neil Aspinall, thanks to whom George would never again have to take his dad's bus to a gig. Aspinall owned a beaten-up van with two rough wooden rear seats and, for the consideration of a pound or two, was only too happy to drive the band wherever they needed to go. After helping them unload their equipment, he'd return to the Bests' house and study for his accountancy exams until it was time to collect them.

Chas Newby's spell as a Beatle ended in January 1961, when Stu Sutcliffe finally returned from Hamburg. Despite the anti-German feeling on his mother's part, of which George had forewarned him, Stu was determined to marry Astrid Kirchherr and settle in Liverpool, having been virtually guaranteed a place on the Art College Teacher Diploma teacher-training course.

Meantime, still unable to disappoint John, he took up his too-heavy bass guitar again.

The Beatles faced a struggle to perform at the Cavern club that the Quarrymen never had. Even after John slipped some Elvis under its guard in 1957, the Cavern had remained dedicated to traditional jazz, an enclave of the acoustic Fifties that winced and covered its ears against the electric din issuing from every other music venue in the city.

Latterly, however, its owner, a former accountant named Ray McFall, had been forced to recognise the decline in jazz audiences and the need for an alternative income stream. He'd therefore let rock 'n' roll into the Cavern, initially in small amounts like spoonfuls of some nauseating medicine. The bands granted this privilege were required to wear suits onstage and jeans were forbidden for customers and performers alike.

As John and George knew from playing there as Quarrymen, the Cavern's lofty attitudes belied its premises, the low-ceilinged brick cellar of three arched bays, in total measuring no more than about fifty by thirty feet. It had no heating (at least not the mechanical kind), no air-conditioning, no limit on the numbers who could be admitted, no extractor fans, smoke alarms, sprinkler system or emergency exit.

No main drainage even: the toilets emptied into a cesspit whose presence never ceased to make itself felt. The competing odours of sewage, disinfectant, mould, mice-droppings, cheeses stored in the warehouse above and rotting rejects from the Fruit Exchange across the street impregnated clothes beyond rescue by any drycleaner; you could identify someone fresh from the Cavern at several yards' distance.

Mona Best had been urging McFall to hire the Beatles since their return from Hamburg, and after their triumph at Litherland Town Hall, Bob Wooler – subsequently hired as the Cavern's compère and deejay – added his wholehearted recommendation. But the cautious McFall wasn't yet ready to grant them parity with Kenny Ball's Jazzmen or the Clyde Valley Stompers by giving them the Cavern stage at night.

Mathew Street, the cobbled lane of Victorian warehouses where the club was located, lay barely a minute's walk from busy thoroughfares like North John Street and Whitechapel. Every lunch hour young office and shop workers thronged the area, gazing into shop windows or eating their sandwiches on the steps of Victorian monuments but with nothing else to fill the time until they returned to duty. McFall's recent brainwave had been to give them lunchtime live music at the Cavern.

Somewhat grudgingly, the Beatles were offered an appearance at this seemingly unrewarding time of day for a collective fee of £5 per performance, which at first it seemed they would have to turn down. In his zeal to placate his father, Paul had joined the maritime coil-winding firm of Massey and Coggins where, singled out as potential management material, he'd been put into the office on a – for then – very healthy wage of £7 per week. Absenting himself for at least three hours in the middle of the day would be impossible.

John unwound him from Massey and Coggins by offering a stark choice: 'Your dad or me.' An immeasurable talent thus escaped throttling by a white-collar office job in Liverpool docks.

The Cavern's facilities for its performers were no better than for its customers. The stage, at the inner end of the central bay, was barely two feet high, its only lighting a crude wooden batten studded with ordinary 60-watt bulbs directly overhead, the few electric sockets in constant jeopardy from the condensation coursing down the walls. Behind it was a single communal dressing room-cum-tune-up area, from which Bob Wooler, aka 'Mister Big Beat', introduced the various acts over the PA and played records from his large personal collection during intermissions.

When the Cavern was full, as it nearly always was, the heat was stupefying. Former club members fondly recall how, as they came down the eighteen steps from the street, it coiled up around their legs like a serpent. Girls regularly fainted, sometimes boys too; in the crush of bodies, the only way to get them to fresh air was to pass them in supine bundles over people's heads.

Many of the Beatles' first lunchtime audience were there solely out of curiosity, for rumours were still circulating of the 'German group' at Litherland Town Hall. 'It was a shock to find out they were Scousers just like us,' recalls Debbie Greenberg, who was there as a fifteen-year-old schoolgirl. 'They blew us away, they had such energy. They didn't stop in between each number like bands usually did. And they were wearing jeans, which had never been allowed at the Cavern. What struck me most was how young George seemed to be, and a bit lost with McCartney and Lennon doing most of the talking and John pulling plenty of faces.'

The Beatles became just one of numerous bands playing the lunchtime sessions by rota, many almost matching them in popularity, such as Gerry and the Pacemakers ('pacemakers' in those days synonymous with long-distance running races rather than dicky hearts) fronted by the irrepressible Gerry Marsden.

The difference was that these rivals had nine-to-five jobs which could tie them up during the daytime. The Beatles were under no such handicap, so always available to plug sudden gaps in the Cavern's schedule. Pun-loving Bob Wooler dubbed them 'the world's first rock 'n' dole group'.

Their Cavern repertoire included few of the original songs accumulating in John and Paul's school exercise book. So far, these had tended mostly to be ballads such as Paul's 'Like Dreamers Do' but what their audience demanded were familiar rock 'n' roll standards. Yet even as a largely 'covers' band, they managed to be continually fresh and unpredictable.

In Wooler's record collection they found American R&B tracks too spiky for British radio, like Barrett Strong's 'Money' or Chan Romero's 'Hippy Hippy Shake'. Thanks to John and Paul's powers of mimicry and George's ability to decrypt chords and riffs, there was nothing they couldn't replicate, whether Larry Williams's 'Slow Down', Carl Perkins's 'Glad All Over', the lusty call-and-response of Gary U.S. Bonds' 'New Orleans' or the weird blues harmonica waltz time of James Ray's 'If You Gotta Make A Fool Of Somebody'.

'You never knew what was coming next,' Debbie Greenberg recalls. 'From "Long Tall Sally", they might go into something my mum and dad liked, like "Besame Mucho" or "Red Sails In The Sunset".'

Daringly in that super-macho culture, they also took to doing songs by black American female groups, like the Marvelettes' 'Please Mister Postman' or the Shirelles' 'Boys' without bothering to alter the girlie lyrics. They'd cover current pop hits, sometimes even by the singing cotton buds who still dominated the charts. Though the lead vocal would usually be John's sourness or Paul's sweetness or the sweet-and-sour blend of the two, George's version of Bobby Vee's 'Take Good Care Of My Baby' had an adenoidal charm all of its own.

Every major Liverpool group boasted a fanatical female following, but from the beginning the Beatles resembled a fully formed movement. At their every performance, the rows of kiddie-size wooden chairs in the centre bay would be packed with beehive hairdos, balloon skirts and black-caked eyes. This was a very Liverpool kind of fandom, adoring yet not in the least reverential – and with no hint of screaming yet. The devotees of each Beatle clustered below his invariable place on the stage. Many would arrive with newly washed hair in rollers which they didn't remove until the last seconds before their darling made his entry.

One of the regulars at the lunchtime sessions' was sixteen-year-old Frieda Kelly, then a typist in a city office. 'I'd always come to the second show, from 1.15 to 2.15,' she recalls. 'In the first, one of them might turn up late – usually George.'

Frieda's 'spec', or regular vantage point, was against the left-hand wall, level with where George always stood and also enjoying a partial view into the band room behind the stage. 'I had to stand up for an hour, but it always seemed to go by in about five minutes.' In addition to the tropical heat and variegated stench, the air would be bright blue with cigarette smoke. 'All the Beatles were dragging on ciggies while they played,' Frieda recalls. 'George would always have a spare one behind his ear or wedged in the head of his guitar.'

They were as much a comedy act as a musical one, singing and talking in cod-German, French or Speedy Gonzales Mexican accents, John giving full rein to his routine of demented grimaces and pretend-claw hands which in those days offended no one. The two-foot-high stage was no barrier: throughout their performance, they would carry on conversations with friends, or foes, in the audience and accept, or reject, song requests.

When, as often happened, a dodgy plug fused and their amps died into silence, John and Paul would do a *Goon Show* or Morecambe and Wise routine or sing the television jingle for Sunblest bread while George mustered what electrical knowledge he'd acquired as an apprentice to try to fix the problem.

None of them had mentioned the Cavern at home, but the number of sodden, strange-smelling shirts left out for the wash launched Jim McCartney, John's Aunt Mimi and Louise Harrison on their own separate bits of sleuthing.

When Jim found his way there from his nearby workplace, the Liverpool Cotton Exchange, he couldn't even get through the crowd around Paul.

On another day, Aunt Mimi and Louise happened to turn up at the same moment, when the Beatles were onstage. Louise instantly started bopping around as excitedly as any teenage fan. 'Aren't they marvellous!' she shouted above the din.

'I'm glad someone thinks so,' Mimi sniffed.

Bob Wooler was to calculate that between 1961 and 1963, when they left Liverpool, a rock 'n' dole group no longer, the Beatles appeared at the Cavern 292 times.

'[We] were no big deal then,' George would remember after they'd become the world's biggest deal and nothing seemed sweeter than obscurity. 'It was fun . . . just pure fun.'

The Reeperbahn's door had not irrevocably slammed behind the Beatles the previous December. Their engagement at its Top

Ten Club remained open if some way could be found around the one-year ban imposed on Paul and Pete Best for allegedly trying to burn down Bruno Koschmider's Bambi cinema with a lighted condom.

Paul wrote to the West German Foreign Office, using all his powers of diplomacy to plead that Koschmider had wildly exaggerated a foolish but harmless prank. Similar representations were made by Allan Williams to the country's consulate in Liverpool and by the Top Ten's young owner, Peter Eckhorn. The ban was lifted on condition that Paul and Pete promised to be of good behaviour and Eckhorn reimbursed the cost of flying them home when they'd been deported.

With George, there was no more threat of trouble from the authorities: his eighteenth birthday in February made him legal to play on the Reeperbahn at any time of night. So, dealing directly with Eckhorn, the band accepted a thirteen-week engagement, beginning on 1 April.

For Stu Sutcliffe, it was to have been an unrancorous parting from rock 'n' roll as he began the Art Teacher's Diploma course he'd been all but guaranteed by Liverpool College of Art. But despite his previous brilliant record at the college, the interviewing panel turned him down. Although no official explanation was given, it seemed he was being blamed for the disappearance of the amplifier he'd persuaded the college to buy for the Quarrymen when they were regularly playing there. So, to Stu's huge disappointment and frustration, he was still stuck with playing bass in the Beatles.

As well as headlining at the Top Ten, they were to act as back-up to the singer/guitarist Tony Sheridan, who'd been the first Brit to find stardom on the Reeperbahn. Born Anthony Esmond

Sheridan McGinnity, Sheridan had had a promising career in early British rock 'n' roll prematurely cut short when he had to flee abroad to escape hire-purchase debts and prosecution for forgery. He was awe-inspiring to George for having appeared onstage with the great Eddie Cochran and actually played the Grescht guitar that George had ogled from afar at Cochran's Liverpool Empire show.

Sheridan was essentially a rhythm guitarist, but with a unique way of slipping unusual chords into the standard rock sequences. 'For me, it was always better to play an E7 than an E,' he recalled. '[I thought] George was the most interesting Beatle as he reminded me of myself at that age. He was always asking me "How do you do that? What's that funny chord?" the way I used to ask Eddie Cochran. Now and again in the Beatles' music you can hear one of the chords that George picked up in St Pauli. Listen to the start of "Come Together" – that's *my* chord, man.'

The Top Ten was far more fun than the Kaiserkeller, with Tuesday talent nights when the Beatles could take a rest from *mach schau* and enjoy the spectacle of drunken customers trying to imitate them. 'They knew the sound of the words but they couldn't really get them, especially if it was something like "Tutti Frutti,"' George would recall. 'Back when we were we were still performing the latest records, one was Johnny Kidd and the Pirates' "Shakin' All Over", but they thought we were singing "send him to Hanover", the German equivalent of send him to Coventry.'

The bunk-bed accommodation above the club was far from luxurious, but this time the toilets had an attendant, an elderly frau named Rosa who, along with soap and clean towels, dispensed Benzedrine 'uppers' from an outsize candy jar. Peter Eckhorn's chief bouncer, a former featherweight boxing champion named Horst Fascher, who'd once accidentally killed a sailor in a street brawl, ensured no retrospective reprisals from Bruno Koschmider.

It was on this visit that they discovered something new to keep them going all through each neon-crazy night, used by punters and workers alike. It was a slimming tablet named Preludin whose high amphetamine content accelerated the body's metabolic rate but also dried up the saliva, magnifying their craving for beer and creating the fizz of a dozen Alka-Seltzer tablets if taken at the same time. 'We were frothing at the mouth,' George would recall. 'We'd be up there, foaming and stomping away. I remember lying in bed [later], sweating and thinking, "Why aren't I sleeping?"'

His memories of John high on 'prellys' and beer together could sound almost like those of a child with an abusive father. 'He'd come in in the early hours of the morning and be ranting and I'd be lying there, pretending to be asleep, hoping he wouldn't notice me.'

John, however, remembered George as a much less timid character. 'We had no time to eat, so we used to eat onstage. George threw a plate of food over me once ... The row was over something stupid ... mainly because we were tired and irritable and working too hard. I said I would smash his face in for him ... but that was all. And I once threw a plate of food over George. That's the only violence we ever had between us.' Not quite, as it would turn out.

But even that other, aggressive George shied away from the murkiest episode in the Beatles' Reepherbahn residencies. All five were drinking away their weekly wage, equivalent to about £20, and chronically hard up so John proposed they should 'roll' a sailor, luring him away from the Kaiskerkeller with the promise of a better bar around the corner, then mugging him and stealing his wallet.

Pete Best, the band's one genuine hard man, was persuaded to leave his stripper girlfriend for once and join in the enterprise but neither George nor Paul would have anything to do with it. The whole thing petered out into farce when John and Pete's chosen victim turned out to be not as helplessly drunk as he'd first appeared and armed with a tear-gas pistol, at the sight of which both would-be muggers turned and fled.

The exis had transferred from the Kaiserkeller to the Top Ten en bloc, their queen bee, Astrid Kirchherr 'made up' – the Liverpool term for overjoyed she already knew – to have Stu back so soon.

Many young men in that era remodelled their girlfriends to fit their fantasies but with Astrid and Stu it was the opposite: the boyishly beautiful blonde turned the delicate little Scot into a mirror-image of herself. A fashion design student before turning to photography, she made him a black leather jerkin and jeans like hers, giving them the appearance less of lovers than creaking conjoined twins.

John, Paul and George loved the look and it was an ideal outfit for the round-the-clock Reeperbahn, which could be worn both on- and offstage, absorb sweat, beer splashes and other stains without trace and be slept in if necessary. They had similar suits rather less well-made by a local tailor, over-accessorising them with elaborately tooled cowboy boots and little pink 'cheesecutter' caps in homage to Gene Vincent's Blue Caps. A famous photograph of them in a row like urban cowboys on some anonymous rooftop is the first showing George an equal to the other two rather than just a tag-along kid.

There was no such rush to copy Astrid's next creation for Stu, a high-buttoning, lapel-less jacket with a round collar, inspired by Pierre Cardin's recent Paris collection but to young Liverpudlian eyes too much like the upper half of an older woman's tweedy matching jacket and skirt. 'Borrowed Mum's jacket again, Stu?' John and Paul would jeer, little suspecting the round-collared future that lay ahead for them.

Most of the male exis wore their hair wedged on their fore-heads and extra long at the sides in what was known throughout Europe as the 'French' style. When Klaus Voormann was Astrid's boyfriend, she'd cut his leonine locks that way, mainly to hide his rather protuberant ears. Stu insisted that Astrid do the same for him, so one night she unpicked his Teddy Boy cockade and reshaped it into a shallow busby with a fringe that barely cleared his eyes.

Neither John nor Paul was yet ready to sacrifice the style they'd lovingly tended, and fiercely defended, since Elvis had gifted it to them. Only 'sweet baby George', as Astrid thought of him, had nerve enough to follow Stu in her barber's chair.

Stu's new persona helped restore the self-confidence and cre-ative drive that Liverpool had crushed and he began to attend drawing classes at Hamburg's large and impressively equipped art college. Fortuitously, its tutors included the Scottish-Italian sculptor Eduardo Paolozzi, whose work had been lauded by the likes of Giacometti and Braque. Stu's talent so impressed

Paolozzi that he put him into his own hand-picked class and even secured him a grant from Hamburg's city council.

Stu's growing absorption in his classes with Paolozzi inevitably affected his commitment to the Beatles; his playing became sloppy and he'd often be late for rehearsals or fail to turn up at all. This was a huge vexation to the super-efficient Paul but for John it was outweighed by the avant-garde touch Stu's new hair and leather gear gave to the line-up and he refused to hear a word against him.

The atmosphere of the Top Ten engagement was civilised enough for John and Paul to invite their girlfriends, Cynthia Powell and Dot Rhone, to Hamburg for a week's visit. Paul and Dot stayed on a houseboat on the River Elbe that was used as a crash by various musicians including Tony Sheridan; Cynthia stayed with Astrid, but spent several nights heroically sharing John's bunk at the Top Ten. George occupied the bunk below, so had to listen in while they made love, just as John had to listen to him losing his virginity at the Bambi Kino.

It was during the girlfriends' visit that Paul's resentment of Stu boiled over. One night when they were onstage with Tony Sheridan, he made a snide remark about Astrid and the usually mild and inoffensive Stu physically attacked him. The incident caused no lasting ill-feeling between the two, but it made Stu realise how untenable his presence in the Beatles had become and he bowed out soon afterwards while still remaining devoted to their interests and close to all of them, George almost as much as John.

In the debate over Stu's successor, George took an unusually firm line, saying they should not recruit another fifth Beatle.

Since neither he nor John wanted to take over on bass guitar, the job went to Paul by default. Stu lent him his Höfner President until he found an instrument of his own, the German Höfner violin bass, like a giraffe-necked Stradivarius, that would become his trademark.

The band had voted not to pay Allan Williams his usual management commission since they'd arranged the Top Ten residency for themselves. It was shabby treatment for a man who, in his chaotic way, had done more than anyone else to bring them to where they were. But Williams's reproaches and threats to get them blacklisted in Liverpool counted for little against the seeming career leap that now lay ahead.

Thanks to Tony Sheridan's performances with and without the Beatles, he'd recently been signed up by the German Polydor record label. His producer there was to be Bert Kaempfert, an internationally known orchestra leader and composer whose instrumental 'Wonderland By Night' had been a number one single in America the previous year. Sheridan had asked the Beatles to extend their Top Ten role by backing Sheridan on his first Polydor recording session.

This took place on 22 and 23 June 1961, disappointingly not in a proper recording studio but the assembly hall of a Hamburg infants school with the equipment trucked in. Nor were the Beatles to play under their real name, which Bert Kaempfert considered too reminiscent of the German word 'peedles', meaning little boys' willies; instead, they were retitled the Beat Brothers.

Despite his eminence, Kaempfert had little idea how to produce rock 'n' roll and thought that only the simplest English language material would be understood by West German record-buyers. Two of the five tracks on which they backed Tony Sheridan – and in which their producer clearly had greatest faith – were the most hackneyed of bierkeller singalongs, 'When the Saints Go Marching In' and 'My Bonnie Lies Over The Ocean' both set to the same anonymous, Reeperbahn-rousing beat.

Yet even the composer of 'Wonderland By Night' couldn't miss the raw talent fizzing under his nose. At the end of the session, Kaempfert allowed them to record two numbers as themselves: the old jazz standard 'Ain't She Sweet', with John on lead vocal, and an instrumental originally known as 'Beatle Bop', now retitled 'Cry For A Shadow' in a dig at Cliff Richard's backing group for whom there was no reason for anyone to cry.

'Cry For A Shadow' was credited jointly to George and John, but there was no mistaking the authorship of its mock-plaintive lead guitar riff, foreshadowing the heartfelt one in 'My Sweet Lord' a decade later. Despite that exercise book bulging with Lennon–McCartney songs, the first original track the Beatles recorded was by George.

Their second, unenforced homecoming from Hamburg couldn't have been more different from their first. During their absence, John's fellow art student Bill Harry had started a paper named *Mersey Beat* to cover a music scene Harry – rightly – equated with 'New Orleans at the turn of the century'. They found they'd already been headlines in the 20 July edition, with the one-year agreement to which they'd put their names as Bert Kaempfert's bit-part players becoming inflated to BEATLES SIGN RECORDING CONTRACT. Though Harry conscientiously covered scores of other Liverpool bands, there was no mistaking his primary allegiance. *Mersey Beat* was always full of the Beatles, here a eulogy to them by the deejay Bob Wooler, there a zany article by John on their 'dubious origins' or a column of his spoof small ads.

All four now outfitted in neck-to-ankles black leather, they were the unchallenged kings of the Cavern. Lunchtimes and evenings alike, the queues of their following stretched the length of Mathew Street: a long line of beehive hairdos, buzzing with excitement – yet still with not a scream to be heard.

'We were overwhelmed by the change in them, George especially,' the former Debbie Greenberg says. 'It was as if he'd gone to Hamburg as a boy and came back as a young man. And he was still the only one with what became the Beatle cut. We'd never seen anything like it before, but we went with it. The important thing was the music.'

Then, suddenly, everything they had built up in the past year seemed to go down the Cavern's inadequately disinfected toilet. When John turned twenty-one in October, one of his relatives made him the munificent gift of £100, worth something like £2,000 in today's money. He decided to spend it on a hitch-hiking trip to Spain for Paul and himself and the pair took off without a word to George or Pete and despite the imminence of several important bookings.

Once in France, they agreed to forget Spain and hitch-hiking and, instead, took the train to Paris, where their exi friend Jürgen Vollmer was studying photography. They spent a week hanging out with Jürgen on the Left Bank and frittering away John's birthday money. Jürgen wore his hair in the French style Astrid had given Stu and George, which no longer seemed so outrageous here with Frenchness all around, so they both asked him to cut theirs the same way, saying goodbye to their fore-heads without remorse.

Their disappearance was their most pointed exclusion of George to date and this time he wasn't having it. While, as always, showing no outward sign of disappointment or hurt, he let it be known he was actively seeking a place in some other band.

The news reached Stu Sutciffe in Hamburg in slightly garbled form. 'Last night I heard that John and Paul have gone to Paris to play together,' he told Astrid. 'In other words [the Beatles] have broken up. It seems mad to me, I don't believe it.'

Altogether, there couldn't have been a better moment for Brian Epstein to step in.

8

'IT WAS THE BEST BUZZ OF ALL TIME'

In the crowded calendar of Beatles anniversaries, none is more sacred than Saturday 28 October 1961. It was the day a teenage customer in the record department that Brian ran at his family's electrical goods store asked him for 'My Bonnie' by Tony Sheridan and the Beatles.

Actually, Bert Kaempfert's first choice for the single had been Sheridan's own song 'Why?' with 'Cry For A Shadow' on the B-side, but he'd decided it was too adventurous for his home market. George came that close to being the first Beatle to have an original composition released commercially.

Brian had been aware of the Beatles since the appearance of Bill Harry's *Mersey Beat* newspaper the previous July. He'd stocked *Mersey Beat* in his record department from the first, noting the preferential coverage Harry gave them and the speed with which his stack of copies always disappeared. Latterly, he'd even contributed a record-review column to the paper, which often appeared in the same issue as their latest adulatory spread.

That the single turned out to be on the German Polydor label was no problem since Brian's policy was to order any record that was requested if he didn't have it in stock. But the name of

Sheridan's backing group was given as the Beat Brothers, leading him to the widespread assumption that they were German. It needed his regular customer, and George's unofficial roadie, Tony Bramwell, to clarify matters.

His first reaction was merely that of a zealous retailer who'd built up what he proudly called 'the Finest Record Selection in the North'. If Liverpool had a group who were actually making records, it was clearly good business to make contact with them. Only then did he learn from Bill Harry that his family's NEMS store in Whitechapel and Mathew Street, where that group could often be seen in action twice daily, were only a couple of hundred yards apart.

The innumerable books, television documentaries and articles about Brian Epstein have all dwelt at length on his predicament as a gay man of particular vulnerability in an era of savage homophobia – a vulnerability that managing the Beatles only increased – and his mysterious, lonely death. All but forgotten is the brilliance he brought to a job for which no rulebook yet existed.

At twenty-seven the dapper disc salesman with the curly hair and uncertain smile had so far been the despair and mystification of his highly respectable Jewish family. He'd attended eight expensive private schools without gaining a single qualification, had a problematic career in the army as a National Serviceman and nurtured worrying ambitions to be an actor and a couturier before reluctantly going into the family business and discovering a talent for selling records and the presentation and promotion that went with it.

His brisk business efficiency by day contrasted with a gay life that could be led only after dark, in secrecy and shame. For in the Britain of 1961, homosexuality, even between consenting parties in private, was illegal, punishable by imprisonment and regarded with especial loathing in conservative northern cities like Liverpool. In Brian's case, it was also a sin that could never be revealed to his orthodox parents.

His first exploratory visit to the Cavern, accompanied by his personal assistant, Alistair Taylor, took place on 9 November, by which time the Beatles had recovered from the contretemps around John's twenty-first. Assaulted at once by the music, the all-over black leather, the heat and the smell, Brian lost his heart four times over.

Bob Wooler announced his presence over the PA and later introduced him to the Beatles in the scruffy band room behind the stage. The only quote that survives from this encounter is George's rather uppish 'What brings Mr Epstein here?'

Even the most diplomatic of the four made a point of not seeming overawed by 'Mr Epstein' when the first meeting to discuss Brian's possible management was convened at the NEMS store after closing time. John, George and Pete Best showed up at the appointed hour, bringing the deejay Bob Wooler with them, but not Paul: after a few minutes, a phone message was received that he was still at home, 'in the bath'.

'He's going to be very late,' Brian said, irritated by this casual attitude at so early a stage.'

'But very clean,' said George, hardly smoothing matters.

With the four all present, and Mr Epstein's annoyance dispelled, matters proved amazingly straightforward. Paul asked whether they'd be expected to change their music in any way and was assured that they wouldn't. 'Right then, Brian,' John said, 'manage us.' Despite George's earlier readiness with a smart-alecky quip, he went along unquestioningly with the others.

Brian's parents were horrified by his involvement with a grubby pop group, but consoled by the thought that he'd quickly tire of it, as he had of acting and dress-designing in the past. His father allowed him to set up a management company called NEMS Enterprises in partnership with his younger brother, Clive, on condition it would take him away from record-retailing for no more than two half-days a week.

All the Beatles but John being under twenty-one, parental permission had to be given for them to be put under contract. Like Jim McCartney and even John's combative Aunt Mimi, Harold and Louise Harrison were hugely impressed by Brian's social status, educated accent and obvious affluence, and put no difficulties in his way.

Nor was there any trouble with the two people who could legitimately claim to have been their managers at different times over the previous three years. Allan Williams, still seething over their non-payment of his Top Ten club commission, willingly ceded them to Brian without any financial compensation while advising him 'not to touch them with a bargepole' (so earning immortality of a kind as The Man Who Gave The Beatles Away).

He expected sterner resistance from Mona Best, whose Casbah Club had saved them from extinction in 1959 and been almost their only source of income and encouragement through many lean months. But Mrs Best, too, stepped aside for the sake of the benefit she believed would now accrue to Pete.

Brian embarked on his new career with creditable humility,

recognising how much he needed the help of people already close to and trusted by the Beatles. He therefore made NEMS Enterprises' first employees the small entourage that had formed around them post-Litherland Town Hall. Neil Aspinall gave up training as an accountant to become their full-time driver; Tony Bramwell exchanged a promising future as a draftsman with the Ford Motor Company for being paid to carry their guitars; Frieda Kelly, their Cavern devotee-in-chief, became Brian's secretary and, before too long, the organiser of their fan club.

He recognised, too, his inexperience of Liverpool's music scene and the handicap his tailor-made suits and 'BBC' accent would be in talking to the tough dance-promoters who were the Beatles' main employers outside the Cavern. Here he turned for help to a tall, quietly spoken man named Joe Flannery, another of Liverpool's necessarily covert gays, with whom, some years earlier, he'd had his only stable domestic relationship.

Flannery himself now managed a Mersey Beat group, Lee Curtis and the All Stars, fronted by his younger brother. Still deeply in love with Brian, he agreed to become a silent partner when it came to negotiating the Beatles' bookings.

'Flo Jannery', as John instantly dubbed him, became less a backroom boy than an uncle. 'After late gigs, they'd come to my house in Gardner Road and I'd make them beans on toast or cheese on toast, then they'd go to sleep all around my living room,' he recalled. 'Even there, I noticed there was a peck-order: John always took the couch and Paul had the two armchairs pushed together.

'George didn't seem to need as much sleep as the others, so I'd take him out in my car and teach him to drive. He told me he was worried about Brian being so upper-class and how he might let himself down if they ever had a meal and he wouldn't know which fork to pick up.'

Brian went about managing the Beatles with the same bureaucratic efficiency and visual flair he did his record department. Before even the lowest-paying gig, they received a lengthy typewritten briefing from his office about the promoter, the venue and their start and finish times. Arriving at the most far-flung Cheshire village hall, they would find it swathed in posters, personally designed by Brian and at once hyperbolic and tasteful.

Often, Frieda Kelly noted, it could be like trying to control puppies that refused to be housetrained. 'One day, Ray McFall phoned from the Cavern to say only three Beatles had turned up and Gerry Marsden was singing with them standing on an orange-box so that they needn't bother to let down the microphone to his height.'

In that city rife with homophobia, there naturally were not-so-quiet whispers behind Brian's back that all the time and money he was lavishing on these four fetching young men had little to do with their potential as musicians.

The whispers were right up to a point, as Joe Flannery knew. With his aptitude for fatally wrong choices, Brian had fallen in love with John – or, rather, the tough street-kid that the middle-class Woolton boy pretended to be. And while John could not have been more belligerently hetero, he'd play Brian along, to gain further advantage for the group or from pure devilment.

Paul unsettled him, too, but in an inverted way: he felt guilty for *not* fancying someone so surpassingly pretty. For a brief spell, he became fixated on Pete Best, to the point – Pete would later allege – of directly propositioning him.

George alone seemed to have no part in this complex sexual equation: one form of exclusion he wouldn't have minded a bit. Only once were there ever whispers about him, as recounted in Tony Bramwell's rollicking memoir, *Magical Mystery Tours: My Life with the Beatles*. He was invited to spend the day alone with Brian at the Epstein family home in Queens Drive, Childwall.

'Everyone was smirking and saying, "Ooh, George has been there all day, what do you think they've been up to?"' Bramwell writes. 'Now George always appeared quiet and laid back, but he had quite a temper. He . . . snarled that he and Brian had just talked and he wouldn't discuss it.'

It's easily forgotten that Brian was only six years older than John, for to be twenty-seven in 1961 was already to be nudging middle age and his attitude to the Beatles was less managerial than paternal. Collectively, they became a substitute for the children a gay man in that era normally couldn't hope for, and as such he could love them, safely and blamelessly.

Although the term was already somewhat inappropriate, he would always refer to them simply as 'the Boys'.

The way for Brian to prove himself to his boys, even before formally putting them under contract, was to get them a record deal. And at first this seemed a straightforward matter thanks to the NEMS shops' importance as record retailers in the north-west.

From the logo-ed names displayed around his department, he chose Decca, the largest and best-known British label, whose vast roster included major pop names like Tommy Steele, Bill Haley and the Comets, Buddy Holly, Little Richard, the Everly Brothers and Duane Eddy as well as timeless greats like Louis

Armstrong, Bing Crosby, Sammy Davis Jr, Billie Holiday and the Glenn Miller Orchestra.

On the strong recommendation of its sales department, Decca agreed to give the Beatles a hearing, sending a young staff producer named Mike Smith into the wilds of Merseyside to see them live at the Cavern. Smith reported back positively and a formal audition was arranged at Decca's London studios on 1 January 1962.

The audition's 10 a.m. start time meant travelling down the day before, in bitterly cold, snowy weather. Brian, whose devotion to his boys did not extend to sharing Neil Aspinall's unheated van, made the journey separately in a First Class train compartment.

Neil had never driven to London before and lost his way several times en route, so that a journey which ought to have taken around five hours lasted more than ten. They didn't arrive at their small hotel in King's Cross until late evening, when the capital's New Year's Eve jollifications were well advanced.

Brian was staying the night with his aunt in Hampstead, so wouldn't join them until the next morning. They brought in the New Year that would be the making of them wandering around the riotous West End streets, shivering in their skimpy overcoats and looking for somewhere they could afford to eat. George's enduring memory was of first seeing boots with elasticated sides and Cuban heels – the future 'Beatle boot' –in the window of the ballet shoemakers Anello & Davide.

At one point, they were approached by two men and offered something called 'pot' if they could all 'smoke' it together in the back of Neil's van. The Liverpudlians bolted.

Their arrival with Brian at Decca's West Hampstead studios

the next morning was anything but promising. First, their producer Mike Smith kept them waiting as he was suffering from a party hangover; then he rejected their amplifiers and made them use the studio's own unsympathetic ones.

Yet from this frigid start they taped fifteen songs demonstrating the extent of their versatility, from R&B and pop through country jazz and vaudeville to Broadway show tunes – and also, daringly, three Lennon–McCartney originals. George had a respectable lead-vocal share with 'Take Good Care Of My Baby', Buddy Holly's 'Crying, Waiting, Hoping' and a jokey version of 'The Sheik Of Araby', a 1921 skit inspired by Rudolf Valentino.

That was the trouble: they were too versatile when what pop record producers wanted from a 'beat group' was simple strum and clang; they were multi- not mono-voiced, funny not frowny. It was as if the young Picasso were applying for a job as a signwriter.

So Decca passed on the Beatles, because they sounded 'too much like the Shadows' – the one thing they *hadn't* sounded like since 'Cry For A Shadow' wasn't included – and because, it was claimed in all seriousness, 'groups with guitars are on the way out.'

Brian strenuously appealed the decision, but the thought of offending the most important retailer in the north-west could not soften the Decca people's hearts. His exit line, greeted with pitying smiles, was that one day his boys would be 'bigger than Elvis'.

He had promised not to mess with their music, but it was his prerogative to tone down the anarchic rocker image that had clearly contributed to Decca's rejection. Paradoxically, there was only one way to do this: he took them to a Shadows concert at the Liverpool Empire, pointing to the polished smiles and synchronised deep bows on display as the only possible formula for success.

The Beatles had just topped a (shamelessly rigged) *Mersey Beat* readers' poll for Liverpool's top group, wearing the all-over black leather they'd scarcely been out of for the past six months. Now Brian said the leather had to go and Shadows-style matching suits with shirts and ties take its place.

John fiercely resisted what he saw as 'selling out'. 'It was a constant fight between Brian and Paul on one side and me and George on the other,' he would recall. 'My little rebellion was to have my tie loose with the top button of my shirt undone, but Paul'd come up to me and pull it straight. I used to try and get George to rebel with me. I'd say, "Look, we don't need these fucking suits. Let's chuck them out of the window."'

As Tony Bramwell points out, the suits in question weren't 'tatty, flash stuff like the other bands wore onstage', but tailor-made in 'grey brushed tweed' and costing £40 each, the equivalent of about £1,500 today. And the Beatle least likely to chuck such an acquisition out of a window would have been George.

He was now nineteen and no one was calling him a 'bloody kid' any more where girls were concerned, least of all the bandmate known city-wide as 'the Boy Romeo'.

Paul had been going out with George's first girlfriend, Iris, Rory Storm's dynamic little sister who'd gone on to be a trapeze artist (or 'aerialist', as she preferred) before becoming a dancer. But he'd always had hopes of reviving their childhood romance. 'If ever Paul and I had a row,' Iris recalls, 'George would be round like a shot.'

Then Paul had a date with a beautiful, blonde-beehived hairdresser named Bernardette Farrell who, with her best friend Joan Griffiths, was always at the Cavern's lunchtime session, sitting directly below the microphone Paul and George shared. 'One of them always tapped his toe in time to the music and the other one his heel; I can't remember which way round it was.'

Bernardette and Paul went to a cinema, where she tried unsuccessfully to slip on the glasses she needed to see the screen without him noticing. Afterwards, Paul introduced her to 'Stormsville', the house Rory's mum, Vi, had renamed in his honour, where his fellow musicians were welcome at any hour.

'George was there and when Paul went into the kitchen for something, he started talking to me,' Bernardette recalls. 'When we all left later, there was snow on the ground and it was very slippery underfoot. Suddenly, George came up behind me and picked me up in his arms and we both went over, right on our backs. Paul looked down at us as if we were a pair of kids.

'The next day, George put a note through the door of my house with his phone number, asking me to call him.'

Their relationship, Bernardette says, was 'a bit more than platonic, but not that serious. We couldn't have many proper dates because at night he was usually playing somewhere. He'd just got his first car, a blue Ford Anglia he was incredibly proud of. I recently found an old diary with the note I made in it when he first gave me a lift from the Cavern to my bus stop. I can still remember its registration, 395 MPF.

'We went to the films a lot, which was fine with me because my mother had been Liverpool's first female cinema manager. And to other clubs, like the Odd Spot and the Blue Angel. He liked the Cabaret Club because it had more old-fashioned acts like Tessie O'Shea, a very big woman who sang and played the ukulele.

'But he'd always get very uncomfortable if anyone recognised him; even if it was just at the cinema; he'd put his head down and rush out.'

Brian would later describe his efforts to interest another national record company in the Beatles like some modern Labour of Hercules: how, month after month, he would travel to London and hawk around the audition tape he'd purchased from Decca; how smug, all-knowing metropolitan executives would ridicule the notion of a Liverpool group being 'bigger than Elvis' and advise him to stick to shopkeeping; how he would always be met off the train at Lime Street station by four expectant faces and have to make them fall yet again.

He certainly suffered rejection and belittlement that would have defeated most people. But it was only three weeks after Decca's formal turn-down that he found his way to George Martin, the head of the EMI organisation's small Parlophone label.

Totally against type, thirty-six-year-old Martin was a gentlemanly figure with an accent more suggestive of the BBC Third Programme than the Top 20. He was also the unusual mixture of a classically trained musician and a producer of comedy albums, often with live audiences.

Although puzzled by many of the song choices on the Decca tape (Fats Waller's 'Your Feet's Too Big' the one he would always quote), Martin conceded there might be 'something' there and agreed to audition the Beatles, without yet giving a firm date.

PHILIP NORMAN

Brian's advent had not severed their Hamburg connection – indeed, it was their most lucrative activity at present – and on 13 April 1962, they were to open a new and superior St Pauli attraction, the Star-Club, billed by him as a 'European tour'. Further to impress *Mersey Beat*'s readership, they were to make the journey by air, George flying for the first time.

At the last minute, rather appropriately, he went down with German measles – caught from Bernardette Farrell, she thinks – so had to leave a day later than the other three, travelling on the same flight as Brian. Waiting for take-off from Manchester Ringway Airport, they met Stu Sutcliffe's mother, Millie, who told them Stu had died from an apparent brain haemorrhage and she was on her way to Hamburg to identify his body.

The catastrophe would always be attributed to Stu's last days as a reluctant Beatle in Liverpool. A year earlier, after a gig at the notoriously violent Lathom Hall, he'd been set on by a gang of Teddy Boys and – he later told his mother – repeatedly kicked in the head until John came to the rescue, fighting the Teds off with such ferocity that he broke one of his own little fingers. Since then, Stu had been suffering from blinding headaches, and fainting fits supposedly from the kicks he'd suffered, but had refused all Astrid's entreaties to seek medical help until it was too late.

However, two witnesses to the Lathom Hall attack, Pete Best and Neil Aspinall, would later recall it as not very serious and its only significant injury to have been to John's little finger.

George's friendship with Stu had not been as intense as John's, but always sincere and steady. The previous Christmas, on what would be Stu's last visit to Liverpool, they had spent time at George's house from which John and Paul, for once, were excluded. 'There was something really warm about his return,' George recalled, 'and in retrospect, I believe he was finishing something.'

Stu's fiancée, Astrid Kirchherr, would later say that the two people who showed her the most kindness in this darkest hour of her life were John and George. John asked to see the studio in the attic of her family home where Stu had gone on turning out brilliant canvases almost to the end. George went too, and the photographer in Astrid couldn't resist capturing the moment.

'John sat in a chair, so full of emotion to be in the same room where his friend was painting that he nearly burst out into tears,' she recalled. 'George was getting a bit worried so I said ,"Just stand behind him." John was just falling to bits there, and when you look at the picture and see George's eyes, they're so full of protection for John.'

The Star-Club was St Pauli's biggest and plushest music venue yet, a 2,000-capacity space with cinema-style raked seating and bars that seemed to run away to infinity, overhung by forests of contemporary tubular lamps. The music went on more or less non-stop, the Beatles working in rotation with Tony Sheridan, pianist Roy Young, aka 'the British Little Richard', and Tex Roburg and the Playboys.

Their new employer, Manfred Weissleder, was the Reeperbahn's biggest strip-club operator and most feared denizen. A huge, fleshy man with a dusting of gold hair, like a Bond villain before his time, Weissleder was rumoured to be closely involved with Hamburg's mafia since his premises were mysteriously immune from the protection rackets and other operational problems elsewhere. He in his turn gave protection to the musicians on his payroll in the form of little star-shaped lapel badges, at the mere sight of which any opportunist mugger or bar-room bully would hastily back off.

The Beatles were under the additional protective eye of Weissleder's club manager, Horst Fascher, whom they'd known as chief bouncer at both the Kaiserkeller and the Top Ten clubs – and who'd paid Brian a substantial bribe for them to renege on a long-standing residency agreement with the Top Ten's Peter Eckhorn.

This extra security was needed since John, in reaction to Stu Sutcliffe's death – and with no Brian around to enforce his new behavioural code – was running wilder through the Reeperbahn than ever before: not just in onstage *mach schau*, like singing with wooden toilet-seats around his neck, but in the much less indulgent world outside.

Early one morning, in the traditional post-performance lurch around Hamburg's fish and livestock market, he persuaded the others they should buy a live piglet to hide in a fellow musician's bed. An indignant crowd accused them of animal cruelty, the polizei were called and they were all locked up until Weissleder could send Horst Fascher to bribe their way out.

The Star-Club was on Grosse Freiheit and the Beatles were accommodated in a nearby flat, which they soon reduced to a squalor that made Bruno Koschmider's Bambi Kino seem like the Reform Club. After George had drunkenly vomited on the floor next to his bed, the mess was simply left there, decorated with matchsticks and referred to as 'the Thing'. When nauseated visitors asked what it was, John would reply, 'Our pet hedgehog.'

Most Sunday mornings, an after-show party would be start-ing at the flat just as the Freiheit's more pious residents were walking to mass at St Joseph's Church, a few doors away. With only one small toilet among many partygoers, it was commonplace for men to relieve themselves from the balcony into the street. The story of John once doing so deliberately onto a group of nuns bound for St Joseph's wasn't strictly true, according to Horst Fascher. 'The people he did it over weren't wearing habits but they were still very, very holy people. If the police had found out, he would have been thrown in jail or deported for sure.'

Fascher's innovation at the Star-Club was to alternate Liverpool bands with pioneer American rock 'n' roll stars of the Fifties, now in eclipse in their homeland. The first with whom the Beatles coincided was Gene Vincent, their greatest hero after Elvis and Buddy Holly.

Though not yet thirty, Vincent had been prematurely aged by shock-celebrity, quick-following decline and the physical injuries life had heaped on him, but he still sang 'Be-Bop-A-Lula' in the same wheedling lisp that had transfixed Paul and George as Inny schoolboys, even if it now it took three half-bottles of Johnnie Walker whisky to get him onstage.

At close quarters, their hero turned out to be a borderline psychopath who always carried a loaded handgun ('Not much point in carrying it if it ain't loaded,' as the Be-Bop-A-Lula voice reasoned) and enjoyed demonstrating the unarmed combat techniques he'd learned in the US Navy, particularly applying pressure-points to make people temporarily lose consciousness.

One day, Vincent forced George to accompany him by taxi to the flat where he was staying, handed him the gun with a peremptory 'Hold this', then began hammering on the front door and – still in the Be-Bop-A-Lula voice – shouting, 'Henry! Henry, you bastard!'

'He thought the tour manager was bonking his girlfriend,' George recalled. 'I thought to myself, "I'm out of here." Gave him the gun back and cleared off quick.'

Back in London, meanwhile, Brian had finally wrung a definite audition date for the Beatles from George Martin at Parlophone. Characteristically, the telegram he sent them made the eagerness seem all on Martin's part and didn't mention it was merely to be an audition:

CONGRATULATIONS BOYS. EMI REQUEST RECORDING SES-
SION. PLEASE REHEARSE NEW MATERIAL

Martin and the Beatles finally met on 6 June 1962, at EMI's studios in Abbey Road, north London. For them, it began as a thoroughly intimidating experience, since British recording studios in those days were more like laboratories with their soundproofed hush and white-coated technicians. Particularly at EMI, which had much the same solemn atmosphere as the BBC, extreme formality pervaded every studio session, when even jazz drummers had to wear suits and ties.

Outside of a tiny elite, recording artists had no creative input; they did what they were told and felt fortunate just to be there. The producer, more commonly called an Artist and Repertoire or A&R man (and always a man), chose the material and backing musicians, decided which take was best and how it should be edited and mixed. Few other professions could show anyone more like God.

The tall, handsome Martin and his cut-glass accent seemingly had little in common with four hard-boiled Scousers, although the class-divide between them was far less than it appeared. The producer actually came from a modest north London background but, like many other young men of his generation, had acquired a patrician manner during wartime military service. Studying the oboe at the Guildhall School of Music and a spell working in the BBC's Music Library had finished off the veneer.

They began the day with the age-old status quo firmly in place; Martin delegating the recording of the Beatles' audition to two subordinates and only coming in later to deliver judgement.

From then on, things warmed up considerably, the Beatles' charm tinged by genuine respect. It impressed them hugely that Martin had produced albums by the Goons, a demented radio-comedy team who had gloriously disrupted their adolescence before there was rock 'n' roll. In an unusual concession, he even took them into the control room to listen to their playback and told them to say if there was anything they didn't like. Whereat George, with that too-ready tongue of his, said, 'Well, I don't like your tie for a start.'

Although since portrayed as ice-breaking Liverpool cheek, it was gratuitous rudeness at the worst possible moment and many an old-fashioned prima donna producer would have taken great offence, possibly even walked out of the session and wanted nothing further to do with them. Fortunately for the future of Western culture, George Martin laughed.

Martin that day had been prepared to use his omnipotence to the full. Parlophone had enjoyed some pop success, with Adam Faith, Matt Monro and the Temperance Seven, but hardly compared with EMI's Columbia label, whose Cliff Richard and the Shadows scored hit after effortless hit. His first thought was that the Beatles could be his very own 'Cliff and the Shads', with Paul as lead singer.

However, he appraised them as a trained musician as well as an A&R man, instantly recognising the potential of their three voices together. With that same hat on, he became the first to pay serious attention to John and Paul's songwriting.

One producer's prerogative Martin did exercise, brooking no argument: he took Brian aside to say that Pete Best wasn't a good enough drummer to record and he wanted to use his own session-player on the Beatles' first single, whatever it might turn out to be.

He didn't say Pete had to be fired from the band, which would have been equally in his power. Pete could continue with them for live shows where no one had ever found fault with his playing. But the others seized on this neat solution to a problem they'd had since their first time in Hamburg; that Pete's handsome face had never really fitted, and Ringo Starr's homely one did perfectly.

To a large section of their Liverpool following, Pete was the most popular Beatle and dumping him, especially at such a moment, would cause the most ferocious outcry. George later admitted being 'quite responsible for stirring things up [against Pete]' and even visiting Ringo's mother to get her onside for the transfer.

Nothing was said to Pete throughout a summer consciously planned by Brian as a run-up to fame. He would bring nationally, sometimes internationally, famous pop stars to Merseyside and its environs, with the Beatles second on the bill as if already snapping at their heels. Among them was the Cockney Joe Brown whose hit single, 'A Picture of You', was currently George's favourite 'cover'. 'He loved Joe's music-hall songs, too,' Klaus Voormann says. 'Like "I'm 'Enery the Eighth I Am".'

The downside for him were the crowds who mobbed them after these much-expanded shows, and having to arrange his own getaways if he didn't want to leave with the others in Neil Aspinall's van. 'When the Beatles played at Southport Floral Hall, he sent me a ticket, telling me to make contact with his mum there,' the former Bernardette Farrell recalls. 'She and I got into his Ford Anglia, with Tony Bramwell behind the wheel.

'The plan was for Tony to drive past the back entrance where the fans were waiting, then George would run out and take his place. Only the change-over went a bit wrong and George's arm got shut in the door.'

On 23 August *Mersey Beat* announced that Pete Best had left the Beatles by mutual 'amicable' agreement and Ringo had succeeded him. By then, it was widely known that Pete had been fired in the most brutal manner: his bandmates for the past two years had chickened out of breaking the news personally and left it to Brian, who in turn had blamed George Martin. To rub in Pete's humiliation, the story footnoted that the Beatles would be recording their first single for Parlophone on 4 September.

The day Ringo made his debut with them at the Cavern, there were pro-Pete riots in Mathew Street. Unluckily, a film crew from Granada Television in Manchester happened to be present, taking the only footage there would ever be of them on the Cavern stage.

Granada's sound-recordist also involuntarily picked up

shouts of 'Pete Best for ever – Ringo never!' to which George responded into the microphone at his most sarcastic. When he came offstage, a Pete supporter from West Derby known only as Bruno, retaliated by 'nutting' (i.e., headbutting) him in the face, giving him a spectacular black eye.

Intrigued though George Martin was by John and Paul's original songs, he thought none yet strong enough for release as a debut single by an unknown group into the hugely competitive pre-Christmas market. So, in time-honoured fashion of the A&R man, he'd gone to a 'professional' songwriter, Mitch Murray, and been supplied with a perky little ballad entitled 'How Do You Do It?' originally intended for Parlophone's previously most successful recording star, Adam Faith.

The 4 September session in Abbey Road's Studio 3 got off to a bumpy start, for the Beatles hated 'How Do You Do It?' whose Pollyanna tone, they said, would make them a laughing stock back home. Martin standing frostily firm, they demoed it in the spirit of a Merseyside industrial go-slow, George's guitar solo only a fraction more inventive than the twanging of a rubber band.

Martin was not a man to give in to such pressure. But it happened that a Lennon–McCartney song from their audition tape had improved sufficiently to merit his reconsideration. This was 'Love Me Do', dating from about 1959 and written by Paul. The main improvement was a harmonica riff and solo played by John like those on Bruce Channel's recent big hit, 'Hey Baby'.

In this form, George's lead guitar was eliminated and Paul and John hogged the vocal between them, meaning he was excluded from their first single other than as an inaudible strummer. All that mattered was 'Love Me Do' being scheduled for release on 5 October with Paul's far subtler 'PS I Love You' as the B-side.

EMI's interest in the single was negligible. When Martin's superiors learned that Parlophone were recording a group named the Beatles, they'd assumed it was for another of his comedy records. And after hearing the stop-start beat and slightly droney harmony of 'Love Me Do', some still thought so.

Even in Liverpool, sales prospects were doubtful, for many of the Beatles' Cavern following were making each other promise not to buy it. 'We didn't want it to be a hit,' Debbie Greenberg recalls, 'because if it was, we knew we'd lose them.'

NEMS Enterprises newly appointed press officer, Tony Barrow, was instructed to prepare questionnaire-style 'Life Lines' on each Beatle like those on established performers that appeared in the *New Musical Express* and *Melody Maker*. Under the heading 'Greatest Musical Influence', George answered 'Carl Perkins'; under 'Dislikes' he answered 'black eyes' (referring to the shiner he'd acquired during the Pete Best riots) and under 'Ambition', 'to retire with a lot of money, thank you'.

Brian's publicity launch surpassed anything EMI might have organised. A week after the single's release, he presented a marathon of Mersey Beat bands at the New Brighton Tower Ballroom, with the Beatles second on the bill to their screamingest rock 'n' roll idol, Little Richard. The message couldn't have been clearer: his boys were just one step short of legendary.

With the BBC still meanly rationing pop music, the crucial launch pad for a new single was Radio Luxembourg, which gave advance notice of the exact time it would be premiered (i.e., '9.51 p.m.'). So George heard the first broadcast of 'Love

Me Do' at home in Speke, with Harold, Louise and his brothers cheering him on as ever.

Though there wasn't a trace of him to be heard, it still 'sent me into shivers all over', he would recall. 'It was the best buzz of all time.'

PART TWO

9

'I WAS ALWAYS RATHER BEASTLY TO GEORGE'

Before 1963, individual members of British beat groups were largely unknown. Only the Shadows, the most housetrained one, had distinct personalities: bespectacled lead guitar Hank B. Marvin, blond, brooding bass-player Jet Harris, stolid rhythm guitar Bruce Welch, boy-drummer Tony Meehan. But asked to name the line-ups of the Tornados or the Ramrods or Johnny Kidd's Pirates or the Fabulous Flee-Rekkers, most of their fans wouldn't have had a clue.

So now, the Beatles remained merely a collective noun for around six months after 'Love Me Do' which, despite all Brian's efforts at chart-fixing, had only just squeezed into the Top 20 at number 17. Such reviews as appeared had dwelt mainly on the absurdity of their name and there'd been little time to do publicity before their return to Hamburg for their final stint at the Star-Club.

Their follow-up, 'Please Please Me', was released on 11 January 1963, when the whole of Britain was snowed in by the harshest winter for decades. This ensured a bumper audience when they performed it on the nationwide TV show *Thank*

Your Lucky Stars, and an instantaneous chart topper. Yet attention remained focused on them as an entity shocking in every possible way, from the outlandish fringed foreheads and round-collared suits to the broad grins in place of standard pop-star scowls and the bizarre bass guitar like a violin with its neck pointing the wrong way.

Even their brief period of press notoriety, the following month, named no actual names. While on tour with the schoolgirl chanteuse Helen Shapiro, they were ejected from a golf club dance in Carlisle for wearing black leather jackets, which older Britons still equated with Nazi stormtroopers.

Not until April when 'From Me To You', their second single, reached number one did the names John Lennon and Paul McCartney begin to appear in print, usually to note the surprising fact that, like its two predecessors – and a number of other songs currently on release by ostensibly rival performers – it had been written by the two of them. Individual vocalists, like their fellow Liverpudlians Billy Fury, Johnny Gentle and Russ Hamilton had written songs before but never members of the same group and none ever so prolifically.

The two songwriters' surnames struck a novel note for being so clearly genuine in a business awash with silly pseudonyms, yet having a certain indefinable classiness. At the other extreme, Ringo Starr was such a blatant Wild West pastiche (the Ringo Kid meets Belle Starr) as to be instantly endearing.

But George Harrison? In those days, long before it came back into vogue for royal babies, George was an old-fashioned, uncle-y name which still held up its trousers with braces and at the seaside wore a knotted handkerchief instead of a sun hat. It was the sort of name a pop manager traditionally changed to something more dramatic, as George himself had once changed it to Carl.

The Beatles' first album – known in those days as an LP, for 'long-player' – was now at the top of *Record Retailer* magazine's definitive chart, where it would stay for thirty weeks. Previously, LPs had merely been a way of further milking a hit single, in this case 'Please Please Me', by reissuing it amid a medley of lacklustre tracks that few buyers listened to more than once. This one benefited from George Martin's expertise as a producer of live-performance records: in a single thirteen-hour session, he replicated their Cavern stage act, with cover-versions still far outnumbering Lennon–McCartney originals.

George's only lead vocal appearances were Gerry Goffin and Carole King's 'Chains', originally recorded by a female group, the Cookies, and Lennon and McCartney's 'Do You Want To Know A Secret?', a coded signal that, like much of Liverpool, they knew all about the secret Brian strove to conceal. As John would explain, 'It only had three notes and [George] wasn't the best singer in the band.' He sounds almost painfully shy and thickly Liverpudlian ('You'll never know how much I reelly cu-ur . . .') yet his version has far greater charm, as well as a surer falsetto, than the later hit single by Billy J. Kramer.

For the present, Martin had absolute control of what the Beatles recorded. With the unsmiling attention of a schoolteacher, even wearing what looked suspiciously like an old school tie, he would listen to John and Paul play over their latest composition on acoustic guitars and, as likely as not, change its speed or invert its verses and chorus.

The two claimed 95 per cent of their producer's time in the studio. At a certain point, with palpable dwindling interest,

Martin would call for the solo George had worked out on a further upgraded guitar, a black Gretsch 'Country Gentleman' like the one used by Carl Perkins. If he didn't like what he heard, he'd go to the piano and brusquely improvise a compulsory alternative. Years later, with great remorse, he would admit, 'I was always rather beastly to George.'

At the time of 'Please Please Me', Brian had stumbled on a publisher for Lennon and McCartney's prodigious output, a former dance-band singer named Dick James, best known for warbling the theme song to the 1950s children's TV series *Robin Hood*. With remarkable vision, James had set up a company called Northern Songs to handle their work exclusively, in which he and they would be (almost) equal partners.

Since George had co-written with each of them in the past ('In Spite Of All The Danger' with Paul, 'Cry For A Shadow' with John), they discussed making him, too, a supplier of Northern Songs and adding his name to their joint credit.

'I remember walking up past Woolton church with John one morning and going over the question,' Sir Paul McCartney would recall. 'Without wanting to be too mean to George, should the three of us write [together] or would it be best to keep it simple? We decided we'd just keep the two of us.'

For the first seven months of this so-called Beatlemania year, there was little mania and much hard work. The beginning of 1963 found the Beatles still based in Liverpool but with a fast-growing reputation outside it. After a Cavern lunchtime session, they would pile into Neil Aspinall's van and head for some theatre or ballroom at the opposite end of the country, often with as little as £30 at stake, for Brian insisted on honouring agreements he'd made before they were in the charts.

There also were repeated trips to London for live appearances on nationally-broadcast BBC radio shows like *Saturday Club* and *Easy Beat* (local radio in Britain then being non-existent), still demonstrating their extensive repertoire as a covers band more than John and Paul's songwriting.

Even now, individual personalities were slow to develop in the public mind because they were usually interviewed together as a comedy team as interdependent as Merseyside Marx Brothers, transforming the accent Britain had looked down on for generations into the most charming of novelties. Middle-class John, who'd formerly possessed it only in its mildest form, was now having to 'put it on', to the pained puzzlement of his Aunt Mimi.

The questions were always about their appearance, which still intrigued people far more than their music: did they find it hard to keep up so comprehensively different a public image? 'Our image is just ourselves, as we were,' George insisted with something less than total accuracy. 'We didn't try to make an image – we just remained ourselves.'

Occasionally, a stray detail about the Beatles' inner life would emerge, as when George revealed Brian paid each of them a weekly wage in a brown envelope (delivered by his childhood friend, Tony Bramwell) as if they were factory workers or shop assistants. 'It's nice when the next one comes before you've spent all of the last one.'

When they needed to stay overnight at a hotel, it would be a small, inexpensive one, two to a room and usually in total anonymity. Here, George showed the thoughtfulness of which he could be capable by always doubling up with Ringo: he felt largely responsible for bringing their new drummer into the group and wanted him to be in no doubt about his full emancipation.

The Arctic winter lasted into late March and their marathon road journeys were often through horrendous conditions. One night, when a blizzard shattered the windscreen of Neil Aspinall's van and the snow blew in horizontally, the four staved off hypothermia only by sharing a bottle of whisky, then lying in a pile like penguins, taking turns to be the warm one at the bottom.

Extraordinary good humour usually prevailed; the only friction Ringo would call to mind was a stand-off between Paul and George about who should take a turn at driving. 'We'd stopped somewhere to eat some grease. When we came out, Paul had the keys [to the van] but George was behind the wheel. It went on for about an hour and a half: "I've got the keys" ... "Well, *I'm* behind the wheel" ... No one was going to give in.'

Outside the charts, the clearest sign of their steady ascent were the package tours in which, as a rule, imported American stars were the gift and the supporting British acts little more than disposable wrappings. The Beatles made two such tours in quick succession, the first with Tommy Roe and Chris Montez, the second with Roy Orbison, both times starting out near the bottom of the bill but soon promoted by audience demand to show-closing headliners.

Orbison was a hero to the Beatles for his sub-operatic anthems to loss and loneliness and George in particular felt bad about being ranked higher. He would recall standing in the wings, watching the solitary figure in funereal dark glasses saturate the auditorium in multi-octave melancholy without moving a muscle. 'He didn't even twitch. He was like marble.'

Yet the Beatles were still only the lead attraction in a Mersey Beat stable that made Brian Epstein the most successful pop impresario Britain had ever known. Brian had gone on to sign Gerry and the Pacemakers and hand them, too, over to George Martin, who'd allotted them the Beatles' reject 'How Do You Do It?' and seen it become their first of three consecutive number ones, something the Beatles themselves hadn't managed. Similar success under Martin's tutelage was to follow for Billy J. Kramer and the Dakotas and the Cavern's former cloakroom attendant Priscilla White, renamed Cilla Black, though, sadly, not for Rory Storm, long believed to be the most charismatic of them all.

For the Beatles to maintain success in the pop market of 1963 meant observing conventions as restrictive as their little round-collared suits. It was, for instance, a given that a male pop star with a wife, or even a steady girlfriend, risked alienating his overwhelmingly female following, with catastrophic results for his career. Here, they harboured what amounted to a ticking – or, rather, kicking – time-bomb. The previous summer, John had married his art college sweetheart, Cynthia Powell, after she'd fallen pregnant and ever since Brian had striven to conceal the fact – for a time even from Ringo.

George was still seeing Bernardette Farrell, but in Liverpool only and in the 'bit more than platonic' fashion, as she describes it, that attracted little notice. When he exchanged his Ford Anglia for a Jaguar Mark 2 – a model usually associated with middle-aged bookmakers – the spin for which he took Bernardette also included her sister and brother-in-law. 'And he brought round the Silver Disc he'd got for "Please Please Me" to show us,' she recalls. 'My mum made him laugh by asking him if he could play it.'

Not long afterwards, he suddenly reappeared in Liverpool for a reason confided to Bernardette but very few others. A couple of nights earlier, at a live broadcast from the Royal Albert Hall, Paul had met the seventeen-year-old actress Jane Asher. The immediate changes in his private life included no longer needing his car in London and he'd asked George to ferry it back up north. That was the kind of mates they used to be.

In April, the Beatles took the first foreign holiday of their career. Paul, George and Ringo went to Tenerife, where the mother of their German friend Klaus Voormann owned a house. Despite the imminent birth of John's baby, he went to Spain alone with Brian, starting rumours of a gay affair to which none of his bandmates gave the slightest credence. Never again would any of them be able to slip out of the country and back like this without a single scream or exploding flashbulb.

Liverpool at the time was in the throes of an invasion by London record company executives who'd scoffed at Brian and the Mersey Sound six months before, now desperate to sign any bit of it he might have missed. In their vanguard was the Decca label's Dick Rowe, who'd passed on the Beatles and instead signed a north London group of only limited lifespan named Brian Poole and the Tremeloes.

One night at the city's Philharmonic Hall, Rowe found himself judging a competition for Cheshire and Lancashire groups in company with George, just returned from Tenerife. Surprisingly, he bore Rowe no ill-will for rejecting the Beatles, saying their audition on New Year's Day 1962 had been so bad that he himself would probably have done the same.

Magnanimously he gave the Decca man his personal tip about the next big thing in pop. It wasn't to be found on Merseyside, however, but in the back room of a pub in Richmond, south-west

London, where he and the other Beatles had recently been blown away by an R&B band called the Rolling Stones.

So, thanks to George, The Man Who Turned Down the Beatles found last-minute redemption as The Man Who Signed the Stones, and John, Paul, Ringo and himself were soon to be faced with their greatest rival.

It began in August of 1963, as suddenly as if some giant switch had been thrown, turning enjoyment into obsession, excitement into frenzy, applause into mayhem.

It was the screaming of very young women, yet far beyond any directed at Frank Sinatra in the 1940s or Elvis Presley in the 1950s; off any known scale of rapture or arousal. It was more a wail or ululation, toneless, eerie, almost dehumanised, that nothing could make stop or draw breath and in the end seemed hardly related to the four little figures who'd released it.

Its trigger was the Beatles' fourth single, 'She Loves You' – John and Paul at this point believing there had to be a 'you' or a 'me' if they were to have a hit – whose 'Yeah Yeah Yeah!' chorus tripled pop music's most familiar trope. But this one they hardly needed to sing; just shaking their hair and shutting their eyes with a falsetto 'Oo!' was enough to send the Wail into fresh transports. To begin with, the Beatles found this monstrous overreaction hilarious; even George seemed to enjoy it, smiling his widest smile, shaking his luxuriant hair and going 'Oo!' as zealously as the others.

Nothing evokes the Sixties at their most innocent like the black-and-white street-scenes outside theatres the Beatles are expected to enter or leave; the buckling all-female crowds held in check by tolerant, unmilitarised police the only violence an occasional Victorian helmet knocked askew.

These early- and pre-teens regarded these veterans of Hamburg's Reeperbahn as cuddly toys whose tummies you pressed and they went 'Oo!' They succumbed to their infantilisation, even embroidered it as when George, in one knockabout multi-interview, claimed to be fond of jelly babies.

It literally backfired: at every subsequent Beatles live show, volleys of jelly babies were hurled at the stage. Soft though their sugar-dusted gelatin, they made an unpleasant missile, particularly en masse. 'Couldn't you just eat them yourself?' he replied aggrievedly to fifteen-year-old Lynn Smith, who'd written to him boasting about her own recent jellykazi attack. 'Besides it is dangerous, I was hit in the eye with a boiled sweet once and it is not funny.'

The Wail and its makers became the topic of the hour, with psychologists and behaviourists jostling to provide explanations. '[It] is one way of flinging off childhood restraints and letting themselves go,' opined one in the patronising tone they all adopted. 'The fact that thousands of others are screaming along with her makes the girl feel she is living life to the full with people of her own age ... The girls are subconsciously preparing for motherhood. Their frenzied screams area rehearsal for that moment. Even the jelly babies are symbolic.'

These hardcore Beatles fans – which all were – not only played their records, ogled their photos in teen magazines like *Mirabelle* and *Fabulous* and rent the air at their concerts, they wore them, boys and girls alike, in Beatle haircuts and the polo-necks that particularly suited George; in deep-collared shirts, shin-high elasticated boots and the corduroy they'd made more chic than velvet. They spoke like them, in faux-naïve Liverpudlian like 'fab' for fabulous, 'gear' as an adjective for 'good', 'ciggies' for the cigarettes so often hanging from George's mouth especially, and 'Crimble' for Christmas.

They bought them in every conceivable form as themed merchandise, a market which pop music hitherto had barely exploited; in Beatles plastic guitars, Beatles miniature drums, Beatles record-racks, Beatles lockets, Beatles badges, Beatles belts, Beatles buttons, Beatles handkerchiefs, Beatles jigsaw puzzles, Beatles shoulder-bags, Beatles trays, Beatles bedspreads, Beatles sunbeds, Beatles kitchen aprons, Beatles pencils, Beatles chewing gum and guitar-shaped Beatles cakes.

All this meant the end of privacy or peace for their families since the fans soon discovered their home addresses in Liverpool and inundated them with fan mail and gifts, ringing their publicly listed phones dozens of times a day and collecting outside in force at the slightest rumour of one in residence. Paul's father, Jim, and Ringo's mother, Elsie Gleave, accepted this resignedly while John's Aunt Mimi turned it into a new form of martyrdom. But to George's parents it was a joy.

Harold and Louise Harrison still lived in Speke but, a year earlier, had moved from Upton Green to one of the superior council houses in Mackets Lane, recently built for workers at the Ford Motors factory. George was the last of their children to be living at home, albeit nowadays away on tour for long periods, their small front drive distinguished from their neighbours' by his parked Jaguar Mark 2.

Harold now had the less arduous job of driving school buses, which allowed him to be home in the middle of each day, but even with the growing status of a 'Beatle mum' there had been no such deceleration for Louise. As for many years past, she worked for a printing firm named Bembrose in Aintree, making the fourteen-mile journey by bicycle. The recent snows hadn't stopped her getting through every morning, although she'd once been docked fifteen minutes' pay for being late.

She always knew where George would be at any given moment and often went by herself to see the Beatles perform, travelling as far afield as Ireland. When she'd redecorated her kitchen during his holiday in Tenerife, it had been with 'Beatle' wallpaper, covered with guitars and dancing figures, at the same time having his bedroom papered all in black, as he'd specified, like Astrid's in Hamburg. At the top of the stairs she kept a life-size photographic blow-up of him in full Beatle-suited and -booted glory that no visitor could miss.

Once, the Harrisons even invited a photographer into the house while George was home, to snap Harold – a magnificently fashion-free figure with pullover tucked into thick leather belt – serving his son cornflakes for breakfast, then two peak-capped postmen arriving with the day's fan mail in four large wicker hampers, then Louise and Harold valiantly setting about answering it in a kind of grotto made from the giant teddy bears and WE LOVE GEORGE placards he'd been sent.

If a letter-writer was particularly charming Louise would slip some little souvenir of him with her reply, like a scrap of lining from one of his jackets. Many posed the same question: after George, who was her favourite Beatle? John, she said, 'because he dances the Tango with me in the kitchen and makes me laugh.'

A question that had grown increasingly bothersome to George, asked most often by *Mersey Beat*'s editor, Bill Harry, was why wasn't he writing original songs like John and Paul?

In truth, anyone would have felt inhibited by the sheer volume the pair turned out together in hotel rooms or at the back of tour buses, each one seldom taking more than minutes. Paul, especially, had always been able to pluck song ideas out of the air; George remembered how, as Quarrymen, they'd seen an advertisement for furniture aimed at young couples 'thinking of linking' and Paul had instantly seized on it as a song title.

But while he himself could come up with tunes – witness 'Cry For A Shadow' – he felt he fatally lacked that same facility with words and rejected Bill Harry's repeated suggestion that he try writing some in partnership with Ringo.

In August 1963 the Beatles were on a tour of South Coast seaside resorts with Billy. J. Kramer and the Dakotas and Brian's latest signing, Tommy Quickly. During a five-night stint at the Gaumont cinema in Bournemouth, George complained of chronic fatigue (hardly surprising), was seen by a doctor, prescribed a tonic and ordered to stay in bed at their hotel.

Alone in his room, weighed down afresh by the songwriting question, he turned to one of his few confidantes. In a long letter to Astrid Kitchherr in Hamburg, he noted that 'John and Paul are going to be rich very soon when they collect what they have earned from writing all these songs' and put forward the idea of earning some extra income himself by putting together a book illustrated with her photographs, because 'I don't think that you would want to see me poor and hungry.'

He added that the tonic he'd been prescribed was like 'liquid Preludin' and, with very George gratuitousness, that 'my balls have been aching, too, and hanging around onstage.'

In the end, boredom drove him to what, as a hedge against failure, he called 'an exercise' to see whether he could write a song. Its title was a seeming, rather irritable response to all those who'd been on at him to do it: 'Don't Bother Me'.

That autumn of 1963, Brian transferred his NEMS organisation to London, taking along the pick of his Liverpool staff – and his principal asset. Indeed, the move was largely for the Beatles' benefit, to be close to EMI's studios and harder for intrusive fans to find.

John moved into a flat with his 'secret' wife, Cynthia, and their baby son, Julian, in Emperor's Gate, Kensington, while the others initially shared one in Green Street, Mayfair. However, Paul soon left to become a permanent guest of Jane Asher's family in Wimpole Street, Marylebone; a hideout that, unlike the others', was never to be discovered.

George and Ringo then took up residence in a second-floor flat at Whaddon House, a modern block in William Mews, Knightsbridge, where Brian himself lived on the top floor. To this point both had been looked after by doting mothers so possessed no domestic skills – another reason why the highly domesticated Paul had jumped ship. Luckily, the couple in the flat downstairs, Harry and Carol Fitzgerald, provided them with regular meals and Brian was up above, ready to answer their smallest need.

Here they acquired two flatmates, both of whom were aspiring pop stars although at the moment subsisting on small roles in children's television. One was an East Ender named Mark Feld, later to be reborn as Marc Bolan; the other, Gregory Phillips, would remain Gregory Phillips yet merit his own small footnote in pop history.

Almost a second home to George and Ringo was the exclusive Saddle Room club on nearby Park Lane, run by the actress and TV personality Helene Cordet, whose lovers were rumoured to include the Queen's husband, Prince Philip. VIP members living in the vicinity who might have drunk a little too much would be offered a ride home by horse-drawn open carriage. The lads from Speke and the Dingle often returned to Whaddon House that way at daybreak like Edwardian rakes, clip-clopping through Hyde Park.

Among their neighbours in Green Street had been a deejay named Tony Hall who often had the job showing visiting American stars around London. At one of Hall's parties, George met Phil Spector, the first record producer to be better known than his artists, and Spector's latest discovery, a female vocal trio named the Ronettes whose 'Be My Baby' was currently challenging 'She Loves You' in the charts.

George was drawn, not to their waif-like siren of a lead singer, Veronica 'Ronnie' Bennett but to her older sister, Estelle, said to be the 'quiet one' of the group like himself in the Beatles. 'We kept running into each other at parties and always found our eyes meeting, no matter how many other people were in the room,' Estelle would recall. 'We found we liked the same things, long walks wearing comfortable clothes and being with people who liked us for ourselves, not because we were in showbusiness.

'I think I was happiest when I talked with George. There was something about him that made me open up and spill out everything that was on my mind. I think he felt the same way because he'd often call late in the evening and stay on the phone for hours.' By her account, they were 'inseparable' until his life changed dramatically early the following year.

By now, only one stratum of British society couldn't tell John apart from George and Ringo from Paul – or, rather, didn't care to. The attitude of Fleet Street newspapers to young people's music was still that formed in the rock 'n' roll era: it was an atrocious din and its performers grubby con-artists with the longevity of fruit flies. So had they regarded four Liverpool upstarts with laughable nomenclature, unthinkable hair and fascistic black leather jackets back in February.

Now they were in the unusual position of having too much news and too little entertainment. Firmly lodged in the headlines all summer had been the final phase of the Profumo scandal in which a government minister had been found to be sharing a mistress with a Russian spy, his far more heinous offence lying to the House of Commons about it.

From that had come the resignation of Prime Minister Harold Macmillan and vicious infighting in the Tory party over his successor. In addition, the country had suffered its first potato famine in a century, virtually wiping out the fish and chip trade, and a Post Office mail train had been robbed of £2 million, the biggest heist in British history.

Every Fleet Street news editor was casting around desperately for some light relief, and found it in those same black leather-wearers, in excelsis.

On 13 October, the Beatles headlined ATV's *Sunday Night at the London Palladium* show, on which George had caught his one fleeting glimpse of Buddy Holly and the Crickets five years earlier. The hugely powerful right-wing *Daily Express* devoted its premier Photo-News page to the '1,000 screaming fans' said to have besieged the Palladium, though actually it had been a rare occasion when all but a handful stayed at home.

Then on 5 November came the *Royal Variety Performance* in the presence of Queen Elizabeth the Queen Mother, when John captivated their top-drawer audience by requesting those in the cheaper sets to clap and the rest to 'rattle yer jewellery', fortunately omitting the four-letter word he'd threated to insert before 'jewellery'.

The next morning, the six-million-selling *Daily Mirror* ran an editorial that was part overweening eulogy, part health certificate and gave the Wail a name at long last:

BEATLEMANIA
YEAH! YEAH! YEAH!

You have to be a real sour square not to love the nutty, noisy, happy, handsome Beatles.

If they don't sweep your blues away – brother, you're a lost cause. If they don't put a beat in your feet – sister – you're not living . . .

How refreshing to see these rumbustious young Beatles take a middle-aged Royal Variety Performance by the scruff of their [sic] necks and have them Beatling like teenagers . . .

The Beatles are whacky [sic]. They wear their hair like a mop – but it's WASHED, it's super clean. So is their fresh young act . . .

From then on, papers that hadn't had a good word to say about pop music hadn't a bad word to say about the Beatles.

They seemed the perfect exemplar of what the commentator Malcolm Muggeridge had called 'the slow, sure death of the upper classes', a tonic for the whole nation after the sleaze of Profumo and the mildew of Macmillan. Stories about them began appearing on a daily basis, often several per edition; their latest feat in the charts or weird-wailing live show or perfectly judged bit of cheek.

Envy, that British original sin, was entirely absent, replaced by a benign voyeurism as they exhibited their presumably ballooning wealth in new cars and clothes; Ringo now reportedly possessed thirty-seven shirts. A whole article was built around George's having recently tasted his first avocado and his Beatle-ishly down-to-earth opinion of such stuff. 'I've had caviar and I like it, but I'd still rather have an egg sandwich.'

Any parliamentarian seeking the spotlight or pontifi-cating cleric had only to utter the magic B-word, ideally throwing in a 'Yeah yeah yeah', to win instant saturation coverage. They were a topic on which every public figure, from the Archbishop of Canterbury to the war hero Viscount Montgomery of Alamein, was expected to pronounce and all took care to do so positively.

British newspapers traditionally build up celebrities only to tear them down again, but now it was in their interests only to build the Beatles up and up. It would have been a simple matter for any investigative reporter to look closely at what their 'fresh, young act' had been like on Hamburg's Reeperbahn, but no editor would have printed it.

Likewise, the interviewers given virtually free access to them knew better than to mention the moments when cloven hoofs popped out of corduroy sleeves; for instance, John beating up the Cavern deejay Bob Wooler at Paul's twenty-first birthday party for a caustic reference to his Spanish 'honeymoon' with Brian. As with the White House press corps and President John F. Kennedy's sexual buccaneering, there was an unspoken pact to suppress any disillusioning truth.

Their second LP, *With The Beatles*, was released in November, its half-million advance sale taking it instantly to number one to displace *Please Please Me* – ultimately giving them a total of fifty-two weeks there and even reaching number 11 on the *singles* charts.

The *Please Please Me* cover had been a straightforward colour photograph of four hard-to-tell-apart young men, looking cheerily down from a balcony at EMI's Manchester Square headquarters. For *With The Beatles*, fashion photographer Robert Freeman used their faces only on a plain black field, half-shadowed, polo-necked and serious, more like art students or denizens of the Parisian Left Bank. Departing from their normal order of precedence, George's floated beside John's, just as Astrid Kirchherr had shot him, so concerned and protective of John after Stu Sutcliffe's death.

With that, the LP become the *album*, no longer a ragbag but a showcase and, increasingly, an art object; pop music broke out of its blue-collar ghetto, seeping into grammar schools, university common rooms, even Burke's Peerage; thereafter, every age and class would be with the Beatles.

The tracklist was a mixture of Lennon–McCartney, taking another giant leap forward, as in 'It Won't Be Long' and 'All My Loving', and one or the other's cover-versions of American R&B and early Motown that many listeners wouldn't have heard before, like the Marvelettes' 'Please Mister Postman' and the Miracles' 'You Really Got A Hold On Me'.

George was represented by two covers, his Hamburg staple 'Roll Over Beethoven' and the Donays' 'Devil In Her Heart', and his 'exercise' in songwriting, 'Don't Bother Me'. For the first time, reviewers noticed and praised his soloing: the unexpected Chet Atkins-style Country picking on 'All My Loving', the nimble acoustic work so perfectly suited to Paul's cover of Peggy Lee's 'Till There Was You'.

But 'Don't Bother Me', though constructed from some interesting chords, seemed under-produced (George Martin being 'rather beastly' again?) and lacked the flourish of John-and-Paul backing vocals. To say nothing of the surprise that a thrice-blessed Beatle could sound this curmudgeonly ('so go away, leave me alone, don't bother me . . .').

It nonetheless begat a cover-version, though not at a very elevated level, artist or label-wise. George's flatmate Gregory Phillips recorded it on Pye with a female chorus that gave it a far better temper. The backing was by a yet-to-be (and never-quite) famous Liverpool band, the Remo Four, whose lead guitarist, Colin Manley, had seemed impossibly superior to George when they'd both been pupils at the Inny.

And it earned him his first songwriter's royalties, though nowhere near the scale of John and Paul's. When he next bumped into Bill Harry, he thanked Harry for pushing him into writing 'Don't Bother Me', which had just brought him a cheque for 'over a thousand pounds'.

On 27 December, the classical music critic of *The Times* – a paper hitherto thought deaf and blind to pop – named John and Paul 'the year's outstanding British composers' for accomplishments of which they'd had been wholly unaware: the 'chain of pandiatonic clusters in "This Boy"', the 'melismas with altered vowels in "She Loves You"', the 'Aeolian cadence' at the end of 'Not A Second Time' which 'correspond[ed] exactly with Mahler's "Song of of the Earth"'.

For some time, Brian had worried that George was receiving so much less media attention that John or Paul, though even his resourceful brain could think of no remedy. He was therefore instantly receptive when the *Daily Express*, the Beatles' main cheerleaders in Fleet Street, proposed running a weekly column under George's name, starting on their visit to Paris early in the New Year.

The ghostwriter was to be the *Express*'s northern drama critic, Derek Taylor, practically a fellow Merseysider since he came from Hoylake in Cheshire, who'd written rave reviews of Beatles shows throughout the months when other nationals wouldn't touch them.

Taylor's audition was a specimen column without George's input, in which his idiosyncratic turn of mind – and phrase – might have cost him the assignment. He improvised a conversation between George and Harold Harrison in which Harold told him, 'You keep playing your guitar and I'll keep driving the big green jobs.'

'And George said, "What are big green jobs?"' Taylor recalled. 'I said, "Um, buses, Liverpool buses." George said, "I didn't know they were called big green jobs." I said, "Well, I don't know that they are, I just made it up", which is what happens on newspapers. I passed the test by admitting I'd made up "big green jobs". George said, "I'll help you with the column – we'll do it together."'

Beatling could be fun, as when all four appeared on a special Christmas edition of BBC-TV's *Juke Box Jury*, impishly mixing up the name plaques in front of them. Among the new singles to be reviewed was 'Hippy Hippy Shake' by the Swinging Blue Jeans, formerly known in Liverpool as the Blue Genes, whose leader, Ray Ennis, had swapped his Club 40 guitar for George's Höfner President.

George was complimentary about the record, adding that he was a fan of Chan Romero, the American R&B singer who'd written and first recorded the song as a seventeen-year-old in 1959. Suddenly, knowing such things looked cool.

But not remotely describable as fun was the Beatles Fan Club (Southern Area) convention at Wimbledon's Palais ballroom, where the first 1,000 who bought tickets would be allowed to shake hands with them. First, they had to do a show, not on the ballroom's stage but a specially built wooden platform behind a steel cage against which the crowd pressed so ardently that John said they'd 'soon be coming through it as chips'.

'Halfway in, George said, "I'm not doing this" and he packed up, went to the stage door and began looking for a cab,' Neil Aspinall recalled. 'I ran after him and said "What are you doing? You can't walk out, we've got to finish." Then John turned up with his guitar . . . and said, "Well, if he's going, I'm going."

'But they did finish the gig and they shook hands with all the fans – about 10,000 actually, because [the fans] kept going to the end of the queue and coming round again.'

School used to feel like a cage to George with its uniform, its endless rules and regulations and orders that had to be obeyed. Despite the Wail, the fan mail, the Jag, the avocados, the dawn carriage-rides and piles of new shirts, was being a Beatle so very different?

10

'I HAD TO LEARN TO THINK LIKE A SPY, LEAVING NO TRACE'

Before the Beatles conquered America, George was the only one to have been there and before they played a note on US soil, he'd already played many with a different band.

It was all because of his eleven-year-older sister Louise, who'd doted on him when he was a baby and given him his first lessons in spelling and arithmetic at the family's tiny Upton Green house in preparation for her career as a schoolteacher. After two years' teacher-training in Newcastle upon Tyne, she'd decided it wasn't for her and abandoned her course – and convention. Until her little brother grew up, Lou – blonde and beautiful with his same facial bone-structure – would be the Harrison with the most eventful life.

She decided to try journalism and managed to pass the rigorous selection-process for a traineeship with the BBC despite lacking the university degree and middle-class accent then expected of candidates. But, in contrast to their later whole-hearted supportiveness of George, her parents were firmly opposed to what they saw as a disastrous comedown from teaching. Being under twenty-one, so still subject to their authority, she had to refuse the BBC and take employment as a dental nurse.

Drills of another kind entered her life when she fell in love with a mining engineer named Gordon Caldwell, twelve years older and already married with three children, plus two more from previous relationships. Caldwell wanted to marry her, but said the only way to force his wife into a divorce was for them to elope.

Lou consented and disappeared with him to Gloucestershire in the far-distant West Country, leaving Harold and Louise no clue to her whereabouts, and not contacting them again until she turned twenty-one. They immediately forgave her and attended her wedding to Caldwell in Cheltenham in 1954.

Thereafter, Caldwell's job as an engineer took her to Inverness in Scotland, then to Ontario in Canada, where he worked for a gold-mining company, then to La Oroya, Peru, a city 12,000 feet above sea level, then back to Vancouver, then to the small town of Benton, Illinois.

Her mother's weekly letters kept her informed of every stage in George's rise with the Beatles. When Louise sent her a copy of 'Love Me Do', Lou wrote to Brian Epstein, volunteering to be their 'ambassador' in a land which at that stage they had no hope of ever seeing for themselves.

Like the journalist she'd once wanted to be, she began sending Brian detailed reports on the American record charts for whatever pointers they might offer; he in turn sent her the Beatles' next two singles and promo material which she hawked around local papers and radio stations in about a 200 square-mile radius of her home.

Although America's prestigious Capitol label was owned by

EMI, it had turned down 'Please Please Me' and 'From Me To You' even after each made number one in the UK, declaring with lofty omniscience, 'We don't think the Beatles will do anything in this market.' The two singles had then been picked up by an obscure Chicago-based label named Vee-Jay and released to utter indifference. When it happened with 'From Me To You', Lou decided to check out Vee-Jay for herself. 'I drove to their address, only to find an abandoned parking lot,' she recalled. 'I wrote to Brian informing him of this and urging him to find a decent record label.'

Fittingly, it was just before the Beatles recorded 'She Loves You' that George wrote to her asking if he could 'pop over' and stay with her in mid-September, on a trip also to include 'maybe call[ing] in at Nashville to see Roy Orbison (whom we met on tour here) and possibly Chet Atkins'.

His original plan was to take Ringo along but, exhausted by the shrieking summer and aware of Lou's lobbying on the Beatles' behalf, Ringo told him: 'I'm not going if she's going to make us work.' So his older brother, Peter, went with him instead.

Benton, Illinois, where Lou and Gordon had settled, was a city of only 7,000 inhabitants, yet had everything calculated to awe and fascinate a young Englishman in 1963: enormous cars in ice-cream colours, with variegated fins, supermarkets that seemed to stretch to infinity, television on multiple channels that went on from early morning till late at night and – even more interesting to George than the cars – a vast choice of every kind of music on the radio.

Other than people acquainted with Lou, no one in Benton had heard of the Beatles and when, on the very day of his arrival, 'She Loves You' was released in America by the small Philadelphia-based Swan label, that state of affairs continued. For the first time in months, George could walk down a street without fear of ravening female pursuit.

The energetic Lou had organised a programme for her brothers' two-week stay that left no time to visit Nashville and call on Roy Orbison: there were visits to drive-in movie-theatres and restaurants where one was served by female carhops on roller skates; barbecues of enormous T-bone steaks; even a camping trip to the Shawnee National Forest with their young nephew and niece, Gordon and Leslie. George and Peter were still young enough to be impressed by Gordon and Leslie's American toys, so different from those they'd grown up with in post-war Liverpool, and they spent hours playing with the children.

At this time, almost every American male of any age sported a crewcut that looked more planed than scissored. George's Beatle cut caused general amazement but none of the hostility it might well have done in such conservative circles. Only once did his choice of topping get a bad reaction: when an attractive young woman delivered pizzas to Lou's house – two other huge novelties – he asked her for a date but was refused. 'I wouldn't want to be seen with him,' she told colleagues at the pizzeria.

He had long coveted an American Rickenbacker 420 guitar like the one John had been playing since their latter days in Hamburg. Fenton's Music Store in nearby Mount Vernon proved to have just one 420 in stock, though with a dark red 'Fireglo' finish rather than the black 'Jetglo' he wanted. The store's owner, Red Fenton, sensing an important customer, offered to repaint it and Lou paid the $400 price tag as a gift for his imminent twenty-first birthday.

She also introduced him to South Illinois's leading semi-pro pop group, the Four Vests – 'vest' in America meaning waistcoat rather than undershirt, as in Britain. These waistcoat-wearers were all some bit older than George, and nowhere near the Beatles' level, but it was nice to be top dog for a change and he happily played a few local gigs with them, mostly in accord with their Hank Williams repertoire but stopping every show with his version of 'Roll Over Beethoven'. 'If that guy's trying out with you,' one audience member advised the other Vests, 'you oughta hire him.'

He became particularly friendly with their bass guitarist, sheet metal-worker Gabe McCarty whose surname was close enough to his Beatle counterpart's to be spooky. 'We were at his sister's house, just picking around a little bit, and George asks if I ever wrote any songs,' McCarty recalls. 'I said, no, I never did. He runs upstairs and comes down with a leather bag, and he has about sixteen handwritten songs and some chords and lyrics. And he says, "If this'll help you, you can take these and use 'em." He gave me a long-play album that the Beatles did and I stuck 'em all in there, inside the cover.'

Were these songs that John, Paul and George Martin had rejected, that George hadn't liked to submit or simply hadn't finished? We can never know. Nor did the Four Vests ever get around to making use of the trove.

'About a year or so later, I had a fire in my trailer and the album was in there,' McCarty says. 'Burned up every dam' thing.'

*

In January 1964, the Beatles were not feeling much like conquerors. Capitol had finally been persuaded to release their fifth single, 'I Want To Hold Your Hand', in the US, but seemingly with no great enthusiasm or hope. They were currently appearing at L'Olympia in Paris and receiving a tepid response from French audiences while, back home, the song had been bumped from the number one spot by the Dave Clark Five's 'Glad All Over'.

The British press were speculating whether this might be the beginning of the end, the Mersey Sound supplanted by Clark's 'Tottenham Sound', when Brian received a telegram from New York; 'I Want To Hold Your Hand' had reached the top of the *Cashbox* chart.

Even a British pop act as big as Cliff Richard had never achieved an American number one, few had dared to perform live there, none had had any real success and the rest of Britain hadn't cared one way or the other. But when the Beatles flew to New York on 7 February, the whole country was behind them in a way previously seen only with prime ministers en route to summit conferences or the England cricket team to overseas Test matches.

Their descent from their aircraft at newly renamed John F. Kennedy Airport, astounded by the shrieking terraces awaiting them, is perhaps the happiest memento of their career. Those earlier British popsters who yearned to 'crack' America had never dreamed of finding it thus pre-cracked, ready caramelised and positively begging to be gobbled up.

The reason had to do with much more than music. Only a little over two months earlier, a burst of rifle shots in Dallas, Texas, had extinguished an inspirational and glamorous young

President whose hair came a little way down his forehead. John F. Kennedy's assassination had dealt a shattering blow to America's pride in itself, not to be equalled until the terrorist attacks of 9/11; moreover, none of the huge panoply of American novelties and crazes seemed able to relieve the shamed aftershock and lighten the pall of mourning.

It was now, when the nation could find no home-prepared balm for its wounded soul, that the Beatles deplaned in their skimpy little coats, with the dual power of beguiling it with song and making it smile.

Brian's pride in his boys was somewhat marred by yet further concerns over George's health. He'd been laid up with stomach trouble brought on by overtiredness in Bournemouth the previous summer and also complained of feeling unwell during the Paris trip, though it hadn't stopped him visiting the Pigalle nightclub and describing the event in his *Daily Express* column through his attendant Boswell, Derek Taylor: 'There are hundreds of marvellous chicks here – neat and very much in control of themselves. (I'm still looking for a Brigitte Bardot, the wild, reckless type) . . . I think girls are here to stay.'

At the Beatles' famous first encounter with the American media – bent on demolishing them but instantly won over – he seemed fine, cigarette in hand, getting off as many crisp comebacks to the asinine questions about their hair as any of the others. He seemed equally so later, in their besieged suite on the twelfth floor of the Plaza Hotel, despite the jet-lag of a seven-hour flight, talking animatedly by phone to journalists back in Britain about all the other (Lennon–McCartney) songs now turning into US hits after 'I Want To Hold Your Hand'.

Among the suite's hand-picked American friends was the

Ronette Estelle Bennett, but there would be no resumption of their rather private romance during George's early days in London. Privacy had become a thing of the past for him; besides, Brian knew the consequences in 1964 America of one of his boys having an interracial relationship.

On their first day in New York, a full complement of Beatles attended the first rehearsal for their live appearance on CBS-TV's *Ed Sullivan Show* two evenings ahead. But the next morning George was absent from their mass photocall, in Central Park and, later, Neil Aspinall stood in for him at the second Sullivan show rehearsal as he was said to be suffering from 'influenza'.

His sister, Lou, had just checked into the Plaza to find a message to go straight up to the Beatles' suite. Emerging from the elevator at '12', she found a table blocking the corridor and a detail from the Burns Detective Agency on watch. When she told one of them she was George Harrison's sister, he laughed and said, 'Do you know how many times that's already been tried today?' Even a Polaroid photo she'd taken of George in Benton failed to move him. 'Luckily, my brother came out into the corridor at that moment,' she recalled, 'and as we hugged and spun each other round, all the detectives broke into applause.'

George was evidently suffering from something more than the mild flu that the press had been told, and Brian had just reluctantly sent for the hotel doctor. 'He said, "This is a very sick boy, he has a severe strep throat and a temperature of 104. I will have to send him to the hospital."'

The prospect of George missing the Beatles' American debut live on *The Ed Sullivan Show*, the most crucial performance of their career, and possibly spending the rest of their visit in hospital, terrified Brian out of his usual calm resourcefulness, as Lou was to recall. 'He was saying, "Oh no, this cannot happen … We can't allow the press to hear of this … Can he be cured by Sunday night?"'

To preserve the awful secret, the doctor was persuaded to let George's sister nurse him in hopes of an improvement over the next twenty-four hours. It came naturally to her to look after him, just as it used to when he was a toddler at 12 Arnold Grove, Wavertree, where the toilet was outside next to the chicken coop and the bath, made of tin, hung on a hook outside the back door. 'The doctor had given him a shot, and he gave me a whole bunch of medications and an ice-collar plus a long list of instructions.'

Lou's care succeeded in averting Brian's worst nightmare. The audience of 73 million who tuned in to *The Ed Sullivan Show* for their first sight of the Beatles got the complete line-up, irradiating revolutionary charm. She herself watched their performance from the studio audience, as young and not-so-young women went berserk all around her, 'trying to will my energy into my brother to make sure he could keep standing up through the show. He still had a temperature of 104.'

Back then, before the emergence of anything resembling a British rock 'culture', the Beatles had been absorbed into conventional show business, their rise and rise measured by *Sunday Night at the London Palladium*, the *Royal Variety Performance*, Novello Awards for John and Paul's songwriting, and guest appearances on television comedy shows like Morcambe and Wise's *The Two of Us*.

In March 1964, the Variety Club of Great Britain made

them its own by voting them the 'Outstanding Show Business Personalities of 1963' and they received their award from soon-to-be Labour Prime Minister Harold Wilson; the first in a long line of politicians seeking to ingratiate themselves with young voters by greasing up to pop stars.

The Beatles had no objection since it allowed them to socialise with entertainers they'd always revered. George was especially thrilled to meet the actor John Mills, star of innumerable war movies like *The Colditz Story* and *Ice Cold in Alex*, and readily agreed to escort Mills's daughter, Hayley, to a charity premiere of the film *Charade* soon after the band's return from America.

Hayley Mills had herself been a huge child star and had recently played her first almost grown-up role in Disney's huge-grossing comedy *The Parent Trap*, but nonetheless was thrown into as great a panic as any seventeen-year-old at the prospect of a date with a Beatle.

The premiere was to be at the Regal cinema in Henley-on-Thames – a town that George would come to know well – and he collected Hayley from her parents' home in his new black E-Type Jaguar. 'He reminded me of a little foal peering out from under a bearskin rug,' she later confided to her diary. 'His smile is rather wicked; when he laughs it's as if there's a tiny leprechaun sitting on his shoulder who pulls the side of his mouth up.'

When they reached the cinema, she found herself in 'a snake-pit of shrieking, scratching' Beatles fans, 'who almost tore the clothes off our backs'. Even in their VIP seats, George continued to be mobbed while the star of *Whistle Down The Wind* and *The Parent Trap* sat there, totally ignored, one woman kneeling in her lap to get to him.

He had turned twenty-one on 25 February, when the Beatles were already back recording at Abbey Road. His mother phoned him from Liverpool at 12.10 a.m., the exact time of his arrival via the same bed as three siblings before him.

Fifty-two sacks of congratulatory fan mail were delivered to the Beatles Fan Club's office in Monmouth Street, along with menageries of teddy bears, regiments of jelly babies, a hand-embroidered greeting card four foot by three and, from a group of even more ingenious needlewomen, a six-foot-high replica of double doors fashioned in felt. 'We know you have enough keys,' said their message, 'so here's the door.'

After success with an album, the traditional next step for every pop act was to appear in a feature film, several usually lumped together in what was no more than series of musical numbers connected by the flimsiest plot and clunkiest dialogue. Only Cliff Richard's *Summer Holiday* and *The Young Ones* had broken out of this cheapskate niche with big-budget locations and elaborately choreographed song-and-dance routines underlining Richard's so far unique transition from flimsy pop to family entertainment.

Accordingly, Brian had contracted the Beatles to make such a self-confessed exploitation movie for United Artists which, like all Hollywood studios then, maintained an office in London. Part of the deal was to be a soundtrack album for UA's record division instead of EMI, ensuring a handsome profit even if the film were to flop.

Both its producer, Walter Shenson, and its director, Richard Lester, were American, but of a deep-dyed Anglophilia common in the UK film industry in those days. Lester had directed *The Running, Jumping & Standing Still Film*, a 'short' by the Goons comedy team, whom all the Beatles had adored since their schooldays. He was assigned a rock-bottom budget of £20,000 and instructed to have the film finished in five months since UA believed they would be 'a spent force by the end of the summer'. Its being in black-and-white with the working title *Beatlemania!* signalled the low level of its ambitions.

Unusually, the Beatles were given a say in the choice of scriptwriter, the Welsh/Liverpudlian playwright Alun Owen. It was to be in documentary style with the four appearing as themselves in Beatle-like situations, among fictitious characters played by trusty British comedy actors. Owen had hung out with them for an extended period in Paris and elsewhere, to get a feel of the atmosphere and the way they talked and interacted.

The film's breakneck production-schedule meant it had to be shot in the order Owen had written it rather than the usual piecemeal fashion. The Beatles' first spell of filming therefore was the opening sequence in which they're pursued into London's Marylebone station by a mob of screaming girls and make their escape on a departing train, acting as if it's all the greatest fun.

The extras on the train for this specially confected journey to Cornwall included four fashion models dressed as uniformed schoolgirls – a touch nobody then considered in the least questionable. The only one given any dialogue (the single word 'Prisoners!') was Pattie Boyd.

Quirkily gorgeous, with a gap in her front teeth and a nose that wrinkled when she laughed (as she often did), nineteen-year-old Pattie belonged to the new breed of 'dolly-bird' models currently storming the glossy heights of *Vogue* and *Elle*, much as the Beatles had the charts, in tandem with brash young Cockney photographers like David Bailey, Terence Donovan and Brian Duffy. She was on the train because of having previously worked with the director Richard Lester on a television commercial for Smith's crisps.

At the lunch break, she sat next to George, thinking him 'the best-looking man I'd ever met' with his 'velvet brown eyes and dark chestnut hair', but he seemed as shy as she was and they exchanged scarcely a word. Then as the train neared London again, he asked her to marry him, which she treated as just Beatly knockabout. 'Well, if you won't marry me,' he said, 'will you have dinner with me tonight?' She replied that she couldn't as she had a steady boyfriend, the photographer Eric Swayne.

Her friends having convinced her of the folly in passing up such an offer, she took the precaution of ending things with Swayne in case it should come a second time. It did ten days later during a photocall at Twickenham film studios when she and the other models from the train scene, still dressed as schoolgirls, had each to pretend to be styling a Beatle's hair. Pattie managed to get to George's first and tell him she was now unattached.

The resulting dinner date was her first taste of the secrecy that had to surround all George's trysts and the paternalism of Brian's management. To ensure complete safety from any intrusive camera lenses, it took place at the Garrick Club, a bastion of male traditionalism where women were barred from membership and even forbidden to use the main staircase.

Not only did Brian choose their food and wine but he joined them for the whole evening, which George seemed to think quite normal. 'We sat side by side on a banquette, listening to [him],' Pattie would recall in her delectable memoir, *Wonderful Tonight*, 'hardly daring to touch each other's hand.'

Contrary to his expectations, George quite enjoyed the

filming apart from the early morning starts and the thick makeup he needed to mask a few lingering adolescent blemishes. In front of the camera, Lester would say, he performed better than his shyness and self-consciousness had promised. 'John had natural talent as an actor, but refused to take it seriously. Paul was so enthusiastic that he perhaps tried too hard. George was the best because he didn't try to do too much, but always hit it right in the middle.'

At the same time, the film's producer, Walter Shenson, normally the most relaxed of men, dreaded any argument with him above all, 'because I never met anyone so intransigent.'

The Beatles improvised much of their own dialogue, notably the running gag about Wilfrid Brambell as Paul's reprobate grandfather being 'very clean', which George had quipped Paul would be after lingering in his bath instead being punctual to the first-ever business meeting with Brian.

However, the scriptwriter, Alun Owen, had taken it on himself to invent a bit of Beatlespeak on top of all that he'd overheard. In the scene with a patronising marketing executive, George is shown some shirts designed for teenagers and opines, 'I wouldn't be seen dead in them, they're dead grotty.' 'He curled up with embarrassment every time he had to say it,' John would recall.

He continued seeing Pattie Boyd – in every sense of that tactful English term – still unbeknown to the most eagle-eyed Fleet Street Beatle-watchers. Pattie's tiny flat in Oakley Street, Chelsea, had only one bedroom, shared with a flatmate named Mary Bee, so George rented a mews house for her, close to his and Ringo's Knightsbridge pad. To avoid any idea of her being a 'kept woman', and as additional camouflage, Mary moved there too.

With some trepidation, she realised she didn't share George's rarefied tastes in pop music. 'The record Mary and I were listening to was Millie's "My Boy Lollipop." He was horrified.' But it proved not to be a fatal flaw.

The formerly self-reliant Pattie now found herself sharing a life from which Brian had removed every mundane pressure or chore. 'I'd never had such fun before,' she recalls. 'It was like being a child, which I'd never felt like even when I was a child. If I was going anywhere with George, we'd be picked up and taken to the airport where our flights had been booked for us; at the other end, we'd be met by a limo and taken to a hotel where our suite would be waiting. We never knew the details. We just knew that the grown-ups would have everything under control.'

Their secret was in greatest jeopardy that Easter when they flew to Ireland with John and Cynthia Lennon for a hopefully relaxing weekend at the Dromoland Castle Hotel in County Clare where President John F. Kennedy had stayed on his one visit to his family's homeland.

Although they went by private plane, so avoiding the most public parts of Heathrow and Shannon airports, John and George both wore disguises and Cynthia and Pattie had to walk several paces behind them. The subterfuge was pointless in Cynthia's case since John's fans had long ago discovered he was married and forgiven him.

The foursome had barely checked into the Dromoland Castle when its manager warned them that the *Daily Mirror* was on to them already. A small army of reporters and photographers swiftly appeared, making any further relaxation impossible. In that pre-mobile phone era, the hacks had to book rooms in the hotel from which to file their copy. The friendly manager tapped the lines so that their quarry could eavesdrop on the stories winging back to Fleet Street, fortunately none yet unmasking George's mystery companion.

With press people now stationed at every exit, the problem was how to leave the hotel before someone identified her. The manager came up with a solution worthy of *The Great Escape*: John and George departed, as expected, by limo while Pattie and Cynthia left by the service entrance crouching inside a pair of wicker laundry-hampers.

The two couples reconvened in May for a month's holiday in Tahiti and sailing around its neighbouring islands, the furthest George could get from screaming crowds and projectile jelly babies. He travelled under the alias of 'Mr Hargreaves', Pattie that of 'Miss Bond' and she and Cynthia Lennon wore wigs and dark glasses.

In Honolulu, there was a hitch in Brian's usually flawless arrangements and they had to wait two days for the connecting boat to the Tahitian capital, Papeete. Beatlemania proving almost as virulent in Honolulu as back home, George and Pattie escaped to a simple beach hotel in the north of the island where no one would recognise George. Or so they thought.

The heat was ferocious, so he asked her to cut his hair as she'd pretended to do at the Twickenham Studios photocall. Afterwards she threw the clippings into the wastepaper basket only to find later that they'd been taken by the cleaners as souvenirs or to sell. 'There and then,' she recalls, 'I learned to think like a spy, leaving no trace.'

The little Pattie was to see of George for the remainder of 1964 ensured that their secret remained secure. Following on from the Beatles' American triumph, Brian had booked them two major overseas tours, the first taking in Denmark, Holland, Hong Kong and Australasia, the second a return to the US to satisfy the nationwide demand created by *The Ed Sullivan Show*.

In June, just before their scheduled departure to Copenhagen, Ringo was rushed to hospital with acute tonsilitis and pharyngitis or inflammation of the throat. Brian decreed the tour was too important to postpone and that a session drummer named Jimmy Nicol should play with them until Ringo recovered.

Ringo himself made no fuss, but George was outraged that he should be so casually dispensed with. It still rankles decades later in his interview for *The Beatles Anthology*: 'Can you imagine the Rolling Stones going on tour [and saying] "Oh, sorry, Mick can't come, we'll just find someone else to replace him for two weeks"? I really despised the way we couldn't make a decision for ourselves.'

Their first Australian stop wouldn't have done much good to Ringo's tonsils. After landing at Sydney's Mascot Airport, where several thousand fans waited in a monsoon-strength rainstorm, they had to parade around the perimeter on a flatbed truck with no protection but short capes and little umbrellas that instantly blew inside out. The lashing rain made the dye in their capes soak through the garments beneath, so that when they undressed later their skin was stained bright blue.

Back in Britain, their big-screen debut was being finished off at Mach speed for release in July before their return to mop up America. The original title, *Beatlemania!*, had been changed to *A Hard Day's Night*, a phrase from John's book of nonsense stories and poems, *John Lennon In His Own Write*, which had become a massive bestseller early in the shoot. It wasn't wholly original: the previous year, the singer Eartha Kitt had written and recorded a song in similar bleary mood entitled 'I Had A Hard Day Last Night'.

A million advance orders for the soundtrack album included in the deal with United Artists made *A Hard Day's Night* one of the few films ever to go into profit while still in production. Even so, UA executives worried that the Beatles' accents might be incomprehensible to cinema audiences and the director, Richard Lester, had to fight off eleventh-hour attempts to have them overdubbed by professional actors.

The eponymous album, their first without any cover-versions, contained their next single, 'Can't Buy Me Love', which was to sell two million in the US in its first week. It also contained such instant Lennon–McCartney evergreens as 'If I Fell', 'And I Love Her', 'Tell Me Why' and 'Things We Said Today'. But there was no George composition to follow 'Don't Bother Me', and he contributed only one lead vocal, 'I'm Happy Just To Dance With You', which John and Paul had written specially for him to sing in the film: 'a bit of a formula song', Paul would later call it, tailored to what they saw as his limited vocal ability.

Even so, he left an indelible mark with the extended, twangling outro to the title track which in the film acts like a travelator to the joyous romp ahead. Not to mention the unrehearsed moment in the pre-title sequence of running from fans at Marylebone station when he trips and sprawls on the pavement, bringing Ringo down on top of him.

A Hard Day's Night was both a commercial and critical smash, grossing £12 million and winning unanimous rave reviews, several hailing the Beatles as 'modern Marx Brothers'. Lester in effect invented the pop video with his inspired framing of the songs, like 'I Should Have Known Better' in the train's guard's van – putting them inside another cage– and 'Can't Buy Me Love' as the soundtrack to their brief escape from confinement into their own speeded-up *Running, Jumping & Standing Still Film* on an empty sportsfield.

The royal gala premiered at the London Pavilion cinema on 6 July and brought the largest crowds into the West End since Victory in Europe Day in 1945, its throng of older celebrities showing the tuxedo-ed Beatles more than ever in the bosom of British show-business. Brian decided that Pattie Boyd still needed to be kept under wraps, so arranged for George to escort Hayley Mills again.

The royals present were the Queen's younger sister, Princess Margaret, and her photographer husband, Lord Snowdon, a hugely glamorous couple who made the occasion somewhat less stuffy than it might have been, even dropping in for a drink at the lavish buffet reception that followed. Nonetheless, there still were strict rules about entertaining a Her Royal Highness and George's tendency to gracelessness, now much magnified by Brian's pampering, caused the film's producer, Walter Shenson, a moment of near cardiac-arresting embarrassment.

'We were all in the ante-room, having drinks before going in to the food,' Shenson recalled. 'Princess Margaret was supposed to have another engagement to go to, but she still stayed on, chatting to people. George caught my eye and whispered, "When do we eat?" "We can't until the Princess goes," I told him. Finally he went over to her and said, "Ma'am, we're starved and Walter says we can't eat until you leave."'

To the notoriously prickly Margaret, it clearly made a refreshing change from the usual servility. 'She just burst out laughing. "Come on, Tony," she said to Lord Snowdon, "we're in the way."'

Four days later, the Beatles flew to Liverpool for the film's northern charity premiere. They might have wowed the world but were all deeply uneasy about their reception in the home city they'd seemingly forsaken.

Since the airport was in Speke, the first part of it they saw was George's home neighbourhood: 'Roads I'd driven down all my life,' he would recall, '. . . lined with people waving.'

They received the freedom of the city from the Lord Mayor, then, like royalty themselves, appeared on the Town Hall balcony, waving to the crowd that jammed Castle Street below. John added a Nazi salute which today might have ended his career but in 1964 aroused scarcely a tut-tut.

It's with *A Hard Day's Night* that the paradox of being George becomes fully apparent – unprecedentedly, ludicrously, suffocatingly famous while at the same time undervalued, overlooked and struggling for recognition.

On 13 July, he's involved in a minor traffic accident in the New King's Road, Fulham, his E-Type suffering nothing worse than a shattered windscreen. Bystanders almost fight to retrieve fragments of its glass from the road.

Yet in the film's elaborate souvenir booklet, his only detailed mention in the text is about his twenty-first birthday and among the many on-set photographs of John and Paul, you could get eyestrain trying to find him.

11

'THE ONLY BEATLE GLARE EVER CAUGHT ON CAMERA'

The last thing the Beatles ever expected was to last. However big they grew, they were always braced for the moment when the fickle pop audience tired of them and moved on to some fresh novelty. The question they were constantly asked, and asked themselves, was 'How much longer can all this go on?'

John and Paul's wholesale circulation of their songs among chart rivals, from Duffy Power to the Rolling Stones, was insurance against the seemingly inevitable day their voices would no longer fit and they'd have to earn their living solely as writers. Since even that promised no certain future, John invested in a supermarket in Hayling Island, Hampshire; Ringo spoke of opening a ladies' hairdresser's and 'trotting around in me stripes and tails'; George was less specific but typically blunt about the need for a post-Beatlemania Plan B: 'I hope to go into a business of my own when we do flop.'

Even with America and the world at their feet, Brian continued milking their popularity to the maximum before it should curdle with virtually back-to-back tours, incessant television and radio work, interviews, personal appearances and a commitment to make a second feature film while the first was still packing out theatres. On the same hit–and–run principle, George Martin demanded a new single every three months and a new album every six.

Far from stunting John and Paul's writing, the ridiculous pressure spurred it to continual leaps forward, so much so that Martin's former headmasterly authority had long since disappeared. Instead, the trained classical musician became the interpreter and enabler of their untrained genius, dazzled afresh by its every new manifestation, and thus more than ever inclined to overlook George.

The *Beatles For Sale* album, released in December 1964, marked the transition of Abbey Road studios from clock-watching laboratory to rehearsal room at their disposal, in the words of its standout Paul track, 'Eight Days A Week'. George had no original song on the album and his only lead vocal, like Ringo's, was a Carl Perkins cover, in his case what he slurs in a half-embarrassed way, perhaps because it was all too true, as 'Everybody's tryin' to be my baby'.

Like Ringo, he'd signed a contract with Northern Songs, the company channelling John and Paul's output. However, he'd soon become dissatisfied with his royalties and minority status, and set up his own publishing company, initially called Mornywork Ltd, then Harrisongs, although his Northern contract wouldn't expire until 1968. But whatever Harrisongs he was writing thus far didn't find their way to Abbey Road and the Star Chamber of John, Paul and George Martin.

Years later, a contrite Martin would acknowledge: 'George was kind of a loner, really. John and Paul had each other to play against and their collaboration was much more a competition;

one would come up with something and the other would go, "Hey, I can do a bit better than that." But George had no one to work with; he was the sole guy.'

In the studio during this era, the Beatles were a two-tier group: John and Paul would arrive with their latest song cache and George and Ringo would fit the guitar and drums around them. 'A kind of attitude came over,' George would recall: "*We're* the Beatles, we've the grooves and you two are just watching."'

If not at the time, the future Sir Paul McCartney was to recognise how crucial the simplest of those off-the-peg George riffs could be. For instance, the gentle acoustic phrase that introduced 'And I Love Her' in *A Hard Day's Night*, both album and film, the latter showing him playing flamenco-style, standing with the guitar resting on one knee:

'It's just four notes, "da–da–da–*dah*." I didn't write that. He made it up on the spot. And if you think about it, *that's* the song.'

The inequality was less obvious on the American tours that followed their first brief promotional visit and the huge trans-atlantic success of *A Hard Day's Night*. These saw live pop music increase in scale, from theatres and halls to giant sports stadiums and arenas, and would forever be unparalleled for the wild excesses of their audiences and the exemplary behaviour of their headliners.

The first, beginning in August 1964, unleashed a Wail mightier than any yet from European or Australasian throats, with which even the Beatles' new 100-watt amplifiers stood no chance of competing. In the general mayhem, few onlookers noticed that from the twelve-song setlist George had only one lead vocal, his same old 'Roll Over Beethoven'.

Among Beatles fans over here, almost the sum total of knowledge about him was his supposed passion for jelly babies. The American version, however, was the hard sugar-coated jelly bean, and the adoring volleys flung at the stage were practically capable of inflicting flesh wounds. With them came other missile love-tokens – shoes, skipping ropes, cartons of cigarettes, metal lighters – and a stream of foot-borne intruders that the wholly inadequate security seemed equally incapable of blocking or removing. George would often find himself trying to play with a demented young woman or two dangling from his neck.

He and Ringo took their equal quarter share of each day's lunacy, discomfort, annoyance and occasional mortal danger: the arrival in city after city under riot conditions; the journey to venue after venue hiding in delivery trucks or ambulances; the moments of sheer terror in their limo with its roof caving in under the weight of screaming bodies while escape was blocked by the screaming bodies pressed against its doors; the frequent rough handling from the very police attempting to clear a path for them. As John would recall, 'We got battered mostly by the people supposed to guard us.'

The constant plane journeys in every type of aircraft were a particular trial to George, who'd once been on a flight from Liverpool when the window beside him had shattered. He was terrified of it happening again and this time being sucked out by the slipstream.

The 1964 itinerary included flying to Jacksonville, Florida, by private Lockheed Electra which at the time had a poor safety record, awakening horrid memories in this undiminished Buddy Holly addict of 'the day the music died'. They landed in the wake of a hurricane and played the outdoor Gator Bowl

Stadium on a twelve-foot-high stage, buffeted by winds still so strong that Ringo's drums had to be nailed to the floor.

The madness was not all adulatory. Death threats against one particular Beatle or all of them together became commonplace, in the American South especially since they always refused to play to racially segregated audiences. In 1964, they were subjected to a burst of anti-Semitism when Ringo's nose was taken as irrefutable proof that he was Jewish. And the naive young Brits – Brian not excluded – had to adjust to a culture in which legal documents giving notice of multimillion-dollar lawsuits were served as casually as people back home served afternoon tea.

In years to come, rock tours would become infamous for the overweening arrogance, capriciousness and volatility of their top names. But so thorough had been Brian's house-training of the Beatles that at every visible moment on the road they were expected to be accessible, friendly, co-operative, patient and charming.

In each new city after their show, they would have to meet and greet a bevy of local dignitaries, mayors, police chiefs or fire chiefs together with wives and children, most of whom they inwardly found detestable or risible, yet still donned smiles and proffered hands as professionally as the Queen at a garden party at Buckingham Palace.

America brought a dismaying new level of worship: at some venues, the front couple of rows would consist of children in wheelchairs, who'd be brought to see them afterwards as if they actually possessed the power to heal. John had a phobia about physical disability, manifested in his parodic leers and limps onstage, but for the others it was hardly less upsetting. And often the 'carers' with the children were merely opportunists who'd grabbed a wheelchair as a passport into their presence.

'Even when we got away from the screaming fans, there were all the screaming policemen and the lord mayors and their wives and the hotel managers and their entourages,' George would recall in *The BeatlesAnthology*. 'The only place we ever got any peace was when we got in the suite and locked ourselves in the bathroom.'

Today's major bands on tour can have entourages and technical-support teams running into hundreds. The Beatles had only Neil Aspinall and Mal Evans, the former Cavern club bouncer who'd lately joined them as a roadie-cum-bodyguard, though the brawny, bespectacled Mal was too soft-hearted ever to bounce anyone with real conviction.

Neil's principal role was to say 'No' – a word the lovely cuddly Beatles themselves never could – as when brusquely clearing their dressing rooms of unwelcome or overstaying visitors, usually at a secret signal from them. He and Mal Evans were the little bit of Liverpool they took everywhere, who stopped their heads ever swelling too much or their feet rising too far off the ground.

On the 1964 tour they also had Derek Taylor, George's Boswell for the *Daily Express* who'd gone on to ghost-write Brian's highly romanticised and sanitised autobiography, *A Cellar Full Of Noise* (known back in Liverpool as *A Cellar Full Of Boys*) and whom he'd since persuaded to quit the *Express* and become their press officer.

The quirky and not notably discreet Taylor thus joined the tiny minority of publicists with no need to drum up interest in their charges and the primary duty of keeping the besieging press under control. He soon discovered that, paradoxically, the Beatles' Achilles heel was not some disreputable secret that needed keeping dark (although they did have plenty of those) but their reputation for infallible charm.

In one city, after they'd gone to sleep, the wife of some mayor or fire chief came to Taylor and demanded they should be awoken to meet her and her children or she'd go to the papers with the story of how the stuck-up Beatles had snubbed her devastated kids (a scenario that was repeated on a larger scale with horrible results two years later in the Philippines).

Taylor's ability to temper his loyalty to the Beatles with professional sympathy for journalists made him popular with the large media contingent who followed the tour, paying for their generous access with rigorous self-censorship. On the road, this restraint chiefly concerned what was referred to obliquely as 'the girl scene' – i.e., the roadies' practice of supplying four sexually active, if not hyperactive Beatles with companions who were not groupies – a fast-expanding constituency – or under the American age of consent or anyone else with the potential to cause trouble after the event.

John would later describe it as 'Satyricon on tour', referring to Federico Fellini's film about orgies in ancient Rome, although these encounters on the road were always one-to-one, sometimes even in earshot of the press, from nearby bedrooms or shower stalls. As far as their readership knew, the Beatles journeyed through the oceans of female adoration and availability like mop-topped Trappist monks.

Taylor was impressed by the way they all handled the constant variegated pressures on them but, as he later admitted, 'There were moments when someone, George in particular, would [say], "Get your bloody arm out and wave for me", "I'm not going up there [i.e., onstage]" or "I'm not meeting Shirley Temple."' The empathy that had developed between them during the writing of George's column deepened during these weeks on the road although, like Walter Shenson, Taylor found that once his mind was made up, he was immovable.

For example, it had been suggested the Beatles might start the tour with a ticker-tape parade, the extravagant salute that New York traditionally gives to American conquering heroes, but in San Francisco, where they were to play the Cow Palace. This being only a year after President Kennedy's assassination in an open car in the midst of mass adulation, George refused to have any part in it, and one must admit good sense was on his side.

To him, the main attraction of this ultimate 'road' was being able to meet his every teenage rock 'n' roll hero, from Chuck Berry to Fats Domino, as well as connect with some of the new American bands the Beatles had galvanised into being, like New York's Lovin' Spoonful, whose songwriting posed a serious challenge to Lennon and McCartney. Asked on BBC radio to name his favourite song of the moment, George chose the Spoonful's 'Do You Believe In Magic?' before it had been heard in the UK.

In Los Angeles, where the Beatles played the Hollywood Bowl, every movie star they'd ever worshipped put out the welcome mat. George wrote excitedly to his parents about visiting Burt Lancaster's house ('which cost a million dollars') and swimming in Lancaster's pool ('which went right into the living room and was as warm as a bath almost').

Generally, he tolerated the photographers who attached themselves to the Beatles like a giant pair of flashing wings. But as Ringo would recall, he had two different personalities that could change from one to the other in an instant: 'There was the love and bag-of-beads personality and the bag of anger. He was very black and white.'

One evening at the super-chic Whisky A Go Go club on Sunset Strip, Derek Taylor temporarily lost his grip on events: the Beatles were lured into an unofficial photo-op with Jayne Mansfield, the monumentally endowed star of their favourite Fifties rock 'n' roll movie, *The Girl Can't Help It*.

When an intrusive lens was turned on George, he couldn't help picking up a glass of water and throwing its contents over the photographer. The man had the presence of mind to click the shutter again while the water was in mid-air, his prize the only Beatle glare ever caught on camera.

The social gulf between George and his now-public 'steady', Pattie Boyd, would once have been unbridgeable but by the mid-Sixties had all but disappeared. Say, rather, a Beatle who'd once lived in a house without an inside toilet now transcended any questions of class.

Born in 1944, to his '43, Pattie had spent her early childhood in Kenya, where her maternal grandfather, a wealthy army colonel, had purchased a large estate for his retirement. The country being still under British rule, it was an idyllic existence, with numerous servants, exotic gardens and thrilling wild animals mostly keeping a respectful distance.

Yet her family life had been as unstable as George's had been unruffled. Her father, Jock, a former RAF officer, had suffered severe burns in a wartime runway accident and consequently was moody and withdrawn. Her mother, Diana, was a glamorous socialite with little interest in children, despite eventually giving birth to five. Pattie spent long periods separated from her younger siblings, Colin and Jenny, farmed out to relatives back in England or crying herself to sleep at a succession of bleak boarding schools.

After the birth of a third daughter, Paula, in 1951, Diana divorced Jock and married Bobbie Gaymer-Jones, an ex-Guards officer with whom she would have two more sons. Gaymer-Jones was a domestic tyrant, given to physically abusing Pattie and Jenny with a streak of inventive sadism. He also began an open affair with the wife of a neighbour, to which Diana turned a blind eye even when the other woman scratched an erotic message on his car windscreen with her diamond ring.

Such stoicism in the face of blatant infidelity had always been expected from women of Diana's class; even the Swinging Sixties would fail to stamp out that peculiarly British quirk. When Pattie's turn came to face an even grosser example, she would at first respond just like her mother.

She had wasted no time in taking George to meet the still-glamorous Diana, now divorced from Bobbie Gaymer-Jones, her sisters Jenny and Paula, her brother Colin and half-brothers David and Robert, the latter nicknamed 'Boo'. 'My mother adored him,' she recalls. 'So did all of them. He was so sweet and natural and funny.'

Even George's usual strictures about privacy were waived for Boo, then at boarding school in Somerset. 'When George would drive down there to take him out, Boo would find out what time he was due to arrive and get his schoolfriends all lined up with their autograph books.'

Pattie, in her turn, instantly warmed to George's parents,

the dynamic Louise and the placid Harold, and to his brothers Harry and Peter. She noticed how even now George deferred to Harry, the eldest, while 'Pete was more like the kid brother than he was.'

Though there wasn't a snobbish bone in her body, she couldn't help noticing the cultural differences between their two families. In her genteel southern one, for instance, 'tea' meant a dainty afternoon interlude with thin bread-and-butter, cake and Earl Grey, whereas in George's northern working-class one, it was an early evening meal of pork pie or cold ham, washed down by a brick-coloured brew that was 'mashed' not made, and 'everyone held their knives and forks like pens.'

Pattie had become the envy of young women all over the world but, equally, the sworn enemy of hardcore George fans who'd come to regard him as their personal property. She received hate mail in many languages – the worst invariably American – whose authors informed her they were already his girlfriend and threatened to kill or put a curse on her if she didn't keep her hands off him.

With her face often shown in both newspapers and magazine fashion spreads, to appear in public without a disguise was to risk physical assault. One night after a Beatles show at the Hammersmith Odeon, as she and Cynthia Lennon left by a side door to rendezvous with John's limo, a group of five girls surrounded Pattie and subjected her to a merciless kicking with their arrow-sharp Italian shoes until rescue came.

At the other extreme, in her public appearances with George, she had to resign herself to virtual invisibility. 'When we were anywhere like an hotel,' she would later say, 'someone would hold the door open for him, then let it shut in my face.'

She had also been inducted – so far as was possible – into the coterie of women whose only bond was that same, burdensome power to excite envy or hatred in millions of young females worldwide.

Pattie found herself most often in the company of Cynthia Lennon, not from any natural affinity but because, when Brian divided up the Beatles for camouflage on their rare holidays, he tended to pair John with George, there being less likelihood of friction than between John and Paul. Cynthia was friendly enough, though always a little distant as well as palpably worn down by John's neglect; nor did it help that he had an obvious soft spot for Pattie, who reminded him of his ideal woman, Brigitte Bardot.

Pattie had most in common with Paul's girlfriend, Jane Asher, who came from a similar middle-class background, her father a renowned consultant physician, her mother a classical musician – and George Martin's one-time oboe-teacher. Jane had no truck with the purdah Brian ordained for Beatles' wives and girlfriends and continued her successful career as a stage and film actor. Pattie, too, continued modelling for the time being, finding herself in much-increased demand thanks to her new dusting of Beatle magic.

Ringo became the second Beatle husband in February 1965, when he married the former Liverpool hairdresser Maureen Cox, whom he'd met at the Cavern. Quiet and shy as 'Mo' was – although would not always be – she reinforced the sense that these women with the most compelling reason for solidarity were riven by a north–south divide.

The fan-nuisance in Central London had become so severe that Brian decided his boys should move to the suburbs in the hope they would afford them more privacy. Only Paul stayed on for the present in his still-secret eyrie at the top of the Asher family's house in Wimpole Street, Marylebone.

The task of finding houses for the other three was delegated to Brian's accountant, a melancholy Czech named Dr Walter Strach, who looked no further than the Surrey stockbroker belt where he himself resided. Accordingly, John and Ringo were each settled in a faux-Tudor pile on Weybridge's St George's Hill estate, a long-time enclave of show business names like Charlie Drake and Eric Sykes.

By the same proxy house-hunt, George ended up in Esher on the London–Surrey border. There Dr Strach had lit on 'Kinfauns', a four-bedroom 1950s bungalow standing in three-quarters of an acre of garden with a swimming pool, tall hedges and a fourteen-foot-high front gate, The price was £20,000, or around half a million in today's money, even then very far from a fortune. 'It was the first house I saw,' George would later recall without nostalgia from the impossible grandeur of his subsequent one. 'I thought, "It'll do."'

He moved from his and Ringo's Knightsbridge pad in the middle of the night, with a police car escorting the removal van. Pattie took charge of furnishing the bungalow from Terence Conran's newly opened Habitat store and joined him there a couple of months later.

She didn't really like 'Kinfauns' any more than George did and they both were embarrassed by the suburban reek of the name. To relieve its stolid conventionality, they covered the exterior with multicoloured graffiti and – in a departure from the traditional visitors' book – invited all their friends to add a scrawl.

The idea that fans who'd journeyed to London from all over Britain and many foreign parts in pursuit of the Beatles would be unable to track them a further six or seven miles across Surrey soon proved illusory. Like John's 'Kenwood' and Ringo's 'Sunny Heights', the entrance of 'Kinfauns' acquired a permanent female picket, waiting at all hours of the day and night and in all weathers for the briefest photo – or screaming – opportunity as its occupants' and their visitors' cars came and went. Since Weybridge was less than five miles away, those with no specific Beatle fixation could stake out each of the three in turn.

Nor did that impressive fourteen-foot-high gate live up to expectations. More practically minded picketers learned to stop it fully closing after some departing delivery person, then insert a small stone into the mechanism so they could reopen it at will. George and Pattie, to begin with, never locked the front door when they went out, so intruders were constantly roaming through their home in search of souvenirs, which could be as little as a square of toilet paper or as much as a Piaget watch.

An early house guest was Arthur Kelly, George's old classmate at Liverpool Institute who'd been in his skiffle group, the Rebels, and an occasional stand-in Quarryman. Kelly was now a trainee office manager in Liverpool but hankered to become an actor and George had offered to introduce him to the Beatles' film producer, Walter Shenson.

'Nothing came of that, but I ended up staying with George for two weeks,' he recalls. 'I reconnected with Paul, too, and we went over to John's house, which was only a couple of miles away. John had just been to Hamleys toy department, bought every bit of Scalextric [miniature slot-racing cars] in the place and had a whole circuit built. We played with that all night, taking various things to help us stay awake.

'Finally George said, "I've got to throw you out because I'm going on tour but how are you off for suits?" He'd had all these suits made for *A Hard Day's Night* and *Help!* that he was never going to wear again, and gave me six of them.'

He had Kelly chauffeured the 225 miles back to Liverpool in the Austin Princess limousine the Beatles used for their domestic tours, asking one small favour in return. He'd recently bought his parents a radiogram, an opulent radio-cum-gramophone in a lacquered cabinet he knew would be more to their taste than an ultramodern hi-fi. It had had to be specially ordered through a Liverpool store and Kelly was to collect it in the Austin Princess and deliver it to them.

Harold and Louise themselves frequently came to stay, which Pattie found no problem for they were model guests and Louise, that indefatigable letter-writer, would immediately settle down to deal with George's accumulated fan mail.

She loved him to take her to clubs like the Ad Lib off Leicester Square and the Pickwick in Covent Garden where British pop's so-called 'new aristocracy' foregathered and all Beatles ranked equally far above any other jukebox duke.

Harold went along with it as amiably as always, though still oblivious to fashion and interested above all in his former milieu of public transport. 'I remember him sitting at the Ad Lib,' Pattie says with undimmed affection, 'explaining the grid system of New York streets to me.'

Bob Dylan had introduced the Beatles to marijuana when they met him at the end of their '64 American tour. Dylan was

PHILIP NORMAN

astonished to discover they weren't already deeply into the substance; in 'I Want To Hold Your Hand', where John and Paul
sang, 'I can't hide, I can't hide', he'd misheard it as 'I get high,
I get high.'

George had brought some home for Pattie and her then flatmate, Mary, to try in the spirit of other transatlantic curiosities like
book-matches or swizzle sticks and, indeed, it felt about as harmless. 'All of a sudden, we were roaring with laughter, and realised
we were stoned,' Pattie recalls. 'Everything seemed hilarious.'

Thereafter, what John always termed 'having a laugh' became
an indispensable part of the Beatles' daily life. These were innocent times when most British police officers couldn't recognise
the smell of pot or distinguish its straggly strands from ordinary
tobacco and were easily persuaded that a joint was just a herbal
cigarette. Going through Customs on foreign trips wasn't a problem either: Neil Aspinall would simply buy packets of cigarettes,
extract their contents, and refill their paper tubes with the pot.
And, anyway, no one then was going to challenge a Beatle.

Pot fumes pervaded their second film, *Help!*, which had a
vastly bigger budget than *A Hard Day's Night*, and an upgrade
from gritty black-and-white to Technicolor with the same winning team of producer Walter Shenson and director Richard
Lester. The latter couldn't but notice his four stars were high
virtually throughout the shoot, but pragmatically gave thanks
for its being 'a happy high'.

What seemed the most lighthearted of romps in 1965 strikes
continuous queasy notes today. A murderous Indian cult finds
itself unable to make its traditional sacrifice of a young woman
because she's not wearing the ring that's essential to the ceremony. The intended victim turns out to be a Beatles fan who's

sent the ring to Ringo to add to his collection, and the cult plots to retrieve it from his finger, severing his hand if necessary. The main Indian roles are played by white British actors in brown makeup, putting on comical singsong voices.

The film's exotic foreign locations included the Bahamas, for no better reason than their tax-sheltering advantages to Brian. The Beatles were shooting outdoors there in February – concidentially on George's twenty-second birthday – when some genuine Indianness interrupted the burlesque; an orange-robed swami suddenly appeared and gave each of them an autographed copy of something called *The Illustrated Book of Yoga*. The swami was Vishnudevananda Saraswati, the world's foremost teacher of hatha yoga, a centuries-old system for 'inner body-cleansing'.

It might have been George's moment of life-changing revelation – but another one had to come first.

For some time, he and the others had been hearing and reading about a narcotic novelty from America named lysergic acid diethylamide, known for short as 'LSD', which was how pre-decimal British pounds, shillings and pence used to be represented. Unlike pot, it wasn't herbal but chemical and possessed hallucinogenic properties said to be 'mind-expanding'. They were all curious to try it even though, unlike pot, and perhaps a little disappointingly, it so far wasn't illegal.

The first to do so were the regular foursome of John, George, Cynthia and Pattie: literally by spoon-feeding. During a break in filming *Help!* they went for dinner at the Bayswater home of John and George's dentist, John Riley, who had many such celebrity patients and was enough of a friend to have visited them on location in the Bahamas. After dinner, they planned to go on to the Pickwick club for the debut of Brian's newest signing, a trio named Paddy, Klaus and Gibson.

They had no inkling of the extra course their host had prepared, despite the four sugar-lumps that were ceremonially set out on the mantelpiece. Dessert over, John and George rose to go because the Klaus of the trio they'd be seeing later was their old Hamburg friend Klaus Voormann and they couldn't be late for his performance. Riley, however, insisted they stayed for coffee and slipped a sugar-lump into each cup. John was the first to catch on: 'We've just had LSD,' he told George.

Riley, too, had 'dropped' it for the first time, and evidently repeated Bob Dylan's mistake of assuming prior experience on their part. Consequently, nobody knew that the one thing *not* to do when an acid trip kicks in is go into London's West End for the evening.

The first to succumb was Cynthia Lennon, for whom the dining room seemed to expand to vast proportions and their host to turn into a savage monster – though many people view dentists that way without help from drugs. George and John were more worried that he'd try to start a sex orgy. As they took off, all packed into George's Mini Cooper, Riley came after them, concerned for their safety, but in their common paranoia he still seemed threatening and they were relieved when he broke off the pursuit.

Still doggedly insisting they mustn't miss Klaus, George ignored every back-double to Covent Garden and drove along Oxford Street, where the usually decorous Pattie was seized with a desire to jump out and smash the windows of a department store.

After all that, the Pickwick passed in a blur, if they were ever there in the first place, and they travelled a short further distance to the Ad Lib where Ringo was waiting along with Mick Jagger and his partner, Marianne Faithfull. The club was accessed by a lift and during its short ascent they shared the hallucination that it burst into flames.

The four stayed there until dawn, babbling to the untripping and mystified Ringo, Mick and Marianne, then George drove them back to Esher 'at about eighteen miles an hour', the caprice of his particular trip being that 'half the time everything seemed normal, then it was back to this craziness.'

John and Cynthia spent the rest of the night at 'Kinfauns', no one able to sleep, make themselves vomit or find any kind of relief until the drug eventually wore off, leaving behind a bleak, bottomless void. As George later admitted, it should have warned him never to touch the stuff again.

As with most films, the last scenes in *Help!* to be shot were the interiors. These included an Indian restaurant with some real Indian musicians, who between takes would leave their instruments lying around the set. One day, George picked up a sitar – that distant Eastern cousin to the guitar with its bulbous body and far longer and broader fretboard – and played with it, but only from idle curiosity.

But for now there was altogether too much else to think about. Working under their usual ludicrous pressure, the Beatles had also been recording the soundtrack album for release with the film's royal premiere in August (Princess Margaret and Lord Snowdon again) and the European and North American tours immediately afterwards.

John's title track seemed in tune with the film's zany spirit, no more than a bubble from the mouth of the cartoon character he'd portrayed onscreen. Nobody at the time recognised it as a genuine cry for help, suffocated as he felt by his mock-Tudor Weybridge mansion and the Beatles' ironbound sweet 'n' smiley image. In their usual competitive spirit, Paul had responded with 'I'm Down', for him simply an exercise in alchemising the most negative thoughts into joy.

And George, for the first time, had *two* Harrisongs on an album. 'You Like Me Too Much' had the same faint air of annoyance as 'Don't Bother Me'; it could have been a subliminal message to the pickets at 'Kinfauns' ineffectual front gate. But it was the first evidence of any interest from Paul and George Martin, both of whom played different parts on the same Steinway grand for its intro.

'I Need You' was on a wholly different level, no longer merely echoing John or Paul but with a character all its own, at once yearning and reproving. In the film, it was his only lead vocal performance, soundtracking the scene where, unable to shake off Ringo's pursuers, the Beatles end up on Salisbury Plain, ringed by tanks and steel-helmeted soldiers. The future convert to Hinduism's precepts of non-violence and universal brotherly love cannot have been comfortable remembering that.

In June, the Queen's Birthday Honours awarded each Beatle the MBE, standing for Membership of the Most Excellent Order of the British Empire: not, of course, the sovereign's personal choice but the recommendation of the Labour Prime Minister, Harold Wilson, in his tireless efforts to siphon off some of their popularity.

No pop act before had ever received any public honour, nor been considered remotely honourable. A few existing

MBE-holders, mostly retired military men and civil servants, sent back their decorations in protest, but to most people it seemed no more than just for reinventing Britain's music industry and hugely boosting its prestige throughout the world. Disgracefully, however, the person fundamentally responsible was passed over; Rumours of Brian's homosexuality already in circulation had excluded him from any such recognition and even the ceremony at which his boys were honoured.

The culmination of their '65 American tour was their historic concert at New York City's Shea Stadium in August to an audience of 55,000 for a gross exceeding $305,000, then the biggest in entertainment history.

The four tiny figures in their round-collared khaki tunics played for just thirty minutes, battling hopelessly against what was no longer a Wail but the roar of a demented ocean. The twelve-song setlist included neither of George's two on the *Help!* album, only his old Carl Perkins standby 'Everybody's Tryin' To Be My Baby'.

'This is the top of the mountain,' Brian told his American co-promoter, Sid Bernstein. And for the Beatle he loved most, the view was evidently too much to bear. 'I felt that on that show, John cracked up,' Ringo would recall. 'Not mentally ill, just crazy.' In the colour documentary of the performance, it's a fine line. With most of his audience barely able to see any more than hear him, he gives up playing his organ and merely crashes the keys with his elbows or under one heel. His face under its sweat-plastered fringe has a look only describable as ecstatic disgust.

Twelve days later in Los Angeles came the Beatles' encounter with Elvis Presley, now an inconceivable thirty years old, long divorced from rock 'n' roll and turning out barely indistinguishable schlock Hollywood movies, yet still the top of *their* mountain.

During the limo ride to Presley's Bel Air mansion, they 'had a laugh' and when their driver lost his way, it sent them into hysterics. That would be one of the memories George would most cherish later on, when they were speaking to each other only through lawyers.

For all the racist pantomime of *Help!*, it had awoken something deeply serious in George, most keenly felt when he'd casually picked up that sitar on the set. It was a malaise unimaginable in 1965 but pithily elucidated by his friend Tom Petty, two decades in the future: 'There's a point where you're successful and you get wealthy and one day the letter comes that says, "None of this is going to make me happy."'

After the film wrapped, George had bought a sitar of his own at the Indiacraft shop in Oxford Street, whose principal stock were the carvings, brasses and incense then just coming into vogue. But it seemed not to be a very good specimen and with no one to help him negotiate that huge wirebound fretboard, he'd soon given up on it. Since then, it had lain in a cupboard in Abbey Road's Studio Two, where musicians down the decades had left an exotic collection of cast-off instruments.

In the months that followed, he'd kept hearing the name of Ravi Shankar, the sitar's greatest virtuoso and composer, and had eventually bought one of Shankar's albums. 'When I first consciously heard Indian music,' he would declare, 'it was as if I'd known it all my life.' Yet he still felt no curiosity about the ancient religions and philosophies it expressed.

By that summer of 1965, it was already starting to infiltrate mainstream British pop, likewise with no religion or philosphies attached. The original version of the Yardbirds' hit single 'Heart Full Of Soul' featured an Indian sitar-player but it didn't really work so Jeff Beck. who'd recently replaced Eric Clapton as lead guitarist, simulated the sound electronically. Then the Kinks' 'See My Friends' had used a raga-ish rhythm and a droney slide guitar mimicking a tambura or Indian lute.

The Beatles were already at work on a new album, *Rubber Soul*, with yet another Lennon–McCartney leap forward in melody and subject matter. Among John's new songs was one with the enigmatic title 'Norwegian Wood', which he'd first played to George Martin months earlier during a winter-sports holiday in St Moritz with their respective wives.

Martin instantly recognised it as a barely camouflaged confession of an extramarital liaison. 'Cynthia's sitting there and John's singing "I once had a girl ... or should I say she once had me? ..."' Martin even recognised the other party: she was the wife of the photographer Robert Freeman, who'd shot the 'half-shadow' cover for the *With The Beatles* album and been the Lennons' upstairs neighbour in London before their move to Weybridge.

The Beatles began recording 'Norwegian Wood' on 21 October, five days before their investiture with their MBEs at Buckingham Palace. They had rehearsed the song with six- and twelve-string guitars, but felt it needed something more attuned to John's edgy playlet.

Usually, it would be George Martin who found the answer to such questions but this time it was already in the studio cupboard – George's cast-off sitar.

12

'WELL, THAT'S IT.
I'M NOT A BEATLE ANY MORE'

LSD-users were the Pollyannas of the drugs world, endlessly willing to forgive bad trips and trust that their next would be a good one. So to George in retrospect the shock and bewilderment detonated by that spiked sugar-lump turned into 'the first feeling I ever had that was strong – *spiritual* feeling. I took one look at the trees and the grass and the sky and thought, "Yeah, man, that's *it*."'

In 1965, the substance was legal and easily obtainable, largely through doctors (or dentists) thanks to its supposed beneficial effects on certain psychological disorders. But in London it hadn't yet been commercialised, its (exclusively American) distributors considering it something between a religion and a right like the Salk polio vaccine in the 1950s. A mansion flat in Chelsea, grandiosely styled the World Psychedelic Centre, offered it gratis on little squares of white bread.

John also soon recovered from their first trip, decided it had been wondrous and – without brakes in this as everything – took around a thousand more, he would estimate, over the next eighteen months. But the cautious Paul, for the moment, hesitated to undergo his own voluntary initiation.

Pattie tried it only once more after her experience with George and the Lennons. 'We were in the back of John's psychedelic Rolls, driving down to Brian's country house in Sussex. When we arrived, we ran around the house like wild things. Brian couldn't control us; he never could. I remember standing at a big, high window, looking down and thinking I could jump and not hurt myself. That warned me off it for good.'

Since trips were safest in the supportive company of someone else, this meant that George and John often took them together. As well as expanding their minds, as they believed, this shrank the age gap that had yawned between them when they first met and never quite gone away. '[On acid] John and I had a very interesting relationship,' George would recall. 'That I was younger or that I was smaller was no kind of embarrassment with him. From then on, I spent more time with John than with any of the others.'

For George alone, there was another, more puzzling side-effect: 'After I'd had LSD, I had this lingering thought, which was just "Yogis of the Himalayas". I'd never thought about anything like that before, but it kept coming back... "Yogis of the Himalayas". It was like someone was whispering to me.'

The idea of using his sitar on 'Norwegian Wood' was quite spontaneous and instantly effective, he would always say. 'We miked it up and put it on and it just seemed to hit the spot.' In fact, Parlophone's brilliant sound engineer, Norman Smith, had to work hard to capture its 'nasty peaks and very complex wave form' without resorting to deliberate distortion.

Having never had anything remotely approximating to a sitar lesson, George simply played John's main melody line on single notes. The experiment almost came to a premature end when he broke a string, as he had no spare and no idea how to fit or tune one. Fortunately, the ever-resourceful George Martin knew of a sitar helpline.

This was the Asian Music Circle, which had been set up in 1954 to promote Indian music, dance and culture and had also introduced the stiff-necked English to yoga. Its founder, Ayana Angadi, a former militant Trotskyite and anti-imperialist, ran it from his home in Finchley, north London, with his wife, the painter and novelist Patricia Fell-Clark.

The Angadis delivered the sitar string to Abbey Road accompanied by their four children. As a mark of appreciation, they were invited to stay and watch the recording and Patricia sketched John and George at work.

While the two of them carried on their LSD explorations together, the Beatles' main communal recreation continued to be 'having a laugh': their private name for *Rubber Soul*, released in December 1965, was 'the Pot Album', and was richly deserved.

As three of them now lived in the Surrey commuter belt, they could do their own special kind of commute to Abbey Road studios. John's Rolls-Royce would first pick up Ringo, who lived only just around the corner from him in Weybridge, then stop in Esher to collect George for the subsequent journey of about an hour. Unfortunately, after a couple of miles the billowing pot-fumes trapped by the Rolls's tight-shut blacked-out windows and its noiseless glide produced nausea rather than laughter.

'By the time we reached Hammersmith, we were pretty loaded with double doses of these reefers,' George would recall.

'When we got to Abbey Road, we'd just fall out of the car.' But they were still sufficiently in awe of George Martin never to do it during recording-sessions.

Rubber Soul, Martin said, was 'the first album to present a new, growing Beatles to the world'. It had John's 'In My Life' and 'Nowhere Man' and Paul's 'Michelle', but the most impressive growth spurt was in the two tracks again ceded to George.

'Think For Yourself' got stuck right in with a left-field D minor: a male-triumphalist chant somewhat like Bob Dylan's 'Positively 4th Street' but mitigated by the melodic energy in place of Dylan's sneering inertia. 'If I Needed Someone' had a jangling riff copied from the Byrds' electric version of an old folk song called 'The Bells of Rhymney' – as George admitted in a note to its player, Roger McGuinn – and a long, flowing 'A-a-ah coda that was like a hymn without a home'.

'If I Needed Someone' became the second Harrisong to generate a cover-version (after 'Don't Bother Me') and gave him his first hit as a writer when Manchester band the Hollies took it to number 20 in Britain. George was said to have described their interpretation as 'rubbish', which sounded in character though he later told their lead guitarist, Tony Hicks, he'd made no such comment.

The sitar he'd chanced to play on 'Norwegian Wood' created a long-lasting fad among other British bands, ultimately to be known as 'raga rock'. Brian Jones, the Rolling Stones' multi-instrumental genius, instantly mastered the instrument for two Stones tracks, 'Paint It Black' and 'Mother's Little Helper', and Traffic would employ it on two hit singles, 'Paper Sun' and 'Hole In My Shoe'.

For these others, it was merely a way of giving the tritest pop lyric an air of mystery and wisdom, but not for George. He and Pattie – who shared fully in his obsessive new interest – became regular visitors to the Asian Music Circle's headquarters in Finchley for long discussions with Ayana Angadi about Indian religion and culture.

There George received some lessons from one of the Circle's sitar-players, ever hoping that Ravi Shankar, its greatest living exponent and a close friend of Angadi, would materialise from India. He and Pattie also sat for Patricia Angadi in what would turn out to be their wedding portrait.

He was twenty-two and she a year younger, in the mid-Sixties a normal marriageable age for both their classes; moreover, John and Ringo seemed to have shown that the taboo about Beatles having wives no longer applied. Even so. George's proposal, just after the release of *Rubber Soul* while they were out and about in London, lacked the usual spontaneity of such moments. 'Let's get married,' he said. 'I'll speak to Brian.'

He drove straight to Brian's house in Belgravia and left Pattie in the car while he went inside. Fifteen minutes later, he reappeared with Brian's blessing: the Beatles having no tour commitments in late January 1966, their wedding could take place on the twenty-first.

Pattie admits she had some qualms about taking on a Beatle husband and everything that went with it. But she was deeply in love with George and his world had its seductive as well as terrifying side. 'In my whole life, no one had ever taken care of me. I'd been the one taking care of my brother and sisters. Now, Brian was looking after me as well as George and it was a feeling of absolute security.'

With that security came absolute control. She had always

dreamed of a traditional church ceremony with bridesmaids and confetti, but Brian decreed it should be as low-key as possible to keep the press furore to a minimum. Nor could she even ask one of the top couturiers she knew through her modelling to design her a dress for fear the secret might leak out of some workroom. She therefore had to 'put herself together' with a ready-made Mary Quant minidress in red shot silk and white stockings.

At her mother's insistence, she'd invited her father, himself long home from Kenya and living in rural Devon, even though she hadn't seen or heard from Jock Boyd for years. 'I'm going to marry George,' she wrote. 'He comes from Liverpool, I'm sure you'd like him . . .' Jock was evidently unaware of the later developments in her life and remained as stiffly Victorian as ever. He forbade her to marry someone so young, whose family he didn't know (i.e., socially) but she ignored the command.

The ceremony took place at Epsom Register Office, as early in the morning as was possible in the vain hope of minimising press coverage. John and Ringo were away on holiday and, surprisingly, didn't seem to think it worth a special trip home to see George married, as he'd seen both of them. Brian and Paul shared the office of best man and Pattie was given away by her mother's twin brother, her Uncle John, a freebooting writer still based in Africa, whom she and her three siblings had always loved more than their father or their explosive step-father, Bobbie.

Afterwards there was a lunch party at 'Kinfauns', where the bride and bridegroom's families mingled with no hint either of class- or north–south divide. When Pattie's two schoolboy half-brothers grew restive during the speeches, Paul took them into the garden and found them George's archery set to play with, not losing his avuncular good humour even when an arrow pinged off his immaculate Rolls-Royce.

In the end, Fleet Street's pressure on Brian became such that there had to be a formal press conference. George laughingly recalled proposing to Pattie the first day they'd met, on the train during the filming of *A Hard Day Night*, but not being taken seriously. He became less genial, as he so easily could, when quizzed about his supposed row with the Hollies over their cover of 'If I Needed Someone'.

The following June, Ravi Shankar returned to Britain on one of his periodic concert tours, this including his historic duet with Yehudi Menuhin, the world's greatest violinist (and the Asian Music Circle's honorary president). George attended Shankar's recital at the Royal Albert Hall and a dinner given for him at their home by Ayana and Patricia Angadi.

Shankar, then in his mid-forties, was a gentle-faced man with the extreme modesty that so often goes with genius. 'I could meet anyone, I could go in all the film stars' houses and meet Elvis but I never met one person who really impressed me until I met Ravi,' George would recall, 'because he never tried to impress me. It was by his being, because he taught me so much without saying a word. It was all by example.'

In a break between concerts, Shankar visited 'Kinfauns' and gave George and Pattie a private recital with tabla player Allah Rahka, which John and Ringo came from Weybridge to watch. He then formally offered his services as teacher, something George had hardly dared to hope. 'It was so nice to find some-body who was such a master being able to start from scratch with a beginner.'

Gentle though Shankar's manner, there was no sense of

fawning around a Beatle who was bound to increase his public profile a thousandfold. 'One thing that happened said a lot. The telephone rang and I put the sitar down, stood up and went to step across it . . . and Ravi whacked me on the leg and said, "The first thing you must realise is that you must have more respect for the instrument."

'There are other things you mustn't do like holding your beads with the first finger or pointing your feet towards someone else or even blowing out a stick of incense with your mouth. It's all part of the discipline and it is true, you can't appreciate anything if you have no respect.'

A sitar made far greater demands on its player than a guitar. One had to sit on the floor cross-legged, left leg over right, not holding it up as one would a guitar but letting it find its own balance so there would be no weight on the fingering hand as there is with a guitar. A whole vocabulary went with it: the pick was a *misra*, 'da' meant a downstroke, 'ra' an upstroke and 'diri-diri' a down-up-downstroke.

Shankar made George play always with eyes shut until he knew every fret in the long labyrinth by touch alone. Even to fingertips hardened by years of sliding up and down a guitar fretboard, the endless-seeming scales were 'murder'.

Yet the da's and the diri-diri's were only part of his training. Fundamental to Shankar's teaching was that 'music has the power to lead you towards God', the oral tradition of Indian music above all. 'The guru', he explained, in his pupil's first-ever encounter with that word, 'passes along not just the technique but the whole spiritual aspect, the meaning of life, philosophy, everything.'

George's last experience of God had been the stringent single

Deity of his early Catholic upbringing. In comparison, the multiplicity of gods invoked by sitar music seemed easy-going, even comforting. 'I couldn't even say the word "God", it embarrassed me,' he would recall. 'But, it was so strange, [when I said it with Ravi] it washed away all those fears and doubts and little things that hang you up.'

Hard on the heels of *Rubber Soul*, the Beatles' so-called Pot Album, came *Revolver*, their so-called Acid Album, considered by many their supreme achievement, on which George's contributions increased to three.

Released in the sweltering late summer of 1966, it seemed the apogee of 'Swinging' Britain and a London lately anointed by America's *Time* magazine as 'the style capital of Europe'. Exactly a decade earlier, following the humiliation of the Suez Crisis, the country had apparently resigned itself to terminal gloom and decay. Now its international prestige was at a zenith, not only through the Beatles but after winning the football World Cup for the first time ever, as if some of their mastery had transferred to the team's boots.

Yet of Revolver's bumper fourteen tracks only Paul's 'Good Day Sunshine' actually conjured up those hot pavements, the barefoot girls in their wasp-striped microdresses and floppy hats, and ruffle-shirted, Beatle-headed boys who suddenly owned the city. The rest of Lennon and McCartney's three-quarters was altogether less euphoric.

'Eleanor Rigby' was a name from a Liverpool gravestone, imagined as a lonely, dying church cleaner like a short story by James Joyce. 'Doctor Robert' satirised a Manhattan physician famous for supplying his moneyed patients with amphetamine shots. 'She Said She Said' was about a near-death experience. 'Yellow Submarine', ostensibly a children's song for Ringo, was the nickname of yellow-coated pentabarbitone 'downers'. It also became a marching song for the industrial strikes that paralysed Swinging Britain as regularly as ever, its chorus changed to 'We all live on bread and margarine.'

George's unprecedented quarter-share of the material brought out the contradictions in his nature to anyone who knew him. 'Taxman', in which John had a hand, kicked off the album in a tone of cold fury over the 95 per cent 'supertax' introduced by Harold Wilson's Labour government, to which all the Beatles found themselves liable. Dreary, expensive hours with accountants were recalled in its advice to 'declare the pennies on your eyes', meaning the big old one-penny coins traditionally used in northern working-class homes to weight the eyelids of the newly deceased.

In contrast, 'I Want To Tell You' referenced the avalanche of thoughts an acid trip tended to unlock, that for someone so normally taciturn were so difficult to share. In each case, the message was reinforced instrumentally, the palpably outraged guitar-lead of one, the other's dissonant piano descant and contrastingly mild, almost apologetic middle eight.

Revolver's most visionary track is always said to be John's 'Tomorrow Never Knows', the result of reading *The Psychedelic Experience* by LSD's American high priest, Dr Timothy Leary. The recording, he told George Martin with typical vagueness, had to be like the Dalai Lama chanting from some distant mountainside – suggesting that George's 'Yogis of the Himalayas' had whispered in his ear, too.

Martin achieved the desired effect with five overlapping tape loops of random noise and by feeding the singing voice that John so disliked through layer after layer of echo and distortion until it had a reedy, robotic quality, the unholy jokester now like a holy man in a trance as he enjoined: 'Turn off your mind, relax and float downstream . . .'

The third song of George's quota, 'Love You To', was introduced by no such sonic arsenal nor multitude of mewling electronic monks, only the languid double ripple of a solitary sitar.

He had created a miniature version of a classical Indian raga in what the author James Gould would later call 'one of the most brazenly exotic acts of experimentation ever heard on a popular LP'. Although it would be credited to the Beatles, he'd recorded it with a trio of Indian musicians, the noted tabla-player Anil Bhagwat and an uncredited sitar- and tambura-player from the Asian Music Circle. He himself played lead sitar, rhythm and 'fuzz tone' lead guitar; Paul augmented the background vocal and Ringo beat on a tambourine.

It had been taped on 11 and 13 April, a month and a half before he first met Ravi Shankar. As with Chuck Berry R&B and Carl Perkins rockabilly years before, he'd put it together jigsaw-fashion by listening to records over and over.

The lyrics were a veritable fly-past of George preoccupations: implicit love for Pattie, acid-inspired musings on the brevity of life, a hippie-inspired exhortation to 'make love all day long' and a resentful mutter, unknown to Indian music, against 'people standing round who'll screw you in the ground'.

In his vocal he'd sought to emulate performers he'd heard in concert with Ravi Shankar; a timbre that can seem flat and monotonous to facile Western ears, being more about prayer than self-projection. Yet somehow this seemingly alien mode suited him far better than his natural glottal Liverpudlian with its edge of self-consciousness, so often on show in 'Everybody's Tryin To Be My Baby'.

India had given him a voice and identity of his own at last.

Half a century on, when their old rivals and friends the Rolling Stones still tour regularly as octogenarians, it's hard to believe that the Beatles' career as an international live attraction lasted only three years. But in common with cats and dogs, a Beatle year equalled seven normal ones, if not more. *Eight Days A Week*, Ron Howard's 2012 feature documentary on the subject, shows them visibly ageing stage by stage as if adulation were corrosive.

The greater their ambition and achievement on record, the more irksome it became to leave George Martin and Abbey Road and go back to blasting out basic old hits which, amid the blizzarding screams, were as inaudible to them as to their audiences. And where people were prepared to listen, the era's limited sound systems meant that almost none of their more complex and subtle recent music could be performed live.

The further their music reached around the world, the less they saw of it; in the words of their aide Tony Bramwell, everywhere boiled down to 'one more stage, one more limo, one more run for your life'.

Early in 1966, John and George had both decided they'd had enough but Paul, that indefatigable showman, was reluctant to break what had always been the strongest link with their fans. 'I'd been trying to say, "Touring's good, it keeps us sharp",' Sir Paul McCartney would recall. '"Musicians need to play. Keep music live."'

To promote *Revolver*, Brian had them locked into a two-segment world tour between early June and late August, the first taking in potential new Asian markets, Japan and the Philippines, the second back to America. Because of the value of the operation, he was not to come and go, as he usually did, but travel with them throughout.

Japan hadn't yet become the contender for the global capital of Beatlemania that it is today. Tokyo's Nippon Budokan Hall, where they gave three shows, was normally a venue for Sumo wrestling and martial arts displays, traditionally religious rites as much as spectator sports. The perceived defilement of this shrine had brought death threats from militarist and right-wing student groups.

For the whole three days, they weren't allowed out of their hotel suite except to perform; at each concert, 3,000 police kept the 9,000-strong audience not only seated but immobile to ensure clear sightlines of any potential sniper; on their motorcade journeys there and back, demonstrators lined the roads, chanting that they were 'bugs who need to be crushed'.

Straight afterwards came the debacle in the Philippines when Brian's usual diplomatic skills seemed to desert him. On the morning before their two concerts at Manila's Rizal Memorial Football Stadium, the Beatles failed to show at a children's party hosted by the wife of the President, Imelda Marcos, to which they were unaware they'd been invited, and awoke to television reports that they'd 'snubbed' the First Lady.

In retaliation, room service was cut off by their hotel, at Manila Airport they were made to carry their own bags, jostled by security guards and prevented from leaving until Brian paid a hefty bribe in cash. Although their oppressors were presidential toadies, in no way representative of national feeling, John later quoted George as saying he'd 'like to drop an H-Bomb on the Philippines'.

George had arranged to break the homeward flight with a first brief visit to India to buy himself a better-quality sitar, accompanied only by Neil Aspinall. But when their plane landed at Delhi, John, Paul and Ringo were told that British Overseas Airways had mistakenly resold their seats for the onward journey, so they decided to join him.

After the mayhem in Manila, George had thought it would be a respite to 'slip into this nice, ancient country and have a bit of peace and quiet'; instead, they found themselves greeted by yet another frantic crowd behind a mesh fence. He was to recall how, waiting for their baggage, without their usual pre-booked luxury hotel, a paraphrase of Christ in St Matthew's Gospel unaccountably popped into his mind: 'Foxes have holes and birds have nests but the Beatles have nowhere to lay their heads.'

This forty-eight-hour stopover barely scratched the surface of the subcontinent. In the hotel suite where the Beatles soon did lay their heads, sitar dealers lined up to show George their choicest wares, as did vendors of souvenirs such as giant chess-pieces carved from forbidden ivory.

An apologetic BOAC staffer arranged guided tours to the old British imperial capital of New Delhi – built of sandstone like Liverpool's posher areas – and scenes of 'local colour' such as a pathetic lone camel drawing water from a well on a treadmill, which particularly upset the tender-hearted Ringo. Eager to use the Nikon cameras they'd bought in Tokyo, they stopped in a village, where even malnourished children covered in flies seemed to know them.

After Manila – according to George Martin later – John and George had told Brian to cancel the tour's American segment in August. The revenues involved, including from a second show at Shea Stadium, were so vast that he persuaded them to go through with it, but recognised that afterwards neither would ever go on the road again.

At the Beatles' press conference after returning from India, they played down their ill-treatment by the Marcos regime and, naturally, nothing was said about dropping an H–Bomb on the Philippines. 'We're going to have a couple of weeks to recuperate before we go and get beaten up by the Americans,' George said, thinking he was joking.

Five months earlier, in an unguarded moment with his favourite interviewer, the London *Evening Standard*'s Maureen Cleave, John had opined that Christianity would 'vanish and shrink' and the Beatles were now 'more popular than Jesus'. In Britain, his remarks had passed almost unnoticed. But reprinted in an American teen magazine on the eve of the tour, they had caused outrage throughout the Southern Bible Belt.

Radio stations by the dozen banned Beatles records, many organising public bonfires of them or ritual smashings on air. Protest demonstrations brought several shows to a premature end and prevented the band from leaving the venue for hours afterwards. The white supremacist Ku Klux Klan nailed a Beatles album to a burning cross and threatened 'vengeance' such as they were wont to wreak on defenceless black people. When a firecracker went off in the audience at Memphis's

Mid-South Coliseum, all four Beatles looked around to see which of them had been shot.

In Cincinnati, Ohio, they had to give a lunchtime show at Crosley Field on a stage still saturated after a rainstorm, so in constant danger of electrocution, then travel 350 miles for an evening performance in St Louis, where they were delivered to Busch Stadium in a steel-lined removal truck without seats or even anything to hold on to. After that, Paul finally conceded that John and George had a point.

The final show was on 29 August in Candlestick Park, San Francisco, with almost a quarter of the 32,000 tickets unsold. Afterwards, they were taken to the airport in an armoured car; quite a change from the ticker-tape parade proposed for the same city only two years before.

On the return flight, George's usual bluntness made it official. 'Well, that's it,' he said. 'I'm not a Beatle any more.'

Two weeks later, he flew back to India, this time accompanied by Pattie and bound for Mumbai, known then as Bombay, the location of Ravi Shankar's Kinnara School of Music. Already, the main stigma of Beatleness had gone: he wore his hair shorter on top and framing his face, and was growing a moustache.

Just as un-Beatle-like was the absence of any aide or roadie to smooth his path and stay around as a security blanket. He and Pattie checked themselves into the Victorian Taj Mahal hotel under the alias of 'Mr and Mrs Sam Wells'. Outside their window was the massive stone arch dating from British colonial days, known as 'the Gateway to India'. Hindu-style asceticism still lay some way in the future: at the super-luxury Taj, room-staff even valeted the guests' toothpaste tubes.

As well as continuing George's private sitar lessons, Shankar brought in a yoga teacher to relieve the agony the playing posture caused his hips while Shankar's personal guru, Tat Baba, taught him about the Law of Karma, or cause and effect, which might be said to have guided the Beatles through all the wrong turns that had taken them to their stupendously right destination.

In India's media capital, Mr Sam Wells's true identity was bound soon to leak out. Besieged by interview requests, George had to hold a press conference at his hotel and, later, give an interview to the BBC's local correspondent. These journalists were the first to discover he was far readier to talk about his new passion than about being a Beatle, though it was with little of his usual laconic wit.

After a month, Shankar took time off from recitals and teaching to give George and Pattie a tour of the country's most famous sights, like the Taj Mahal at Agra, the 'Pink City' of Jaipur in Rajasthan and the holy city of Benares, now Varanasi, where public cremations were held at the ghats or bathing-steps to the River Ganges. They ended up in Kashmir, living in a houseboat on Lake Dal, next to a floating garden with the Himalayas as a backdrop.

For Pattie, a talented photographer since her modelling days, everywhere brought a superabundance of extraordinary material. But her principal subject was George, in knee-length kurta tunics and sandals, tirelessly visiting this or that temple or monument, his face uncloudedly happy as never in his million-and-one Fab Four portraits – though often still with a cigarette between his lips. 'It was the first feeling I'd ever had of not being a Beatle or a number,' he would remember.

He had scarcely opened a book since leaving the Inny but now Shankar's brother, Raju, lent him works on Hindu religion and philosophy, some by real-life Yogis of the Himalayas, that held him fascinated. Time and again he came upon the precept at the opposite extreme of his boyhood Catholicism and its demand that he blindly believe everything he was told. '[It said] if there is a God you must see Him and if there's a soul you must perceive it ... You can't believe anything until you have direct perception of it. That made me think, "Wow fantastic! At last something that really made sense."'

One of his most abiding memories was witnessing the climax of Kumbh Mela, the most sacred of all Hindu festivals, when thousands of pilgrims underwent ritual cleansing in the Ganges. The best possible antidote to Beatlemania was to be part of the enormous crowd that was utterly peaceable and strangely companionable yet at the same time paid him no attention whatsoever.

13

'THE MEDITATION BUZZ'

Psychologists speak of something called 'the group mind', usually occurring in crowds which at moments of high emotion can seem governed by a single intelligence. Utterly different personalities though the Beatles were, their years together had equipped them with a group mind that never stopped working. To see it in action, you need only watch footage of their press conferences as they pick up on one another's thoughts and finish one another's sentences like some tightly scripted comedy team – only there's no script.

With the media they always presented a totally united front, whatever might be going on behind the scenes, never criticising each other or admitting to the smallest disagreement among themselves. Their intercommunication could verge on the psychic: journalists came to recognise the moment when they would close ranks without a word being said and an iron grille seemed to rattle down, leaving all outsiders out in the cold.

The greatest threat to their group mind thus far had appeared in November 1966 at the Indica art gallery in London's West End when John first met the Japanese-American conceptual artist Yoko Ono. But this would take another two years for the full implications to emerge. Meantime, it came under its first real pressure early in 1967 after George had returned to work with the other three and George Martin at Abbey Road.

'I'd just got back from India and my heart was still out there,' he would recall. 'I'd been out of the confines of the group and it was difficult for me to come back into the sessions . . . I'd been through so many major [creative] trips of my own and I was growing out of that kind of thing.'

To follow the hugely praised and successful *Revolver*, John and Paul had planned an album exploring their Liverpool childhood, about which George felt no excitement whatsoever. He was not immune to nostalgia – witness his fondness for George Formby's saucy wartime ditties – but he had no desire to rhapsodise about the bleak, tough parts of the city where he'd grown up.

The childhood album had to be abandoned, however, thanks to Martin's need to release a Beatles single in February (still with the aim of milking their popularity to the maximum before it evaporated). So John and Paul's postcards of their respective pasts, the surreal 'Strawberry Fields Forever' and the cinematic 'Penny Lane', were put together in a double A-side format, probably representing the greatest value ever offered by a puny little '45' disc. Unfortunately, each harmed the other's sales and, shockingly, the record reached only number two, yielding the top spot to Engelbert Humperdinck's 'Release Me'.

But by now, Paul was developing a new idea, suggested by Swinging London's fad for Victorian militaria. 'I felt we were just in the studio to make the next record,' George would recall, 'and Paul was going on about this fictitious band . . . I wasn't really into it.'

Nor would he ever be really into the Beatles' masterpiece,

Sgt. Pepper's Lonely Hearts Club Band, in which they masqueraded as a toy-soldier brass ensemble giving one of the live shows they'd ceased doing under their own name the previous year.

Unprecedentedly for an album, it was to take four months and cost a jaw-dropping £25,000. Hitherto, they had always recorded like a band, in unison with perhaps a novelty instrument like a harpsichord or French horn added on. *Sgt. Pepper* seemed to George more 'an assembly process', not only of vocal and instrumental tracks but esoteric sound-effects like fairground organs and calliopes, noisy farm livestock, a pack of foxhounds in full cry and a forty-one-piece orchestra playing without a score. 'For me [it] became a bit tiring and a bit boring. I had a few moments in there that I enjoyed, but generally I didn't like making the album that much.'

Ringo accepted his marginal involvement, stoically waiting around to do his traditional single vocal; as he would recall, 'I learned to play chess during *Sgt. Pepper*.' For George, it meant being a barely discernible hinterland to this or that Lennon or McCartney tour-de-force, occasionally slipping in an Indian 'drone' effect like the touch of tambura on John's 'Lucy In The Sky With Diamonds'. For the title track, he was even replaced on lead guitar by Paul.

Yet still the group mind seemed to power the project, with Paul now finally initiated into the LSD that permeated it, and all four sporting variations on a sergeant-major's moustache, George adding a small beard like the advance guard of a tonsorial Grande Armée.

Rather than fight for space on the album as usual, he'd put up only one composition, and that far from the mood of Revolver's 'Love You To'. 'Only A Northern Song' was a sour reference to the publishing company set up to handle Lennon–McCartney's output, to which he and Ringo had both been contracted and of which each owned a token 0.8 per cent. Since Northern had been floated on the London Stock Exchange in 1965, it had made John and Paul wealthy – but only them.

Quietly seething over the company's near-irrelevance where he was concerned, George had written an almost deliberately bad Northern song, like a slowed down 'If I Needed Someone', lacking his usual arresting chord changes and sung in a drone less redolent of India than a clothes-peg on the nose. It seemed to have been recorded with a mélange of instruments from Abbey Road's lost property cupboard, with George on Hammond organ, John on piano and glockenspiel, Paul on trumpet and miscellaneous sound effects. Albeit with more deference than he would once have employed, George Martin told George it simply wasn't good enough and to try again.

This might simply have sent him into one of his chilly silences but for the artist/musician Klaus Voormann, the Beatles' Hamburg cheerleader-in-chief, to whom he'd always been especially close. Voormann had since moved to London, shared George and Ringo's flat in Green Street, joined the Manfred Mann band on bass guitar and designed the *Revolver* album cover.

One night after dinner at Voormann's house in Hampstead, George began playing an ancient pedal-harmonium whose wheezing tone unexpectedly conjured up myriad memories of India. It gave him the chords for another raga-esque piece like 'Love You To' but much more ambitious, based on a symphony-length piece Ravi Shankar had written for the All India Radio network.

The title came from a book entitled *Karma and Rebirth* by Christmas Humphrey, a noted British lawyer and convert to Buddhism, published in the 1940s and containing the maxim 'Life goes on within you and without you' ('without' in its Old English sense of outside). From there, unusually for George, the lyric seemed to write itself: 'Try to realise it's all within yourself and to see you're really only very small ... and life flows on within you and without you.'

Ending up more than five minutes long, it was recorded in three parts, with instrumentalists from the Asian Music Circle, George this time yielding the sitar lead and simply playing a tambura as, surprisingly, did the Beatles' faithful roadie, Neil Aspinall. To create a suitable atmosphere at Abbey Road, the participants sat on a carpet; there were Indian tapestries on the walls, low lights and burning incense.

It wasn't easy to see how Indian-inspired mysticism fitted into *Sgt. Pepper*'s psychedelic vaudeville show – but one might say the same of a nocturnal masturbator ('With A Little Help From My Friends'), a traffic warden ('Lovely Rita'), a young woman running away from her parents ('She's Leaving Home'), an old couple who holidayed on the Isle of Wight ('When I'm Sixty-Four') or a fatal car crash ('A Day In The Life'). Now, as then, it seems as indispensable as any of those.

'Within You Without You' would always divide the Beatles' audience into those who found it unbearably solemn and dreary and those who thought it the Sergeant's only meaningful message, 'at once beautiful and severe', to quote *Rolling Stone* magazine, 'a magnetic sermon about materialism and communal responsibility in the middle of a record devoted to gentle Technicolor anarchy'.

Most importantly for George, it earned him his first on-the-record praise from John, although – characteristically – as part of a general disparagement of the album. 'I actively dislike ... bits which didn't come out right ... "Sgt. Pepper" is a nice song, "Getting Better" is a nice song and George's "Within You Without You" is beautiful. What else is on it but the whole concept of having tracks running into each other?'

LSD had been illegal in Britain since the summer of 1966 and now carried penalties for manufacture or possession of up to seven years' imprisonment. It had also awoken the police to the prevalence of already illegal drugs, chiefly cocaine and marijuana, among young people with the barely disguised encouragement of pop music and its makers.

The obvious first target for retribution was a band that had been flouting decent British values for three years past, not through drugs so much as being in every way the opposites of the cute, family-friendly Beatles.

In February 1967, there was a massive police raid on the Rolling Stone Keith Richards' Sussex cottage, where Mick Jagger was staying the weekend with his girlfriend Marianne Faithfull and other non-musician friends. Though the two Stones had taken acid that weekend (Jagger for the first time), both were charged with possession of far lesser narcotics, yet for these first and arguably technical offences were thrown into the judicial system to be ritually disembowelled.

On the day of the raid, George and Pattie Harrison had been among the house party but departed late in the afternoon. 'We'd got drunk and stoned enough,' Pattie recalls, 'and it was a long way to drive back to Esher.'

As the police task force approached Richards' cottage they passed George's psychedelic Mini going in the opposite direction. A legend was to grow up that, rather than bust a sacred Beatle, they'd waited for him to get clear before they went in. However, when interviewed later, none of the officers remembered hearing his name mentioned before the operation or recognising the Mini as his. And if any such immunity had ever existed, it wasn't to last much longer.

Sgt. Pepper's Lonely Hearts Club Band was released in the spring of 1967, to a welcome seldom equalled since in commercial terms and never in emotional ones. In Britain, it spent twenty-three consecutive weeks at the top of *Record Retailer* magazine's chart and in the US, fifteen heading *Billboard's* Hot 100. Highbrow critics competed in superlatives such as 'A decisive moment in the history of Western culture' and 'a harbinger of a Golden Renaissance of Song'. As with the news of President John F. Kennedy's assassination (and of another John still to come), millions would always remember exactly where they were and what they were doing when they first heard it.

Peter Blake's cover was an artwork such as had jacketed no 'LP' before, showing the Beatles as psychedelic silk hussars beneath a collage of Pop Art icons from Marlon Brando to W. C. Fields, each supposed Sergeant Pepper recruit holding a different brass-band instrument. With (presumably) unconscious symbolism, orange-suited George's was the very smallest, a piccolo, which he seemed to be trying to hide in his neighbour Paul's sky-blue sleeve. By way of a consolation prize, it seemed, the motley faces and effigies included a prominent Indian mystic, Paramahansa Yogananda.

The album's London launch produced a second,

as-yet-undetectable threat to the group mind. A rangy blonde photographer named Linda Eastman had come from New York to photograph the band, but seemed interested only in Paul, to whom she remained talking intently long after her cameras were sheathed.

With 'I get high with a little help from my friends', 'I'd love to turn you on', the initial letters of 'Lucy In The Sky With Diamonds' and the clump of cannabis plants at their feet on the *Sgt. Pepper* cover, plus innumerable other aural winks and nudges, the Beatles couldn't have set themselves up in plainer sight as figureheads of the Sixties' drug culture at its apogee.

Yet even the manager devoted to their welfare and safety seemed in no fear of the police crackdown. A few days after *Sgt. Pepper*'s official launch, Brian threw an extravagant party at his new country house in Sussex, attended by John, George and Ringo, plus Mick Jagger – currently awaiting trial – and other top names from the charts, where acid circulated as freely as the champagne and nibbles.

From George's point of view, the most welcome guest was Derek Taylor, the Beatles' former press officer who'd left after a blow-up with Brian on their '64 trans-America tour and now did PR in California for bands like the Beach Boys and the Byrds. Hoping to woo him back to the only worthwhile B-group, Brian had sent First Class round-trip plane-tickets for Taylor and his wife, Joan, then seven months' pregnant.

To Joan Taylor, it seemed a persuasive advertisement for LSD that under its influence John and George were now able to show affection and behave unselfishly as the buttoned-up, self-centred pot-puffers she remembered never could. So when George gave Taylor a tab of acid, Joan accepted one from John despite the advanced state of her pregnancy. 'Both of them took care of Derek and me for the rest of the night,' she recalls. 'They couldn't have been kinder and more attentive.'

In mid-June, the so-called Summer of Love kicked off with the novel concept of an open-air pop festival in Monterey, California, whose big-name bill – except Ravi Shankar – donated their fees to charity. Derek Taylor was one of its organisers, but even Taylor couldn't persuade the Beatles to break their ban on live performances.

Little as George wanted to go back onstage, he'd become increasingly curious about California's hippie movement, centred on the Haight-Ashbury district of San Francisco, and being part of the Monterey Festival would have given him an opportunity to check it out. 'We just took acid in St George's Hill [where John lived in Weybridge],' he would recall, 'and wondered what [Monterey] would have been like.'

On 19 June, Paul admitted to Britain's Independent Television News that he'd taken LSD 'about four times', so putting himself in extreme jeopardy and the whole band with him. To George it was typical McCartney scene-stealing that, having been the last by about eighteen months to try acid, 'one day he's on the television, talking all about it.' But Paul had no bother with the police either, nor did his confession bar his being on show to the world with the others as one of Britain's foremost national assets.

A week later, twenty-five countries joined forces to create the first global live broadcast by satellite with a marathon documentary illustrating the wholesome best of their various societies. The centrepiece of the British segment were the Beatles in a staged scene from Abbey Road where they pretended to be recording their latest single, the instant hippie anthem 'All You Need Is Love'.

The flower bedecked studio was filled with fellow musicians, among them Mick Jagger and Keith Richards – only a few days away from being convicted of their microscopic drug offences and thrown into Brixton and Wormwood Scrubs prisons respectively until sanity returned to the British legal system and they were released pending an appeal.

Clamped between outsize headphones, George was scarcely visible to the transmission's 44 million audience, his incisive solo hemmed in by a full symphony orchestra and more *Sgt. Pepper*-ish sound-effects: the French National Anthem 'La Marseillaise', Glenn Miller's 'In the Mood', King Henry VIII's 'Greensleeves', Bach's Invention No. 8 in F Major and John's jeering parody of 'She loves you, yeah yeah yeah'.

So far were the Beatles themselves swayed by 'All You Need Is Love' that the group mind almost metamorphosed into hippie-style group living.

For a time, they contemplated inhabiting their own private Greek island and went as far as cruising the Aegean, looking for one under the leadership of John's protégé, 'Magic' Alex Mardas, who allegedly had family connections with Greece's fascistic military government, so could expedite any purchase. 'John and I were on acid all the time,' George would recall, 'sitting on the front of the ship, playing ukuleles.' Another short-lived idea was buying an idyllic English village with a green in the centre and having 'one side each'.

In August, George and Pattie flew to Los Angeles, accompanied by Neil Aspinall and 'Magic Alex', to see Pattie's younger sister, Jenny, who'd been helping a friend open a boutique there, and attend a Ravi Shankar concert at the Hollywood Bowl. The Harrisons were also invited to meet Frank Sinatra (who'd once detested the Beatles), first watching him in the studio recording 'My Way', that self-eulogy for bastards ever after, then joining him at a dinner where his several bodyguards all had their own personal bottles of whisky.

Derek Taylor, too, was on hand to arrange George's long-awaited San Francisco visit to check out Haight-Ashbury. But while most others had made that pilgrimage hitch-hiking with bedrolls, he and his party did it by private Learjet.

Their afternoon walkabout, shepherded by Taylor and under the beneficent influence of some 'good shit' from a local deejay, proved a severe let-down. Haight-Ashbury had once been a genuine, caring-and-sharing community but had long since been commercialised and corrupted. 'I went there expecting it to be a brilliant place with groovy gipsy people making works of art and paintings and carvings in little workshops,' George would recall. 'But it was full of horrible spotty dropout kids on drugs.'

He was treated 'like a Messiah', which in this case meant being offered inferior acid from every side, including 'STP', ten times more powerful than the regular kind, with ten times the potential nightmares. The whole experience had the effect of putting him off LSD for good. 'It wasn't what I'd thought – spiritual awakenings and being artistic. It was like alcoholism, like any addiction.'

Having some in liquid form in a bottle, he decided to look at it through a microscope. 'And it was like bits of old rope. I thought I couldn't put that into my brain any more.'

To round off the disillusioning trip, on the return flight

to LA, the Learjet suddenly went into a stall. George, seated behind the pilot, saw its whole control-board light up with the word UNSAFE before the horrific plunge was corrected.

Monterey in the aftermath of the festival also lacked enchantment. Derek Taylor was to recall that in a coffee shop where they'd stopped to eat, the waitress didn't recognise George and made a great show of clearing tables to avoid serving 'the cloud of denim in the corner'.

'Finally, George told her, "We've got the money, you know" and waved about $1,000 in bills under her nose. She recognised him then and dropped every piece of crockery she was holding.'

14

'PLEASE DON'T THINK I'VE GONE OFF MY ROCKER'

It wasn't only George; the Beatles group mind also had begun to feel that universal fame, vast wealth, luxurious homes and limitless toys weren't everything and there surely must be more to life. But it was Pattie Harrison who found a possible route to it.

The previous February, following her return from India with George, Pattie and a friend had begun attending classes organised by the country's Spiritual Regeneration movement whose leader, Maharishi Mahesh Yogi, regularly visited Britain to lecture and recruit new followers.

The Beatles had seen the Maharishi on television, expounding his system of Transcendental Meditation, and been mildly interested; Paul had since had a girlfriend named Maggie McGivern already converted to it, and had then built a 'meditation chapel' in the garden of his new house in north London. Indeed, it was not Pattie but Paul who spotted a press report that the guru had returned to Britain and was to give a talk at the London Hilton Hotel on 24 August.

In a rare instance of women being admitted to the group mind, he not only rounded up the Harrisons but John and

Cynthia Lennon and his own actress partner, Jane Asher. Ringo had to pass because his wife Maureen was in hospital, about to give birth to their second child.

The Maharishi was a diminutive figure with straggly hair and a black-and-white forked beard, whose high-pitched voice seemed to quaver with perpetual mirth. But if his appearance was rather comical, his message was riveting. Through Transcendental Meditation, his listeners could find 'perfect inner peace' at the cost of only twenty minutes per day.

After the lecture, John, Paul and George talked with him in his hotel suite and there and then signed up to the Spiritual Regeneration movement, pledging to contribute a week's earnings each to its funds and make a pilgrimage to the Maharishi's ashram, or religious sanctuary, in India. Meantime, they agreed to attend a ten-day induction course he was holding in Bangor, North Wales, beginning the next day.

In the intervening twenty-four hours, Mick Jagger, his girlfriend Marianne Faithfull, Cilla Black and Jenny Boyd joined the inductees. They left London by the same ordinary train service as the Maharishi on what was the Friday before August Bank Holiday weekend, so ogled by large crowds as well as massed camera-lenses.

It was the Beatles' first journey in years without their manager to smooth their path: John likened it to going somewhere without their trousers. Brian – who was himself in greater need of 'perfect inner peace' than they knew – had been unable to get away for the weekend but promised to join the Maharishi's course afterwards.

That evening found the assorted superstars and their retinue in the spartan accommodation of a teacher-training college, with none of the usual special arrangements made for their reception. Bangor was a small town and at that hour the only restaurant open was a Chinese one.

In London, their meal would have been complimentary but that convention didn't apply in North Wales and since, like royalty, superstars weren't expected to carry money and credit cards were still almost unknown, an embarrassing scene threatened. Finally, George reluctantly prised open the heel of one of his sandals where he kept a secret stash of £10 notes.

Next day, the Maharishi gave each Beatle and their retinue a mantra, or chant, to prevent the meditator's thoughts wandering to worldly things. John, Paul and George then held a joint press conference with their new guru to announce one bit of spiritual regeneration already to his credit: they were giving up hallucinogenic drugs. They also mentioned the plan to go to his Indian ashram in October and spend three months of study there.

In those pre-cellphone days, their only link with the outside world was the telephone in the college office. This was how on Bank Holiday Sunday they learned of Brian's death, seemingly from a barbiturates overdose at his house in Chapel Street, Belgravia, aged thirty-two.

Minutes later, John was asked for his reaction in a glare of television lights. 'I'd never seen him look so devastated,' Pattie recalls. George was equally devastated, having been the last Beatle to speak to Brian, but was fortified by the talk they'd just had with the Maharishi, not to mention his lyrics for 'Within You Without You'. 'There's no such thing as death anyway,' he told the press. 'It's death on a physical level but life goes on everywhere and you just keep going.'

In truth, Brian had quietly been falling apart since the Beatles had voted to stop touring and live their creative life almost entirely in the recording studio, for it meant he could no longer lavish the care and attention of a doting father on his 'boys', as he still insisted on referring to them.

In September 1967, the management contract he had signed with four black-leathern lads in 1962 was due to expire. Despite the five beyond-amazing years since, he half-expected them not to renew it. All the star Liverpudlian acts he'd discovered subsequently — even Cilla Black, whom he'd nurtured almost as tenderly as the Beatles — couldn't have compensated for their loss.

Despite his obvious fixation on John, he fondly imagined his boys were unaware of his sexual orientation. In fact they'd known from the start and never had any problem with it, though Pattie remembers George used to dislike the camp badinage between Brian and the several other gay men he employed.

In the Summer of Love's most meaningful happening, British law had decriminalised gay sex between consenting males over twenty-one. But it hadn't taken away Brian's shame nor his unlucky penchant for violent and exploitative lovers. Lonely and lost, fearful of losing his greatest love of all, he'd become increasingly dependent on alcohol and sleeping pills, the first of which had evidently made him lose track of how many of the second he was taking. The inquest verdict was accidental death due to 'incautious self-overdoses' of barbiturates and brandy.

Major story though Brian's death was, an even bigger one was the revelation that the Beatles hadn't been happy just being Beatles. The general astonishment reached even the highest person in the land: when EMI's Chairman, Sir Joseph Lockwood, arrived at a Buckingham Palace reception, the

Queen greeted him with the words 'The Beatles are turning awfully *funny*, aren't they?'

There was a unanimous media outcry against the Maharishi, now dubbed 'the giggling guru', and his effect on young men who'd once spoken only in wisecracks but now held forth at length about mantras and 'states of bliss'. John and George defended him and meditation in a round of TV appearances including a studio debate conducted by David Frost, with sceptical establishment figures like the barrister and writer John Mortimer. George was moved to an eloquence never seen before by Mortimer's courtroom-style jibes against 'the mystical'. 'There's nothing mystical about it,' he said. 'That's just a word that's been arrived at by people ... who are ignorant of what it entails.'

Knowing how bizarre all this must look to his parents, he wrote Harold and Louise a note to reassure them that the Maharishi hadn't alienated him from them. 'Please don't think I've gone off my rocker because I haven't ... because I now love you more than ever.'

Jewish funerals take place as quickly as possible and it was a matter of some surprise that the Beatles didn't attend the Epstein family's private obsequies for Brian at Liverpool's Long Lane Synagogue when the inquest formalities permitted, but waited for the star-studded memorial service in London five weeks later.

George sent a single sunflower for Brian's American associate Nat Weiss to throw into the open grave – a vaguely cosmic gesture, contrasting with his tenderness to his father and mother, seemed inadequate.

*

Brian's death inevitably left behind a lot of unfinished Beatles business – or rather, *an* unfinished Beatles business.

For it had come in the midst of complex arrangements to mitigate the enormous UK income tax that would be due on £2 million in accumulated royalties about to be paid them by EMI. This could be drastically reduced, however if the money were sunk into a company of which the Beatles themselves were theoretical employees. The company would take control of activities from which others had already made fortunes: records, music-publishing and film-making. Since they were leaders of fashion, a venture into the boutique trade also seemed logical.

The film side was already up and almost running. Only four days after completing *Sgt. Pepper's Lonely Hearts Club Band*, Paul had presented the others with a project that, unlike *A Hard Day's Night* and *Help!*, they would themselves originate and control. Paul saw it as the first in a succession of films that would replace their live tours of yesteryear.

The initial, sensible company prospectus was then elaborated by the Beatles' group mind with rather less clarity. They wanted it also to have a philanthropic dimension unseen in British commerce since the nineteenth century's Quaker chocolate-making families and the Lever Brothers' Sunlight Soap empire.

They wanted profit not to be its primary concern and to give recognition to youthful talent that they'd had to struggle for, the impulse later known as 'giving something back'. To imply freshness and good health and a commercial Garden of Eden – and because John could never resist a pun – it was to be named Apple Corps, pronounced 'core'.

Straight after Brian's funeral, to give the others some focus in their shock and bewilderment, Paul persuaded them to push ahead with his film idea during the autumn they'd meant to spend meditating with the Maharishi. Privately, he told their press officer, Tony Barrow, of his fear that if they went to India in October as promised, they would never again work together as a band.

The film was inspired by a mythic episode in American countercultural history when the writer Ken Kesey and a troupe of hippie exhibitionists known as the Merry Pranksters had crossed the country in a psychedelically painted school bus, dispensing LSD in the soft drink Kool-Aid, with results documented by Tom Wolfe's 'New Journalism' classic, *The Electric Kool-Aid Acid Test*.

Paul's British version had the same seemingly infallible mix of fantasy and homeliness as *Sgt. Pepper*. The Beatles and forty-odd friends and extras journeyed into the West Country by motor coach on one of the 'mystery tours' that had been a staple of their childhood seaside holidays. But, lacking even the fixed purpose of handing out acid, it soon descended into chaos.

Ringo was a central figure in the plot for this *Magical Mystery Tour*, and John and Paul each had cameo scenes, but George was given nothing to do on the journey except sit on the coach, as he later recalled, 'like an appendage'. Always being sidelined seemed, at least, to be expanding his vocabulary.

Apple Corps' first solid manifestation was the eponymous boutique opened early in December in London's Baker Street, the first of a proposed chain. John and George jointly hosted its celebrity launch party – the former rather more enthusiastically than the latter – whose refreshments were apples and apple juice. It turned sour prematurely after other local traders objected to the stunning psychedelic mural covering its exterior, which could have turned Sherlock Holmes's fictional habitat into a new King's Road, and the visionless local authority ordered it to be scrubbed clean.

Worse followed when BBC-TV showed the Beatles' *Magical Mystery Tour* film on the peak viewing day after Christmas. Although since recognised as a forerunner of pop video and *Monty Python*, it baffled critics and audience alike, not least because the colour production was initially transmitted in black-and-white, turning its psychedelic sequences into featureless grey murk.

But no one complained about the songs in the film even though they almost painfully exposed the gulf between two once inseparable composers in John's 'I Am The Walrus' and Paul's 'The Fool On The Hill' and 'Your Mother Should Know'.

George's contribution, 'Blue Jay Way', was the name of the boulevard in LA's Hollywood Hills where he'd rented a house the previous August and, on arrival, had waited in a jet-lagged and sleepy state for Derek and Joan Taylor to drive there through thick fog. It was in Indian style but played by the Beatles on Western instruments, led by George's droning Hammond organ.

The accompanying film clip showed him in an orange suit (but not his *Sgt. Pepper* one) pretending to play an organ keyboard drawn on the ground, with a beggar's paper cup near at hand. Cutaway shots showed Paul, Ringo and himself kicking a football around in Ringo's garden in Weybridge and miming the song's drawn-out chorus of 'Don't be long' deliberately out of sync.

Far more to his taste was a different film project which might not have come his way but for the postponement of the Indian trip. A young American writer/director named Joe Massot had asked him to write a score for Massot's first feature, a psychedelic fantasy entitled *Wonderwall*. When George protested he had no idea how to go about such a task, Massot told him that whatever he came up with would be used in the picture.

Its plot, little more substantial than that of *Magical Mystery Tour*, concerned a reclusive scientist living next door to a glamour photographer. Mysterious fissures that kept appearing in their party wall allowed the scientist to spy on the photographer shooting a beautiful young model as a result of which he became madly obsessed with her. The psychedelic effects turned this into cutting-edge art rather than queasy voyeurism.

Contrary to George's expectations, he wasn't expected to be able to read music, only use his sonic imagination as never before – and time the gaps in the script that Massot had left for him. The project also allowed him to return to Bombay, to use EMI's recording studios there.

His score brought together the classical Indian, on lesser-known instruments like the shehnai and the sarod, and Western idioms like country and ragtime, performed by guest musicians including Ringo and Eric Clapton. A few years later, such fusions would be dubbed World Music.

In 1966, Paul had written the score for a British film, *The Family Way*, with George Martin's help, but not entailing a soundtrack album like George's *Wonderwall Music*. He thus became the first Beatle to release a solo album, which in turn became the first fruit of their new Apple Records label.

Rishikesh is 200 miles north of Delhi in the foothills of the Himalayas beside the River Ganges on one of its holiest

The tiny house where George was born and spent his early years, 12 Arnold Grove, Wavertree, in Liverpool. While John and Paul's childhood homes are now national monuments, George's doesn't even rate a commemorative plaque. (*Thea Trollope*)

George with his mother, Louise: the only Beatle parent to be a Beatlemaniac from the beginning. (*Shutterstock*)

January 1962: Seventeen-year-old George in his Hamburg black leather still looks 'just a kid' when Liverpool's pioneering music paper, *Mersey Beat*, names the Beatles the city's most popular band (after a readers' poll in which they voted heavily for themselves). The dealership that sold George his first car – a much-prized Ford Anglia – lost no time in capitalising on his name. (*Bill Harry Archive*)

At home in Speke, the tough Merseyside suburb where George lived with his parents until well into Beatlemania. His mother kept a life-size photographic blowup of him at the top of the stairs that no visitor could miss. (*Shutterstock*)

George's parents help him pack for the Beatles' Paris debut: note the personalised British European Airways flight bag. (*Shutterstock*)

Paris, January 1964: The fans can still get up close. (*Shutterstock*)

George Martin: the Beatles' inspirational producer admitted to being 'rather beastly to George' before eventually discovering his worth. (*Shutterstock*)

The Ed Sullivan Show, in February 1964, when George performed with a temperature of 40 degrees Celsius. (*Shutterstock*)

Heavyweight PR: clowning for the camera with Cassius Clay (later Muhammad Ali) in Miami, February 1964. (*Shutterstock*)

Marriage to Pattie Boyd, 1966. (*Shutterstock*)

Ravi Shankar's devoted sitar student: 'I never met one person who really impressed me until I met Ravi.' (*Shutterstock*)

The making of Paul's pet project, *Sgt. Pepper's Lonely Hearts Club Band*, in 1967: Relegated to the sidelines, George found it 'a bit tiring and a bit boring.' He still came up with a masterpiece, 'Within You Without You,' that impressed even John. (*Shutterstock*)

The Beatles' first encounter with the Maharishi Mahesh Yogi, 1967. (*Shutterstock*)

John and George with the guru in Rishikesh before their premature exit. (*Shutterstock*)

'Wedding bells are breaking up that old gang of mine . . .': The Beatles and their consorts at the premiere of the cartoon fantasy *Yellow Submarine*, 1968. George's distance from Yoko may be accidental. (*Shutterstock*)

George, far left, with Patti Boyd, and in the foreground, Ringo, sitting to the left of his then wife Maureen Cox – watching Bob Dylan at the Isle of Wight Festival, 1969. (*Shutterstock*)

The solo George: recovering from a six-year bout of creative constipation. (*Shutterstock*)

Madison Square Garden, New York, 1 August 1971: George 'at the height of nobility' with his Concerts for Bangladesh, leading his superstar friends in what remains the most memorable rock charity concert ever. Eric Clapton, whose heroin use almost made him miss the gig, is at the extreme right. (*Shutterstock*)

With Ringo: their friendship survived George's 'depths of disloyalty.' (*Shutterstock*)

With Ravi Shankar and Billy Preston, meeting President Gerald Ford at the White House during the unhappy Dark Horse solo tour of the US, 1974. (*Shutterstock*)

George poses with his second wife, the former Olivia Arias, after their marriage in 1978. With them is fellow Traveling Wilbury Jeff Lynne, the leading light of the Electric Light Orchestra. (*Shutterstock*)

George and Madonna promoting the disastrous *Shanghai Surprise*: 'Never had a minder been more in need of a minder.' (*Shutterstock*)

George with his twelve-year-old son Dhani, named after the sixth and seventh notes in the Indian musical scale. Taught to play the guitar by his father, Dhani made his debut as a producer on George's final album, *Brainwashed*. (*Shutterstock*)

Dhani with Olivia in 2016. Olivia has kept George's memory alive with the rereleases of his albums and has emerged in her own right as a film producer and poet. (*Shutterstock*)

stretches. In February 1968, a twenty-four-year-old Canadian named Paul Saltzman arrived at the Maharishi's ashram on the off chance of being accepted as a pupil. He was told the ashram had been closed because the Beatles were there and it wasn't possible for him to meet the guru in the foreseeable future.

Saltzman said he would wait as he was 'in great emotional pain'. He waited in a tent just outside the gate, conscious of the Beatles' proximity only insofar as it was blocking his way to the Maharishi. On the eighth day, his persistence finally paid off.

He was taken to the Maharishi's bungalow and shown into a large meditation chapel. A moment later, another door opened and the four Beatles came in, accompanied by Cynthia Lennon, Jane Asher, Maureen Starkey, Pattie Harrison, Pattie's sister, Jenny, and their roadie, Mal Evans. 'We all sat down in a row, very close together,' Saltzman recalls. 'My knee was about six inches from George Harrison's.

'When the Maharishi appeared, he noticed George had a little tape-recorder, one of the old-fashioned kinds with buttons that you pressed. He was very humorous; he said to George, "Is that a new song or do you want me to recite the whole of the Baghavad Gita?"

'George switched it on and it played a mix of "The Inner Light" he'd made back in London. Then he starts to sing along with himself on the tape. It's only at that point that I suddenly think "*Wow!*"'

The Beatles had themselves been at the ashram for only a week and Saltzman, to his amazement, found himself part of this farewell appearance of the group mind. The respite from their usual pitiless treadmill was already having positive effects. 'The four of them were like brothers,' Saltzman recalls. 'There was zero friction between them. One morning after they'd left the breakfast table I said to Mal Evans, "Are they always as sweet as this?" He smiled and said, "Well . . . not always."'

From the beginning, Saltzman was drawn to George especially. 'He was the quiet one when the others were around but on his own, he was amazingly open and talkative. "The meditation buzz is incredible," he told me. "I get higher than I ever did with drugs."

'One day, he told me it was time for his sitar practice, and I could go with him if I liked. We went to a little meditation chapel and I sat on the floor beside him. I don't know if he played for ten minutes or forty minutes. I was in a state of bliss.'

Though Saltzman worked in the Canadian film business, he was not a professional photographer, 'just a kid with a camera', yet the Beatles, George included, let him take their picture whenever he liked, much to the chagrin of the world's press camped with telephoto lenses outside the ashram's perimeter.

His cheap Pentax notwithstanding, northern India's balmy winter sunshine invested the white-clad, flower-garlanded figures with palpable tranquillity and harmony. 'It was wonderful,' the then Pattie Harrison recalls. 'The pressure was totally off and all four of the Beatles were getting on so well together.' Cynthia Lennon looked particularly happy, believing as she did that her long-troubled marriage was reviving, even though John had requested separate accommodation for the two of them so that he could 'concentrate on his meditation'.

Saltzman's greatest coup was a kind of super-hippie school photograph including the Beatles' whole party and the ashram's other celebrity students, the actress Mia Farrow, the Scottish folk singer Donovan and Mike Love of the Beach Boys, along with a dozen-odd older Europeans training to be meditation teachers.

However, the regime of meditation in manageable chunks and thrice-daily audiences with the Maharishi brought only a brief pause to the Lennon–McCartney songwriting machine. Before long, they were back at it as competitively as ever, often using their surroundings and fellow meditators as subject-matter, sometimes even composing together on two guitars as they used to at the very beginning. Paul would later say that between them they'd written forty-eight new songs.

'One day I shot them together on a veranda, working on something of Paul's called "Ob-La-Di Ob-La-Da",' Saltzman recalls. 'But he wasn't mad at me. He just smiled and said, "That's as far as I've got."'

George thoroughly disapproved, saying this wasn't what they were here for, and was among the most zealous meditators and attentive listeners at their guru's lectures. But even he couldn't stop two or three new song ideas from breaking his concentration, and on 25 February, his twenty-fifth birthday, he was persuaded to give a mini-recital on his sitar.

The Maharishi did not impose total self-denial. The Beatles' aide Tony Bramwell, based in a luxury hotel in Delhi, kept them well supplied with cigarettes, records, music trade papers and film for their cameras while 'behind the wire', as John put it; a handful of two-rupee notes could procure alcohol and superior grades of marijuana.

Neil Aspinall flew out for a week to update them on developments with Apple Corps and explore the feasibility of making a documentary about the Maharishi, who surprised him with a detailed knowledge of percentages and 'back ends'.

With Aspinall came the newly appointed head of Apple Films, Denis O'Dell, with a project he believed was as perfect for the Beatles as *A Hard Day's Night*. This was a film musical based on J. R. R. Tolkien's *The Lord of the Rings*, then a huge seller on American college campuses yet barely known in Britain. O'Dell had already provisionally cast Paul and Ringo as the Hobbits Frodo and Sam, John as the slithery, sibilant Gollum and George as the wizard Gandalf.

Paul Saltzman had tried not to take advantage of George's friendliness: 'I told myself, "The Beatles' lives are crazy, they don't need any more friends."' But his 'kindness and caringness' encouraged the young Canadian to reveal the 'emotional pain' that had brought him to India, his uncertainty about who he was and why he existed and the letter he'd since received from his girlfriend beginning 'I've moved in with Henry ...'

One observation from George, he recalls, was as much an epiphany as any from the Maharishi. The two were alone at the communal breakfast table when a baby monkey from the flocks that filled the trees jumped down and stole a morsel of food. 'We laughed about it, then George suddenly said, "We [the Beatles] had all the fame we could ever want and all the money we could ever want but it isn't love, it isn't health, it isn't peace inside, is it?"'

Saltzman left Rishikesh after a week to return to Montreal and try to win his girlfriend back from Henry. Ringo went at the same time after only two weeks as his delicate stomach couldn't take Indian food and Maureen couldn't stand the flies. Paul and Jane lasted five weeks, and then the clinging 'Magic Alex' arrived to take over their bungalow.

John, Cynthia, George and Pattie continued with the

supposed three-month course, although John, too, had started to waver. All the time, he'd been receiving postcards from Yoko Ono with messages such as 'Look for me, I'm a cloud in the sky', which Tony Bramwell would intercept in Delhi and put into plain brown envelopes before delivering them so that Cynthia would have no suspicions.

'Paul was on to the next thing which was Apple,' Pattie says. 'Yoko was calling to John from a cloud, but George was dreading going back to London, facing all the stuff connected with their business and trying to find a new manager to replace Brian.'

In any case, the idyll at Rishikesh was soon to be broken up by the Maharishi himself. He was about to move his ashram to a property to Kashmir, whither he expected the keenest of his Beatle converts to accompany him. However, George had already visited Kashmir on his first visit to India the previous year and was planning to go south to meet up with Ravi Shankar and take part in a film documentary about Shankar. Yet the Maharishi, unaccustomed to the finality of a George 'no', refused to take it for an answer.

The situation was rather conveniently resolved when the guru was alleged to have made sexual advances to one of his non-famous followers, a young Australian nurse. In the future, other such holy men would be unmasked as sexual predators, but in the Maharishi's case there was not a scrap of evidence to support the accusation, then or ever.

John immediately saw an excuse to leave the ashram on moral grounds and, with no sense of irony, begin an illicit relationship with Yoko. He had no idea that he wasn't the only one looking for such an excuse. 'When George started thinking [the rumour about the Maharishi] might be true,' he would recall, 'I thought, well, it must be true because if George is doubting him there must be something in it.'

The Harrisons and Lennons travelled back to Delhi with one of the film crews that had been so resolutely kept outside 'the wire'. En route, the songwriting mechanism started up again in John's head although the first words that came were obviously unusable: 'Maharishi, you little twat/ Who the fuck do you think you are?/ Oh you cunt ...' George applied the brakes a little by suggesting 'Sexy Sadie' in place of 'Maharishi'.

He and Pattie then spent a week in Kerala with Ravi Shankar. As usual, she took numerous photographs of George, including one in which he's reclining on a mattress at the simple guest-house where they stayed.

'It's the last image I have of him,' she says, 'looking completely happy and at peace.'

15

'DON'T UPSET THE HELL'S ANGELS'

George and Eric Clapton first met in 1964 when the Yardbirds, the band to which Clapton then belonged, were bottom of the bill in the Beatles' annual Christmas show at Hammersmith's Odeon cinema. Like many before him, he was fascinated by the group mind in evidence not only onstage but when they mingled democratically with their fellow artistes. 'They were like one person,' he would recall. 'They seemed to move together and think together.'

A mere Yardbird couldn't aspire to friendship with a Beatle, however, and they stuck mainly to shop talk as fellow lead guitarists, with George showing Clapton his collection of Gretsch instruments, Clapton introducing him to lighter-gauge strings.

Clapton himself never had time to develop any sort of group mind; for him, a band was simply a vehicle for playing the hardcore Delta blues that obsessed him. Any failing to match his own exalted standards of purity he would abandon without a backward glance.

Hence he had soon left the 'too commercial' Yardbirds for John Mayall's Bluesbreakers, there finding deification even the

Beatles never had when brick walls all over north London were spray-painted CLAPTON IS GOD.

After barely a year with Mayall, he'd formed the supergroup Cream with bassist Jack Bruce and drummer Ginger Baker, spectacularly combining blues, psychedelia, heavy metal and jazz but totally out of its group mind and fated to auto-destruct in less than three years.

Clapton's growing celebrity had brought him into the Beatles' orbit, for example as one of the elite studio audience when they'd played 'All You Need Is Love' to the world and inner space. He'd first taken acid on a night at the Speakeasy club when all the Beatles were there doing likewise; George had given the deejay a test-pressing of *Sgt. Pepper's Lonely Hearts Club Band* to play and everyone danced dementedly to that ultimate good trip.

It being only a few weeks after the Rolling Stones bust, the police were waiting in force outside the club like blue-clad butterfly-collectors. But the Beatles were allowed to drive away un-netted, John even while ostentatiously giving them the finger.

After Clapton had played on George's *Wonderwall* soundtrack and album, the two began hanging out together, although protocol dictated that George would always be the instigator and the relationship kept in the lowest possible key. He became a regular nocturnal visitor to the King's Road flat where Clapton lived with an eighteen-year-old French fashion model named Charlotte Martin and assorted arty male friends.

'George was always very sweet and shy,' one of these, the painter and film-maker Philippe Mora, recalls. 'He and Eric didn't seem to do much guitar-playing together: they'd talk for hours in Eric's room, then go off somewhere, just the two of them.'

Clapton would never forget the authentically magical effect of being in a Beatle's company. 'It felt like basking in a golden light. Walking into a restaurant or anywhere with George, everything that I thought *I* was just shrivelled to nothing.' George on his side envied Clapton's ability to flit from one band to another without being shackled to a public image like his own.

Both at the time were obsessed with a newcomer to the British pop scene, an exquisite expatriate African-American who refused to stay within the traditional 'black' genres of blues and R&B but played hard rock to white audiences, combining breathtaking virtuosity with a blatantly sexual stage act in which he fellated his guitar-strings with his teeth, bestrode, dry-humped then set fire to it and tossed its smouldering shards into his audience.

Jimi Hendrix was so many streets ahead of George and Clapton, and every other British guitar star, that they could feel no envy, only the kind of hero-worship they were accustomed to receive. Clapton, in particular, willingly abdicated from being 'God' and haunted the front row of every Hendrix gig he could find, often with George at his side.

Clapton first met Pattie Harrison backstage after a Cream concert at the Saville Theatre – which, under Brian Epstein's ownership, had become London's foremost live rock venue. 'She belonged to a powerful man who seemed to have everything I wanted ... amazing cars, an amazing career and a beautiful wife. They were like Camelot and I was the Lancelot.'

Away from his guitar, Clapton was a strangely anonymous character who, chameleon-like, took on the appearance of any musician he admired at a given moment. Cream's first year he had spent clean-shaven, with an enormous Jimi Hendrix Afro which at times threatened to float away with his peaky, unanimated face. Now this changed to the same kind of thick downturned moustache and centre-parted hair with weighty side wings that George had worn since Rishikesh. The two mega-macho males were thus obliged to punctuate their speech with little-girlish tosses of stray locks out of their eyes.

'I had very little to do with Apple,' George would say in hindsight. 'I think it was basically John and Paul's madness – their egos running away with themselves or each other.' Actually he had quite a lot to do with Apple, although its supposed new era of creative possibility led only to more frustration and resentment for him.

John and Paul certainly were the figureheads, calling a press conference in New York to expound its novel commercial strategy. 'The aim isn't just a stack of gold teeth in the bank,' said John. 'We've done that bit. It's more of a trick to see if we can get artistic freedom within a business structure [and whether] we can create things and sell them without charging five times our cost.'

Paul defined it as 'a kind of Western communism ... We want to help people but without doing it like a charity. We're in the happy position of not needing any more money, so for the first time, the bosses aren't in it for profit. If you come to me and say, "I've had such and such a dream," I'll say, "Go away and do it."'

Inevitably, there were questions about their sudden break with the Maharishi and focus on an unspiritual commercial enterprise. 'We made a mistake,' John replied tersely. 'We're human.'

'We thought there was more to him than there was,' Paul concurred.

George, meanwhile, who didn't feel he'd made a mistake nor in the least overvalued the Maharishi, was at the Cannes Film Festival with Ringo and their wives for the world premiere of *Wonderwall* with his original score.

From Apple's founding record label, music-publishing and film companies and boutique, subsidiaries began multiplying like amoeba in a psychedelic light show: Apple Electronics, run by 'Magic Alex', an Apple recording studio, a 'spoken word' label named Zapple to indicate its underground affiliations, an Apple Foundations for the Arts to fund struggling artists in every genre, even an Apple school to be attended by the Beatles' as yet unborn children and those of their friends.

The trouble with their partnership structure, George later said, was that 'other people have weird ideas and you have to go along with it.' To be sure, their ruling spirit now might be described as the group half-a-mind.

The round of lavish Apple openings and inaugurations had the incidental effect of revealing that John and Yoko Ono were now a couple. She was by his side at the press launch of a second Apple boutique, this one in Chelsea's King's Road and dedicated to bespoke tailoring (not quite the way they'd later present themselves on the cover of their first album together). George was also there, as if in tacit proof that John hadn't gone completely rogue.

The uproar in the media instantly blotted out their generally positive coverage of Apple. At a pinch, Swinging Sixties and all, this most unruly Beatle might have been forgiven for deserting his wife and young son. But with all the world's most ravishing dolly birds at his disposal, how could he have chosen a dimin-utive Japanese-American, seven years his senior who seemed to care nothing about her appearance and was given to staging seemingly pointless events like swathing Trafalgar Square's lion statues in white canvas or filming anonymous bare bottoms in the name of art?

The Second World War was only twenty years distant and the atrocities committed by the Japanese military on British prisoners of war legitimised the grossest racism against Yoko in the press, from Beatles fans and even John's family, most of all his Aunt Mimi.

Although the band were now theoretically their own record company bosses, the Apple label's product was still to be man-ufactured and distributed by EMI. May 1968 therefore found them back on the treadmill with George Martin at Abbey Road and thirty-odd songs, mostly written in India, to be turned into their next album.

On their first day, the exclusive boys' club that had existed since 1962 was no more. Yoko sat beside John in matching white, on a stool of equal height. Throughout the session, he turned to her for her opinion before consulting his bandmates or Martin. 'I think John told them some kind of sob story, like she was depressed or she was in pain, and he wanted me to be there to cheer me up,' she recalled. 'So George came over and said, "Hello, how are you?"'

'She didn't really like us because she saw the Beatles as some-thing between John and her,' George would say. 'The vibe I picked up from her was that she was like a wedge that was trying to drive itself deeper and deeper between him and us.'

But according to Yoko, John insisted on her being there every

day largely because of his own pathological jealousy and insecurity. 'He was afraid to let me out of his sight for a moment in
case I started an affair with one of the others. There's a legend
that I even followed him into the bathroom – but he made me
go in there with him.'

In fact, the others showed remarkable tolerance to what
they viewed merely as his 'flavour of the month'. 'George was
very nice,' she would recall, 'but he was sometimes very frank
and it could be very hurtful. "That's just George," John used
to tell me.'

Despite appearances, Yoko cast a powerful sexual spell (at
thirty-three, she was already on her second husband) but her real
attraction for John was in a long-dormant area: his mind. For
she awakened the yearning he used to feel around Stu Sutcliffe
to be a 'serious' artist', never thinking that 'Norwegian Wood'
or 'A Day In the Life' or 'Lucy In The Sky With Diamonds' had
since given him that status and to spare.

Yoko's utter indifference to public opinion of her conceptual
art stunts was intoxicating to a Beatle who'd been forced to
guard his tongue over issues like the Vietnam War for the sake of
the band's cuddly image, or cravenly to apologise for not doing
so, as after uttering the truism that they were 'more popular
than Jesus'. In 1968, youthful anti-war protest was convulsing
Europe and America, and it took little persuasion from Yoko to
combine her aesthetic shock-tactics with the magnitude of his
voice to propagate something more than electronics companies
and boutiques.

They started small with the burial of two acorns as peace
symbols in the grounds of Coventry Cathedral, which had been
almost destroyed by bombing during the Second World War.

This being June and the acorn season being autumn, Apple had to scour the country for a supplier of the symbols, then pay a ludicrous price for them.

When John and Yoko arrived at the cathedral, its canon refused to let the acorns be buried in consecrated ground by unmarried cohabitees, so the interment had to take place a little distance away, one facing west to represent John, the other east to represent Yoko. Within hours, they were dug up by Beatles fans as souvenirs and two more had to be buried and put under round-the-clock guard.

All in all it was a relief for George to get away and spend more time with Ravi Shankar: not to India this time but the hippie paradise of Big Sur, California, to film his guest appearance in the still-ongoing Shankar documentary, *Raga*. The sequence at the town's Esalen Institute is the only known footage of him playing the sitar.

In fact, it was to be for the very last time. 'I thought, "Well, maybe I'm better off being a pop singer-guitar-player-songwriter – whatever-I'm-supposed-to-be,"' he would explain, '"because I've seen a thousand sitar-players in India who are twice as better as I'll ever be. And only one of them Ravi thought was going to be a good player."'

While never discounting his ability nor remarkable dedication, Shankar had gently suggested that his primary music ought properly to come from his roots. 'And I realised that was riding my bike down a street in Liverpool and hearing "Heartbreak Hotel" coming out of someone's house.'

His decision to abandon the instrument which had given him his edge in the Beatles was strengthened during a stop-off in New York on the journey home, when he found himself at the same hotel as Eric Clapton and Jimi Hendrix. On their night of drinking together, Clapton told him forcibly he was too good a lead guitarist not to be doing it full-time. He would always be grateful for such encouragement 'from someone like that, who I really rated as a player ... he treated me like a human.' The implication being that the other Beatles didn't.

To encourage the reverse transition, Clapton later gave him what George called 'the best guitar I'd ever had', a one-off red Gibson Les Paul, formerly owned by the Lovin' Spoonful's John Sebastian. He named it 'Lucy' after Lucille Ball, flame-haired star of the 1950s TV sitcom *I Love Lucy*.

Although his *Wonderwall Music* album had been Apple Records' first release, there had initially seemed little room for him there to develop as a producer. Peter Asher, the brother of Paul's now fiancée Jane and one half of the pop duo Peter and Gordon, was the head of A&R but Paul himself was equally involved in building the label, not only as a producer but in talent-spotting, artist relations, even session musicianship, a multitasker before the word existed.

In May, the model Twiggy had phoned Paul to enthuse about an eighteen-year-old soprano named Mary Hopkin who'd just won on the television talent show *Opportunity Knocks*. Paul sent a car to bring her from Pontardawe, South Wales, got her signed to Apple, chose the song for her first single, an old Russian ballad called 'Those Were The Days', produced it and even played acoustic guitar on the session.

Nevertheless, an Apple producing assignment came George's way, albeit not a terribly prestigious one. Among Brian's last signings had been a raw-boned singer named Jackie Lomax, formerly with a Liverpool band, the Undertakers. Lomax's first Apple single was to be a George composition, 'Sour Milk Sea', which he'd written in Rishikesh. It was in the nature of a consolation prize since John and Paul had considered 'Sour Milk Sea' for the Beatles' new album-in-progress but rejected it as 'too spiritual'.

George produced the song as what he called 'a glorified jam session', with Paul on bass, Ringo, on drums, pianist Nicky Hopkins on Hammond organ and himself and Eric Clapton alternating on lead guitar: such a heavyweight ensemble that a nervous Jackie Lomax queried: 'You want me to sing on top of *that*?'

Despite its hard rock setting, 'Sour Milk Sea' was a transparent bit of advocacy for Transcendental Meditation in the face of the other Beatles' disenchantment. The lyric included a paraphrase of Ravi Shankar's recent advice, 'get back to where you should be', destined to be repeated later in an altogether different context.

In July, Apple Corps moved into number 3 Savile Row, a five-storey Georgian house on the Mayfair street hitherto most famous for bespoke tailoring establishments. This former headquarters of bandleader and impresario Jack Hylton, purchased outright for a bargain £500,000, now had its interior repainted white and carpeted in glossy apple-green, its passageways lined with Gold Discs from a seemingly inexhaustible supply, its elegant panelled rooms converted into plush executive offices. The only unfinished area was its basement, where 'Magic Alex' had been assigned a hefty budget to install a state-of-the-art recording studio.

Remarkably even in that less fearful age, a building regularly frequented by the world's four most adored beings, opening directly onto the street and only minutes from the crowded West End, had no security beyond a single young doorman in a dove-grey tailcoat to open the (unlocked) front door for visitors, which he usually did no matter how flimsy their bona-fides.

On either side of the front steps, a small crowd of young women from all over the country, and the world, waited all day, every day, regardless of weather or season, for however fleeting a glimpse of this or that Beatle arriving or departing by white limousine. George's charmless nickname for them was 'Apple Scruffs.'

In fact, this appearance of consolidation on the Beatles' part was wholly illusory and, their multi-faceted business organisation, elegant new offices and ever-expanding workforce notwithstanding, they were drifting rudderless.

Sixteen months after Brian Epstein's death, they still were unable to find a new manager. The task clearly being beyond anyone else in the pop music sphere, exalted figures from finance and industry had been auditioned – mainly by Paul – such as the Queen's banker, Lord Poole, and Dr Richard Beeching, who'd 'rationalised' Britain's railways in the early 1960s by closing down large swathes of them. But all had had the inherent disadvantage of not being Brian.

Following a brief, unsatisfactory trial of Brian's younger brother, Clive, the role was being jointly filled, without the title, by Brian's former aide Peter Brown, who to some degree perpetuated his air of sophistication and calm, and the Beatles' indispensable roadie and friend, Neil Aspinall. In addition, Derek Taylor had been wooed back from California to take charge of Apple's publicity as well as theirs.

Since his death, evidence had been accumulating that, for

all his paternal care for his 'boys', he hadn't been the greatest dealmaker on their behalf. At the height of Beatlemania in America, he'd handed over the granting of licences to manufacture Fab Four-themed merchandise to a group of British marketing novices for only a 10 per cent royalty to NEMS Enterprises, of which the Fab Four themselves would get 10 per cent.

In the end, thanks to a muddle over the contracts that was entirely Brian's fault, a mere fraction of the merchandise had been produced and millions of dollars that might have been generated by plastic guitars, bubblegum and motor scooters with Beatle-wig saddles had been lost. Despite the indifference to worldly things that the Maharishi preached, such revelations sharpened George's sense of having been short-changed from the very beginning.

There was a reminder of earlier, simpler times on 17 July when crowds brought traffic to a standstill around the London Pavilion cinema at the premiere of a new Beatles film. But this time only an animated one, based on Paul's children's song on the *Revolver* album, with their cartoon characters voiced by actors. Despite the group's apathy towards it, *Yellow Submarine* proved a Pop Art masterpiece that gave a boost to British animation after decades of Disney dominance and would be a major influence on George's future friends and beneficiaries, the Monty Python team.

The soundtrack album was considerably less auspicious: only one side consisted of Beatles tracks – among them George's *Sgt. Pepper* reject, 'Only A Northern Song' – and the other of orchestral arrangements of their songs by George Martin, surprisingly including 'Within You Without You'.

Complicated modern times returned with a vengeance on 31 July when the Apple boutique in Baker Street ceased trading after only six months. It had never really recovered from the scrubbing off of its exterior mural; its clothes, created by a design collective known as The Fool, had been too expensive and elaborate for the boutique market and the trendy twilight within had made it a shoplifters' paradise. The Beatles and their inner circle took the pick of the stock for themselves, then the public were let in to scrimmage for the remainder.

The Fool continued to be court decorators to British pop royalty, one of their creations even finding its way into 'Kinfauns'. 'George and I had a huge circular brick fireplace that was a replica of Salvador Dalí's,' Pattie recalls, 'and they painted a most fantastic design on it.' A far cry indeed from that tiny iron fireplace at 12 Arnold Grove, Wavertree, in front of which the Harrison family of six used to take their weekly turns in a tin bath.

The next Beatles album was into its third month, yet still nowhere near completion. Such was the glut of new Lennon–McCartney songs that they'd decided, against George Martin's advice, that it must be in the new double-disc format. But the cohesiveness of *Sgt. Pepper* was no more: at Abbey Road, there would sometimes be three Beatles working on their separate parts of different songs in three different studios.

When they did record together, Yoko's presence was a constant distraction and an exasperation to Martin – although, for the sake of his relationship with John, he managed never to show it. Nor was this the limit of her incursion, for John had made 3 Savile Row double as the headquarters of their conceptual art partnership-cum-anti-war crusade and announced he would be making albums with her as well as with the Beatles on the Apple label.

The fans at the front steps felt no such constraint in expressing their feelings about Yoko, who was invariably greeted with shouts of 'Jap!', Chink!' and 'Yellow!' One day, she was presented with a bunch of symbolically yellow roses, the thorns uppermost so as to gash her hands when she accepted it.

All this variegated tension finally got to the Beatle who'd always been the most patient and stoical one. Although nobody had said a word against Ringo's drumming, he decided it was substandard and that the other three were ganging up on him. On 22 August, during the recording of a Beach Boys pastiche called 'Back In The USSR', he walked out and disappeared on holiday with his family to Sardinia.

Derek Taylor somehow kept the story out of the papers, and the others sent him a wire saying, 'You are the greatest rock 'n' roll drummer. we love you, come home,' which he soon did, his old patient, stoical self again. George, who could strike just the right note when necessary, filled the studio with flowers to welcome him.

Striking the right note, alas, proved impossible in a more serious context. For a single to come out ahead of the double album, Paul had written the seven-minutes-long 'Hey Jude' as a sympathetic message to John's five-year-old son, Julian, following the messy collapse of his parents' marriage.

When 'Hey Jude' was first unveiled to the others, George as usual instantly came up with a lead guitar part, in this case a riff answering each line of the verse. However, Paul had already decided on an arrangement solely consisting of his own piano fortissimo with backing vocals. The result was their first public row in years but not their last nor worst.

On 26 August, Apple Records released four singles at once: the Beatles"Hey Jude', Mary Hopkin's 'Those Were The Days', Jackie Lomax's 'Sour Milk Sea' and 'Thingumybob', the theme from a popular TV show by Yorkshire's Black Dyke Mills brass band, written and produced by Paul.

Special presentation sets labelled 'Our First Four' were circulated to the media and deluxe versions hand-delivered to the Queen at Buckingham Palace, the Queen Mother at Clarence House, Princess Margaret at Kensington Palace and Prime Minister Harold Wilson at 10 Downing Street.

Jackie Lomax got equal billing in the presentation set, but that was about all. 'Hey Jude' became the year's top-selling single in most of the world while 'Those Were The Days' went to number one in the UK, kept from the top spot in the *Billboard* Hot 100 only by 'Hey Jude'. The most 'Sour Milk Sea' could do was beat the Black Dyke Mills band by reaching number 29 in Canada.

Afterwards, George seemed to suffer the same crisis of confidence in his songwriting that he'd recently had over his guitar-playing. But something exceptional was to come out of it.

He was staying with his parents at the house he'd bought for them in Appleton, a quiet suburb of Warrington, Lancashire, after the fan-nuisance in Speke had become too much even for the hospitable Louise. Though modest in size, it had a name, 'Seven Oaks', and a garden which, after the small patches of earth Harold was used to cultivating, felt like a stately home's.

That day George had been musing about the *I Ching* (Book of Changes), the ancient Chinese text which holds that everything happens for a pre-ordained reason and there are no such things as coincidences. Then, opening a book at random, the first words he read were 'gently weeps'.

It was utterly unlike him to write a song about weeping, even through the proxy of a guitar. And in successive early drafts, the lyric was an objective lament about the state of the world. Only by degrees did it become more personal albeit never specific: a lover apparently watching his sleeping paramour, numbed by grief that only a plectrum and six strings could express, apparently of its own volition.

Unconsciously, too, he had absorbed John's blending of the surreal with the everyday, the passive with the piercingly acute, in 'I look at the floor and I see it needs sweeping ... I look at the world and I notice it's turning ...' Even in the rather laboured list of the paramour's faults ('controlled', 'bought and sold', 'diverted', 'perverted', 'inverted'), he opened his touchy heart wide.

Nevertheless, the other Beatles showed only minimal interest in 'While My Guitar Gently Weeps' and put little effort into its first run-through. But this time, George refused to cave in as he had over 'Hey Jude'. When driving into London with Eric Clapton on 5 September, he asked Clapton to go with him to Abbey Road and play on the recording.

It was an astounding suggestion: Clapton had already appeared on record with individual Beatles but augmenting the sacred four was something no one had ever been asked to do and, six months earlier, would have been unthinkable.

George waved away his friend's misgivings and lent him a guitar, since he didn't have one with him. John wasn't at the studio that day but Clapton's presence awoke Paul's interest in the song sufficiently to play a dramatic piano intro to the guitar's grief. Clapton himself, normally the last man on earth likely to weep over a woman, improvised riffs that positively keened.

On 14 October, after more than four months, the double album was finally complete. Female fans who'd kept vigil out in the street for much of that time, were allowed into the empty studio to pick up its litter of Coca-Cola bottles and crisp packets as souvenirs.

Along with 'While My Guitar Gently Weeps', George had three songs as opposed to Lennon and McCartney's twenty-six. Elsewhere, too, the new personal note abounded. His 'Savoy Truffle' was named after a centre in Mackintosh's Good News chocolates, one of Clapton's less harmful addictions. Other centres like Crème Tangerine and Coffee Dessert were referenced as was George's favourite dessert, 'nice apple tart', for which Paul's widowed father Jim McCartney had a particularly nice recipe he would never divulge.

'Long Long Long' was atypically double-tracked and as bland as an English hymn after all those rhapsodic ragas. 'Piggies' was a poke at greedy meat-eaters actually conceived in 1966 but left unfinished. Finding the lyric sheet in his parents' attic, George had completed it with the help of his mother, Louise, who supplied the line 'What they need's a damn good whacking', something he'd never received from her.

Unpredictable as always, he'd also had a hand in a piece by John and Yoko in conceptual art mode, a ten-minute sound-collage entitled 'Revolution 9'. This had redoubled George Martin's fruitless pleas for a single album like *Revolver* and *Sgt. Pepper*, packed end-to-end with quality and all such private self-indulgences left out.

Simultaneously in the works was a love song inspired by Pattie and suggested by one entitled 'Something In The Way She Moves' by the American singer-songwriter James Taylor, later a highly successful Apple Records artist.

But it was coming out so easily that George suspected he might have unconsciously heard it somewhere, so put it aside until he could be certain he hadn't.

He refused to give up on Jackie Lomax after just one single and in October, accompanied by Pattie, he took Lomax to Los Angeles to make an album using the elite group of session musicians known as the Wrecking Crew. Afterwards, he accepted an invitation to stay with Bob Dylan in upstate New York that would turn out to have spared him from major dramas around Apple and John and Yoko.

Since Dylan had introduced the Beatles to pot in 1964, his equally prolific output had acted as both a spur and a threat, to John particularly. George was a less obvious disciple but Dylan's *Blonde On Blonde* was the only Western pop album he took with him to Rishikesh and his 'Long Long Long' showed an obvious debt to Dylan's 'Sad-Eyed Lady of the Lowlands'.

In 1966 Dylan had suffered severe injuries from a motorcycle crash that took him off the commercial market for two years. At the time of George's visit, he'd just completed a Country-influenced album, *Nashville Skyline*, on which his former mocking, sneering folkie voice changed to a lower, fruitier one more suited to the genre, and was now contemplating a return to live performance. 'He'd obviously just bought a new pair of jeans,' the sharp-eyed Pattie noted, 'because the sales ticket from the shop was still stapled to a back pocket.'

Dylan was by no means an expansive host, as George would recall: 'He seemed very nervous and I was a little uncomfortable [until] on about the third day we got the guitars out ... I was saying to him "write me some words" and thinking of all this "Johnnie's in the basement, mixing up the medicine" type of thing and he was saying "Show me some chords, how do you get those tunes?"'

A photograph was taken of them together on a couch, in wide-brimmed Stetson hats that both still wore around the house, collaborating on a song that would be called 'I'd Have You Anytime'. George was even allowed to keep Dylan's lyric sheet, not touch-typed as usual but in a precise, European-looking script.

In the neighbouring hamlet of West Saugerties lived the five musicians who'd steadfastly backed Dylan through his turbulent transition from folk to rock and called themselves simply The Band. They'd just released their debut album, *Music From Big Pink*, a celebration of America's diverse folk and blues heritage that had the itchy-footed Eric Clapton already pining to join up with them.

George was amazed to find himself admired by these multi-instrumental talents, lead guitarist and songwriter Robbie Robertson, bass-player Rick Danko, drummer Levon Helm and keyboards players Richard Manuel and Garth Hudson, for the musicianship that had recently been so little valued in the Beatles. Despite their devotion to Americana, they had a European sensibility, for all of them except Helm were Canadian and Robertson had a Parisian wife. 'They all loved George and he adored them,' Pattie remembers, 'because in their different ways they were all equally adorable.'

Thanksgiving fell during the Harrisons' stay with Dylan, so The Band invited them to dinner at the house-cum-recording studio actually named Big Pink. Here George found no social awkwardness, for the quintet lived together as comfortably as they played together, in an egalitarian spirit he'd never known with John and Paul.

He had not long left London when the Beatles' seeming immunity to drug busts finally came to an end. In the first glare of their joint notoriety, John and Yoko had been living like nomads (one of them albeit in the supertax class), hiding from the press temporarily both at Paul's house in north London and with George and Pattie in Esher, when Yoko's insistence on preparing John's food had left every one of Pattie's saucepans burnt.

The fugitive pair seemed to have found a more lasting sanctuary at a flat Ringo owned at 34 Montagu Square, Marylebone, until Scotland Yard's Drugs Squad raided the property on 18 October and 213 grams of cannabis, approximately half an ounce, was discovered in various superficial hiding places.

Ringo's previous tenant had been Jimi Hendrix and, knowing Hendrix's drug-intake, John had taken the precaution of having the flat deep-cleaned to rout out every incriminating grain. Such a detail was not likely to inhibit the officer in charge, the infamous Detective Sergeant 'Nobby' Pilcher, for whom accumulating other rock-star 'scalps' and the consequent media celebrity had become an addiction rivalling any that he had exposed.

The fact that Fleet Street had been given advance notice of the raid as good as announced it to be a frame-up. Even so John would be convicted, taking sole responsibility to prevent Yoko's probable deportation back to America.

Then on 11 November, Apple Records released John and Yoko's experimental album *Unfinished Music No. 1: Two Virgins*. Its front cover was a selfie of them as full-frontal nudes, taken at Ringo's flat, with a corresponding rear view on the back.

In a coffee-table art book, the image would have attracted little notice but on an unavoidably Beatle-related product, it all but annihilated the wholesome impression of 'Our First Four' with sweet Mary Hopkin and the no-nonsense West Yorkshire brass band. Most of the album's few retailers would sell it only in plain brown paper bags, traditional porn-packaging, and an optimistic shipment of 30,000 copies to New York was pulped by the Customs authorities.

George's morale-boosting American trip meant his missing the release of the Beatles' double album on 22 November which, given his modest showing on it, cannot have caused him much heartbreak. In deliberate contrast to *Sgt. Pepper*'s rampant psychedelia, the cover designed by the Pop artist Richard Hamilton was a double-creamy void; its official title, barely legible and slightly off-centre, was *The Beatles*. But it would always be known as the White Album.

Eric Clapton had learned how easy it was to put a foot wrong with his megastar friend when George sent him an early test-pressing. This he took with him to Los Angeles and played to some musician friends there, thinking George would appreciate his singing its praises; instead, he found himself frostily accused of betraying a confidence, and backed away from their friendship, mortified.

The White Album topped the British charts all through that Christmas season and in America sold 3.3 million copies in the first four days after its release: The media eulogies were led by television director Tony Palmer, writing in the *Observer*, for whom it confirmed Lennon and McCartney as 'the greatest songwriters since Schubert'.

Among the few dissenters was *The Times*'s classical music critic William Mann, the first to recognise them as major twentieth-century composers five years earlier. Mann felt that over-many pastiches and in-jokes had staled their talent; certainly, makeweight tracks like John's 'The Continuing Story of Bungalow Bill' or Paul's 'Honey Pie' would never feature on the everlasting Beatles playlist – and few to the extent of 'While My Guitar Gently Weeps'. George had not outnumbered them on the album, but for the first time he'd outdone them.

He might not have been much involved in Apple's day-to-day running – which Neil Aspinall later compared to 'spinning a top and seeing where it stopped' – but as a director of the company with an equal quarter-share he couldn't help but see how things at its elegant Mayfair townhouse were getting out of control.

With the White Album now added to 'Hey Jude' and 'Those Were The Days', Apple Records was a huge success, one that top talent on both sides of the Atlantic, notably the newly formed Crosby, Stills and Nash, were standing in line to join. But after almost a year, Apple Electronics, Apple Retailing, Apple Book Publishing, Apple Tailoring and the Apple School had accomplished little beyond giving employment to numerous Beatle friends and acquaintances at handsome salaries and burning up prodigious amounts of Beatle cash.

Apple Films, at least, was in capable professional hands with Denis O'Dell, who'd produced *A Hard Day's Night* in 1964, but even O'Dell was unequal to the task of getting all four Beatles at once to agree on a project for themselves and then stick to it. At one point, he'd persuaded them to work with the great French director Jean-Luc Godard, financing from United Artists was in place, but then George had changed his mind and Godard had made the film (*One Plus One*) with the Rolling Stones instead.

That rash Beatle promise of unlimited largesse had attracted spongers and con-artists from throughout the international music business, but not only there. The fortunes lavished on equipping 3 Savile Row and lack of any security meant it was a rare electric typewriter or copying machine that did not develop legs and an irresistible wanderlust a few days shortly after being installed.

In a rare spot-check of those with the right to come and go through Friar Park's ever-unlocked front door, a hippie couple from California were found to have been living in an empty office with their several small children, unnoticed by anyone. A flourishing racket was also discovered among the youthful Post Office messengers who brought telegrams and cablegrams throughout the day. After delivering their missives, they would take the opportunity to slip up to the roof – destined to be the scene of an historic Beatles event but previously unused – and pilfer its valuable lead.

The most glaring under-achievement had been that of the Apple Foundation for the Arts with its supposed mission to support young creative talent in every genre. A few random grants had been made, including to a Punch and Judy show on Brighton's beach, but there remained an immense heap of music tapes, paintings, manuscripts, film treatments and out-right begging letters that Paul, in a series of national press ads, had promised 'won't just be thrown into the wastepaper-basket'.

And they hadn't been. They'd been thrown into what was known as 'the black room', adjoining Derek Taylor's press and publicity department, where they stood as little chance of being sympathetically sifted through as radioactive nuclear waste.

Taylor personified Apple and its welcome to all the world's media, seated in a basketwork armchair with an outsize scallop-shaped back and open-handedly dispensing Scotch and Coke and Benson & Hedges Gold cigarettes, not least to himself. The space was shared with a kitchen staffed by two young women whose Cordon Bleu training was seldom challenged by visiting Beatle snack-orders, such as George's invariable cheese and cucumber sandwiches.

Among Taylor's large staff was a bubbly-haired young American gofer he designated 'the house hippie'; for months, too, with the press officer's indulgence a mysterious personage known only as 'Stocky' sat on top of a filing-cabinet, all day every day, drawing endless pictures of genitalia on the tasteful Apple-crested notepaper.

Taylor was the last court of appeal for those hoping to touch the Apple Foundation for the Arts. He always gave them a hearing, however outlandish and however many times he'd endured the same pitch already. One day, his desk intercom buzzed and a female voice from the ground floor said, 'Derek – Adolf Hitler is in Reception.'

'Oh Christ, not that asshole again,' Taylor sighed. 'Okay, send him up.'

Drugs still circulated among the company's directors and their executives as freely as ever, despite John and Yoko's recent bust and the presence of a large police station a couple of hundred yards further along Savile Row. At the slightest hint of dark blue that wasn't made to measure, a Press Office secretary had been trained to gather the various substances and flush them down a toilet.

'Sometimes George would go in and go crazy because of how many people were just lying around drunk there and living off the company,' John would remember. Yet the most spectacular example of people lying around and living off the company originated with George or, rather, his good humour on his recent American trip.

He would later vaguely remember somebody in New York expressing a wish to visit him at 3 Savile Row and himself agreeing. He then forgot all about it until the week before Christmas when Heathrow Airport notified Apple that it was holding seventeen Harley-Davidson motorcycles whose freight charges the Beatles were supposedly to pay.

He had unwittingly invited an entire chapter of Californian Hell's Angels to stop off en route to Czechoslovakia to 'sort out the political situation' between Soviet Russia and the youthful democracy movement it had brutally crushed the previous spring. It being too late now to turn them back, George hastily circulated a memo to Apple staff, cautioning: 'Keep doing what you're doing but just be nice to them. And don't upset them because they could kill you.'

The Angels' joint leaders were two equally huge, intimidating figures known as Frisco Pete and Billy Tumbleweed. It immediately became clear this was no mere social call in passing but that they expected the entire chapter to be accommodated at the Apple house during their stay in London. Parking their gleaming 'hogs' in Savile Row under the awed gaze of bespoke tailor and Beatles fan alike, they scattered their sleeping-bags around the still-unfinished basement recording studio.

Among the house's other current habitués was the writer Ken Kesey, whose Merry Pranksters had inspired the Beatles' chaotic *Magical Mystery Tour* and whom Apple Book Publishing had brought from New York, provided with an electric typewriter and commissioned to keep a 'street diary of London'.

Apple staff would arrive at work to find Kesey giving a poetry reading in one or other executive office and the place a sea of cracked black leather and fog of pot smoke. The two debutantes in the Cordon Bleu kitchen found themselves providing all-hours room service with sexual harassment as a side-order. Yet carefully worded suggestions to Frisco Pete or Billy Tumbleweed from Derek Taylor or Neil Aspinall that now might be a good moment to move on to Czechoslovakia met with the same baleful glare and growl that George had invited them, saying nothing about a time limit.

Just before Christmas, with its Apple School hat half-on, the company held a party for its employees' children with John and Yoko playing Father and Mother Christmas and a forty-two-pound turkey warranted to be the biggest in Britain. George did not attend 'because I knew there'd be trouble' and he wasn't wrong.

The Hell's Angels gatecrashed the party just as the enormous turkey was brought in. 'It took two people to carry it across the room,' Neil Aspinall recalled, 'and on the way, the Angels ripped it to pieces. By the time it got to the table, there was nothing left.'

Everyone was too scared to protest except the *New Musical Express* journalist Alan Smith whose wife, Mavis, worked in Derek Taylor's Press Office. A single blow from Frisco Pete knocked Smith into the laps of Father and Mother Christmas, leaving tea from the cup in John's hand dripping from his spectacles.

Only George could rid Apple of these perilous guests, which he finally did with a finesse that astonished Aspinall. 'They were talking and George said, "There's Yin and there's Yang, there's in, there's out, there's up, there's down, you're here, you go." So the Angels just went "okay" and left.'

16

'HE WANTED SO MUCH TO
BE A SPIRITUAL BEING'

For the first two years of their marriage, Pattie recalls, 'George was divine ... sweet and kind', adored by her mother, siblings and stepsiblings alike. But things changed drastically after their pilgrimage to Rishinkesh. If the Maharishi's teachings had given him a sense of purpose he'd never found with the Beatles, she felt they also 'took some of the lightness out of his soul'.

His obsessive meditating and chanting and spinning of a prayer-wheel, far from bringing the promised inner peace, seemed only to make him moody and irritable. 'He wanted so much to be a spiritual being, but could never reach the level he wanted to,' Pattie recalls, 'and he felt that all the frustrations with the Beatles and Apple were holding him back.'

All too easily, inner peace could be replaced by outer scratchiness. Derek Taylor was to recall sitting next to him on a transatlantic flight as he was chanting in an undertone and a cabin attendant asked him if he wanted anything. 'Fuck off,' George snapped, 'can't you see I'm meditating?'

Like any well-to-do north-countryman of that era, he hadn't liked his wife 'going out to work', so had made Pattie give up her successful modelling career and its pleasurable social life among the young photographers who were now as glamorous as pop stars.

With her couture background, Pattie might have expected a role at the Apple boutique where her younger sister, Jenny, headed the far-from-overstretched sales staff. She did submit some clothes designs, but they were eclipsed by The Fool's extravagant though insecurely stitched creations, and she had nothing more to do with the place until she went in with the other Beatle wives to rifle its racks the night before it closed down.

Like Cynthia Lennon and Maureen Starkey, she'd never been at Abbey Road save in the most casual, fleeting way, or thought to influence the Beatles' work as Yoko was now doing (although she soon would do so in a far subtler and more lasting way).

On the many nights when George was working there, she'd sometimes be escorted to the theatre or ballet by Apple's temporary joint-MD, the charming (and safely gay) Peter Brown. Otherwise, since George didn't like her 'going to new places or meeting new people', she'd be alone at 'Kinfauns', their face-painted bungalow in Esher. Disinclined to sit at home and mope, she tried various ways of filling the time, running an antiques stall with her sister, after Jenny's job at the Apple boutique disappeared and starting a course of flying lessons.

In India, George had been fascinated by images of Krishna, the love god always depicted amid innumerable concubines, and the discovery that in Hinduism sex did not diminish divinity. As Pattie well knew, the numbers of concubines available to a Beatle would have made even Krishna's jaw hit the floor. During his long absences, she tried not to picture what he might be getting up to, especially in Eric Clapton's company, and took some consolation from planning the perfect suicide if it should turn out to be what she suspected: a leap from the top of Beachy Head, wearing her floatiest Foale and Tuffin dress.

At the occasional get-togethers she and George had with Eric Clapton and his French model girlfriend, Charlotte Martin, she was totally unconscious of Clapton's rapturous gaze, merely thinking him 'rather nice'. The two women became good friends and when Clapton summarily dumped Charlotte at the end of 1968 and she had to leave his Chelsea flat, Pattie invited her to stay at 'Kinfauns' while she considered her future.

In the aftermath of a New Year's Eve party at Cilla Black's house, she recalls, 'everything went swiftly downhill ... Charlotte didn't seem remotely upset about Eric and was getting uncomfortably close to George.' He denied anything untoward and accused Pattie of paranoia, whereupon she fled the house and went to London to stay with friends.

'On about day three, Eric rang me, saying "I know you're on your own. Would you like to come out to dinner?" She refused, 'quite annoyed that he'd done that while George was with his girlfriend ... It felt like a set-up.'

After six days George phoned her to say that Charlotte had gone back to France and begging her to come home, which she did.

Ironically, what would be the first step in the Beatles' two-year-long breakup began as their attempted self-reinvention.

Paul, the one most in love with being a Beatle, had always regretted the loss of intimacy with their fans in 1966 when they gave up touring and disappeared into the recording studio. And, as their de facto leader since Brian's death, it was Paul who came up with a way of rekindling that intimacy without the almighty disruption of going back on the road.

Rather, they would metaphorically let the fans into the studio with a television documentary showing them at work on a new album in the fly-on-the-wall style the medium had barely begun to explore, whose climax would be a one-off live performance.

George felt the least nostalgia for those days when shrieking young women would dangle from his neck as he tried to play. Yet, despite the liberating times with Dylan and The Band the previous summer, Beatleness still ran through him like the grain in old oak; as John and Ringo were both for Paul's plan, he went along with it.

Both album and documentary were to be called *Get Back* after a Paul song, originally a sarcastic riposte to the Tory politician Enoch Powell's rant against immigrants from the Indian sub-continent. Instead, it expressed the Beatles' unanimous wish – in fact, very last unanimous wish – to get back their old simplicity and spontaneity as musicians after years of growing complexity and sophistication at Abbey Road with George Martin.

Symbolising this fresh start, even in George's eyes, rehearsals of material for the album and filming began simultaneously on New Year's Day 1969. The location was Twickenham film studios where, in more carefree times. they had made *A Hard Day's Night* and *Help!*, and where now the head of Apple Films, Denis O'Dell, had arranged the use of a 7,500-square-foot sound stage with a 34-foot-high ceiling. In the harsh January weather, numerous electric heaters only just took the edge off the biting cold.

Symbolically, too, they had elected not to use Martin this

PHILIP NORMAN

time but a younger producer, Glyn Johns, until then best
known for his work with the Rolling Stones. Unfortunately,
no one had informed Martin of the decision and he was also at
Twickenham, though too much of a gentleman to protest about
his treatment; enough of a gentleman, indeed, to stay around in
case they still might need him.

Get Back the documentary was to be directed by twenty-
nine-year-old Michael Lindsay-Hogg, who'd previously filmed
Beatles songs like 'Paperback Writer' and 'Hey Jude' as well
as *The Rolling Stones Rock and Roll Circus*, the Stones' (so far
unaired) 'answer' to *Magical Mystery Tour*. Lindsay-Hogg was a
cut above other documentarians, cherubic and charming, with
connections to high society on both sides of the Atlantic, and
the rumoured out-of-wedlock son of a towering twentieth-
century film-maker, Orson Welles.

He and one assistant, wielding hand-held cameras, were to
have total access to the Beatles' rehearsals and discussions. Since
the band were the producers as well as stars, they could cut out
anything they didn't like at the editing stage.

Gathered with them and their faithful factotums, Neil
Aspinall and Mal Evans, in the chilly, vaulted space, there were
now several powerful deterrents to the group mind. As well as
Yoko, all but superglued to John's side, Paul's new American
photographer girlfriend, Linda Eastman, was busy with her
camera, also with no one to gainsay her.

In fairness, George could have insisted on Pattie's being there,
too, but instead had brought with him a shaven-headed figure
in an orange robe and sandals who sat cross-legged on the floor
at a respectful distance. This was Shyamsundar Das, a founding
member of the Radha Krishna Temple in Britain – actually,

white and American, born Samuel Speerstra in Salem, Oregon. He was to act as a kind of human bookmark, keeping George's place in higher spiritual concerns.

Although Glyn Johns was in the producer's chair, Paul effectively took charge, wearing a new, dark, bushy beard he continually stroked with one hand as he exhorted his band-mates to greater effort in the tones of a gym teacher urging slothful pupils up the wall-bars. To foster the back-to-basics spirit, he'd rather touchingly brought along both the Höfner violin bass guitars he had made his trademark in their Cavern and Hamburg days (one of which would be stolen during the sessions and never recovered).

John by contrast was devoid of his usual wit and abrasiveness and for long spells almost completely silent. There was a good reason: he'd just been introduced to heroin by Yoko, who'd first tried it in Paris some time previously with the jazz saxophonist Ornette Coleman.

None of his fellow Beatles had yet picked up on the clas-sic symptoms of slurred speech and chalk-white facial rictus (known to its initiates as 'pulling a whitey'). Nor had Michael Lindsay-Hogg's access-all-areas camera even when, during an on-set interview with a Canadian TV crew, John's whitey went to the usual next stage and he vomited onto the floor.

It wasn't long, Pattie recalls, before George hated being there. 'He'd come home every night in a terrible mood, complaining about the electrics and sound quality and saying how sick he was of the others.'

On 6 January, he clashed with his bearded gym teacher over the arrangement for Lennon and McCartney's 'Two Of Us'. Paul wanted to get the structure fully worked out while George, in his customary way, was already adding in lead guitar breaks. It was the same dispute they'd had over 'Hey Jude' except that then Paul hadn't wanted any guitar breaks at all.

Lindsay-Hogg's camera was recording the exchange and at Paul's mention of 'Hey Jude', it went in tight on George in a cheery gold polo-neck contrasting with his sotto voce surliness: 'Okay, well I don't mind. I'll play whatever it is you want me to play. Or I won't play at all if you don't want me to play. Whatever it is that'll please you, I'll do it.'

It was just a temporary blow-up, however, no worse than many on previous occasions when cameras hadn't been watching. A few minutes later, Paul went off the subject to confide he was suffering from an 'itchy dick' and receive blokey advice on treating the condition from George and John.

The right arrangement – Paul's – was found for 'Two Of Us'. There was even a run-through of George's latest from his spiritual bag, 'All Things Must Pass', although it clearly wasn't going to get onto this or any other Beatles album.

But his resentment at being 'curtailed' by Paul, as he put it, ran too deep to be so easily dissipated, though never again revealed on-camera. George Martin was the sole witness to actual physical violence between two Beatles whose only previous fisticuffs had been on Hamburg's Reeperbahn circa 1962. 'George and John actually came to blows,' Martin would recall. 'You'd think it would have been with Paul, but it was John. It was hushed up afterwards.'

On 10 January, a Saturday, the morning was partly spent in watching Paul on guitar vamp the chords to the project's keynote song, for which he still had only the words 'Get back . . .' Then Michael Lindsay-Hogg went for lunch with John and

Ringo in the small VIP restaurant just off the sound stage. George didn't join them until a few minutes later and the director, who'd sensed something coming to the boil in him again, thoughtfully had a bug concealed in a nearby pot plant.

But this time there was no boiling over, as with Paul four days earlier. He merely said. 'Okay, see you around the clubs,' then left the building and drove home. John shrugged it off, ordering Neil Aspinall to 'get Eric Clapton. He's just as good and not so much of a headache.' Lindsay-Hogg's concealed microphone unfortunately picked up none of it amid the clash of cutlery from surrounding tables.

'George was very sombre when he came home,' Pattie recalls. 'It was obvious that he hadn't just walked out on an album like Ringo a few months before – he'd walked out of the band.'

Over that weekend, however, there was what he later described as 'an intervention' from John, accompanied by Yoko. 'They turned up both wearing sunglasses even though it was January,' Pattie says. 'John kept asking, "Why's it so *dark* in here?"'

After further discussions at Ringo's house, George agreed to return, on two conditions. First, they must leave their present cheerless surroundings and continue recording the album in the basement studio at 3 Savile Row. Secondly, the breach in their sacred line-up he'd made by having Eric Clapton play on 'While My Guitar Gently Weeps' was to be repeated on a larger scale.

The Beatles had met Billy Preston in 1962 when Brian put them second on the bill to Little Richard at New Brighton Tower Ballroom and fifteen-year-old Preston had been the virtuoso keyboard-player in Richard's band. Early in the *Get*

Back sessions, George and Eric Clapton had gone to a Ray Charles concert at the Royal Festival Hall, where George spotted Preston playing back-up organ so brilliantly that he vowed himself never to touch the instrument again.

Now he insisted Preston should temporarily join the Beatles as a *named* supernumerary, unlike Clapton: not just for his musicianship but the good humour George remembered, hoping it would help banish the toxicity of Twickenham.

There was a major hitch when the state-of-the art studio Magic Alex had supposedly been installing under the Apple house proved nowhere near completion and ever-supportive George Martin had to be asked to supply the equipment it still lacked from Abbey Road. After that, Martin could hardly not be invited back as the album's lead producer.

He was briefed by John in terms that as good as wrote off all the ways he'd nurtured Lennon and McCartney's genius (albeit failed for a long time to see any similar potential in George). 'John came to me and said, "On this one we don't want any of your production crap,"' he would recall. '"It's got to be an honest album, okay? I don't want any overdubbing or any of the editing that you do. I want to do it so that when we listen to it, I know *we* did it."'

Despite much pleasanter working conditions and the beaming magic of Billy Preston, tension soon began to seep back. Recording whole tracks in one go without editing or overdubbing was something the Beatles hadn't done since Martin had wrung their first album out of them in 1963. 'And it became terribly tedious because they couldn't give me what I wanted – a perfect performance ... After about the sixty-first take, John would say, "How was that one?" and I'd have to say, "John, I honestly don't know." "No fookin' good then, are you?" he'd say. That was the general atmosphere.'

As well as recording, they were also supposedly getting back into trim for the one-off live show planned to climax Michael Lindsay-Hogg's TV documentary. However, Paul's former efforts to run a tight ship seemed to evaporate; they wasted miles of film and tape in jamming old rock 'n' roll numbers, show tunes, even Liverpool's bawdy sea-shanty 'Maggie May', often so sloppily that future listeners could easily mistake them for a particularly inept Beatles tribute band.

The 'no females at recording sessions' rule was completely forgotten, with Yoko sometimes adding a shrieking vocal of her own – inspired by overhearing female servants of her wealthy parents in childbirth – and Linda Eastman now close enough to Paul to bring along her six-year-old daughter, Heather (who'd sometimes mischievously imitate Yoko) but still only the briefest look-ins by Pattie.

'It all began to feel like Sartre's play *No Exit*,' Lindsay-Hogg would recall. 'Characters trapped together in a room, uncertain why they were there. No one seemed to know any way of stopping it.'

There was also inconclusive discussion of possible settings for the live show, with suggestions including north London's Roundhouse arena, Liverpool's still-extant Cavern, an orphanage and the deck of an ocean liner at sea. Lindsay-Hogg very nearly sold the idea of a 2,000-year-old Roman amphitheatre in Tunisia, to which its audience would be transported on the just-launched liner *Queen Elizabeth II*, but George refused to go anywhere outside Britain.

In the end, they barely had to go out of doors, giving the

comeback show that would be their farewell one on the roof of the Apple house on 30 January. 'I wasn't invited to be there either,' Pattie recalls. 'George told me, "It won't be interesting. It's nothing."'

The Beatles by this point were no longer 'in the fortunate position of not needing any more money', as Paul had proclaimed a year earlier. Their accountants had issued a stark warning that their business was threatening to bleed them whiter than the cover of the double album which had helped launch it.

Characteristically, John couldn't keep from sharing this news with the trade paper *Disc and Music Echo* early in the Twickenham rehearsals: 'We haven't got half the money people think we have. It's been pie in the sky from the start. Apple's been losing money every week because it needs close running by a big businessman. If it carries on like this, all of us will be broke in six months.'

The resulting headline, BEATLES IN CASH CRISIS, created almost as great a sensation as he had with BEATLES MORE POPULAR THAN JESUS three years earlier. But this time, far from recanting, John followed it up by telling America's new music magazine, *Rolling Stone*, that he personally was 'down to his last fifty thousand [pounds]'. That £50,000 in 1969 was equivalent to about two-thirds of a million today hardly dispelled the awful vision of a Beatle with a begging-bowl.

Concerned to limit the damage to the company's image and its employees' morale, Paul for once offered little or no public comment; it was therefore to George that reporters turned for further amplification. Possibly mindful of the Hell's Angels episode, he was less moralistic than he would once have been.

Apple, he said, had 'become a haven for dropouts. But some of our best friends are dropouts.'

As to the 'big businessman' to whom John had sent out that generalised *cri-de-cœur*, Allen Klein had seen the *Disc and Music Echo* story's many follow-ups and was circling ever nearer like a shark scenting blood in the water.

Klein was a New Jersey-born accountant who'd carved a profitable niche from the reluctance of young pop stars, especially British ones, to bother their shaggy heads with business matters. Turning to management, he had scooped up several major names from the 'British Invasion' of the mid-Sixties, culminating in the Rolling Stones in 1965, while never hiding the fact that the Beatles were his ultimate goal.

Outwardly he was the antithesis of rock 'n' roll: squat and podgy with unfashionably greasy hair, and given to smoking a malodorous pipe to signify respectability and trustworthiness. In New York entrepreneurial circles, his ruthlessness in dealmaking was as legendary as his rudeness: his desk proudly displayed a plaque with a paraphrase of the Old Testament's Twenty-third Psalm: 'Yea, though I walk through the Valley of the Shadow of Death I shall fear no evil for I am the biggest bastard in the valley.'

His effect on the somnolent British record business of the mid-Sixties was akin to a pit bull savaging chihuahuas. Re-signing the Stones to the Decca label just after his takeover of the band, he'd secured them an advance of $1.25 million, something the Beatles had never thought of demanding from EMI (although what happened to that $1.25 million thereafter would be shrouded in mystery).

Two days before the rooftop concert, unbeknown to the other Beatles, John and Yoko met with Klein at the Dorchester

Hotel. With the 'straight talking' on which bent people so often pride themselves, he made John two offers. Firstly, he would clean up the mess at Apple and secondly, magic away all the Beatles' financial problems so completely that from here on their motto could be 'FYM', or 'Fuck You, Money.'

Having conscientiously studied John's peculiar susceptibilities, he soon mentioned how his mother had died when he was small and he and his sister had spent a miserable time in Newark's austere Hebrew Orphans Shelter. He also took care to show the same respect for Yoko's conceptual art as for Beatles music. There and then, John scribbled a note to EMI's chairman, Sir Joseph Lockwood: 'Dear Sir Joe, from now on Allen Klein handles all my stuff.'

It was the grossest breach of the Beatles' one-for-all-and-all-for-one spirit; moreover, technically speaking, Klein was too late for Paul had already found a manager candidate, seemingly acceptable to them all. This was his fiancée Linda Eastman's father, Lee, a New York entertainment lawyer whose firm, Eastman & Eastman, handled an impressive range of American musician clients from the 1940s swing legend Tommy Dorsey to the super-contemporary rock band Chicago.

At the end of 1968, Paul had persuaded the others to appoint Eastman & Eastman general counsel to Apple, a role tacitly expected to enlarge to their management. Seemingly in confirmation, Linda's twenty-eight-year-old brother, John, who'd lately joined Lee in the firm, was now based at 3 Savile Row.

The first repercussions from John's unilateral appointment of Klein mostly passed George by. Ever the most sickness-prone Beatle, he was suffering from acute tonsilitis and underwent a tonsillectomy on 7 February at London's University College

Hospital, where Ringo had undergone the same procedure four years earlier. His hospitalisation for several days in medically prescribed silence was an opportunity for further concentrated meditating, only slightly disrupted by the hair appointment Derek Taylor arranged for him.

Once he'd got his voice back, he met both John's and Paul's nominees to become his manager. As Ringo had already been, George was won over by Klein's 'straight' talk and the prospect of being able to say, 'Fuck You, Money'. On the other hand, the urbane and sophisticated Lee Eastman reawoke an old inferiority complex, seeming to him an archetypal snobby New York WASP (though in fact Eastman came from poor Jewish immigrant stock and, by a bizarre coincidence, had been born with the surname of Epstein).

The majority vote for Klein held, despite Paul's protests and vows to have nothing to do with him, based on the damning evidence gathered by the Eastmans. In New York, he was currently involved in some fifty lawsuits and recently had had dealings in his ABKO company suspended on the New York Stock Exchange and been investigated by its watchdog, the Securities and Exchange Commission, following allegations of dodgy share-dealing.

Rather than prejudicing his annexation of the Beatles, all this and more was dismissed by John as malicious gossip stirred up by the losers in the race for the ultimate managerial prize. Both he and George even derived a perverse thrill from the idea of Klein as a real-life criminal, possibly even with connections to the Mafia. George was also irrelevantly amused by his resemblance to Barney Rubble in *The Flintstones*.

*

The conflict inside the Beatles as yet was nothing to that in Cream, where George's now best friend Eric Clapton was caught between two colleagues, drummer Ginger Baker and bass-player/vocalist Jack Bruce, whose mutual loathing had led each to try to kill the other in mid-performance – and keep trying.

By the time of Cream's breakup in November 1968, the trio couldn't be in a room together long enough to do a cover photograph for their *Goodbye Cream* album. Instead, their heads were superimposed on different bodies in silver tail suits, flourishing matching top hats in a jovial Busby Berkeley-style finale.

With them had gone another potential outlet for George's songs, for he'd recently written one entitled 'Badge' as a rare lead vocal for Clapton. It had nothing to with badges; Clapton had misread the place on the lyric sheet where George had written 'bridge'.

Unable to live without a band any more than with one, Clapton had immediately started Blind Faith, the seeming last word in supergroups, with Ginger Baker, Stevie Winwood from the Spencer Davis Group and Traffic, and Rick Grech from Family, moving George to new envy of his ability to travel through the musical dimensions leaving no boot-print behind.

At around the same time, Clapton had learned he was next on the hit-list of the Drug Squad's witchfinder general, Detective Sergeant Norman Pilcher, and had fled from his King's Road flat-share only minutes ahead of Pilcher's arrival without bothering to warn his two flatmates about it. Deciding he would be safer as far as possible from Central London, he'd bought an Italianate country mansion named Hurtwood Edge in Ewhurst, Surrey, just eight miles from George in Esher.

His next girlfriend represented a far greater social leap than

George had taken by marrying Pattie. She was the Honourable Alice Magdalen Sarah Ormsby-Gore, daughter of the fifth Baron Harlech, a former British Ambassador in Washington. That she had only just turned sixteen and was still a virgin while he was twenty-four and steeped in drugs, alcohol and groupie sex, in those days excited no adverse comment whatsoever.

Now as good as neighbours, George and Clapton took to spending long hours at each other's houses, usually closeted with their guitars but Clapton, his super-posh, super-young love notwithstanding, still secretly smitten by his best friend's wife.

Detective Sergeant Pilcher's failure to collar Clapton had only spurred him on to larger quarry. On 12 March – the day Paul McCartney married Linda Eastman by civil ceremony in London, to the anguish of young women around the world – Pattie Harrison opened the front door of 'Kinfauns' to find Sergeant Pilcher with the same heavy back-up he'd used to bust John and Yoko five months earlier.

After an enthusiastic search with a sniffer dog, a lump of hashish was allegedly found in one of George's shoes, although the house's supply was always kept in a pot in the sitting room. A surreal touch was added by the dog's name being Yogi, in this case not referencing an Indian holy man but the picnic-pilfering bear in the Hanna-Barbera cartoon.

Tellingly, none of the other Beatles was to attend Paul's wedding and Pattie telephoned the bad news to George at the Apple recording studio. When he got home, accompanied by Derek Taylor and a lawyer, the raiders were sitting around, drinking tea – made by the one female member of the team as Pattie refused to do it – and the younger ones trying to pump her about his next record.

That evening, rather than Paul's wedding reception, George and Pattie had been invited to a 'Pisces party' given by the painter Rory McEwan. After Pilcher had charged them both with drug-possession and they'd been fingerprinted by the local police (who'd never given a thought to raiding them), they decided they'd still go to the party, taking along Pattie's 18-year-old youngest sister, Paula.

Their fellow guests included those staunch attendees at Beatles film premieres, Princess Margaret and Lord Snowdon, and George took Snowdon to one side, hoping he might be able to pull some strings over the drugs bust. Just then, Pattie caught sight of Paula handing the chain-smoking princess a freshly lit joint. Fearful that Sergeant Pilcher might still be in the vicinity, Pattie managed to warn her that it was a different kind of cigarette, and the royal couple made a hasty exit.

Even in this unfamiliar notoriety, George was to experience all-too-familiar inequality. On the day he and Pattie were arraigned and made bail at Walton and Esher magistrates court, the immeasurably bigger news story was John and Yoko's spur-of-the-moment marriage in the quaintly British colonial setting of the Rock of Gibraltar.

From there the newlyweds flew to Amsterdam for a week-long 'honeymoon' in bed at the Hilton hotel to which the world's media had been invited, expecting to watch them have sex, but which proved to be part-performance art event, part-anti-war seminar. The resultant howls of disappointment and derision almost equalled the shrieks of Beatlemania six years earlier. Three decades would have to pass before Tracey Emin turned her unmade bed into an installation shortlisted for the Turner Prize and later sold for £2.5 million.

On 31 March, George and Pattie pleaded guilty to possessing cannabis, having realised the futility of challenging Sergeant Pilcher's 'evidence', and were fined £250 each with 20 guineas (£21) costs. Again, the same day brought an infinitely more newsworthy John and Yoko spectacle: ending their Amsterdam Bed-In, they flew to Vienna for the television premiere of their film *Rape*, a satire on intrusive media, where they talked to reporters while crouching together inside a white sack.

Like John before him, George's conviction meant having to return his passport to the American Embassy in London for a permanent notation that he'd committed what the American government called 'a crime of moral turpitude'. In years to come, even when his prestige in the country stood at its highest, this would still cause delay and earn him hostile looks at the US border.

The Apple rooftop performance intended to crown the Beatles' self-reinvention had instead brought it to an ignominious halt. Afterwards, they had abandoned *Get Back* – the first of their albums ever to suffer such a fate – leaving George Martin and Glyn Johns to make whatever they could of it.

The two had combined their formidable skills to weed out the many good things among that vast slush-pile and put together the requisite 'honest' production, free of all editing or overdubbing. But only Paul had shown any glimmer of approval and neither John nor George could now bear even to hear its name. Apple Films were therefore at a loss over what to do with the mass of equally honest film footage Michael Lindsay-Hogg had shot for the accompanying television documentary.

Martin had thought his career with the Beatles was over, nor was he altogether sorry, but only three weeks after *Get Back*'s final death-throes he received a visit from a contrite Paul, asking him to 'Come back and make an album with us the way we used to do it.'

He responded with a touch of his old headmasterly strictness. 'I said, "If the album's going to be the way we used to do it, then all of you have got to be the way you used to be."'

And, extraordinarily, it happened. During that spring and early summer of 1969, their internecine conflict over Allen Klein was put on hold, the boredom with each other that had hung over *Get Back* evaporated, rampant individual egos took a step back and the group mind made one final, glorious appearance. The intimacy and spontaneity vainly sought in their own recording studio came surging again at Abbey Road, their old home, whose institutional corridors, canteen and washrooms had fitted as comfortably as an old tweed jacket.

It didn't mean starting completely from scratch since much of the content had been developed during the *Get Back* sessions. Paul's atypically sick 'Maxwell's Silver Hammer' was part of the session when George and he had their on-camera falling out. Ringo's contribution, a children's song called 'Octopus's Garden', had been finished off at the same time with help from George (on piano) over its chord structure.

It happened, too, that Lennon and McCartney's offerings mainly consisted of small fragments, individually brilliant but collectively rather like the spillage of an odd-sock drawer. This allowed George's songwriting to shine as never before on two tracks as close as he would ever come to direct autobiography, one as close as he would to genius.

'Here Comes The Sun' was the product of a day in Eric

Clapton's garden at Hurtwood Edge when they'd walked round together with their guitars – Clapton slightly self-consciously – and George had seemed to feel a 'long, cold, lonely winter' of inter-Beatle strife melting in the sunlight through the trees, even some hope of 'smiles returning to their faces'. His down-spiralling guitar leitmotif, a distant descendant of Buddy Holly's in 'That'll Be The Day', would be widely considered the most elegant he ever played.

And now at last, having been left off both the White Album and *Get Back*, came the placement of 'Something'. George had written it about Pattie during a time in their marriage when she'd had little to fear from 'concubines', although even then he'd informed her she was his muse as matter-of-factly as if saying 'We're out of detergent.' Until recently, he still hadn't completed the first line after 'Something in the way she moves' and had been singing 'attracts me like a pomegranate'.

It was like nothing he'd written before, nor that either John or Paul ever had, a love song with the brevity and mystery of a Japanese haiku, rather typically not naming the 'she' who had won his adoration and saying more between the lines than was in them. His voice was in a passionate register never previously heard, not even in Indian contexts, his softly burbling guitar its perfect proxy.

'Something' would be his first song released as the A-side of a Beatles single, topping the charts in Britain, America and around the world and winning a Novello Award as the best song, 'musically and lyrically', of 1969. Over time, it would become the second most-covered Beatles track (after Paul's 'Yesterday') and be ranked the twentieth century's seventeenth-most-performed song, inspiring some 150 versions by, among others, Frank Sinatra, Elvis Presley, Ray Charles. James Brown, Smokey Robinson, Lena Horne and Shirley Bassey. Sinatra, that former rabid Beatlephobe, called it 'the greatest love song of the twentieth century – though he mistakenly attributed it to Lennon and McCartney.

Despite the Beatles' immaculate behaviour throughout, the album wasn't quite 'the way we used to do it'. In one of the several extended breaks between sessions, John took Yoko on a trip around the Scottish Highlands, where he'd spent childhood holidays, and put their rental car into a ditch. Yoko suffered a back injury that needed complete bed-rest, so he had a bed from Harrods delivered to the studio, allowing her still to be at the recordings in a prone position and comment on them through a microphone rigged above her.

Only now there were no SOS calls for Eric Clapton or Billy Preston; once more, no need of anybody but that essential four with their indispensable producer. They had once been closer than brothers, closer than lovers, close enough to share body-heat that night in the back of a freezing van when they'd kept hypothermia at bay by lying in a pile like penguins, taking turns to be the warm one at the bottom. Yet in the intricately layered vocals of 'Because' and 'Sun King', they seemed closest of all. As George said, to general agreement, it felt good to be 'performing like musicians again'.

But in early August, when time came to package the album, terminal ennui returned. Since it had no obvious theme, it was named after the leafy road where EMI's studios had always seemed so incongruous. And for a cover photograph, the Beatles bestirred themselves no further than for their rooftop concert, in the same 'fuck it' spirit walking single file over the zebra crossing a few yards from EMI's front entrance – little dreaming how reverently both 'fuck its' would be copied by other bands for evermore.

17

'THAT WAS MINXY OF GEORGE. HE COULD BE VERY MINXY'

George's involvement with Apple increased during that summer of 1969 as its hippie idealism vanished from 3 Savile Row pip by pip, to be replaced by greasy hair and malodorous pipe-smoke.

Nothing could persuade Paul to accept Allen Klein as the Beatles' manager in place of his new father-in-law, the New York entertainment lawyer Lee Eastman. In May, when the other three had signed Klein's management contract, the only protest left to him was to walk away from the business he'd done the most to establish.

Since then, John had given numerous interviews in praise of Klein and waxing optimistic about Apple's future in a slimmed-down, efficient form. His old wit still lurking under his Old Testament beard, he said, 'The circus has left town, but we still own the site.'

Only, so far as the media were concerned, the circus named not Barnum & Bailey but John and Yoko continued to pull in the crowds with their demonstrations of 'Bag-ism' or 'total communication', performing and giving press conferences crouched together inside a sack; incinerating naked plastic dolls with napalm in the King's Road as a protest against the Vietnam War; or screening their latest film collaboration, *Self-Portrait*, a forty-two-minute study of John's partially erect penis.

While still a titular Beatle, John had formed an alternative group with Yoko called the Plastic Ono Band, flaunting the name that enraged so many people and flouting the Fab Four convention of a fixed, unchangeable line-up: any number of musicians could belong on an ad-hoc basis and its only permanent feature was a quartet of mute Perspex robots.

At 3 Savile Row, the couple occupied a ground-floor office with hand-lettered placards saying BED PEACE and HAIR PIECE taped to its elegant panelling, a Plastic Ono Band robot in one corner and a naked plastic doll that had survived the King's Road napalm event, upside-down in the fireplace.

Sharing the same executive-sized desk, eating brown rice from a wooden bowl or Beluga caviar from nearby Fortnum & Mason at £60 per pot, they combined media interviews about their newest exploit with a kind of walk-in clinic for all the world's wrongs. A constant stream of visitors came seeking their support for humanitarian causes from the persecution of Europe's Romany communities to the exploitation of Hispanic workers in Californian vineyards to the campaign to prove the innocence of James Hanratty, one of the last men to be hanged for murder in Britain. No one was ever refused a hearing and almost no one left empty-handed.

In May their second album together, *Unfinished Music No. 2: Life With The Lions* was released on Apple's avant-garde label, Zapple, this one without their genitalia on the cover but arousing little less scorn and derision than its predecessor. Virtually unnoticed on Zapple that same month was George's second solo album, *Electronic Sound*, like *Wonderwall Music* a solely instrumental work in which he played two lengthy pieces on the newfangled Moog Synthesizer. It was still a highly specialised instrument but, with his usual determination, he'd got the hang of one in time for the Beatles to use on *Abbey Road*.

With Paul no longer around, John and Yoko deep in multimedia conceptual art and Ringo reluctant to leave Maureen and their two young sons in Weybridge, George was often the last one doing Beatly things around the Apple house. An August morning that summer, for instance, found him at a photo session in its attic studio with the German magazine *Bravo*. In deference to his Indian interests, an elaborate bower of yellow and orange flowers had been assembled; then an elderly workman staggered in with a cardboard box containing an eight-armed Hindu deity still in pieces, which he and the photographer gamely began trying to assemble.

Even George was impressed by the preparations. 'If I'd known it was going to be like this,' he said, 'I'd have washed me hair.' He decided his denim top wouldn't do for *Bravo* and sent his assistant, Terry Doran, to the nearby Mr Fish boutique to buy two shirts for him to choose from.

In this mellow mood, he could be philosophical about the way Apple had turned out or, rather, hadn't. 'It was like a game of Chinese whispers really. We said one thing, it was passed around a lot of other people and what came back to us wasn't anything like we'd meant.'

Lee Eastman's son John having left with Paul to become his personal lawyer, Klein now had absolute control, flying over from New York for several days each week. Since business then was still mainly conducted on paper, he brought all his filing cabinets with him each time for fear of sudden raids by US fiscal authorities during his absence. Even in the few steps from his limo to number 3's front door, he'd be poring over a balance-sheet, oblivious to the shouts of 'Mafia!' from the George-baptised 'Apple Scruffs' perpetually stationed there.

Klein's consuming priority was to rid Apple of the free-loaders and con-artists held chiefly responsible for its financial plight, Since the three remaining Beatles seldom questioned his judgements (any more than Henry VIII used to challenge his wives' death warrants), this was a perfect opportunity to get rid of anyone close to them who might threaten his own position, regardless of their value to the company.

Indeed, his earliest victims included the two executives who presided over its one profitable division. Ron Kass, the newly hired American boss of Apple Records, was let go with a hefty payoff, giving over his office to John, Yoko, the Plastic Ono Band robot and the upside-down doll, while Peter Asher, the spectacularly successful head of A&R, jumped before he could be pushed, taking with him the label's main asset after the Beatles, singer/songwriter James Taylor. As a result, George had the scope to find new talent and produce, until now limited by what he'd regarded as a Paul clique.

Billy Preston, that civilising influence on the *Get Back* sessions, had already signed with Apple and George produced his first album for the label, *That's The Way God Planned It*, with celebrity backing musicians including Eric Clapton and Ginger Baker, now of Blind Faith, and Keith Richards of the Rolling Stones. The single of the same name, a spiritual as sweet as its singer/composer, was an international hit, reaching number 11 in Britain.

Among Preston's backing chorus was the American singer/ songwriter Doris Troy, who'd recently moved to London after a long fallow period since her biggest hit, 'Just One Look'. Just one listen was enough for George to offer her a contract with Apple Records both as a performer and writer. She was given her own office at 3 Savile Row with a piano to compose on: the most significant example of Apple keeping that promise to nurture talent.

His next Apple signing literally came off the street or, to be precise, Oxford Street. A year earlier, the San Francisco-based Radha Krishna Temple, a Hindu/Christian sect dedicated to dancing and singing, had sent six converts to start a branch in London. Their success was demonstrated by the salmon-robed, shaven-headed troupe daily to be seen progressing locomotive-style up and down London's busiest shopping thoroughfare, ringing little bells and chanting the mantra 'Hare Krishna hare Rama' or praise be to Krishna and Rama.

Selecting the troupe's more tuneful members, George produced an arrangement of its mantra during breaks from recording *Abbey Road*, with himself on harmonium, guitar and bass. The unworldly, sandalled chanters received a full publicity build-up from Apple Records and in August found themselves in the British Top 20 and appearing on the BBC's *Top Of The Pops* show. 'Hare Krishna' became a catchphrase throughout 3 Savile Row, weirdly counterpointing the fear and insecurity being generated by Allen Klein.

On 20 July humankind had finally succeeded in travelling to the Moon. Young people, however, seemed more preoccupied with getting as close as possible to Earth via a series of open-air rock festivals – not only free of charge but of any violence or criminality – that seemed to grow bigger each time.

On 7 June Eric Clapton's new supergroup Blind Faith had made their debut before a pacific crowd of 150,000 in London's Hyde Park. The following month, the Rolling Stones had picked the same location but this time attracted around 250,000 to what was in part a requiem for Brian Jones, their former lead guitarist who'd been found mysteriously dead in his swimming pool two days earlier.

Allen Klein had been with the Stones in Hyde Park, unaware of the plot they were hatching to get rid of him. They'd recently discovered that each of them owed vast sums in British income tax, which they'd assumed he'd been paying on their behalf, and could avoid bankruptcy only by becoming tax exiles in France. Mick Jagger and Keith Richards, a songwriting partnership almost as prolific as Lennon and McCartney's, had further learned he'd covertly acquired every one of their copyrights up to 1971.

Jagger, though normally no altruist, had called at 3 Savile Row to warn the Beatles about Klein, but lost his nerve when faced with them all around a boardroom table. What remains mysterious is why the far more fearless Richards didn't deliver the warning to George while they were working on Billy Preston's album.

Thunderous with alfresco guitars, a-sparkle with sunshine and acid, drenched in pot and joss, cheerfully roughing it under canvas with minimal catering or toilet facilities, frolicking naked in foam or mud, these festivals were the last dreamy hurrah of the hippies, the 'flower children', the 'gentle people'. But well before summer's end, the climate was already changing and the music, which above all had stood for innocent joy, was being appropriated for darker purposes.

Early in August, news of a horrific crime came from America's West Coast where the gentlest people were supposedly found. The film actress Sharon Tate, pregnant wife of the Polish director Roman Polanski, and six friends had been hacked to death at Tate's rented home in Benedict Canyon, Los Angeles.

The perpetrators were followers of a runtish thirty-four-year-old with a record of petty crime and incarceration named Charles Manson. Frustrated in his ambition to be a pop singer/songwriter, he had started a hippie-style 'family' of urban terrorists, guided, as he claimed, by the New Testament's Book of Revelation and Beatles songs on the White Album.

Paul's raucous 'Helter-Skelter', titled after a harmless fairground ride, was Manson's codename for the murder rampage to which Sharon Tate and her friends first fell victim. And George's jokey 'Piggies' gave it added barbarity, spurred by the line his mother Louise had suggested: 'What they need's a damn good whacking.'

The night after the Tate massacre, Manson's family – mostly consisting of middle-class young women – struck at random a second time, butchering a supermarket executive named Leno LaBianca and his wife Rosemary at their home in a different part of town. 'Political Piggies' and 'Death To Pigs' was written on the walls in the victims' blood and they were stabbed with their own cutlery in a seeming re-enactment of 'clutching forks and knives to eat their bacon'.

The Beatles, who all knew Tate's husband, Roman Polanski, were sickened by the crimes and appalled to be thus linked with them. George felt additional dismay that Manson 'portrayed the long hair and beard kind of image as well as that of a murderer ... Everyone attaches themselves to us whether it's our fault or not.'

On 22 August, the four posed for what would be their last-ever-group photograph, in the grounds of Tittenhurst Park, John's newly purchased stately home near Ascot. 'George was miserable from frame one to 500,' the photographer, Ethan Russell, would observe. 'I don't think he did anything but scowl for three hours.'

That was the point at which Paul effectively disappeared from the line-up. Very different was the atmosphere between the others a week later when Britain's biggest rock festival yet took place, of all places, on the sleepy Isle of Wight headlined by, of all people, Bob Dylan.

Dylan's first live performance since his motorcycle accident had been expected to be at America's recent Woodstock festival, when a 500,000-strong crowd gathered in a muddy cow pasture almost in his backyard (and the Beatles turned down an invitation to appear for any fee they cared to name). Instead, the Isle of Wight event's promoters, two young brothers named Ronnie and Ray Foulk, diverted him 3,500 miles by telling him that one of his favourite poets, Alfred Lord Tennyson, used to live on the island.

Tennyson or not, Dylan had last-minute doubts about the journey. 'He asked George whether he should come and George said yes, he should,' Pattie recalls. 'The festival came that close to losing him.'

George and Pattie were not just to watch Dylan close the festival on 31 August but they were to spend the preceding couple of days with him, his wife Sara, and The Band at their secluded quarters, Forelands Farm, near Bembridge. 'We thought it was a good idea for Dylan to have a friend there,' Ray Foulk recounts. 'I remember walking through the sitting-room and he and George were sitting on a sofa with their guitars, singing the Everly Brothers' "Dream." It was incredibly charming.'

George's arrival proved timely, for Dylan had forgotten to pack a harmonica. A call was made to Apple and a trusted aide, Chris O'Dell, dispatched to the island by helicopter with a couple of the crucial silver bars. John and Ringo had promised to follow later; Paul's absence was explained by the recent birth of his first child with Linda.

George's reunion with the five equally charming and admiring members of The Band was balm for the inferiority he still felt, despite his recent songwriting breakthrough. 'He'd brought an acetate of *Abbey Road* with him, and played it to the other guys as they sat around the swimming- pool,' Ray Foulk recalls. 'He was going on about how hard-done-by he felt because of only having two songs on the album. Even two songs like "Here Comes The Sun" and "Something".'

John and Ringo with their respective spouses didn't show until the festival's final day, arriving by separate helicopters. Ringo and Maureen's landed in the field adjoining Forelands Farm, but John and Yoko's in its garden. 'The wind from the blades decapitated every flower in sight,' Foulk says. 'I remember thinking they were too grand just to land in a field.

'John, Ringo and George immediately went into a huddle. "Excuse us for talking shop," John called out to me, "but we don't see one another very often."'

The chilly photo session with Paul at Tittenhurst Park eight days earlier clearly hadn't counted as actually seeing each other. Indeed, the festival atmosphere and sea air, seemed to turn George and Dylan back into schoolboys, for they both kicked off their shoes and started playing a hilarious game of tennis on the lawn.

It's hard not to feel a twinge of pity for Allen Klein at this point. After years of coveting the Beatles, he'd finally got them into his net only to discover their breakup wasn't just inevitable but well underway.

Their contract with their American record label, Capitol, was about to expire and in renegotiating it Klein planned to demand a colossally increased royalty that would change even Paul's opinion of him. If news of their disintegrating state were to leak out, it could capsize this biggest deal of his career – for in 1969 no one conceived that a band could go on selling records after ceasing to exist.

Beatles fans had felt growing anxiety about its future ever since John took up with Yoko, Paul's marriage to Linda and the Klein takeover. They would have felt still more had they known that Paul hadn't just disappeared from Apple but from London, and was sequestered with his new family on his small farm in the remote Scottish Highlands of whose existence the media were still unaware.

Nor was this once supremely self-assured Beatle merely sulking like Achilles in his tent: his outvoting and marginalisation by the others had simultaneously brought on an emotional collapse and incipient alcoholism.

It was this long, uncharacteristic invisibility that ignited the 'Paul is dead' rumour. Planted by a college students' newspaper in Des Moines, Iowa, it went viral two decades before there was an internet, evolving into pop's most famous conspiracy theory. Not just dead but long dead: he was said to have been killed in a car crash in 1966 and impersonated ever since by an actor named William Campbell.

Almost as troubling to Klein was John's formation of another band implicitly as a substitute for the Beatles and his keenness to perform with it as he no longer would with them. Hence, early in September, he accepted an invitation to take the Plastic Ono Band to a one-day rock 'n' roll revival festival in Toronto even though it meant leaving at twenty-four hours' notice and the only rehearsal time would be on the flight.

Temporary sidemen were easily added to Yoko and the Perspex robots: Eric Clapton, John's old Hamburg friend Klaus Voormann on bass and session drummer Alan White. George had been John's first choice as lead guitarist but had turned him down despite the chance to share a stage with cherished rock 'n' roll idols like Chuck Berry, Little Richard and Bo Diddley. George suspected that, even so, the festival would have an 'avant-garde' element, and the disruption of getting away and the minimal rehearsing were equal deterrents.

He and Ringo happened to be in the Apple Press Office as Derek Taylor tried to arrange a North American entry visa for John, an uphill struggle thanks to his drug conviction, as it would have been for George, too. 'Do you fancy going to Australia to play?' he quipped sourly to Ringo. 'We get back yesterday.'

It was on the return flight from Toronto that John told the London *Evening Standard*'s Ray Connolly, ahead of any other Beatle or Klein, that he was leaving the Beatles, but

persuaded Connolly to sit on the story so as not to jeopard-
ise Klein's negotiations with Capitol. With George along,
it's safe to say, no such hostage to fortune would have been
taken.

Abbey Road was released on 26 September. 'They're together
just like they used to be,' Taylor told journalists on the telephone
dozens of times a day and 'Here Comes The Sun', above all,
encouraged that belief with its lines about ice slowly melting and
smiles returning to faces. Beatles albums usually became hits
amid high excitement but this one did amid massive (though
short-lived) relief, selling four million in its first two months,
spending a total of seventeen weeks at number one in the UK
and eleven straight in the US.

Its cover-image, the band's single-file march over a pedestrian
crossing, gave fresh ammunition to Paul-is-dead conspiracy-
theorists, for whom their visual 'fuck it' represented a funeral
procession with white-suited John as the minister, pinstriped
Ringo the undertaker, Paul marked as deceased by his bare feet
and blue-denimed George the gravedigger. In other words, the
only working man.

The album's undisputed showpiece track, 'Something', merited a video to itself, albeit not personified solely by Pattie, who
had inspired it but by the whole band and their wives in separate
vignettes: John and Yoko as twin black wraiths at Tittenhurst
Park, Ringo and Maureen riding motorcycles, Paul with Linda
under a faraway Scottish sky, clearly in better shape now and
romping with his Old English sheepdog.

Of the four couples, George and Pattie looked the least compatible, she with her corkscrew curls and floaty scarf, he with
shoulder-length hair and heavy beard like some nineteenth

century evangelist, as if deliberately blotting out all trace of the song's passion.

George's best friend was behaving very much in character. Having co-founded Blind Faith, the last two words in super-groups, Eric Clapton had wearied of the surrounding ballyhoo and hype, and now hankered to be a mere backing guitarist for people he seriously thought more gifted than himself.

On Blind Faith's only American tour, they'd been supported by the husband-and-wife country-blues duo Delaney and Bonnie Bramlett. Captivated by the Bramletts' downhome acoustic style, Clapton had spent as much time 'picking' with them and their backing band – modestly styled 'and Friends' – as with his own multimillion-dollar one.

That was the end of Blind Faith and in December, Clapton brought Delaney & Bonnie and Friends to Britain on tour, with himself an incognito member of the line-up. On its northern leg, there was a second unbilled extra guitarist in a black Stetson hat and fringed buckskin jacket who played only chords and onstage kept so far to the rear that most audiences never realised who he was.

George had attended the opening concert at the Royal Albert Hall in hopes of signing the Bramletts to Apple. But back-stage he'd suddenly offered to join them on the road, 'unless you have too many guitars'. It was a surprising offer from one who'd loathed the Beatles' tours with such a passion and lobbied Brian so insistently to end them. Now, after the strife among the Beatles and the pressures at 3 Savile Row, the idea seemed positively therapeutic.

George still had no inkling of Clapton's infatuation with

Pattie any more than did she herself. There was little reason to suspect it since he'd recently become engaged to his seventeen-year-old girlfriend, the Hon. Alice Ormsby-Gore, thereby creating a perfect snapshot of the Sixties' tumbling class-barriers.

Clapton could only look on and long as every echo of 'Something' in the Harrisons' marriage was chased away by George's coldness, obsessive meditating and increasingly blatant infidelities. In the words of the love songs to Pattie he too would write, he 'tried to give [her] consolation' with the attention she no longer received from her husband if only on a social level, like compliments about her clothes or cooking.

But joining Delaney & Bonnie and Friends was a boys' jaunt when Clapton's guilt about wanting Pattie could be paused. And George entered fully into the spirit of it, travelling on a tour bus for the first time since early Beatlemania, standing in line in motorway cafeterias, searching for things that didn't contain meat. If not onstage, he was instantly recognised in such places and besieged with paper napkins to autograph while Clapton was – happily – ignored. If anyone asked who *he* was, he replied 'Just a hanger-on.'

The atmosphere was relentlessly juvenile, with black-bearded Delaney Bramlett the ringleader. In Leeds, the whole band bought little wind-up figures in the shapes of fruit with which they held races on the floor of their communal dressing room and sent toddling across the stage to distract their warm-up act, Ashton, Gardner and Dyke. At their succession of grand hotels, the lavish cold buffets provided for them after the show were destroyed by food fights worthy of the Marx Brothers. There was even a little mild vandalism, as if to make the experience thoroughly authentic for George, although the

Beatles on their most punitive tours had never given way to such behaviour.

It wasn't all so carefree: Bramlett turned out to be ferociously envious of his golden-haired, angel-faced, smoky-voiced wife and frequently assaulted her in front of the whole company, some shows – the Albert Hall among them – having to be postponed until her bruises went down. Violence against women was considered a male prerogative in those times, in downhome rock circles especially, and George, who'd never felt the least such impulse, could only watch and wince.

Before going onstage one night, Clapton swept all his hair back with water into a 1950s cowlick, the others followed suit and they inserted a run of the old rock 'n' roll classics George had missed playing in Toronto. By their end, the cautious beard under the black Stetson wore a broad smile. 'I'd forgotten what a trip live playing could be,' he said. 'That Little Richard medley is in E, isn't it?'

Pattie had seen the show without George at the Albert Hall and thought that would be the end of it. But when it reached the Liverpool Empire – that storehouse of Beatle memories – he invited her to come up and see it again, this time accompanied by her eighteen-year-old sister, Paula.

As the baby of the Boyd family, Paula had received the affection withheld from her three older siblings by their mother, Diana, and escaped the physical abuse inflicted on them by their stepfather. Consequently, while just as beautiful as Jenny and Pattie – whom she resembled the more – she had none of their insecurity and self-restraint.

Insufficiently tall to follow them into modelling, she had gone to drama school and afterwards landed a couple of parts in children's televison series. What she really wanted was the racy rock 'n' roll lifestyle they both now had, for Jenny's boyfriend and later two-time husband was Fleetwood Mac's co-founder and drummer, Mick Fleetwood.

George had already shown more than a brother-in-law's interest in Paula, not caring if Pattie noticed – indeed, positively flaunting it With the Krishna-like rights he felt to any female, and in a spirit of competitiveness with Clapton's seventeen-year-old Hon. Alice, he laid plans to seduce Paula after the Liverpool Empire show.

The problem of Pattie's presence was dealt with by offering her to Clapton for the night as casually as he might lend a guitar, still totally unaware of Clapton's feelings for her. Then at the last minute his innate caution got the better of him and it was Clapton who ended up spending the night with Paula, fantasising that she was her big sister.

Pattie herself never knew of the stratagem at the time and now smiles forgivingly. 'That was minxy of George. He could be very minxy.'

18

'BEATLE GEORGE'S NEW PAD – TURRETS AND ALL'

When George was still taking LSD, but Pattie no longer partici-pated, he'd sometimes go into the park next to their psychedelic bungalow and take a solitary trip, sitting under a tree. The park belonged to Esher's Claremont Estate and was part of an expen-sive private school. One evening, he was spotted by an elderly caretaker while locking its gates, not recognised as one of the world's four most famous faces and rudely ordered to leave.

The incident killed what little fondness he still felt for 'Kinfauns'; in any case, Esher's commuter-belt atmosphere had begun to oppress him and he now hankered after something more on the lines of Hurtwood Edge, Eric Clapton's Tuscan-style mansion hidden away in Surrey woodland.

For the best part of a year, Pattie drove all over southern England viewing likely properties. George would sometimes go along but her usual companion was Terry Doran, the personal assistant he'd taken over from John after Yoko's arrival.

Curly-haired, affable Doran was a former Liverpool car salesman who'd supplied George's first-ever set of wheels, that cherished pale blue Ford Anglia, and later partnered Brian in a short-lived luxury-car dealership, giving rise to the (mistaken) belief that he was the 'man from the motor trade' mentioned in Paul's *Sgt. Pepper* song 'She's Leaving Home'.

The only guideline from George was that he wanted 'his own park' where he'd be safe from officious caretakers. However, in the upper reaches of Britain's property market the word park took a capital P and signified more than tracts of grass and trees. With them almost invariably came the 'big mansion house' of which he'd once dared to daydream while living in a tiny one without an indoor toilet.

In this world of underplayed grandeur, a 'Place' ranked with a 'Park' and George nearly became the owner of Plumpton Place in East Sussex, a moated Elizabethan manor house with gardens laid out by Sir Edwin Lutyens, the architect of New Delhi, and the great Victorian landscaper Gertrude Jekyll. Then at the last minute, its female owner jibbed at handing it over to a rock musician (though nothing could halt the rise of landed-gentleman guitar gods; it was later bought by Jimmy Page of Led Zeppelin).

Finally, in genteel Henley-on-Thames in upmarket Oxfordshire, close to the annual scene of Britain's most class-ridden regatta, the house-hunters came upon Friar Park.

The late nineteenth-century passion for Gothic-style architecture had produced many fanciful creations but few to compare with this terracotta-and-white jostle of spires, turrets, pinnacles, cathedral-size windows, pointed arches and grimacing gargoyles. Despite the eccentricity and excess in almost every stone, no Liverpudlian could look on Friar Park without a pinch of déjà vu: it was as if the Picton Clock, just around the corner from George's childhood home in Wavertree, had migrated 200 miles south and given birth to an enormous, clamorous litter.

It had been built in the 1890s by a wealthy London solicitor named Sir Frank Crisp, whose many passions included horticulture, collecting microscopes, world travel and the study of medieval England. What Sir Frank intended merely as a weekend retreat had twenty-five bedrooms, a library and a blue, white and gold ballroom with cherubim cavorting on the ceiling and stained-glass windows designed by the Pre-Raphaelite painter Edward Burne-Jones. Dominating its entrance-hall/reception area was a fireplace twenty feet high and an immense curving staircase to a minstrel's gallery. Its gatekeeper's lodge was large and ornate enough to be mistaken for the main house and there were two more outlying lodges for guest accommodation.

Its name derived from the monastery on whose site it reputedly stood and the wandering holy men in medieval times whose tonsured hair somewhat resembled a Beatle cut. The friar motif was everywhere, in paintings and tapestries and carved on wood and stone with faux medieval inscriptions. Even the brass light-switches were friars' faces, operated by tweaking their noses.

The grounds, extending over some sixty-five acres, were a theme park a century too early, with a Japanese garden, an Elizabethan garden, a rhododendron garden, an Alpine rock garden, innumerable bushes sculpted into animal or bird shapes, and a maze. In surreal proximity to each other were a miniature but still climbable version of the Matterhorn, constructed from 20,000 tons of Yorkshire granite, and a replica of Capri's Blue Grotto.

Sir Frank Crisp had generously thrown his creation open to

the public and reminders of his quirky humour and Disneyesque showmanship were all around. House and grounds were connected by a warren of tunnels and caves, one filled with plaster gnomes, another with model skeletons, another containing fairground distorting mirrors, another a wishing-well. The lake had stepping-stones set just below its surface so that visitors could enjoy the Christ-like sensation of walking on water. Reversing the usual strict stately-home protocol, there were signs reading: 'Please *Don't* Keep Off The Grass.'

Sir Frank had died in 1919, with no family members interested in preserving it, and Friar Park had fallen on progressively harder times, its wonders and oddities forgotten except by ageing Henley locals. Latterly, that Gothic explosion of a house had belonged to the Salesian Sisters, a teaching order of nuns who'd turned it into a school, but by the time George and Pattie came for a viewing, its only remaining occupants were four nuns and a monk. It was in appalling disrepair, outside and in, and the Sisters had allowed local building firms to use its garden and lake as a rubbish dump. If no buyer could be found, it was to be demolished.

George was instantly captivated by a verse etched into a garden wall, commemorating Sir Frank Crisp's subsidiary passion for microscopes: 'Scan not a friend with a microscopic glass/you know his faults so let his foibles pass.' 'He felt as if Sir Frank was speaking directly to him,' Pattie recalls. 'Telling him not to feel resentful towards the other Beatles.'

His first thought was to turn the house into 'a religious institution' of some Indian kind. On reflection, misgivings set in 'that I was going beyond my means completely and karmically, the way only I could have done.' Brian almost certainly wouldn't have approved, but it gave Allen Klein the opportunity to suck up to a Beatle of whose support he wasn't completely sure.

Klein therefore made the funds available for him to offer £140,000, around £1.75 million in today's money and £20,000 more than the asking price. 'Beatle George's new pad – turrets and all,' was the *Daily Mail*'s headline over murky newsprint images of the implausible skyline.

He and Pattie moved in in March 1970, just after his twenty-seventh birthday, together with the indispensable Terry Doran. As no bedrooms were usable yet, the three had to make do with sleeping bags in the front hall, warmed by crackling logs in its twenty-foot-high fireplace.

One night, in a horrible portent of things to come, Pattie heard a noise from above and ran up the grand staircase to find a man climbing in through a second-floor window. But at her shout of 'Burglar!' – unlike the future intruder – he hastily retreated.

As a small boy, George had had a feeling for architecture long before any for music, and now he set about restoring Friar Park to its Victorian pomp, aided by the maps and blueprints from its construction that Sir Frank had thoughtfully left in the library.

It was a delicate as well as costly process, ultimately taking four and a half years, to preserve the house's myriad curiosities while turning it into a fitting rock-star home and a centre for his music. Most importantly, the redevelopment was to include a professional recording studio in which to pursue his parallel career as a producer and to free him from the sometimes oppressive bureaucracy of EMI at Abbey Road.

His family had enjoyed the luxury of both a front and back garden after moving from Wavertree to Speke and his father made a great success of them, producing impressive crops of both vegetables and flowers. He'd been used to helping Harold with the planting and picking and come to like the feeling of earth under his fingernails.

Still, his ownership of Friar Park's gardens felt like taking the helm of the *Titanic* after a few turns in a rowing skiff. There were acres of lawn to be tended and flowerbeds to be coaxed back into bloom; hundreds of exotic plants and shrubs that Sir Frank had brought home from his foreign travels, each one with its own special needs; menageries of topiary to be clipped; avenues of hothouses full of grape vines or orchids to be superintended.

The vexed question of where to start was answered one day when he and Terry Doran saw a solitary magnolia flower, 'growing off a tree, battling its way through the weeds, brambles and undergrowth,' as he would recall, 'so Terry and I set about clearing around [it] to let it breathe.'

The eminent horticulturalist Beth Chatto was hired to identify and prescribe treatment for the rarest or most sensitive plants and George's former gardener at 'Kinfauns', Maurice Milbourne, followed him to Henley, soon heading a ground staff numbering around eight, the equal of any conventional stately home like Chatsworth or Longleat.

George could be generous about big things – like buying Pattie's mother, Diana, a house – but as an employer he was less than munificent. It was a trait familiar to his childhood friend Tony Bramwell, at this point still working for Apple. 'His dad had never earned more than about ten quid a week as a bus driver. And George didn't see why he should pay anyone much more than that.'

Nevertheless, he inspired absolute loyalty from his ever-expanding staff, the gardeners especially. Nor was it solely due to the prestige that working for a Beatle afforded. In the garden there was nothing of the rock superstar about him, no prickliness but in the brambles they cleared together. He treated them as equals and was eager to learn everything they could teach him.

Pattie loved Friar Park as much as he did, and delighted in choosing luminous silks and glass-shaded Tiffany lamps to break up the Gothic gloaming and omnipresent friars' faces. This mutual passion for the place might have produced rock 'n' roll's answer to the writers Harold Nicolson and Vita Sackville-West, both of whose sexual strayings ceased to matter as they created their celebrated garden at Sissinghurst Castle in Kent.

But whenever some new phase of the improvement programme needed discussion, it wouldn't be Pattie he turned to but Terry Doran or Maurice Milbourne. 'At Kinfauns, though he'd bought it before I went to live there, I thought we'd had an equal partnership,' she recalls, 'but at Friar Park, I felt it was George's house and he made the decisions.'

The garden came in time to be a sanctuary from the Beatles' acrid final days together which George's minor role made no less of an ordeal.

Despite the great rip in the band, their usual relentless production cycle still churned on. A new album had to come out that spring and it would have to be *Get Back*, which they'd abandoned in January 1969, accompanied by Michael Lindsay-Hogg's film documentary of the same name, likewise in limbo ever since.

Two perfectly releasable versions of the album had been put

together by Glyn Johns, but John and George had rejected both and demanded a completely new approach. Paul, who'd broadly approved of them, was no longer around to voice an opinion.

It happened that John and George had recently worked with Phil Spector, the American producer whose thrilling Wall of Sound technique in the early Sixties, epitomised by the Ronettes' 'Be My Baby' and Ike and Tina Turner's 'River Deep-Mountain High', had caused the Beatles to throw many an uneasy glance over their shoulders.

Famously gangster-like and paranoid, Spector had faded from view after the demise of his Philles record label but had lately resurfaced to produce 'Instant Karma', John's first single with Yoko and the Plastic Ono Band on which George had finally been persuaded to play with them.

Wall of Sound meets Beatles had instant allure, so Spector was given the job of remixing *Get Back*. But the so-called Svengali of Pop was never likely to be content merely with that sonic teaspoon.

The two outstanding tracks on the album as it stood were Paul's, 'The Long And Winding Road' and 'Let It Be', the latter a phrase used by generations of Liverpool mothers to calm fractious children. Indeed, it was an almost hymn-like evocation of the 'Mother Mary' he had lost as a fourteen-year-old, whose spirit he believed to have comforted him during his troubled self-exile in Scotland.

As recorded, both had the simple voice-and-piano arrangement that had taken 'Hey Jude' into the stratosphere. This Spector turned into a Wall of Saccharine with an enormous orchestra containing eighteen violins and a sub-operatic female choir. Paul, who'd never had so much as a semiquaver altered by George Martin, was outraged – but outvoted yet again.

Since Klein fancied himself as a film producer, the documentary originally meant for television was upgraded to cinema length and, in an unintended compliment to Paul, both film and album were retitled *Let It Be.*

By now, three-quarters of the Beatles had declared their individuality while insisting less and less plausibly that it didn't stop them being Beatles. John had put out two singles and a live album from the Toronto festival plus three other offerings with Yoko; Paul had made a solo album at his London home with Linda his sole, and much more restful, collaborator; Ringo had recorded a selection of standards largely aimed at pleasing his mum in Liverpool.

George already had two solo instrumental albums to his credit and had talked vaguely about making his first vocal one as early as the *Get Back* sessions. But since then he'd seemed content to remain a producer for Apple, working with Doris Troy and Billy Preston and being an occasional sideman for friends.

He had so far managed to stay out of the battle over Klein's appointment, but now inter-Beatle conflict shifted to Apple Records and he found himself in it up to the polo-neck.

After Apple's release of Ringo's *Sentimental Journey* album on 27 March, Paul's partly home-produced *McCartney* was to have followed on 17 April. But so zealous had been Phil Spector's work on the Beatles' *Let It Be* (largely in sugarifying Paul's two best tracks) that it could be released on 8 May, perfect timing for the film's world premiere in New York on the thirteenth.

The problem was that Paul's debut album appearing just before it was scheduled could be expected to eat into its sales.

In their capacity as Apple directors, John and George wrote him a joint letter, headed 'From Us To You' (a reference to their Beatlemania hit, 'From Me To You'), announcing that *McCartney* was to be put back until June. They signed off with an attempt to soften the high-handed tone, redolent of George at his most gauche: 'We're sorry it turned out like this – it's nothing personal. Hare Krishna. Love John & George. A Mantra A Day Keeps Maya [Indian goddess] Away.'

Indicating the depth of their remorse, the letter was left at Apple reception to be delivered to Paul's north London home impersonally by messenger. Ringo noticed it there and, rather than entrust it to 'some office lad', he did it himself. This latest belittlement pushed Paul over the edge and the guiltless Mister Postman found himself ordered out of the house. Kind man that he was, he returned to the others and talked them into giving *McCartney* back its 17 April slot.

Nowadays, a squad of paparazzi would have jumped on the encounter; in 1970, its only witness was an 'Apple Scruff' who reported back to her companions outside 3 Savile Row that when Ringo left Paul's she thought he had a bruise on one cheek (although Paul would always deny having lashed out physically.)

The young women whom George had given that contemptuous nickname did not confine their watch to Savile Row but were to be found outside the individual Beatle's homes, Abbey Road studios and anywhere else they happened to be, convening by the same instinct that enabled African big-game hunters to detect wildebeest or Native Americans to follow the buffalo.

In modern terms, they were stalkers of the most extreme kind, but with none of the modern stalker's malevolence. On the contrary, each was deeply respectful towards her chosen Beatle (whose first name she often adopted, as in 'Sue-John' or 'Linda-Ringo') and felt a duty to shield him from mere tourists and other kinds of non-vocational gawpers.

Aside from the consuming obsession that took no account of day or night, heat or cold, snow or rain, they could be intelligent, sensible and humorous, even about that consuming obsession. Their title, calculated to infuriate any modern feminist, they wore with pride; they considered themselves an exclusive club to the point of issuing membership cards, even produced their own monthly newsletter headed 'Steps, 3 Savile Row.'

The Scruffs' George faction was led by an Englishwoman known only as Lucy and a tall Texan from Dallas named Carol Bedford. All of them regularly offered 'their' Beatles gifts and Carol's introductory one to George had been a cake in the shape of Texas from her home city's famous Neiman Marcus department store.

Knowing his temperament, she and Lucy were models of decorum when asking him to pose for the photographs of which they could never have enough. On one occasion, at least, he'd been pleased enough to see them: when his cannabis-possession charge came to court, Derek Taylor had recruited them to trek out to Walton and Esher magistrates court as a supportive presence. And he was eventually to owe them and their co-Scruffs much more than that.

If the Beatles were recording all night at Abbey Road, Carol would be in the group that settled down on the forecourt with sleeping-bags and flasks of coffee, hoping for the briefest of sightings the next morning before going straight to their various places of employment.

They were not allowed into EMI to use the toilets, so had to make do in the shadows, terrified of emulating the colleague who'd been floodlit in mid-flood by George's car headlights as he drove in. 'Abbey Road was our home away from home,' Carol recalled. '3 Savile Row was our home.'

These mobile Scruffs therefore could watch the final count-down to the end of the Beatles through successive windows and doorways. They were outside Abbey Road when Paul failed to turn up for a session, making the excuse that it was his wedding anniversary and he couldn't miss having dinner with Linda. A friendly EMI security man told them how John had stormed round to Paul's house, only a couple of streets away, wrenched one of his own paintings off a wall where it had had pride of place and 'put his foot through it'.

They were outside Olympic Studios in Barnes when George arrived hours later for some postproduction work and John came out of the entrance 'looking as if he wanted to punch him but then only yelled'. What had detained him so long became clear when Carol and Lucy looked through his car window and spotted 'the cardboard cone from a candyfloss and a souvenir brochure from Battersea Fun Fair'.

They were back outside 3 Savile Row to watch a turbulent band-meeting in mime through the uncurtained and brightly lit ground floor window of John and Yoko's office, with Yoko and Linda both present and the Plastic Ono Band robot completing the quorum. At one moment they saw John and Paul appear close to blows and George 'look depressed and walk to the other end of the room'.

For his twenty-seventh birthday Carol bought George a hand-carved pipe 'from a drug-paraphernalia shop'. Her visitor's visa was about to expire but before returning to Dallas, she asked him to sign one more photograph of himself. He put 'Love from George' and an x.

She was soon to return – and go where no Apple Scruff had gone before.

By the time the *Let It Be* album and film were released in May 1970, the world had already deduced that the Beatles had broken up from the *McCartney* album they'd allowed to go first. The announcement took the form of a printed Q&A with Apple's Peter Brown in which Paul formally disowned Allen Klein and seemed to terminate the career of the century in a couple of monosyllables:

> Q. *Are you planning a new album or single with the Beatles?*
> A. No.
> Q. *Do you foresee a time when Lennon–McCartney become an active songwriting partnership again?*
> A. No.

However long expected, it was still shattering to the generation for whom they'd lit up almost every year of the decade only just ended, which already seemed a millennium away. But their farewell album hardly seemed equal to the moment.

As always, Lennon and McCartney were the overwhelming presence, although now plainly beyond any hope of reconciliation, harmonising their buddy song 'Two Of Us' like squabbling schoolboys whom their teacher had ordered to shake hands. The stand-out tracks, 'Let It Be' and 'The Long and Winding Road', were those with the greatest pall of sadness; suddenly,

Phil Spector's over-the-top orchestration and celestial choir seemed only commensurate with the worldwide grief.

George's two songs came nowhere near the level of his *Abbey Road* tours de force. 'I Me Mine' was a dirgey attack on self-ishness and egotism dating from the *Get Back* sessions – when those qualities, as he saw it, were so strong in John and Paul – and wavered between a waltz and a belligerent rocker. 'For You Blue' abandoned his usual chordal inventiveness for the three timeless compass points of 12-bar blues. He seemed already to have started saving his best stuff for later.

Elsewhere were some future Beatles classics, notably John's 'Don't Let Me Down', his acidic elegy-cum-warning to Yoko, and Paul's 'Get Back', the cod-Western ballad that had evolved from their desire to return to their roots. But also much obvious padding, like 'Dig It', where John's shouted shit-list of institutions from the CIA to the BBC (with Harrison for once added to the Lennon/McCartney credit); and two leftovers from the Quarrymen's skiffle songbook, 'Maggie Mae' and 'The One After 909'.

A rare light-hearted moment, surprisingly, came from George as John played lap-steel guitar in 'For You Blue'. 'Go, Johnny, go!' he ad-libbed, invoking Chuck Berry's 'Johnny B. Goode'. 'Elmore James has got nothing on this, baby.'

Never before had a Beatles album been so thoroughly trashed by the music press. Alan Smith in the *New Musical Express* called it 'a cheapskate epitaph, a cardboard tombstone, a sad and tatty end to a musical fusion which wiped clean and drew again the face of pop.' Still, by what was now almost a law of Nature, it instantly went to number one in Britain and the US and its single, 'The Long And Winding Road', became a monster, tear-touched hit (as 'Let It Be' already had been when issued in pre-Phil Spector form). As a soundtrack album, it would win at the next Oscars for 'Best Original Song Score'.

Michael Lindsay-Hogg's feature documentary had a double British premiere, at the London Pavilion – though, unlike previous Beatles films, with no royal attendees or good-humoured police controlling the West End crowds – and at Liverpool's Gaumont cinema. None of the Beatles showed up for either event.

Let It Be the movie was a revelation to anyone who'd ever thought their lives to be Heaven on earth. No attempt had been made to hide the discomfort and friction that had gone into making the album, particularly where George was concerned. There on the big screen were the chilly wastes of Twickenham film studios and his sullen gold polo-neck telling schoolteachery Paul: 'Look, I'll play whatever it is you want me to play. Or I won't play at all . . .' There was John in a run-through of 'I Me Mine' showing his indifference by waltzing Yoko around the cable-strewn floor.

Climactically, there they were with Billy Preston on the Apple roof that chill, windy midday in January 1969: the final 'fuck it' showing just how great they were and why they could never have stayed together any longer.

There was the performance being cut short by police officers from the nearby Savile Row station, who'd never taken the least interest in a house full of drugs but were now responding to complaints from surrounding businesses about the noise. And there was George in a shortie 'fun' fur, clearly not having any but still making every note count for as long as the power lasted.

The *Sunday Telegraph* compared sitting through it to 'watching the Albert Hall being dismantled and replaced by National Coal Board offices'. Penelope Gilliatt in the *New Yorker* called it 'a very bad film and a touching one about the breaking-apart of this reassuring, geometrically perfect, once apparently ageless family of siblings'.

Yet to many of their fans, it was so like them. On top of the music and laughter and love they made, they'd been cherished for their honesty and that was the note on which they chose to go out. As John said by way of a sardonic health-warning, 'This is what we are like without our trousers on so would you please end the game now?'

PART THREE

19

'GARBO SPEAKS – HARRISON IS FREE'

A couple of months earlier, George had come home late from a day at Apple accompanied by a young American woman he introduced as Chris O'Dell, his new live-in personal assistant. Her ringletty blonde hair and wide smile had such a look of his favourite film star Goldie Hawn, that Pattie wondered if the job description was just a cover for him to start competing with Krishna under their very roof.

That wasn't to happen until later with someone else, but in twenty-year-old Chris's case the suspicion was pardonable. Since joining Apple in 1969, she'd been pursued by several of George's musician friends and had a passionate affair with the one currently at the top of his list, the singer/songwriter Leon Russell, who'd combined her workplace and all-important astrological sign to nickname her 'the Pisces Apple Lady'.

George, in fact, had already made several moves on her, which she'd parried with sufficient tact for them to stay on good terms. Her greater appeal to him now were her formidable efficiency, absolute trustworthiness and seemingly limitless tolerance of rock superstars' funny little ways.

At Friar Park, she found a household still made up only of

himself, Pattie and his existing personal assistant, Terry Doran. But since her job was to run his diary and Doran's to be his shadow, there was no rivalry between them.

That spring was unusually cold and the house's only warm place was its huge, antiquated kitchen. Chris privately thought it 'a mausoleum' while loyally enthusing about it to George. Doran firmly believed it was haunted and claimed to have seen the figure of a strangely dressed man in the minstrel's gallery which vanished when he called out to it. Chris encountered no actual ghosts but never felt quite comfortable among the myriad friars' faces that stared out even from the light-switches.

At these relatively close quarters, she discovered three very different Georges. One was friendly, funny and gossipy, another was uptight, hypercritical and given to witheringly sarcastic personal remarks, the third was either chanting under his breath or delivering 'spiritual rants' to which she would dutifully stay up listening long after Pattie and Doran had made their excuses and retired. She embraced his strict vegetarianism with the same pragmatism, occasionally sneaking off to Henley's town centre to gaze longingly into the windows of butcher's shops

Initially, she found Pattie somewhat cool towards her thanks to that mistaken assumption that she had designs on George. And though Pattie clearly loved Friar Park and all its curiosities as much as he did, her life with him there seemed to have had a dampening effect on the fun-loving person Chris had met socially.

Pattie had imagined brightening the Gothic gloom with flower-arrangements from the vast choice outside, but George would never allow it. 'He called it robbing the garden. I had to order what I wanted from the florist in Henley.'

Outwardly the former rock star had all but disappeared; he spent all day every day in old gardening clothes, shapeless hats and rubber boots and at meals talked only about his redevelopment of the house and grounds, sometimes repairing an agricultural implement at the table. 'It was as if there were no world outside Friar Park,' Chris would later write in her memoir, *Miss O'Dell*, 'and as time went by the walls seemed to close in shielding us from all outside influences.'

The outside world did manage one noisy incursion when George invited three families from the Radha Krishna Temple to stay indefinitely. Thanks to him, their singers had enjoyed a second British Top 30 hit and appearance on *Top Of The Pops* with 'Govinda', an ancient song from north India performed in the original Sanskrit.

The idea was that the women would cook and the men help out in the garden. They moved into the top floor of the house, turning its dining room into an extension temple and wafting a scent of incense or dal to the most faraway friar-face.

Between them they had several small children whom they allowed to play in the fountain on the south side of the house without supervision, evidently trusting in the Law of Karma to do the job. On two different occasions, a toddler had to be rescued from drowning by Terry Doran and resuscitated by the local doctor, who told Pattie forcibly he wouldn't be responding to any more such SOS calls.

For Pattie's twenty-sixth birthday party on 26 March, she persuaded George, with Chris's support, to have a party to show off the newly renovated caves. Twenty-some guests, including his staunchest allies in Beatle-land – Ringo, Neil Aspinall and Derek Taylor, and their wives – were conducted by torchlight past the grottoes full of gnomes and skeletons and distorting mirrors and out onto the far side of the lawn, below the mini-Matterhorn.

It was after the party that Pattie finally lowered her guard with Chris. She explained how, since marrying George, she'd been unable to have any women friends without suspecting they were really after him. '[I said] "Chris, I'd really like to be your friend [but] you will only be my friend as long as you don't let George have you." "Okay," she said. "That's a deal. I'd much rather be your friend."'

Such were the Pisces Apple Lady's diplomatic skills that she managed this without any disloyalty to George – or 'Geoffrey', as she and Pattie took to calling him behind his back. Now the house became less mausoleum and more adventure playground: they'd go on expeditions in search of passages to forgotten rooms – of which several still remained – or try to make out if the nude cherubim on the ballroom ceiling really did wear diapers, painted on for modesty's sake by the nuns formerly in charge here. As Chris had also discovered, meditation, architectural over-stimulation, even his garden hadn't taken away 'Geoffrey's' need for a certain outlawed white powder.

'Pattie would say to me in the morning, "What's he got his hands in today, the prayer-beads or the cocaine?"' she recalls. 'If he was in his spiritual place, you couldn't reach him. But if he was doing coke, he'd want to drink and party.'

Like something in a Friar Park hothouse, George's third solo album, but first vocal one, had been germinating throughout his final two years as a Beatle, fertilised variously by Bob Dylan's new country style, The Band's and Delaney & Bonnie's folk-rock, Billy Preston's gospel-soul and the mantras of the Radha Krishna Temple.

Its starting point had been the *Get Back* album sessions, when he'd brought in a meditative offering entitled 'All Things Must Pass', prompted by a line in the Tao Te Ching, the founding text of Taoism. John and Paul had run through it with an apathy unequalled since George Martin forced them to demo 'How Do You Do It?' as a second single rather than 'Please Please Me' in 1962.

Although they passed on 'All Things Must Pass' for *Abbey Road*, then again for *Let It Be*, George had persisted in the same vein. During his spell on tour with Delaney & Bonnie, he'd set out to write a spiritual like the Edwin Hawkins Singers' 'Oh Happy Day', which Bonnie Bramlett would often sing back-stage. But where the Hawkins song mentioned Jesus by name, George's was about an unspecific 'sweet Lord' open to any faith.

Other Harrisongs had continued piling on top of those already piled up, like 'I'd Have You Anytime', co-written with Bob Dylan in Woodstock, and 'Behind That Locked Door', a supportive message to Dylan on the eve of the 1969 Isle of Wight festival. He and Pattie paid a second visit to Woodstock, from which he returned with a new Dylan composition, 'If Not For You', that he wanted to cover. 'We were supposed to have gone on to LA,' Pattie remembers. 'But there was still a lot in the press about George's song "Piggies" being used in the Manson killings and we were warned that if he went there, he might be arrested.'

His fantastical new home had also begun working its way into his music, through lyrics coloured by the whimsicality and wordplay of its creator. 'The Ballad of Sir Frankie Crisp' (aka

'Let It Roll') celebrated the 'fountain of perpetual mirth' he had inherited, referencing its caves and maze, even using Sir Frank's ubiquitous faux-medieval 'ye' instead of 'the'.

Yet turning all these ingredients into vinyl had taken second place to taming Friar Park until Paul's de facto announcement of leaving the band. John and George were furious at what seemed to them typical headline-grabbing when both of them had already left in spirit long before but kept silent about it for the common good. George's quieter fury refocused him on his album and a few days later, he was back at work at Abbey Road.

A formidable array of talent was on hand to help him prove he could make it without the Beatles. Eric Clapton had volunteered to head a studio band containing the pick of Delaney & Bonnie's American 'Friends' augmented by Ringo in his own new solo capacity, Billy Preston, Klaus Voormann, Cream's Ginger Baker, Procol Harum's Gary Brooker and younger admirers like Peter Frampton from Humble Pie and Genesis drummer Phil Collins.

Phil Spector had agreed to co-produce the album, a role in which the Svengali of Pop would be unable to take the liberties he had with Paul's tracks on *Let It Be*. Coincidentally, John had secured Spector as co-producer of his debut solo album with the Plastic Ono Band, also to be made at Abbey Road – and with Ringo, Preston and Voormann part of its line-up – on some of the same dates George had booked. But he was determined not to let this inhibit him in any way.

For a title he chose that of his two-time Beatles reject, though *All Things Must Pass* took on a less mystic meaning as he played his seventeen main tracks to Spector, together with around twenty further demos and out-takes dating back to 1966. It would feel, he said, 'like recovering from a four-year dose of constipation'.

The recording sessions were designed to be totally unlike the bleak, undemocratic ones he'd often experienced here with the Beatles. To encourage feelings of harmony and egalitarianism, he set up a small Hindu altar in the studio and again had a Radha Krishna Temple member looking on like a monitor. Contrasting with what he remembered as Paul's dictatorial ways, every member of the outsize band was encouraged to make suggestions and express their individuality in performance.

It took more than an altar and a Hare Krishna to keep the peace where Phil Spector was at work. While doctoring *Let It Be*, Spector had been relatively well-behaved but now his celebrated paranoia ran wild, fuelled by the approaching trial of the Charles Manson family in California. Believing himself next in line on a homicidal hippie hit-list, he refused to go anywhere without a bodyguard and carried a gun which he had to be prevented from bringing into the studio.

At the mixing desk, George recalled, 'He couldn't start work until he'd had about eighteen cherry brandies,' and at one point, blind drunk and drugged, fell over and fractured an arm. Periodically he would disappear without warning to a clinic in Palo Alto, California, where he was trying to kick his addictions, then equally suddenly reappear showing no noticeable improvement.

The pressure on George increased after John's arrival with the Plastic Ono Band to make the album Spector was also co-producing and for which he would be requisitioning Ringo, Billy Preston and Klaus Voormann. Just beforehand Spector had again disappeared to Palo Alto, staying out of touch for so long that Allen Klein was reduced to advertising in *Billboard* magazine: 'Phil! John is ready this weekend.'

John's presence in an adjacent studio inevitably stirred memories of those six years of creative constipation. 'What are you doing here?' George demanded icily when he and Yoko looked in on *All Things Must Pass* but thawed a little when John said he liked what was going down.

In the Plastic Ono Band's case, the main disruptor was not Spector but John himself. He regarded the album as a therapy session in which to lay bare childhood traumas and insecurities that still tortured him. Tapings frequently came to a stop as he burst into rage or tears.

George was feeling similar emotions, his suppressed and for very different reasons. The previous year, his mother, Louise, had suffered recurrent headaches which doctors at first dismissed as 'psychological', then finally diagnosed as a brain tumour. It had seemed to go into remission but had returned that spring. While trying to keep the album and his co-producer on track, George was making frequent 400-mile round trips to the Cheshire Wirral, where Louise was receiving treatment at Clatterbridge Hospital's cancer centre, the prognosis not good.

Carol Bedford had returned from Dallas to London in May – with a work permit this time – to find the Apple Scruffs still traumatised by Paul's apparent breakup announcement. Soon after her arrival, she was among a small group to whom John gave tickets to *Let It Be*'s Beatle-less London premiere. It made them feel little better.

The George faction keeping day and night watch on the Abbey Road forecourt had observed his comings and goings, sometimes with Phil Spector, sometimes Eric Clapton, but mystified as to what they were doing together. At the first opportunity, Carol handed him a large bouquet of yellow flowers and to her amazement discovered that he remembered her.

Not only that, he seemed to like seeing her, much to the chagrin of her fellow arch-Georgephile, Lucy, who'd been 'waiting out' for him since 1967. One chilly evening when he arrived, the group were trying to keep their spirits up with a teeth-chattering 'Hare Krishna'. He wound down his car window and handed Carol an incense stick 'to help you with your chanting'.

The attention from George continued, to her increasing amazement and confusion. During an afternoon Abbey Road-watch, she was approached by the roadie Mal Evans who told her George wanted to know where she lived. Usually this was just a ruse for Evans himself to get someone's address, turn up there later and offer her preferential Beatle vantage-points in exchange for sex. But in Carol's case the request proved to be genuine.

Another morning, having watched George drive off after an all-night session, she was walking straight to her secretarial job when she saw his white Mercedes parked ahead. This time, a more substantial gift came through its driver's window, a copy of *The Autobiography of a Yogi* by Paramahansa Yogananda which he told her he'd read seven times.

After another all-nighter, he helped a clearly worse-for-wear Phil Spector into a limo, then walked over to the Scruffs' bivouac and sat down on the oily concrete beside Carol in her sleeping bag for an extended chat. He seemed to like her forthright Texan manner: while as reverential as a Scruff could be, she would still reprimand him for flashes of discourtesy towards her and her colleagues or the chain smoking that no amount of meditation seemed able to cure.

When whatever he was doing temporarily moved to Trident Studios in Soho, her Scruff's instinct led her there with a kindred spirit named Cathy. George emerged for a break unusually without roadie-cover and the two found themselves taking a stroll with him, unnoticed among the afternoon crowds. He seemed particularly interested in the sex-workers' cards stuck inside telephone boxes, saying almost nostalgically that they reminded him of the Hamburg Reeperbahn.

On 8 July his mother, Louise, died from brain cancer in Warrington General Hospital aged only fifty-nine. His father, Harold, was also a patient there, receiving treatment for leg ulcers, and George had been dividing his visits between them, assuring each that the other was getting on well, though with less and less conviction in Louise's case.

On 4 July, the day that 'Something' won a Novello Award, he'd driven up to see her for the last time and stayed at her bedside until the end. She had predicted at the moment of his birth that he'd grow up to be 'special', imperilled the family's food budget to give him the cutaway guitar of his dreams, sat up with him into the small hours as he struggled to find its first chords, loved his Beatle fame so much that she'd kept a life-size photograph of him in his mop-top and shawl collar at the top of the stairs for every visitor to marvel at. The final cruelty of her illness was to make her unable to recognise him.

Outwardly impassive as always, he would later write a song called 'Deep Blue', reliving his feelings of helplessness as he watched her suffer, with a breath of the Catholicism she'd never forced on him: 'When I think of the life I'm living/Pray God help me, give me your light.'

Louise was mourned not only by her family and huge circle of friends but by hundreds of women whose fan mail to George she had answered and with whom she'd then kept up a regular correspondence. Afterwards, in all kinds of faraway places, total strangers would come up to him and say, 'I used to write to your mum.'

His older sister, Lou, returned from Illinois for the first time in many years to attend the private family funeral at St Wilfrid's (Anglican) Church in Grappenhall, Warrington, close to the house he'd bought his parents, followed by cremation at Walton Lea Crematorium. The many floral tributes included a huge bunch of white carnations from John – always Louise's favourite Beatle bar one – and a bouquet from the Apple Scruffs. George sent them a thank-you note, addressed to 'Steps, 3 Savile Row' and quoting Sir Frank Crisp: 'The speech of flowers excels the flowers of speech and we thank you all very much for your love.'

Not all his following showed the same delicacy. After the funeral, word reached him that the Beatles' American Fan Club, which, like its British counterpart, still refused to acknowledge their disintegration, was advertising trips to visit Louise's grave. He immediately withdrew his endorsement of the club and the other three did likewise.

Quiet, unassuming Harold Harrison was lost without his dynamic soulmate of thirty-nine years. Although Harold was reluctant to leave the home he'd shared with Louise, George persuaded him to come and live at Friar Park, where Pattie gave him the warmest of welcomes. One day, he brought Harold on a visit to 3 Savile Row, taking time to introduce him to the Apple Scruffs on the way in.

With Louise no more and Lou back in America, the Harrison brothers drew together. Harry, the eldest, also came to Friar Park to run the estate for George, moving into its grandiose gatehouse with his wife, Irene, and two children; Peter settled in Henley with his family, easily finding work at his trade of garage mechanic.

George was now back working on *All Things Must Pass*, finishing up a track he once would never have imagined recording. But first, it seemed, some further field-research was needed.

One evening, when Carol Bedford reluctantly left her place at the Savile Row steps to pay a rare visit to her home, he was waiting for her in his white Mercedes again and offered her a lift. No Scruff had ever been in any of his cars and at these close quarters Carol smelled him for the first time, like a pilgrim entering a cathedral. 'It was an incense smell, but flowery-fresh as opposed to powdery.'

She'd been able to find a tiny flat only a couple of streets from Abbey Road. Instead of just letting her out there, which would have been miracle enough, George switched off the engine and talked to the tall Texan with an openness withheld from even his closest family and friends: about the loss of his mother, the pressures on him both from the album and the still-unresolved situation with the Beatles, even the state of his marriage, which the Scruffs already knew to be 'slipping'.

No attempt at a Krishna-like pounce was made; instead, Carol impulsively threw her arms around his neck then, horrified by her own temerity, tried to open the passenger door and run. The long scarf she was wearing caught in her seat-back and as George leaned across trying to free her, it suddenly came loose, flew up and clipped him across the face.

Later that week she and four other Scruffs were watching the dawn break over Abbey Road when Mal Evans appeared and, to their astonishment, took them into the studio to hear the track George had just finished. It was called 'Apple Scruffs' and was a tribute to their steadfastness 'in the fog and in the rain/through the pleasure and the pain'. The worshippers he'd once cast in the most dismissive of terms had become muses.

Recording *All Things Must Pass* was originally to have taken only eight weeks but, thanks to George's perfectionism in the studio and the interruption of his bereavement, it lasted five months, eventually racking up as much studio time as *Sgt. Pepper's Lonely Hearts Club Band*, though at a vastly higher cost.

Phil Spector did not see the album through to its conclusion, bowing out in late summer for what were described as 'health reasons'. Yet underneath the cherry brandy-swilling and gun-waving, his producer's instincts were still second to none. For this time around, he hadn't built his customary Wall of Sound but demolished one of Inhibition.

Previous beneficiaries of the Spector technique like Tina Turner or the Righteous Brothers had had vocal power enough to flatten any real wall, but George's singing at first seemed to get lost in his all-star backing, if not his own guitar riffs. With a respect – and tact – Paul's work had never received, Spector sent him a detailed breakdown of the record as it stood, highlighting the places where his voice seemed 'buried' and reiterating: '[It] has got to be heard throughout so that the greatness of the songs can really come through.'

Even praise at this level couldn't reassure George about the project as a whole. In September, he'd somehow found time to co-produce Billy Preston's second Apple album, *Encouraging Words*, and given Preston 'All Things Must Pass' and 'My Sweet Lord' to perform on it two months before record-buyers would hear his versions, testing the water with the most cautious of elbows. Encouraging words about both tracks did indeed result, but no chart action for Preston.

Carol and the other hardcore Georgeists were waiting outside, as ever, the night that *All Things Must Pass* finally wrapped. In another note addressed to 'Steps, 3 Savile Row', he told them he didn't know if it was good or bad, but 'even during my worst moments I always felt that encouragement from you was sufficient to make me finish the thing.'

It was released late in November as one of the first triple albums seen on either side of the Atlantic. Two of its discs consisted of songs in conventional sequence, the third of extended jam-sessions allowing its virtuoso sidemen to take centre studio. The only one with a vocal, 'It's Johnny's Birthday', was a greeting to mark John's thirtieth that George had delivered personally while they were both working at Abbey Road as if to make up for his earlier frigidity.

Barry Feinstein's black-and-white cover was a repudiation of all rock-star glamour and mystique. George sat alone in the rain in his Friar Park garden, wearing old clothes, a shapeless hat and rubber boots, surrounded by four plaster gnomes taken from their dedicated cave, beardily gnome-like himself except in his unsmilingness. Readers of album-cover symbolism, grown to huge numbers in the Beatles' era, quickly guessed whom the grotesque quartet were supposed to represent, lying prone on the wet lawn while he radiated tension and purposefulness.

No imagery could have been more archaic yet after a year full of speculation about where pop music might go in the Seventies, this seemed to be the answer: a seamless fusion of Eastern and Western musical styles that lightened the solemnity of one while giving new soul to the other. A voice with no particle of its former glottal Liverpudlian and now (thanks to Spector) vibrant with passion and devotion. Luminous slide–guitar riffs as eloquent as voices. Just as compellingly, chord–changes set free to fashion almost an aural Friar Park with their continual diversions and surprises.

Not since *Sgt. Pepper* had an album made such an impact: it topped the British and American charts for eight and seven weeks respectively, far outstripping *John Lennon/Plastic Ono Band*, which had appeared a week after it, and the *McCartney* album back in April. 'My Sweet Lord' became the first single by a solo Beatle to reach number one, in this case simultaneously with the album in both the UK and US en route to going Platinum six times over.

For its magnitude and ambition, *Rolling Stone* called it 'the War and Peace of rock 'n' roll . . . Wagnerian, Brucknerian – the music of mountain-tops and distant horizons.' *Melody Maker's* reviewer Richard Williams equated the moment with the first onscreen words of Hollywood's most enigmatic silent-movie goddess: 'Garbo speaks – Harrison is free.'

Yet it was to land George in legal trouble for its least consequential feature, the congratulatory message on John's thirtieth birthday. For this he'd jokily used the tune of 'Congratulations', with which Cliff Richard had won the 1968 Eurovision Song

Contest and which had since become a birthday anthem to Queen Elizabeth the Queen Mother.

However light-hearted, it had been conscious plagiarism and the song's composers, Bill Martin and Phil Coulter, promptly entered a claim for a share in George's royalties and a credit on the record that, fortunately for him, was settled out of court. Before long, in a much trickier plagiarism case, he wouldn't be so lucky.

Although all four Beatles by now put out a solo album (and Ringo already a second), millions of their fans still clung to the hope that they might still sort out their differences and, in their own words, get back to where they once belonged.

Paul was held solely responsible for the schism and attacked from every side – even publicly heckled by Apple Scruffs – for what was seen as overweening vanity and selfishness in timing the announcement of his exit to ensure maximum publicity for *McCartney*. In vain did he protest, 'I didn't leave the Beatles. The Beatles have left the Beatles, but nobody wanted to be the one to say the party was over.'

John had since said much worse in a song called 'God' on *John Lennon/Plastic Ono Band* which asserted the self-belief Yoko had given him by listing everything he no longer felt a need to believe in. At the very end, after 'magic' and 'I Ching' and 'Bible' and 'Tarot' and 'Hitler' and 'Jesus' and '[John F.] Kennedy' and 'Buddha' and 'mantra' and 'Gita' and 'Yoga' and 'Kings' and 'Elvis' and 'Zimmerman [Bob Dylan]' came 'Beatles', diminished by the deliberate absence of a definite article and not so much sung as spat out.

Meanwhile, Allen Klein was clutching at straws. Having

accepted he was powerless to prevent the breakup, Klein now hoped for a stay of execution to allow them to work off some of the whopping new recording contract he'd negotiated with Capitol in America. And in November, he convinced John and George that it was in their best interests to seek some kind of rapprochement with Paul.

He attempted his own rapprochement by inviting Paul to a meeting in the Harlequin Suite at the Dorchester Hotel, where he'd so easily captivated John and Yoko two years earlier. It ended after only minutes when Paul's brother-in-law, now lawyer, John Eastman called him 'an asshole'.

Shortly afterwards, Klein persuaded George to reach out to Paul when the two happened both to be in New York. But with *All Things Must Pass* topping charts around the world, George was in no mood to be diplomatic with his supposed constipator-in-chief and told him, 'You're staying on the fucking [Apple] label. Hare Krishna.'

20

'I SUPPOSE HE IS STILL A PERSON OF CONSIDERABLE MEANS'

For Paul the main driver at this point was not egotism, as so many supposed. Under the partnership agreement the Beatles had signed in 1967, all proceeds from their individual projects went into their collective coffers; Paul's royalties from his solo album therefore were under Klein's control and for the present as unreachable as his Beatles ones. As a result, the one-time boy millionaire was running out of resources and having to be partly supported by his wife.

Eastman's advice was that the partnership agreement had already been breached by the appointment of Klein against Paul's wishes, which under British law could be grounds for its dissolution. But taking legal action against Klein was not the proper course since the agreement in question predated his arrival. Paul would therefore have to sue the other Beatles and Apple, the company he'd done more than any of them to build.

The suit was launched in the Chancery Division of the British High Court on New Year's Eve 1970, with an application for the appointment of an official receiver – a measure usually seen in commercial bankruptcy cases – to take the Beatles' finances out of Klein's control. Attached to the writ was a personal affidavit from Paul, asserting that they'd ceased to function as a group, that his artistic freedom would be compromised so long as the partnership continued and that no accounts for it had been compiled since its inception.

John, George and Ringo fought the dissolution of the partnership, not from any sentimental reasons but because of the tax implications for them if Paul were successful. This placed John and George in the bizarre position of wanting out of the Beatles as much as he did, yet having to pretend the band was still a going concern with no serious personality problems.

During the short interval between the opening of the case and the full hearing, John guaranteed it maximum attention with a lengthy interview with *Rolling Stone*'s editor, Jann Wenner, portraying his life as a Beatle as a refined form of torture from which he'd been lucky to escape with his life.

He was surprisingly easy on Paul, but loftily condescending towards George and *All Things Must Pass*. 'Every time I put the radio on, it's "Oh My Lord" . . . I'm beginning to think there must be a God.' What others were hailing as a masterpiece, he rated no higher than 'all right. At home I wouldn't play that kind of music . . . George has not done his best work yet. His talents have developed over the years and he was working with two fucking brilliant songwriters and he learned a lot from us.'

Nor did his breakout Beatles songs 'While My Guitar Gently Weeps', 'Here Comes The Sun' or even 'Something' merit even a namecheck. 'The best thing he's done is "Within You Without You" still for me.'

The interview's most rancorous moments were about the other Beatles' supposed hostility towards Yoko – when in fact their tolerance had been extraordinary. To be sure, the only example given was an unpleasant remark from George during the *Get Back* sessions, for which John said he'd almost hit him. (Note that 'almost'.)

The partnership dispute resumed in the High Court on 17 February before Mr Justice Stamp. The only Beatle present in the flesh was Paul, who wore a sober dark suit and sat through the entire eleven-day hearing, paying close attention as John Eastman had instructed, knowing how favourably it would impress the bench. John, George and Ringo, acting on less good advice, submitted written statements to be incongruously read out by barristers with wigs and gowns in drawly upper-class accents.

John's statement reflected little credit on the man soon to write a song pleading 'Gimme Some Truth'. It set the necessary Pollyanna-ish tone by observing that, while Paul had 'always preferred pop-type music '[George and I] preferred what is now called underground ... this contrast in our tastes, I am sure, did more good than harm and contributed to our success.' After a half-truth (Lennon having written many a soft ballad and McCartney the ultra-underground 'Helter-Skelter') came a flat-out lie: that the majority decision to hire Klein had been normal Beatles practice.

George's bewigged ventriloquist's doll spoke in an authentic George tone of 'the superior attitude which for years past Paul has shown to me musically'. But he represented his walk-out from the *Get Back* sessions as having cleared the air, not left it even heavier with resentment 'Since the row, Paul has treated me more as a musical equal. I think this whole episode shows how a disagreement could be worked out so that we all benefited.'

The only unvarnished truth came from Ringo as he recalled Paul's misplaced fury with him over the postponement of the *McCartney* album. a rather glaring example of how disagreements had tended to be worked out since Brian's death. Ringo, too felt – sincerely in his case – that the band's conflicts had made for 'really great products' and that 'all four of us together could even yet work out everything satisfactorily.'

By now these were not the only Beatle court proceedings being reported in the British press. On 23 February, George was up before Wells Street magistrates in Central London for driving his Mercedes three times at a police constable who was signalling him to pull over after causing an obstruction in one of the new yellow traffic-control 'boxes'. It was conduct far removed from the spirit of 'My Sweet Lord', but fortunately he had only bumped the officer, causing no injury.

Disqualifying him from driving for a month with a £35 fine, the presiding magistrate, Iain McLean, referred drily to the larger case he was involved in: 'I suppose he is still a person of considerable means despite what one reads in the newspapers.'

Klein was not formally on trial, but nonetheless came to the High Court to mount an aggressive defence by proxy. Apple's counsel read an affidavit from one of its senior accountants stating that under his management the Beatles' assets had increased from around £1 million to £6.5 million and that Apple was now fully solvent and able to meet its tax liabilities, something which had previously been in doubt.

The lawyer went on to read a statement by Klein rebutting all Paul's charges against him and running to forty-six pages. Along the way it pointed out a major benefit to Paul from the partnership he sought to dissolve: 25 per cent of George's royalties from *All Things Must Pass*.

On 12 March 1971, after a week of deliberation, Judge Stamp ruled that the Beatles had 'long since ceased to perform as a group, that Apple was not a Frankenstein set up to control the individual partners' and the situation with regard to the partnership accounts was 'quite intolerable'.

Klein received stinging personal criticism for having taken management commission 'grossly in excess' of his due and tried to camouflage it with 'the irresponsible patter of a second-rate salesman'. Since no one else around the Beatles seemed capable of handling their finances, Paul's application for an official receiver would be granted.

Almost a year after the Beatles' coded breakup inside a record album, this was the real thing, certified by the highest court in the land. It turned Savile Row into a battleground of reporters, TV news crews and tearful young women. When George tried to make a discreet exit from number 3, he found himself trapped by arc lights and outthrust tape-recorders until a posse of Apple Scruffs led by Carol Bedford came to the rescue, not hesitating to kick or bite anyone who obstructed them as they escorted him to his car.

21

'I HAVE TO TELL YOU, MAN, I'M IN LOVE WITH YOUR WIFE'

The letter addressed to Pattie Harrison at Friar Park, marked 'Express' and 'Urgent', was as enigmatic as any of the mottoes and maxims bequeathed by Sir Frank Crisp. Addressed to 'Dearest L' and written in tiny italic script, it demanded to know whether she still loved her husband or had 'another lover', and 'if there is still a feeling in your heart for me'. It was signed 'all my love e'.

The 'e' stood for Eric as in Clapton, her husband's best friend, confessing his long-concealed adoration. Not recognising the 'e' and mystified by the 'Dearest L', Pattie mistook his letter for some stray bit of George's fan mail until Clapton followed it up with an impatient phone call. She told him in all honesty that she'd had no idea he felt that way and the call ended in mutual embarrassment.

What with the chill now emanating from George and the affairs to which she continually turned a blind eye, such overtures from an almost comparably glamorous man were a huge boost to Pattie's morale. But the two men's close friendship made any encouraging response doubly risky.

There was a further complication dating from the Delaney &

Bonnie tour when George had offered her to Clapton without her knowledge to divert her attention from his intended seduction of her youngest sister, Paula, then aged eighteen.

Clapton had ended up sleeping with Paula, fantasising that she was Pattie, and then begun an affair with her despite being engaged to Alice Ormsby-Gore, who was not only the same age but a good friend of hers.

Though Pattie still knew nothing about George's targeting of Paula, his 'minxy' side seemed to enjoy letting her know his feelings for her sister were more than brotherly-in-law. If the two were walking together in the Friar Park gardens and he saw her watching from a window, he'd casually slip an arm around Paula's shoulders.

Pattie began what she thought a passing dalliance with Clapton, paying George back mildly and discreetly for his wholesale Krishna-ising. In any case, the relationship was limited by its intricate background politics. It had to be kept completely away from Friar Park, which Clapton visited frequently to hang out with George, nor could Pattie go to Clapton's house in Surrey, where Paula might be staying or, if not, Alice Ormsby-Gore.

They managed one visit to a cinema in Central London, at an off-peak time when no one recognised them. Otherwise, their trysts mainly took place in Guildford, a couple of miles from Clapton's home, where they'd meet under the Town Clock like a blue-denim and platform-heeled *Brief Encounter*.

All of this was going on while George made the intensely spiritual *All Things Must Pass* with Clapton heading the all-star studio band, often in a palpable haze although it never affected his playing. For his chronic insecurity combined with guilt over pursuing Pattie had made him turn to heroin. As if challenging

Fate, he'd take it publicly in the EMI cafeteria where the Beatles had never so much as smoked a joint.

Clapton continued to change musical partners as restlessly as sexual ones. While the *All Things Must Pass* sessions were still in progress, he began rehearsing the studio band's three best American musicians to become the first line-up where he'd be frontman rather just a virtuoso soloist. Even here, his strangely self-effacing nature kicked in: in a pastiche of some New York doo-wop group of the 1950s, they were called Derek and the Dominos.

After *All Things Must Pass* wrapped, the new quartet needed a London base so Clapton borrowed George's assistant, Chris O'Dell, to find them a flat in South Kensington and keep the letting agents well dosed with money as it fell into rock 'n' roll squalor. It also became a regular meeting place for Pattie and him, although she still insisted on keeping things platonic.

His longing for them to be more even led him to seek help from the supernatural. Derek and the Dominos' debut gig was in company with the white blues singer/pianist known as Dr John, a sinister-looking figure who performed in the Mardi Gras costumes of his native New Orleans and was said to possess Voodoo powers.

After the show, Clapton asked Dr John to invoke those powers to make Pattie leave George for him. The supposed witch doctor gave him a small box made of plaited straw to carry in his pocket and written instructions for a secret ritual warranted to cast the necessary aphrodisiacal spell.

In fairness to Voodoo, it wasn't given much chance to get going. A couple of weeks later came the West End premiere of the scandalous *Oh! Calcutta!* revue, produced by Clapton's manager, Robert Stigwood. George and Pattie were invited but since George had other – unspecified – plans, she was escorted by Peter Brown, the suave Apple executive who'd recently fled from Klein into Stigwood's employ.

Unknown to her, Clapton was also at the *Oh! Calcutta!* first night. When she returned to her seat after the interval, she found him in the one next to hers having persuaded its previous occupant to change places.

George hadn't bothered his head about where Pattie would be that evening. But as the hour grew late, in a syndrome common with faithless husbands, he felt a surge of possessiveness. He turned up at the after-show party at Robert Stigwood's house and found her in the garden with Clapton. 'He asked what was going on,' she recalls, 'and, to my complete horror, Eric said, "I have to tell you, man, I'm in love with your wife."'

George didn't reply – probably because it was no great surprise – but merely asked Pattie which of them she'd be ending the night with. She replied, firmly, 'I'm coming home with you, George.'

There was no time to pursue the subject as immediately afterwards Clapton went off to Miami to make Derek and the Dominos' first (and, it would prove, only) album. With him went Pattie's sister, Paula, whom he made little secret of regarding as a substitute for her.

Knowing only too well the temptations she would be exposed to, Pattie tried to stop her, as did her other sister, Jenny, and their mother. 'But she couldn't wait to get into the rock 'n' roll lifestyle like Jenny and me. If someone is that determined to go out and play, there's nothing you can do about it.'

Those Miami sessions included one of Clapton's still-rare ventures into songwriting and singing. He'd become obsessed by the twelfth-century Persian tale of a young man named Majnun who falls hopelessly in love with a high-born maiden named Layla. But her father won't hear of the match and marries her off to someone more suitable, sending Majnun insane with grief.

Clapton had already cast himself as Majnun and Pattie as Layla, hence the 'Dearest L' to whom he'd addressed his confessional letter. Now he wrote a song that was partly a desperate plea for her love, partly an overt criticism of George: 'I tried to give you consolation when your old man let you down . . .' Through it ran a wailing riff shared by Clapton and the brilliant (and soon-to-die) Duane Allman, like sexual tumescence in sound.

When Clapton returned to London, he asked Pattie to meet him at the South Kensington flat for which the Dominos had George's PA, Chris O'Dell, to thank. There he played a cassette of 'Layla' three times over, studying her face carefully for her reaction. As she recalls, it was a mixture of awe that 'the most powerful, moving song I had ever heard' should have been written about her and consternation that its lyric would be instantly decoded, not only by her husband, family and friends but by the tens of thousands of strangers who would buy the album.

Most distressing of all was the knowledge that Paula had been with Clapton throughout the song's evolution and must soon have realised she wasn't its subject. 'She really believed Eric was in love with her,' Pattie would say later, 'And then finding out that he had written a song about me and not her and finally getting to understand how she'd been used . . . I think it broke her heart.'

As bad as she felt about Paula, 'the song got the better of me, with the realisation I had inspired such passion and such creativity. I could resist no longer.' But her surrender, she made clear, had been just a momentary lapse.

Since the excruciating scene in Robert Stigwood's garden, George had remained strangely passive, never seeking any further explanation from Pattie (which she would have welcomed as a sign that he still cared) nor confrontation with Clapton. The closest they came was a rock 'n' roll version of the 'pistols at dawn' a wronged Victorian husband would have demanded – in this case, guitars after dusk.

One evening, he invited Clapton to Friar Park for what Clapton expected to be a lordly cards-on-the-table discussion about Pattie. Instead, George was waiting in the huge front hall with two guitars and two amplifiers set up as if for a show, although the only audience consisted of Pattie, the actor John Hurt, who happened to be staying with them, and the numerous friar-faces staring out from light-switches.

Scarcely exchanging a word, Clapton and he began to trade licks on the two guitars. It had the semblance of a jam but on George's part was clearly a duel over Pattie. Knowing himself unable to best Clapton on a level playing field, he had the better of the two guitars and plied Clapton with brandy while himself drinking only tea. No winner was declared and George never mentioned the episode afterwards.

When Derek and the Dominos' album, *Layla And Other Assorted Love Songs*, was released, Clapton's previous diffident love note became a 1,000-watt confession; the songs he'd written in Miami with Paula looking over his shoulder were largely about his guilty pursuit of Pattie, her continuing resistance and the undignified extremes to which, like Majnun in the Persian fable, he felt himself driven.

'Bell Bottom Blues', ostensibly about some jeans he'd brought her from America, melodramatically demanded: 'Do you want to see me crawl across the floor to you?' 'I Looked Away' defiantly asserted: 'If it's a sin to love another man's woman ... I guess I'll keep on sinning.' 'I Am Yours' adapted a poem by Nizami Ganjavi, the Persian author of *The Story of Layla and Majnun*: 'However distant you may be/There blows no wind but wafts your scent to me.' And as usual there was a blues to fit any size of yearning and frustration: 'Have you ever loved a woman/So-o-o much that you tremble in pain?'

The album cover was the biggest giveaway of all, a painting by the Franco-Danish Émile Théodore Frandsen de Schomberg, entitled 'Fille Au Bouquet' (Young Girl With Bouquet). Its secretively smiling face in a heart-shape of golden hair and white flowers bore an uncanny resemblance to Pattie.

Having thus thoroughly prepared the ground, as he thought, Clapton turned up without warning at Friar Park when George was away and Pattie was alone in the house. He told her he couldn't live without her and she had to come away with him this very minute. When she refused, he took a small packet from his pocket and said it contained heroin, which he'd start taking if she didn't do as he wanted (although he was already well into it).

Horrified, she tried to grab the packet, but he held it in a clenched hand in his pocket. After a brief struggle, he broke away and disappeared into the night. She wasn't to see him again for eight months.

All Things Must Pass was doing the very opposite of its title. After 'My Sweet Lord', it had spun off a second blockbuster single, 'What Is Life', likewise half-spiritual, half-love song but infused with a *joie de vivre* of which George had never seemed capable, on or off a record.

Having trounced John and Paul in the singles charts himself, he made the same happen for the bandmate who'd never complained about being eclipsed by them. Ringo had been trying since 1968 to complete a song appropriately titled 'It Don't Come Easy'; now George helped him finish it (without asking for a credit), produced it with generous slabs of his heaviest guitar and saw it go to number one in America, where John's 'Power To The People' reached only number 11 and Paul's 'Another Day', number 5.

He still had a working relationship with Phil Spector and a pile of his songs unused on *All Things Must Pass*. Instead of saving these for its sequel, he offered them as a debut album for Spector's wife, Ronnie, who'd recently left the Ronettes to go solo.

This return to co-producing with Spector found the Svengali of Pop at his most unstable yet and resulted only in a single, 'Try Some, Buy Some', which failed to chart. Ronnie Spector would go on to write a hair-raising memoir of her life with a spouse so frantically possessive that he surrounded their house with barbed-wire and guard dogs, confiscated all her shoes to prevent her from escaping and threatened to kill her and display her corpse in a glass coffin he already had waiting in the basement if ever she tried to leave him.

'Where there's a hit, there's a writ,' the saying goes. But for a long age in pop music, plagiarism was rarely a courtroom issue: songs were generally so simplistic that they couldn't help duplicating themselves and few of their writers earned more than a pittance in publishing royalties.

What raised the stakes immeasurably was youthful performers, the Beatles especially, writing their own original material and the advent of singles and albums selling by the multi-million. When 'Yesterday' had come into Paul's head in 1965, he'd spent weeks checking that its melody wasn't just one he'd remembered and might be sued over. Nor did plagiarism necessarily apply to complete songs: the opening line of John's 'Come Together' used that of Chuck Berry's 'You Can't Catch Me' almost verbatim, for which the avaricious Berry would eventually demand a price.

But George's turn came first. At the very height of his dual triumph in achieving a worldwide smash and giving a two-finger salute to Lennon and McCartney, he found himself being sued for copyright infringement. An American publishing company with the artless name of Bright Tunes Music claimed that the three-note phrase running through 'My Sweet Lord' plagiarised 'He's So Fine' a hit by a black female vocal group, the Chiffons, in 1963.

Before the Bright Tunes writ, there had been some doubt as to whether 'My Sweet Lord' was all George's handiwork. He'd begun it while touring with Delaney & Bonnie, under the joint influence of the Edwin Hawkins Singers' 'Oh Happy Day' and Delaney Bramlett's slide-guitar style. Bramlett claimed to have supplied its riff and the ready-made words 'My Lord . . . Oh my Lord,' for which George promised him a co-writer's credit that had never materialised.

Despite the warning of 'It's Johnny's Birthday' and 'Congratulations', no thought of legal trouble from 'My Sweet Lord' had ever crossed George's mind. Though he certainly recalled the Chiffons' 'He's So Fine', it seemed remote from his interdenominational spiritual, besides which Billy Preston's gospel-ish version had come out two months ahead of *All Things Must Pass* without causing any legal trouble.

By an unlucky coincidence, during the album's gestation a new version of 'He's So Fine' by the American country chanteuse Jody

Miller had done moderately well on both sides of the Atlantic. Several members of George's studio superband had remarked on its similarity to 'My Sweet Lord', but he'd shrugged it off.

'He was mortified to be sued,' Pattie recollects; 'I was with him when he wrote it and it took him a long time to finish. He stopped me listening to the radio in case he heard something, put it into a song without realising and got sued by someone else.'

Allen Klein initially saw the lawsuit as no big deal and arranged for George and himself to meet with Bright Tunes' president, Seymour Barash, with a view to an out-of-court settlement. Klein's typically grandiose proposition was that George should acquire the rights to 'He's So Fine' (whose writer, Johnny Mack, had died just after it became a hit) by buying up the publishers' entire back catalogue. But Barash wanted the 'My Sweet Lord' copyright transferred to Bright Tunes, in return for which George would be allocated 50 per cent of its revenues.

No agreement could be reached and the litigation was to meander through the American courts for the next four years, with his royalties from one of the greatest pop hits of all time held in escrow.

Despite the many unforgotten grievances of his Beatle years, he refused all requests to be interviewed about the breakup, reinforcing the public view of Ringo and himself as the unfortunate children in a particularly messy divorce.

He saw a lot of John, whose Tittenhurst Park in Ascot was only minutes by car from Friar Park, and avoided all social situations where there was the slightest chance of bumping into Paul. To Paul's offences in their eyes was added the music he'd chosen to play with his new band, Wings, and his decision to turn his wife Linda into the creative soulmate John had once been.

In May 1971, Klaus Voormann was in the throes of separating from his wife, so George invited him to stay at Friar Park for as long as he needed. 'I asked him what he thought of Paul's new album with Linda,' Voormann recalls. 'All George said was "Oh well, I suppose it keeps him off the streets."'

The album was called *Ram* and its cover, showing Paul gripping the curly horns of a blackface ram on his Scottish farm, clearly owed something to George's anti-glamour portrait on *All Things Must Pass*. Yet, while selling in similarly huge quantities, it stirred none of the same critical rapture.

Rolling Stone called it 'incredibly inconsequential', 'monumentally irrelevant' and 'emotionally vacuous'. The *Village Voice* called it 'a classic form/content mismatch'. *Playboy* magazine charged Paul with 'substitut[ing] facility for substance' and likened the effect to 'watching someone juggle five guitars ... it's fairly impressive but you keep wondering why he bothers.'

One of the tracks, 'Too Many People', was an oblique reference to John's relationship with Yoko and all that Paul felt that she'd made him throw away: 'That was your first mistake/You took your lucky break and broke it in two.'

John at the time was making his first solo album without the Plastic Ono Band whose title track was an appeal to 'imagine all the people, living life in peace.' His response was to cut an extra song answering Paul's pinprick with a nuclear strike entitled 'How Do You Sleep?' whose verses competed in ludicrous unfairness: 'The only thing you done was "Yesterday",' was the monstrous charge. Inside the album sleeve, parodying the *Ram* cover, was a photograph of John gingerly gripping the ears of a bewildered pig.

'How Do You Sleep?' had a slide guitar solo by George,

nothing like the sweet, swooning 'My Sweet Lord' riff but a raw and shivery tirade that seemed in full agreement with John's verbal one. Truly, a case of 'vengeance is mine saith the Chord.'

That summer, the Indian subcontinent that had so enriched George's life focused his attention on something higher than scoring points off his former bandmates or fighting for the ownership of single musical notes. This time, his engagement was not with its music or religions but its history and politics.

The chaotic end to British colonial rule in 1947 had created the new nation of Pakistan for a Muslim-majority population to sit alongside Hindu-majority India. Pakistan itself had then been split into two segments on opposite sides of the subcontinent, the easterly one encompassing the former fiercely individualistic state of Bengal.

West Pakistan, the bisected country's administrative and economic hub, had always discriminated against far poorer East Pakistan, starving it of funds for development, scorning its political and legal processes and trying to suppress its vibrant Bengali language and literature. Finally, in March 1971, it had unilaterally declared independence, renaming itself Bangladesh.

The ensuing civil war between Bengali insurgents and a West Pakistan military that frequently resorted to genocide was only one of Bangladesh's multiple birth-agonies. Battered by the ruinous Bhola Cyclone a few months earlier, it was now hit by torrential rain and apocalyptic floods. Millions of terrified refugees were caught in the crossfire of guns and the elements, and starvation and disease, including cholera, were omnipresent.

George at the time was in Los Angeles with Ravi Shankar, finalising the music soundtrack to *Raga*, the oft-interrupted film about Shankar's life and music. The horrors unfolding in Bangladesh suddenly seemed close to home, for Shankar came from a Bengali brahmin family and several of his relations were among the victims.

Shankar had some thoughts of holding a benefit concert with his own Indian ensemble and former sitar-pupil, but hesitated to take advantage of his friendship with George by suggesting it. George, however, jumped at this opportunity to give something back to the subcontinent and support the man he esteemed most in the world. It would also exercise his new freedom to take a public stand on a moral issue which he'd never been allowed to do as a Beatle.

He immediately proposed a concert combining Shankar's Eastern and his Western music – something rarely attempted before – for which he would persuade a selection of his superstar friends to play for charity. The obvious venue for an event of such scale was New York's 20,000-capacity Madison Square Garden. But the Garden's only available slot was Sunday 1 August, just five weeks away.

Despite this desperately short notice, the project expanded far beyond a one-off performance. To supplement the ticket sales, which George hoped would raise about $25,000, there would be a live triple album and a film. He would also write and co-produce (with Phil Spector) a single aimed both at publicising the concert and raising awareness of Bangladesh's ordeal internationally.

His former PA, Chris O'Dell, now back in America, worked on the concert while his old ally Neil Aspinall, who'd survived the Allen Klein purges at Apple, dealt with setting up the album and film. But the crucial celebrity-recruitment was handled by George personally for hour after hour on the telephone. 'He'd never put on a show like this before,' Aspinall would recall. 'To my mind, it took a lot of humility for him to call around with the obvious risk of being turned down.'

The promotional single, 'Bangla Desh', a common alternative spelling at the time, was in the anthemic style of 'My Sweet Lord' and 'All Things Must Pass'. Its lyrics hardly did the subject justice – 'now won't you give some bread? To get the starving fed?' – but probably none could have done. Adding further emotional weight, the B-side was 'Deep Blue', about his mother's death and his anguish in watching her fade.

He also somehow found time to produce a selection of Ravi Shankar's music entitled *Joi Bangla* and including some of the Bengali songs that had been banned during West Pakistan's rule. A delighted Shankar greeted it as 'a miracle'.

'Bangla Desh' reached number 10 in Britain and peaked at 13 in America. Don Heckman in the *Village Voice* drew favourable comparisons with other ex-Beatles at that same moment: 'I have no quarrel with John Lennon's endless clattering around inside his psyche or Paul McCartney's search for sweetness and light, but at the moment I have to have stronger feelings about George Harrison's active efforts to do something about the misery in the world around him.'

In late July, the back pages of the *New York Times* carried a modest advertisement for an appearance by 'George Harrison and Friends' at Madison Square Garden on the evening of 1 August, making no mention of its purpose. The tickets sold out so quickly that an afternoon show had to be added.

At a mobbed press conference George identified those 'Friends' as Ringo Starr, Leon Russell, Billy Preston, Eric Clapton and Bob Dylan. Beside him sat Allen Klein, who had rallied to the project for his first-ever experience of being on the side of the angels.

It was only four months since the Beatles' breakup and the mention of Ringo's name touched off rumours of an onstage reunion sans Paul that no amount of weary denials by George could scotch. In fact, John had initially agreed to appear, then pulled out on discovering the invitation didn't include Yoko.

A questioner rather patronisingly asked George how it felt 'to be the number one guy, the star'. 'I prefer to be part of a band,' he said. 'But we had to do it like this to get the money [for Bangladesh]. I had to put myself out there and hope my friends would come and help me out.'

The two foremost of his capital F friends actually did rather the opposite of helping him out before they finally shared the Garden's stage.

Eric Clapton had soon tired of Derek and the Dominos, as he did of every band, and was holed up at home in rural Surrey with nineteen-year-old Alice Ormsby-Gore and his heroin habit, the peer's daughter repeatedly imperilling her father's good name by scoring the smack, then giving it all to Clapton while she sought her own oblivion by drinking two bottles of vodka a day.

Despite the shenanigans with Pattie, George could not conceive of leaving Clapton out of the Concert For Bangladesh. For a whole week, he had him booked on successive flights to New York and limos waiting for him at Kennedy Airport in vain. Many other top lead guitarists were hanging around in hopes of the gig and finally George gave it to Jesse Ed Davis from the bluesman Taj Mahal's backing band. But when Terry Doran went to Clapton's house to tell him his services were no longer required, he insisted he would be coming.

It being too risky to try to smuggle his daily fixes through US Customs, George had had to promise a supply would be waiting for him at his hotel. Unfortunately, this proved to be 'street-cut' – i.e., mixed with talcum powder or baby-milk formula – and only about 10 per cent of the strength his system demanded. Clapton spent the next three days locked away in his room in the sweating palpitations of cold turkey while Alice and George's minions sought a dealer with merchandise of sufficient purity. Such was his condition, he barely registered Pattie's arrival in New York to be with George at this huge moment and she wisely steered well clear of him.

Bob Dylan's participation in the concert seemed in equal jeopardy. The last time Dylan had played live in New York had been when folkie purists had booed him for 'going electric', and the experience still rankled.

A recce of Madison Square Garden with George on the night before the concerts only increased his unease. '[Dylan] looked at all the film cameras and lights and the size of the place and said "No, man, this isn't my scene,"' George would recall. 'I said it wasn't mine either: "This is the first time I've ever done anything like this on my own. You at least have been a solo artist for years."'

Each of the two shows attracted a capacity crowd of 20,000 and their combined ticket sales totalled $250,000, ten times what George had hoped. for. But there was none of the screaming he used to find so repugnant as a Beatle. Both audiences watched in silence appropriate to the gravity of the cause they were supporting and applauded in a reverent low key, the first house even doing so when Ravi Shankar and his musicians finished their preparatory tune-up.

George himself had been racked with stage-fright, prey to

vomiting and diarrhoea and strongly tempted to flee in Dylan's footsteps until the knell of Showtime. Yet, wearing a white Stratocaster over his ice-cream suit, there was something almost saintly about him as he emceed with aplomb and performed his first-ever live versions of 'Here Comes the Sun', 'Something' and 'Wah-Wah'. And, although the audience never knew it, two small miracles were to happen up on that stage.

Clapton had been incapable of attending a single rehearsal and, heavily dosed with the heroin substitute methadone, was not expected to produce a single coherent chord. But when time came for 'While My Guitar Gently Weeps', he stepped forward to play a single-string duet with George as mutually warm as their plectrum-duel over Pattie at Friar Park had been edgy.

The running-order taped to George's Strat read 'Bob?' and until almost the last minute, the answer seemed to be 'No'; indeed, he was so taken by surprise when Dylan materialised in the wings, guitar and frame-mounted mouth organ at the ready, that he could barely stammer out an introduction to 'your friend and mine'.

As if it had never been in doubt, Dylan performed a superb five-song set including 'A Hard Rain's Gonna Fall' (no surprise to any Bangladeshi) and 'Just Like A Woman' with George and Leon Russell on backing vocals and nary a feminist protest at the line 'She breaks just like a little girl.'

Rolling Stone called the concerts 'a brief incandescent revival of all that was best in the Sixties'. The *New Musical Express*'s Bob Woffinden said they were 'a declaration of faith' and that George had 'put rock back on track'. Ravi Shankar and his musicians also received due credit, the *Village Voice* calling Shankar and his distinguished sarod-player, Ali Akbar Khan, 'a pairing as unique as Dylan and Harrison'.

'And the next day,' Shankar would declare, 'the whole world knew the name of Bangladesh.'

The proceeds from the Ravi Shankar/George Harrison Emergency Relief Fund, derived from the concerts, live album and film, were to be channelled via the United Nations Children's Fund (UNICEF), a neutral body that could not offend any political sensitivities in the disaster area and deliver help where it was most needed with maximum efficiency.

George had unknowingly done far more than relieve a specific humanitarian crisis. He had altered the whole conception of rock stars as motivated solely by greed and egotism and shown that an industry could also be a community and a potent force, if it chose, for doing good. The Concert For Bangladesh would be a blueprint for similar events in decades to come, from Live Aid to No Nukes and Rock Against Racism, many bigger, starrier and higher grossing but none to compare.

22

'BY THE GRACE OF KRISHNA, YOU ARE ONE OF THE GREAT MEN'

George had meant to start work on his follow-up to *All Things Must Pass* at the beginning of 1972. But he'd reckoned without the Concert For Bangladesh's lengthy aftermath and the many ways in which it would confirm the old adage that 'no good turn goes unpunished'.

The first and most serious stemmed from Allen Klein's inexperience in this strange new world of doing things for free. Klein had failed to register the Bangladesh project in America as a tax-exempt charity before it commenced operations, as the law required. Consequently, the Internal Revenue Service refused to treat it as such and decreed that between $8 and $10 million of the proceeds from its film and triple live album should be held in escrow until the matter was resolved (which it wouldn't be for around ten years).

In Britain, official hearts proved equally flinty. George had expected the government to waive its usual hefty purchase tax to make the album affordable to the largest possible public and so maximise the relief to Bangladesh. He took the request personally to a Treasury minister, only to be treated with amused condescension. 'Sorry,' the minister told him, 'it's all very well for your high ideals, but the country needs the money.'

There was also a dispute over which record company should release the album: Capitol/EMI, which distributed Apple product in the US, or Bob Dylan's label, CBS, on the grounds that Dylan was its head-headliner. Capitol won, at the price of giving CBS domestic tape-distribution rights and record and tape distribution in the rest of the world.

The album pulled no punches: its cover showed a malnourished Bangladeshi child sitting beside an empty food-bowl. Capitol marketing people thought the image 'too depressing' but George told them that was the whole point and refused to let it be toned down.

Packaged with the three discs was a sixty-four-page booklet, charging the West Pakistan military with 'a deliberate reign of terror' against East Pakistan's Bengali population and calling it 'the greatest atrocity since Hitler's extermination of the Jews'. Different indeed from the Beatle whose lip had had to stay buttoned throughout the worst years of the Vietnam War.

Most of the participants' record companies entered into the charitable spirit by charging no fees or percentages for their artists' performances. The one exception was Capitol itself, all the more surprisingly since its new CEO, Bhaskar Menon, was the first person from the Indian subcontinent to have reached such heights in the industry and might have been expected to feel a special empathy for George's cause.

However, the company that had once floated happily on seas of Beatles profits was now in financial trouble and Menon's brief was to turn it around by whatever means were necessary. He therefore insisted it should earn 25 cents on each copy of

George's charity album and even demanded that Apple pay Capitol around half a million dollars towards the high costs of its packaging.

George had done his utmost to get both the album and film documentary released while the memory of the concerts was still fresh. Whereas the recording of the music had gone perfectly, the filming had been seriously botched; one stage-side camera was afterwards found to have been out of focus throughout the show and another blocked by hanging cables. He'd therefore spent most of September in New York with the director, Saul Swimmer, editing the footage to conceal its gaps as much as possible, assisted in the latter stages by Bob Dylan.

Thanks to Bhaskar Menon's haggling over contractual minu-tiae the album missed its deadline for the Christmas market and bootleg versions began to proliferate. Capitol issued record stores with sublimely tasteless posters reading: 'Save a starving child – don't buy a bootleg.'

Finally, George was driven publicly to challenge his own record-company boss from the set of Dick Cavett's primetime TV talk show where he was supposed to be plugging the finally released Ravi Shankar documentary, *Raga*. Only half-jokingly, he threatened to give the album to CBS, and dared Menon to sue him.

That prompted its release on the cusp of 1972, to reviews that made its three-month hold-up and awkward timing irrelevant. *Circus* magazine could not find praise enough for 'music that practically jumps out into your life'. *Rolling Stone* described it as 'rock reaching for its manhood' and *The Guardian* as 'rock's greatest act of magnanimity'. In every one, George himself seemed close to canonisation. 'The spirit he creates through his own demeanour is inspirational,' wrote the critic Jon Landau. 'Concert for Bangladesh was George's moment. He put it together and he pulled it off.' Even with British purchase tax grimly added on, it sold in massive quantities and would win Album of the Year at the 1973 Grammys.

Outside the music business, the only public recognition he received, in tandem with Ravi Shankar and Allen Klein, his titular co-organiser, was UNICEF'S Child Is The Father Of The Man award for 'pioneering in fundraising'.

This rare flattering portrayal of Klein was soon undermined when *New York* magazine accused him of creaming off $1.44 from every album, one of a list of covert beneficiaries allegedly including Dylan (25 cents per copy) and the publishers and songwriters (50 cents).

Klein denied any such misappropriation, saying that in fact the album was costing him money and filing a lawsuit against the magazine for $150 million in damages. After an initial burst of publicity, the suit was dropped. Not so easily disposed of was the music industry joke, paraphrasing Pepsodent toothpaste's 'You'll wonder where the yellow went' jingle: 'You'll wonder where the money went/When Klein runs a charity event.'

On the evening of 28 February, George and Pattie were to have had a rare evening out together in London, hopefully recalling happier times. They'd been invited to an after-concert party for Rick Nelson, the former Fifties teen-idol Ricky whom Pattie had once swooned over. George would often tease her about it when his teasing used to be gentle.

This night, they barely made it out of Henley. On a slip-road to the M4, the traffic flow had been changed since George had last used it and, going too fast as always in his white Mercedes, he drove straight across a roundabout and into a concrete lamp post.

Neither of them was wearing a seatbelt and both could easily have been killed, for the impact crushed the whole front of the Mercedes. Pattie suffered severe concussion and badly bruised ribs and George a gashed forehead. He had to climb over her unconscious body to get out and flag down help with a face so bloodied, the first driver to stop didn't recognise him.

The couple were taken to Maidenhead General Hospital – where an opportunistic staff member managed to photograph the blood-streaked George in the ambulance – and kept in overnight; then he was allowed home and Pattie transferred to a private clinic for what would be a two-week stay.

He was prosecuted for careless driving and lost his licence for the second time in a year. Mortified by what had happened to Pattie, he seemed to return to his former sweet self during the weeks it took her bruised ribs to heal when the slightest movement was agony. But once she was back to full mobility, the ice re-formed around him.

There were lots of people at Friar Park these days as the finishing touches were made to the recording studio where George intended to do most of his work in future. Often, he was so preoccupied with that or the gardens that Pattie would have to communicate with him via Terry Doran.

These people, almost exclusively male, treated him with a deference that couldn't have been further from the verbal snap-and-crackle of the Beatles' circle. 'I asked him once, "Why do you have all these yes-men around you?"' she recalls. 'He said, "Because it's better than having no-men."'

Allen Klein paid only one visit to Friar Park that she can call to mind, but it was enough for her to get his measure. 'For some reason, we all played Happy Families, that innocent children's card-game. And I realised Allen was cheating.'

As the person who'd started him on his meditation journey, Pattie felt sad to be excluded even from that. His Hare Krishna friend and studio-sentinel Syamsundara had recently introduced him to A. C. Bhaktivedanta Prabhupada, the movement's seventy-seven-year-old founder, who was taking him far further than the modest gurus of the Asian Music Circle.

The Hare Krishnas were in need of a permanent British home and, with the munificence of which he was sometimes capable, George bought them a faux-Tudor house named Piggotts Manor near Watford, Hertfordshire, to serve as the headquarters of the International Society For Krishna Consciousness (ISKCON).

He regularly visited the renamed Bhaktivedanta Manor by himself for lengthy consultations with the swami that were often less spiritual than self-analytical. A recording has survived of one in which he showed an awareness of the two contradictory sides of himself – what Ringo called 'the bag of beads and the bag of cocaine'.

'I go around in circles,' he tells the swami. 'Maybe it's something to do with me being, you know, the Pisces. [Its symbols] show one fish going this way, the other that way. There are periods when I can't stop chanting and there are other periods when, you know, I turn into a demon again.

'You are not demon,' says Bhaktivedanta Swami, who knows how to lay it on. 'You are demigod. You have somehow got attached to Krishna. That will help you.'

He says he's been trying to read the Bhagavad Gita in the original Sanskrit, but finds the 'dots' (i.e., pronunciation marks) endlessly confusing. Syamsundara suggests he should listen to a tape of the swami reading and learn the pronunciation by ear. 'I can learn anything by ear,' George says.

Syamsundara reads a passage aloud, then translates: 'Whatever action is performed by great men, common men follow in his footsteps. And whatever standards he sets by exemplary acts, all the world pursues.'

'So there is your instruction,' the swami tells him. 'By the grace of Krishna, you are one of the great men.'

George was never outright cruel to Pattie, but wounding insensitivity had always been part of his nature. She was no longer his sole creative muse for he'd written a song about Chris O'Dell, the one employee who could get along with him without a trace of sycophancy, and he was determined to let her know it.

'Miss O'Dell' had none of the shy erotic charge of 'Something'; it was a jaunty Country number pleading with Chris to phone him, as he still did even now she no longer worked for him, to sort out some problem anyone else would find insoluble. Nonetheless, he deliberately played it to her while Pattie was in the room as if trying to stir up some kind of muses' catfight. The two women's friendship thwarted him, however: Pattie merely hugged Chris and said she was delighted George had paid her such a tribute.

At such moments, she often found her thoughts turning to Eric Clapton, who'd broadcast his adoration of her to the world so brazenly in 'Layla'. By rights, she ought to have wanted nothing more to do with Clapton since his brief affair with her teenage sister, Paula, as a substitute for her, had left Paula heroin-addicted as well as broken-hearted. Pattie tried her utmost to suppress the thought that now, for however short a time, he was available.

Yet all George's coldness and neglect hadn't succeeded in killing her love, nor the hope that he might somehow miraculously revert to the person she'd married in 1966. Besides, she'd seen how ruthlessly a Beatle ex-wife could be cast into outer darkness when Cynthia Lennon had divorced John on the grounds of his adultery with Yoko and received a settlement of just £100,000.

That August, in another withering snub to Pattie, George announced he was to drive to the South of France and Portugal with his front passenger seat 'reserved for Krishna'. 'I drove for about twenty-three hours,' he later told Swami Prabhupada proudly, 'and chanted all the way.'

Two months later, he began his long-delayed follow-up to *All Things Must Pass* in the ballroom-sized home studio henceforward to be known as FPSHOT (Friar Park Studios Henley-on-Thames).

It was supposed to have been another co-production with Phil Spector, once more brought over from New York at colossal expense. But since *All Things Must Pass*, Spector's alcohol-fuelled paranoia had taken a quantum leap and after a couple of exploratory sessions he holed up in his suite at London's Inn On The Park hotel whence he could not be enticed by telephone or telegram.

Reluctant to lose him, George got the hotel's permission to go onto the roof at a place where he could climb into Spector's window and plead with him to return to work, a considerable risk in view of the gun Spector never left or stayed home without. But after a couple of these death-defying clambers, he had to admit defeat.

It was just as well for, after the Himalayan distances and studio orchestra of *All Things Must Pass*, he wanted a more intimate feel with a scaled-down group of friends like Ringo, Klaus Voormann and pianist Nicky Hopkins. Nor would there be an Eric Clapton to compete with this time as Clapton was finally trying to rid himself of his heroin habit.

Enough unused material had been left over from *All Things* to give the new album a powerful lift-off, especially as it was to consist of only a single disc. But George had written an almost completely new set of songs, most dealing openly or obliquely with the question that increasingly weighed on him. How could being the world's biggest rock star, as he indubitably now was, be reconciled with the simplicity and humility that were his only path to being a truly spiritual being?

Its title track, 'Living In The Material World', had been inspired by long conversations with Bhaktivedanta Swami about the illusoriness of human existence and the need to escape the endless cycle of birth and rebirth to achieve the Hindu state of *moksha* or ultimate transcendence.

George's lyric was, for George, extraordinarily personal, touching on the particular material world he had fallen into with 'John, Paul and Ritchie' (the name by which everyone close to Ringo knew him), and confessing to having used his body 'like a car' (which wasn't saying much, given his recent displays of driving).

Whereas he'd been like a global prayer-leader in 'My Sweet

Lord', now he was vulnerable and uncertain, hoping 'I don't get lost or go astray' before seeing 'the Spiritual Sky . . . by the Lord Sri Krishna's grace'.

As the album neared completion, however, the material world thrust itself back into the foreground. In April 1973, Allen Klein's four-year management contract, which had continued in force with all the former Beatles except Paul, came up for renewal.

George and Ringo naturally looked to John, who had hired Klein in the first place and always defended him against the multiple accusations of crookery that had followed him from New York. But now a drip-feed of damning evidence about his tenure at Apple was making even John concede that Paul might have been right about him all along.

For George, the last straw had been Klein's failure to insulate the Bangladesh project from the Taxman he'd hated with particular virulence since the Beatles' *Revolver* album. In the coming summer, he would find himself signing a cheque from Apple to Britain's Inland Revenue for one million pounds.

So Klein's contract was not renewed and, by way of limbering up for the inevitable court battles to come, he immediately sued George for an alleged outstanding loan of around $270,000 from his ABKCO company and also claimed that Harrisongs Inc., which handled George's publishing in the US, rightfully belonged to ABKCO.

One of many ways in which the pop world had changed since 1969 was that someone at George's level no longer needed an all-purpose manager but a highly specific financial adviser. His friend the comedian Peter Sellers recommended an expatriate American lawyer named Denis O'Brien who'd sorted out

Sellers' complicated finances following his appearances in the *Pink Panther* films.

In contrast to the squat, oily-haired street-fighter Klein, O'Brien proved to be angular and bald with outsize spectacles and the permanent fixed smile of a ventriloquist's doll. He impressed George with extravagant compliments to his intelligence rather than the usual predictable ones to his music. 'The Chairman of Shell, of Rio Tinto Zinc, of IBM, of Ford ... I've met all these people and I've never met anyone so together.'

George in turn was mightily impressed by O'Brien's civilised air and seeming mastery of superstar economics: 'In twenty minutes,' he said, 'Denis can get more from a balance-sheet than most people do in twenty hours.'

Which would prove only too true, although not quite in the way he'd meant.

Not since *All Things Must Pass* had an album been awaited as eagerly as *Living In The Material World*. Two days after its US release on 30 May, the Recording Industries Association of America certified it as gold with more than half a million copies sold. For a second time, George achieved a '*Billboard* double' with the paper showing both the album and its single, 'Give Me Love (Give Me Peace On Earth') at the top of their respective charts.

For the most part, the album reflected the teachings of Bhaktivedanta Swami and George's own spiritual quest, with cosmic but uncatchy titles like 'The Light That Has Lighted The World', 'The Day The World Gets Round' and 'The Lord Loves The One (That Loves The Lord)'. Often his vocal almost seemed to liquefy into a chant while his slide guitar does the talking.

The mood was not exclusively devotional. His wittier demon was on display in 'Sue Me Sue You', a blues tune invoking such disagreeable discoveries as escrow and serving of legal papers. 'Miss O'Dell' was also included where once there might have been a love note to Pattie. The only bit of recycling was the anomalously anti-drug 'Try Some Buy Some', already recorded by Phil Spector's wife Ronnie, which George now revoiced over Spector's Wall of Sound orchestration.

Obedient to the swami's strictures about humility, or so it seemed, he refused to promote the album in the usual form of press and television interviews; his closest to a related public appearance didn't come until two months after its release when he joined the swami in a religious procession through Central London.

Rolling Stone led the ecstatic American reviews, saying 'it stands alone as an article of faith, miraculous in its radiance'. In more cynical Britain, it was felt to have a preachiness that *All Things Must Pass* had avoided. The *New Musical Express*'s Tony Tyler called it 'pleasant and competent, vaguely dull and inoffensive. Also breathtakingly unoriginal and – lyrically at least – turgid, repetitive and so damned holy I could scream.'

By contrast, despite all its monkish memorabilia, domestic life at Friar Park could not remotely be described as holy. In the past, George had always been reasonably discreet about his infidelities but since Eric Clapton's public declaration of being in love with Pattie, he seemed to feel entitled to pursue them openly, now sometimes with women friends of hers and even under their own roof.

One of his current musical side projects was with the soon-to-be Rolling Stone Ronnie Wood, then still lead guitar with

Rod Stewart and the Faces. George helped Ronnie write a song, 'Far East Man', for his debut solo album, contributing slide guitar and backing vocals, and started an affair with his wife, Krissy.

The Woods lived in nearby Richmond and while Ronnie was on the road with the Faces, Krissy would often spend nights at Friar Park. Yet George repeatedly told Pattie nothing was going on between them and accused her of paranoia.

Early in that summer of '73, he refused to go on holiday with Pattie to Portugal and instead went to Spain with Krissy Wood, allegedly to visit the surrealist painter Salvador Dalí. While they were away, Ronnie turned up at Friar Park and stayed a few days purely as a friend. He seemed not at all put out that George was off with his wife and his easy-going nature was like a tonic to Pattie. He might have felt differently had he known George was also trying to arrange a threesome with Krissy, himself, and the girlfriend of another first-echelon guitarist, Alvin Lee.

In his autobiography, *Ronnie*, he recalls a night when he and Krissy were both house guests and the Seventies pastime of wife-swapping reached a peculiarly macho pitch. 'I took George aside and told him that when it was time for bed I would be going to Pattie's room. Seemingly unflustered he pointed at the room Krissy and I were staying in and said, "I shall be sleeping there."

'When the time came, we stood outside the respective bedrooms. "Are we going to do this?" I asked George. "I'll see you in court," George replied and in we went.'

Whatever the current political climate between John, Paul and George, all three remained equally fond of Ringo and felt a responsibility to help him navigate their new life apart. George, in particular, had mentored him as a songwriter from his own hard-won experience, co-writing and producing his two hit singles, 'It Don't Come Easy' and 'Back Off Boogaloo' without taking any credit.

Ringo now had a successful film career after his appearances in *Candy* and *The Magic Christian*, but in 1973 he decided to pause it and make a solo album in Los Angeles. A crowd of well-wishers had rushed to lend a hand, among them Billy Preston, Harry Nilsson, Marc Bolan and four members of The Band. And, true to his mollifying influence, it was to bring all the ex-Beatles together on a record for the very first time.

John happened to be in LA on the drunken furlough from Yoko he would later call his Lost Weekend; at the same time George was there to work on an album project with Ravi Shankar. Stopping by Ringo's recording sessions, he noticed they included 'Photograph', a song they'd written together two years earlier and test-recorded during breaks from *Living In The Material World*. Also scheduled was a new John Lennon song called 'I'm The Greatest', on which John had agreed to play.

For a brief space, the old Beatle enchantment was back and the producer, Richard Perry, and all the other session stars could only watch and marvel as John and George sang backing vocals on 'I'm the Greatest'. Paul was currently denied entry to the US following a conviction for growing cannabis on his Scottish farm – and anyway not yet ready for a rapprochement with John and George. But he too offered a song, 'Six O'clock', which Ringo later recorded backed by Linda and himself at Apple studios in London.

The single picked from the album was 'Photograph' and it became an international hit, certified gold in America for sales of more than a million. Yet again George had been the means of building up the friend he was soon to let down so grievously.

Hitherto, Ringo's wife Maureen had been the least noticeable of the four Beatle spouses. A Liverpool hairdresser when he picked her out of the Cavern crowd, she was small and quiet, with huge, panda-rimmed eyes. Since their marriage in 1965, she'd kept dutifully in the background, seemingly content to stay home and look after their sons, Zak and Jason, and daughter, Lee.

She was not quite as mouse-like as she seemed, especially when other women showed too much interest in Ringo. After George's then PA, Chris O'Dell, had chatted innocently with him at a party, Chris discovered Maureen had phoned Pattie for a detailed description of who and what she was.

Chris was impressed by what seemed an unextinguishable romance between the couple. 'They were always holding hands. Every time [Maureen] picked up a cigarette Ringo would suddenly appear next to her with his silver lighter. He'd look at her adoringly, she'd look at him lovingly and when she exhaled she'd lower her eyes as if the moment was too intimate even for a man and woman who'd been married for eight years.'

When John had moved to New York with Yoko, he sold Ringo Tittenhurst Park, his Georgian stately home in Ascot, only thirty minutes by car from Henley. And somewhere between the two houses known as parks, George had broken the First Commandment of Beatlehood that was binding for always: Thou shalt not have it off with another Beatle's wife.

Pattie's suspicions were first aroused when she returned from a visit to her mother in Devon and found some photographs

George had taken of Maureen at Friar Park during her absence. She further discovered that a necklace Maureen often flaunted in front of her had been a gift from him. But even confronted with such evidence, he would admit nothing.

Before long, he wouldn't even wait for Pattie to be out of the house. Late at night when she was alone in Friar Park's great hall with only its friar-faced light-switches for company, Maureen would show up on the pretext of 'listening to George in the studio' and would still be there the next morning without the least sign of shame or apology. 'Her attitude was very much that she had the right to spend the night with George if she felt like it,' Pattie recalls.

Then the affair moved to daytime: he disappeared with Maureen into the house's upper regions while musicians were waiting to begin work with him in his recording studio. 'I thought, "This is being deliberately rubbed in my face,"' Pattie says. '"He and Maureen want me to know this is happening."'

Pushed beyond endurance at last, she sought out the guilty bedroom – a lengthy process since there were more than twenty to choose from – and hammered on the door. George opened it to reveal Maureen on a mattress on the floor, but still would not admit any guilt. 'Oh, she's a bit tired,' he explained. 'She's having a rest.'

A French or Italian wife at this point might have resorted to a loaded revolver. Pattie's milder English response was to attack Maureen with a brace of water pistols and then give two fingers to the Hare Krishna piety that George could put on and off as it suited him.

From Friar Park's tallest spire flew an OM flag, signifying that meditation was practised within. Pattie remembered that put away downstairs was another flag, left over from some fancy-dress party in jollier times: a pirate skull-and-crossbones. With the help of two sympathetic studio engineers, she hauled down the OM and ran up the Jolly Roger.

Christmas was approaching and Chris O'Dell had been invited to spend the holiday at Friar Park after an exhausting American tour with the Rolling Stones as Mick Jagger's PA. She sensed something wrong on her first evening as she and Pattie sat together in the library with a visiting Ronnie Wood while George and Maureen shared a small sofa in the front hall, 'looking very private and intense'. Next morning, when George brought her a cup of tea in bed, he told her he was in love with Maureen.

She then had the full story from Pattie: how George and Maureen had been carrying on under her very nose; how when she'd tried to tell Ringo what had been going on totally without his knowledge he'd flown into a rage – something no one had ever seen before – and refused to listen to her.

Corroboration came the next evening while George, Pattie and Chris were having supper with Ringo and Maureen at Tittenhurst Park, seated around the long kitchen table where John and Yoko had planned their final European exploits before seeking, and finding, greater tolerance across the Atlantic.

With his famous disregard for conversational subtleties, George told Ringo: 'I'm in love with your wife,' in a voice loud enough for all the others to hear. They were almost the exact words Eric Clapton had used to him about Pattie, but at least those had been in private.

'There was absolute silence,' Chris O'Dell recalls, 'as if everyone's hearts had stopped beating at once. Finally, [Ringo] looked at George. "Better you than someone we don't know," he said.'

Despite the steep decline in festive spirit this naturally brought about, Ringo still threw a lavish New Year's Eve party at Tittenhurst. As George, Pattie and Terry Doran were setting off in George's car, Pattie realised she'd forgotten something, dashed to her bedroom to fetch it and through the window saw the car's tail lights disappear into the night; George, at his most brutally dismissive, had gone without her.

She had to drive herself to Ascot through thick fog that reduced traffic to a crawl. When midnight struck, she was marooned in a seemingly immovable jam and all the drivers got out of their vehicles and wished each other a happy 1974.

In her case, this seemed doubtful. George's only greeting when she finally arrived at the party was 'Let's have a divorce this year.'

Yet their marriage stumbled on for several months more. George's grand passion for Maureen burnt itself out, leaving her and Ringo so estranged that they would divorce the following year. John had described the episode as 'virtual incest' and from now on if anyone dared raise the subject with George, he would use the same term, minus the 'virtual', to check them from probing further.

He had said nothing further to Pattie about getting a divorce but with Eric Clapton's reappearance in their lives, the prospect came several steps closer. Clapton's heroin addiction had been cured by a process called neuroelectric therapy, a kind of acupuncture which counteracted the drug's horrible withdrawal symptoms. Part of the process had been his enforced separation from Alice Ormsby-Gore, who'd been unable to kick the habit permanently (and, lacking a rock star's protective layers, would die from a massive overdose aged only forty-two).

Now Clapton's career was back on track; he had a new band with whom he'd made his second solo album as a named vocalist, *461 Ocean Boulevard*. Later that summer, he would score his first number one single with a cover of Bob Marley and the Wailers' 'I Shot The Sheriff'.

Yet a different addiction had proved immune to neuroelectric therapy. After five years of spasmodic pursuit, propositioning and pleading, none to any lasting effect, he remained as guiltily obsessed as ever with his best friend's wife.

He became a regular caller at Friar Park again, ostensibly to see George but taking every opportunity to woo Pattie with senses now unimpaired. 'George must have realised we were having an affair, but he never said so,' she would recall. 'I felt he wanted to break us up, he wanted to get rid of me. We were like chopsticks, joined together and cracking apart.'

Clapton was about to begin his first American tour since beating heroin and under his own name. Before setting off, he showed up at Friar Park with two musician cronies, Pete Townshend and Graham Bell, who had instructions to keep George talking in his studio while Clapton had one last try at persuading Pattie to go off with him. He was 'passionate, desperate and compelling', but still she hesitated.

Not until July could she nerve herself to go to George late at night in his studio and say she could stand no more of their 'ludicrous and hateful life . . . Half of me wanted to believe him when he said he would make it better, but I was at the end of my tether . . . When he came to bed, I could feel his sadness as he lay beside me. "Don't go," he said.'

The next day, she left the madcap mansion she loved as much as he did, her only immediate plan to fly to Los Angeles to stay with her sister, Jenny, who, somewhat following family tradition, had married Mick Fleetwood, the drummer and co-founder of Fleetwood Mac. To add to her distress, the credit cards George had allowed her had already been cancelled.

Clapton, on the road in America, soon learned what had happened and telephoned her at Jenny's, asking her to meet him the next week when he'd be appearing in Boston – but clearly not just to watch a performance.

This time, she said yes.

23

'IF PEOPLE WANT THEIR MONEY
BACK, THEY CAN HAVE IT'

George would later say that he and Pattie had lived virtually separate lives for so long that the final break came almost without him noticing. On the contrary, there could hardly have been a greater embarrassment for a former Beatle and an idol to millions than to be walked out on by his wife.

The reality was that it brought on a spell of heavy drinking like a quieter version of John's Lost Weekend even with the same tipple, Courvoisier five star brandy, of which he would put away a whole bottle at a sitting, added to a much-increased intake of cocaine and weed.

His new uncoupled status made women's hearts worldwide beat faster with the thought that it mightn't be too late for them after all. But not for long. Within a couple of weeks, he was dating the model Kathy Simmonds who'd formerly been with Rod Stewart, so now had to make a hasty adjustment to meditation and vegetarianism from football, beer and boogie.

For consolation during the bleak finale with Pattie, he'd turned back to India and to Ravi Shankar, his mentor, surrogate father and protégé. He flew to Mumbai to attend a ceremony of blessing for Shankar's new house, then stayed on for two months.

During 1973, he'd produced an album bringing the pick of Shankar's Indian virtuosi, including his son Shubho and sister-in-law Lakshmi, together with Western rock-star friends like Ringo and Billy Preston for another pioneering experiment in World Music. This became the genesis of Ravi Shankar's Music Festival from India, a travelling revue with George's sponsorship and regular participation.

MFI's appearance at the Royal Albert Hall was the first event in support of George's Material World Charitable Foundation, set up at the time of the album's release 'to promote diverse artistic endeavours and philosophies' and support a range of welfare organisations. To ensure it a reliable income stream in perpetuity and avoid the tax complications that had dogged the Concert For Bangladesh, he assigned it nine of *Living In The Material World*'s eleven song copyrights.

Shankar's *Family And Friends* album was supposed to have been for Apple Records, where George by now had almost sole responsibility for finding and developing new talent. But in 1974, Apple was winding down and there was only one other way to give so precious a charge the kind of launch he wanted.

By that point, several leading British pop names had emulated the Beatles in starting their own record labels, notably the Rolling Stones after finally breaking free of Allen Klein. Following the Apple model, such labels were not self-sufficient organisations but satellites of major record companies that were paying increasingly vast sums for the prestige of manufacturing their product and handling its marketing and distribution.

George's contract with Apple as a recording artist still had two years to run, but there was nothing to stop him having his own label and working purely as a talent scout and producer until he was free to appear on it.

Despite the offer of a much larger advance against future royalties from Apple's distributors, Capitol/EMI, he accepted $1 million for four albums from the much smaller A&M label in whose Hollywood studios the *Shankar Family & Friends* album had been made. He was still seething over Capitol's uncharitable handling of the *Concert For Bangladesh* album, and felt that A&M would be a more empathetic partner. The A stood for its co-founder, the trumpet-player Herb Alpert, who had a hugely successful parallel career with the Tijuana Brass.

George called his label Dark Horse, the racing fraternity's name for a rank outsider that suddenly surges past the odds-on favourite to leave it far behind, just as he'd outstripped Lennon and McCartney. For a logo, he turned to Hindu mythology and found the Uchchaihshravas, the seven-headed flying horse ridden by Indra, the god king of Heaven.

Ravi Shankar with his Family & Friends became Dark Horse Records' first signing, along with Bill Elliott and Bobby Purvis, two young singer/songwriters from South Shields who performed as a duo named Splinter. although more a shaving from George's debut as a feature film producer.

Because there was no one else to do it, he'd been given Apple Films' final project, a screen adaptation of David Halliwell's sex-comedy *Little Malcolm and His Struggle Against the Eunuchs* which he'd seen onstage with Pattie only two weeks into their marriage, rather scandalised by all its jokes about erections. He was also responsible for the film's music soundtrack and when Splinter came his way via the Beatles' former roadie, Mal

Evans, he put them into a pivotal scene, performing their song, 'Lonely Man'.

A quality production co-starring John Hurt and David Warner, *Little Malcolm* almost didn't get released when it was found to be among the Beatles' collective assets impounded by the Official Receiver after Paul's High Court action in 1971. The director, Adam Cooper, gave George credit for retrieving it, to enjoy critical success and win prizes at festivals in Berlin and Atlanta. All valuable preparation for the later career in the film business that would almost edge music out of his life.

From a cameo appearance in *Little Malcolm*, Splinter graduated to making an album at Friar Park with George not only producing but playing several instruments to boost their two acoustic guitars. Awed though they were, they couldn't help noticing his heavy consumption of Courvoisier and that the lonely man they'd sung about, 'holding on to what's past and gone', often seemed manifested in front of them.

His own next album, though still for Apple, was also to be named *Dark Horse*. And the obvious thing to do to give it and his new label maximum exposure was to tour. Before 1971 he would have rejected the idea out of hand. But the Concert For Bangladesh had reawakened his appetite for live performance and shown how much audiences had changed since the Beatlemania years.

Tour promoters had changed, too, and the obvious candidate for this highly sensitive one was Bill Graham, the creator of San Francisco's celebrated Fillmore auditorium and the first member of his profession to possess anything resembling a soul. After lengthy negotiations at Friar Park, Graham secured George's agreement to go back on the road in North America only, playing forty-three major venues in twenty-six cities during November and December 1974.

But a very different road was in prospect from any he'd travelled with John, Paul and Ringo. Rather than cranking out the same old songs against a barrage of shrieks, he'd be developing his collaboration with the coterie of musicians that had grown up around his solo albums. Above all, it would be a way of drawing further attention to someone he considered far worthier of attention than himself. He agreed to Graham's daunting schedule only on condition that Ravi Shankar plus orchestra were his co-headliners.

Among the band he assembled for the tour was Tom Scott, a young jazz saxophonist from California who'd studied Indian rhythms under one of Shankar's most distinguished pupils, Harihar Rao, and played on the *Shankar Family & Friends* album. 'On the first day in the studio, George came up to me and said, "You're the guy who studied with Harihar, right?"' Scott recalls. '"Would you like to hang out with me after the session?" Duh! Hang out with George Harrison in the flesh? You betcha!'

They met up again when Scott and his jazz-rock band the L.A. Express backed Joni Mitchell in her concert at London's New Victoria theatre. George invited him to Friar Park and the offer to join the tour along with the L.A. Express's drummer, John Guerin, quickly followed.

'He was a delightful person, kind, funny and self-effacing,' Scott recalls. 'His melodic slide guitar style was instantly recognisable, within two or three notes you knew it was him but, believe it or not, he thought he was merely an okay guitarist. It was an odd situation, trying to convince someone so world famous to give himself more credit.'

The news that the first ex-Beatle to tour under his own name was to be the one largely responsible for ending the Beatles' touring days in 1966 caused a sensation in the music press on both sides of the Atlantic. Coincidentally, it appeared in the same *Melody Maker* as a large picture of Paul, whose band, Wings, had finally hit its commercial stride as part of the Glam Rock craze.

All George's latter triumphs and the admiration of young musicians like Tom Scott had not softened his rancour against the person he held most responsible for his travails in the Beatles. 'I had no confidence in myself [when they broke up] having spent so many years with Paul McCartney,' he told an interviewer around this time, ''cause he ruined me as a guitar-player.' All one can say to that is: it didn't show.

Bill Graham was soon able to report that George Harrison's Dark Horse Tour had 'gone clean' – i.e., sold out all its forty-three dates. The international media flocked to a press conference at the Beverly Wilshire hotel in Los Angeles to hear from George what the tour wouldn't be. It wouldn't be a repeat of the Concert For Bangladesh, he told them, still less at any point a Beatles reunion despite a recent offer of $15 million for the band to give a single performance.

'One of the reasons I'm doing [the tour] is that I was turning into a lawyer or an accountant,' he said. 'I want to try and get back to being a musician.'

Inevitably, the questions soon moved on to the Pattie/Eric Clapton affair. George was first asked if he intended to write 'a rebuttal to "Layla"', the song with which Clapton had wooed his wife in the concert hall and on record.

He made no attempt to dodge the subject. 'Eric Clapton's been a close friend for years and I'm very happy about it.'

'How can you be happy about it?' the questioner persisted.

'Because he's great. I'd rather she was with him than some dope.'

And was he now intending to get a divorce?

'No,' he said, 'that's as silly as marriage.'

As so often, however, he spoke too soon.

The Dark Horse label got off to a flying start worthy of Pegasus. Its first release, Splinter's album *The Place I Love* with George's multi-instrumental backing, charted in *Billboard* and the single taken from it, 'Costafine Town', reached the Top 20 in Britain, Australia and South Africa.

From the beginning, George was determined to avoid any of the extravagance that had brought down Apple. Dark Horse operated from the Mayfair offices of his business manager, Denis O'Brien, and had only the minimum of staff. In another shining contrast with Allen Klein, O'Brien occupied himself solely with his EuroAtlantic company, which serviced every aspect of George's professional and personal life, and made no attempt to interfere with his choice or promotion of artists.

In August, Dark Horse opened a similarly modest office in Los Angeles, sharing the facilities of its parent company, A&M. Several times thereafter, George had occasion to speak on the phone to a member of the latter's marketing department named Olivia Arias. Intrigued by what he heard, he asked Chris O'Dell, who by now was back in LA, to take a Polaroid photograph of her 'to see if she's as beautiful as she sounds'.

Chris managed to sidestep the awkward chore, but George found out for himself in October when he flew out to meet his new West Coast staff. No one was expecting him and when he arrived at A&M's offices alone in a modest rental car, only Olivia Arias spotted him and hastily turned herself into a one-person welcoming committee.

Then twenty-six, Olivia had been born in Los Angeles of a family originally from Guanajuato in central Mexico. Her background was as working-class as George's, her father a dry-cleaner, her mother a seamstress. But she had a natural elegance and dignity that connected with him more immediately than any wide, inviting California smile.

She also turned out to be heavily into meditation and a follower of the so-called Boy Guru Maharaj-Ji. When she met George, she'd been due to quit her job at A&M and the music business to join a commune. This plan was shelved when he asked that she work exclusively for him.

Sometime earlier, while he was still with Pattie, an astrologer had predicted 'a dark-haired woman' would become of importance in his life. He'd always thought it meant someone Indian, but as soon as Chris saw Olivia Arias, 'I knew this was she. They went on one date and from then on they were never apart.'

The album called *Dark Horse* was largely autobiography in the Lennon or McCartney mode and a misnomer, for there was very little that it kept dark. George even told his pre-tour press conference where to find two salient references to a recent lifestyle he likened to the steamy American blockbuster novel, movie and TV series *Peyton Place*.

The first was 'So Sad', which laid bare how he'd really felt about the collapse of his marriage to Pattie while never making the slightest effort to rescue it: not 'a rebuttal of Layla' but of the most optimistic song he'd ever written, 'now the winter is here to eclipse out the sun.' The second was 'Simply Shady', a first-person confession of his 'bit of a binge' when '[I] came off the rails so crazy/My senses took a dip.'

That consoling return to India had prompted 'It Is He (Jai Sri Krishna)' after a visit to the holy city of Vrindavan, when George, Ravi Shankar and their companions had kept up a *bhajan*, or devotional song, for five straight hours as they explored its temples and shrines. But the blissful-seeming 'Māya Love' showed even India no longer quite working for him: '*Māya*' is Sanskrit for illusion.

The Pattie/Clapton affair was there, too, in the forgiving spirit the press conference had found so hard to credit, though not with the lightest of touches. It was a cover-version of the Everly Brothers' 'Bye Bye Love' with one verse rewritten as 'I hope she's happy/Old Clapper too.'

Seemingly incongruous and context-free was 'Ding Dong, Ding Dong', an attempt at an everlasting holiday hit like Slade's 'Merry Xmas Everybody' and Wizzard's 'I Wish It Could Be Christmas Every Day', with words borrowed from another of Sir Frank Crisp's inscriptions at Friar Park: 'Ring out the old/ring in the new/Ring out the false/ring in the true.'

If not exactly a confession it was a footnote to the mortifying moment when Pattie had caught him in flagrante with Maureen Starkey and been unconvinced by his explanation that Maureen was just 'tired and having a lie-down'. The video included a sequence in which a crowd of elaborately attired buccaneers surged up to Friar Park's highest tower, hauled down the skull-and-crossbones Pattie had flown to signal enough was enough, and restored the OM flag to its rightful place.

The very album cover forswore any hint of horsiness to settle a long-rankling personal score. It showed a panoramic Liverpool

Institute school photograph from 1956 cupped in a giant lotus flower with the Himalayas in the background. Thirteen-year-old George had been moved from the anonymous middle of the assembly to its senior back row and given a blue face, while his old headmaster 'the Baz' – that ruthless enforcer of school uniformity – wore a roundel like a target in a shooting gallery.

This sudden plunge into the personal took most critics by surprise, but not pleasantly so. *Dark Horse* received savage reviews, some of the worst in publications that had praised *All Thing Must Pass* and *Living In The Material World* to the skies yet now seemed to have completely forgotten them.

In a piece headed 'Transcendental Mediocrity', *Rolling Stone*'s Jim Miller said that 'In plain point of fact, George Harrison has never been a great artist. The question becomes whether he can ever become a competent entertainer.' The *New Musical Express*'s Bob Woffinden, another former eulogist, dismissed it as 'stuff and nonsense'.

His public seemed to agree. In America, *Dark Horse* peaked at number four on *Cash Box*'s chart, enough to earn a Gold Disc, but quickly subsided and disappeared; in Britain, it failed to chart.

This was nothing like a Beatles tour when the four would circle their crazy world attended by two roadies. George headed a company of seventy, travelling in a chartered airliner with OM symbols painted on its fuselage and including his new companion Olivia Arias, his business manager Denis O'Brien, the tour promoter Bill Graham, his friend, and now PA again, Chris O'Dell, and his father Harold.

He brought with him nine Western musicians accompanied

by wives or girlfriends; Ravi Shankar brought fourteen Indian ones many of whom had never been out of India before, without wives or girlfriends but with their own cook and three portable kitchens to meet their various dietary needs.

For George, indeed, there was no question who the tour's real headliner was. He'd originally wanted the posters to read 'George Harrison and Ravi Shankar' and carry the warning 'Don't come if you don't like Indian music'. Though Graham managed to talk him out of that, the hugely expensive souvenir programme was full of Krishna quotations and imagery and encyclopaedic biographies of every last sitarist.

He introduced Shankar and the orchestra onstage each night with a *pranam*, or ceremonial bow, instructed rather than requested the audience to pay close attention, and fumed over any signs of restlessness.

Rock tours, like politics, are largely a matter of luck and this the Dark Horse tour seemed to lack from the start. Fielding questions at his press conference, George had been suffering from a sore throat, a habitual problem for him all his life, and by the opening show it had developed into acute laryngitis. Despite constant gargling and sips of herbal tea, his singing voice all but disappeared and at high-register moments (unfortunately including 'What I feel, I can't say') he could only gasp like a stranded guppy while ever-supportive Billy Preston descanted the missing notes. The press gleefully dubbed it the Dark Hoarse tour.

Taking one's father on the road was unprecedented in those days although, after four years of living with George at Friar Park, Harold Harrison was unrecognisable as the conventional, cautious pilot of Liverpool buses for decades without a single scrape. Now Harold's hair curled around his shoulders and he sported gaudy rock 'n' roll threads, among them a rose-embroidered satin jacket matching George's.

At sixty-five, he was still strikingly good-looking and received many backstage overtures from women not solely as a way of getting to his son. But since Louise's death, despite encouragement from all three sons, he had never looked at anyone else.

If anything, it was thirty-one-year-old George who seemed a bit out of date in the denim dungarees he usually wore onstage, his hair now a little too curly and moustache a little too bushy, the former best-looking-but-one Beatle skinny and sallow from eating too little, drugging too much and, despite his stricken throat, still chain smoking acrid French Disque Bleu cigarettes.

The Beatles had never played on stages furnished by anything but three matching Vox amps but rock audiences in the Seventies demanded light shows and spectacle. Even the Rolling Stones, that one-time pure blues band, had had to glitz and camp themselves up with Mick Jagger taking the role of a stripper as much as a singer.

Yet George's stage visuals consisted only of a Dark Horse logo and an OM banner. It particularly irked Graham that he didn't open with a song but with the rather meandering instrumental 'Hari's On Tour (Express)' he'd evolved for the album with Tom Scott.

This was followed by a set containing just three of his Beatles songs, 'Something', 'While My Guitar Gently Weeps' and 'For You Blue' plus, surprisingly, John's 'In My Life', whose nostalgic mood might have seemed to have little appeal for him. There was no 'Here Comes The Sun' or 'If I Needed Someone' or 'I

Want To Tell You' or 'Taxman' despite his many new grudges against that grasping entity both British and American.

In the cold light of the Seventies, other performers of his generation had come to realise how lucky they were still to have fans and that a little graciousness did not come amiss. Even that synonym for ungraciousness Bob Dylan on his own recent return to touring had played a selection of his oldies with scarcely a sneer.

But for George, songs beloved by millions seemed a tiresome chore to be got through with gritted teeth (and he was very good at gritted teeth) as quickly as possible. Nor were they quite the songs they'd loved for he'd altered their lyrics as if to cleanse them of uncomfortable memories: 'while my guitar gently smiles . . . if there's something in the way we move it, find yourself another lover . . . in my life, I love God more.'

He remained impervious to Bill Graham's pleas to bump up the Beatles quotient, usually conveyed by Tom Scott. 'He told me to tell Graham, "These are the tunes we're gonna play,"' Scott recalls. '"If people want their money back, they can have it."'

His determination to push *Dark Horse* to the maximum likewise seemed to downgrade his other solo music: *All Things Must Pass* was represented by only two tracks. One night when an audience member called out a request for 'Bangla Desh', he snapped back, 'Don't just shout "Bangla Desh", give them something to help.'

The press sniping continued relentlessly, particularly from *Rolling Stone* whose correspondent, Ben Fong-Torres, was travelling with the tour. After another crushing *RS* headline, 'Lumbering In The Material World', George relaxed his usual

PHILIP NORMAN

no-interview rule to set Fong-Torres straight. 'I don't care if
nobody comes to see me or if nobody ever buys another record
of me,' he said. 'I don't give a shit – but I'm going to do what I
feel within myself.'

On top of the tour's manifold pressures, he couldn't help
thinking back to 1966 and the Beatles' final tour when they'd
been pursued by death threats across half the world. Though
none of his 1974 audiences showed him the slightest animosity,
whatever his stinginess with Beatles songs, he told Chris O'Dell
he never went onstage without wondering whether all these
years later he might be the first of the four to get shot.

Olivia had had an instantly beneficial effect on him, sooth-
ing the annoyances and neuroses of travelling and performing
that he multiplied by the hundred and doing her tactful best to
curtail his drinking and drugging. With her he was more physically demonstrative than Chris had ever known him and, just as
surprisingly, didn't care who saw it. 'They were always holding
hands, heads touching as they talked, [George] snuggling up to
her at every opportunity.'

In Tulsa, Oklahoma, the silvery-bearded Leon Russell came
onstage to play piano in the show's finale, 'My Sweet Lord'. The
claim that it plagiarised the three-note riff from the Chiffons'
'He's So Fine' still hadn't gone away and throughout the tour
George had used the Billy Preston soul arrangement in which
it was less noticeable, hoping thereby to avoid additional claims
for damages.

Bad luck struck again on 30 November in Chicago when
Ravi Shankar suffered a mild heart attack and had to leave the
tour for its entire Canadian leg, handing over the orchestra
to his sister-in-law, Lakshmi. However, he was back by 13

422

December to join George, Billy Preston and a hugely proud Harold in the first visit by a British rock star to an American President at the White House.

This was Gerald Ford who'd replaced Richard Nixon after the Watergate scandal forced Nixon's resignation: a 'safe pair of hands' said to be so dense that he couldn't walk and scratch his ass (or, some preferred, chew gum) at the same time. George presented him with an OM badge and in return received a lapel-button inscribed WIN, standing for the current presidential initiative 'Whip Inflation Now'.

Beatleness could not be completely kept at bay for John by now was back in New York, angling for a reconciliation with Yoko but still living with May Pang, the young Chinese-American she'd sent with him on the Lost Weekend in the dual role of girlfriend and guardian.

The couple attended George's show at Nassau Coliseum, Long Island, on 15 December and afterwards had dinner with him and Olivia in a suite at the Plaza. The hotel had borne the first shock of Beatlemania in America and it was there that the final papers dissolving the band's partnership were due to be signed in four days' time.

Under the Plaza's benign influence, John and George both forgot their usual repugnance for their Fab Four past and reminisced about the snowy day in February 1964 when half of New York seemed to be shrieking in the street below and the only privacy their suite afforded was the bathroom. After dinner, Maureen Starkey joined them unexpectedly, having just arrived from London, and George chatted to her as casually as if that shaming interlude on the floors of remote Friar Park bedrooms had never been.

The tour was to culminate with three performances at Madison Square Garden, the scene of his triumph with the Concert For Bangladesh. It had also witnessed a more recent triumph for John, who'd made his own nervous return to live performance with a surprise walk-on at Elton John's Thanksgiving concert, been cheered to the rafters and afterwards half-persuaded Yoko to take him back.

He was therefore in a mood to waive his 'no reunions' rule and was so persuasive that George relaxed his also. It was agreed John would join him onstage during his final show at the Garden on 19 December, ironically the day they were to sign the final papers terminating their business partnership.

George was yearning to get the papers signed but on the morning of 19 May Pang telephoned with the news that John's astrologer had told him his stars were in an unfavourable alignment, so he wouldn't be showing up at the Plaza. In that case, George shouted, he could forget about playing together that evening: 'I started the tour without him and I'll finish it without him.'

The signing of the sixty-seven-page document took place in one of the Plaza's most gilded salons with a gravity somewhat undermined when John sent along a balloon to represent him. Since Ringo was in London and would be signing there, only George and Paul were present and at the time happened not to be on speaking terms, although Paul would be at the Garden later with Linda, both of them heavily disguised.

The film footage of the ceremony shows George signing page after page while pretending not to see Paul six feet or so away. 'I've no idea what I'm signing,' he mutters, teeth never more tightly gritted, 'I just want this to be over.' It was the saddest of postscripts for the two Liverpool Institute boys who used to swap views about Elvis and guitars so eagerly on the morning bus ride into town from Speke.

After the tour ended, George went to Hawaii to decompress with Olivia and the band's percussionist Emil Richards and his wife. Out of the trip came a sequel to 'While My Guitar Gently Weeps', only this time without the tears its title implied. Rather, 'This Guitar (Can't Keep From Crying)' was a riposte to the critical maulings, from Ben Fong-Torres in particular, which the song claimed had only strengthened him 'to get up when I fall ... even climb *Rolling Stone* walls', though in reality they'd done nothing of the kind. Never again would he trust any writer from the magazine.

Afterwards, he and Olivia went their separate ways for the present and, in spite of their Hawaiian break, he returned to Britain just before Christmas in a far worse condition than from any tour with the Beatles. When he reached Friar Park, he went straight to the gardens whose flowerbeds held audiences he knew would never fail him. 'It was,' he would say, 'the nearest I ever got to a nervous breakdown.'

Now there was time to reflect on what the stresses of the past two months had largely blotted out: that his wife and his best friend had themselves recently been on the road in the US together as a prelude to living together, so keeping his humiliation even longer in the headlines.

Pattie had never been allowed to accompany him on tour while he was in the Beatles and, after her Rapunzel life at Friar Park, found it exalting to stand at the side of a different stage each night as Eric Clapton conjured wizardry from a slab of electrified wood. And when he came to 'Layla', the song he'd written in adoration of her, she was possessed by 'an intoxicating, overwhelming passion ... quite different from the deep, gentle love I'd felt for George.'

But with Clapton, it was the reverse. For the five years he'd pursued her in utter hopelessness, she'd been the only woman in the world for him but now that he'd finally won her over, other temptations began to beckon on every side. The night before she joined the tour in Boston, he'd slept with one of his show's backing singers.

Pattie's overwhelming passion turned to consternation when she discovered he'd kicked the heroin habit with which he'd once tried to blackmail her by becoming an alcoholic. Like George, his tipple of choice was Courvoisier, in his case drowned in 7Up, and he started on it straight after breakfast.

'Even though I was madly in love with Eric, I realised what a wreck he was,' she recalls. 'I thought, "What have I done, joining this group of mad people that he led?"'

Before she left Friar Park, in a last-minute resurgence of tenderness, George had told her she could always come back if things didn't work out. To make amends for his nonchalant 'Bye Bye Love' cover, he'd later sent Clapton and her a note reminiscent of the sweet person she'd once known: 'E+P God bless us all. Love from G.'

That summer, she'd been with Clapton in Jamaica while he recorded in the new reggae mode that had provided his breakthrough single 'I Shot The Sheriff'. There she received a welcome visit from Chris O'Dell, her one female confidante at Friar Park who flitted from one rock megastar camp to another like a ringletted Ariel from *The Tempest*.

With Chris's encouragement, she placed a telephone call to Friar Park, but Clapton came into the room at that moment and thought she was plotting to go back to George. The resulting furious row ended with Pattie locking herself in the bathroom and Clapton kicking the door so violently that he fractured a toe.

By December, she'd moved into his Surrey mansion, Hurtwood Edge, whose mere six bedrooms and couple of acres of garden felt bijou after Friar Park. In contrast with the self-sufficient, resourceful George, Clapton had a feather-bedded existence, shielded by his manager, Roger Forrester, from all of life's tiresome realities, even his driving test taken for him by a lookalike roadie. He was unequal to the smallest chore: all over the house, Pattie found drawers full of cheques for performance fees totalling hundreds of thousands of pounds that he hadn't bothered to cash.

While her whole family had adored George, they had little time for Clapton after his affair with her youngest sister, Paula, as a substitute for her, and he reciprocated their froideur. 'He hated my mother or sister Jenny even phoning me,' she recalls.

While George had never been the jealous type, at least until the very end, Clapton was ferociously proprietorial and would pursue her car into Guildford, their one-time trysting-place, when she went shopping to check that she wasn't keeping a tryst with someone else.

She hadn't expected to hear from George after his return from the Dark Horse tour, but on Christmas Day he turned up unexpectedly at Hurtwood Edge while she, Clapton and assorted guests were in the middle of lunch.

Clapton being an unapologetic carnivore, she'd had to give up the vegetarianism she used to practise with George and now couldn't help feeling guilty that he'd caught her eating turkey. But he made a joke of it, accepted her offer of some wine and Christmas pudding and they chatted with no trace of awkwardness. Only later did she think it rather sad that he'd seemed to have nowhere else to go on Christmas Day.

There was an awkward transitional period when Clapton felt a need to keep apologising for what had happened. 'I didn't get annoyed at him and I think that has always annoyed him,' George would say years later when finally addressing the subject in detail. 'I think that deep down inside he wishes it had really pissed me off but it didn't .... because otherwise [Pattie and I] would have had to go through all these rows and divorces. And ... she went off to live in the same style she'd become accustomed to and it really was very convenient for me.'

It helped that he had a new romantic interest of his own that engaged him on a deeper level than any before. The stoicism he'd learned from India also undoubtedly came in useful although even the Yogis of the Himalayas might have scratched their heads over the bizarre new triangle that replaced the former conventional one. But then, yogis knew nothing of infinitely entitled rock stars, or that the most blatant sexism for them was still no crime.

George and Clapton didn't just stay friends, they became still closer ones while the woman for whose favour they'd once duelled with their guitars found herself all but invisible.

'Those two were so tight,' Pattie recalls. 'I was just the one in the middle.'

24

'Introducing George Harrison'

Before 1974 was out, George had brought Olivia Arias to Friar Park in the white Rolls-Royce he'd inherited from John and Yoko and begun introducing her to the almost horizonless gardens, the omnipresent benevolent ghost of Sir Frank Crisp and his many playful riddles and conundrums. Despite their incalculable distance from Olivia's Mexican-American upbringing, she managed the transition effortlessly.

But there was to be only the briefest pause in George's work schedule, caught as he was between two record labels. Barely four months after the Dark Horse tour, he had to return to A&M's studios in Hollywood to make the final album for Apple that would free him to make the first under his own logo. He therefore missed the first eruptions of a new sound that would transform Britain's music business as completely as the Beatles had in 1963, although this time without tunefulness or charm.

To be sure, Punk Rock was a rebellion against the sort of complexity and experimentation they'd introduced into pop, chiefly through their most celebrated album. *Sgt. Pepper*'s early-Seventies heirs had been bands who took themselves as seriously as symphony orchestras and made absurdly pretentious concept albums like Yes's *Tales From Topographic Oceans* or Rick Wakeman's *The Myths and Legends of King Arthur and the Knights of the Round Table* (whose live version was performed at Wembley Arena on ice).

Punk bands, born of the harder economic times that had soon followed the flowery Sixties, were like a mass mockery of that so-called 'pomp rock' with their shaven heads, masochistic body-piercings and habit of spitting at their audiences rather than bowing. That most possessed not even a glimmer of vocal or instrumental talent was the whole point; a new unprivileged, nihilistic generation cared nothing about the bum notes and basked in the flying spittle as if it were stardust.

The Sixties' biggest names – the likes of the Who, Led Zeppelin, Pink Floyd or Eric Clapton – escaped classification as 'dinosaurs' and kept, even increased, their followings. But there was only one for whom that had never been in doubt.

In 1973, EMI issued a double-disc compilation of Beatles hits from 1962 to '70, afterwards known as the Red and Blue Albums for their coloured translucent vinyl, which peaked at number three in Britain and America and went on selling briskly for the rest of the decade.

This was good news for all the ex-Beatles except the one long-hardened to losing out. The tracks had been chosen by Allen Klein with his dismissal looming and George already in his sights as the first of the Beatles he'd sue. So with patent malice he'd chosen only Lennon–McCartney songs, ignoring 'Taxman', 'Here Comes The Sun' and even 'Something'. His further exclusion of hit cover-versions like 'Twist And Shout' left George virtually mute.

The ex-Beatles dealt with Punk Rock in different ways, apart from John in New York where it had come and gone in a milder form some years earlier. The significance of 1975 for him was in winning his long fight against the US government's campaign to deport him as a 'subversive', acquiring a Green Card and stepping away from music to take care of his newborn second son, Sean, while Yoko took care of his business.

Ringo didn't have to adjust to Punk either, for now that he no longer had George to feed him hit songs and produce him, his recording career began to falter. He became almost as well known for his cameo roles in Hollywood films and appearances on TV talk shows, always sidestepping the one subject, beginning with a capital B, the host wanted to talk about.

And Paul simply rose above it: at the apogee of the screaming, swearing and spitting, he wrote a song named 'Mull Of Kintyre' eulogising the headland near his remote farm in south-west Scotland, released it as a single with a bagpipe accompaniment and saw it reach number one.

Thus it was the former Quiet One who had most to say about Punk Rock and the music business in general, often in a curmudgeonly tone that was taken as a symptom of his advanced age (thirty-two) though it had always been there. During the Dark Horse tour, for instance, he'd met David Bowie, the androgynous godhead of Glam Rock (which also carried on post-Punk) and afterwards merely commented that Bowie 'looked dopey'.

He might have felt some affinity with the Punk bands as an echo of the makeshift skiffle groups that had given John, Paul and himself their entrée into music. But he dismissed them as 'just rubbish ... no finesse in the drumming ... just a lot of noise and nothing', sounding very like so many grown-ups at the beginning of the Beatles.

His last album for Apple, and Apple's last album, released in September 1975, was *Extra Texture (Read All About It)*, a title at once suggesting some superfine tailored garment and a trashy newspaper headline that gave notice of its conflicted character.

Nobody could accuse him of repeating himself. There was not a breath of the spiritual ardour that had flooded every George Harrison album since *All Things Must Pass*, nor philosophising of any kind apart from 'The Answer's At The End', a quotation from his favourite pensée by Sir Frank Crisp: 'Life is one long enigma my friend/so read on, read on, the answer's at the end.'

In place of his almost sermonising slide guitar were keyboards and a 'chicken' sax, that unholiest voice of early rock 'n' roll, lately given a new chic by the young Bruce Springsteen's E Street Band.

Yet for all this instrumental exuberance, most of the songs were about disillusionment, exhaustion and the still-unhealed wounds of the Dark Horse tour: 'This Guitar (Can't Keep From Crying)', 'World Of Stone', telling the listener 'lucky man you won't be/to follow the likes of me,' 'Grey Cloudy Lies' with its palpable yearning to 'leave the battlefield behind/get out of the fight', 'Tired of Midnight Blue' with its jadedness and self-disgust at the 'Peyton Place' interlude he'd so successfully concealed from the world.

Not everything was doom and gloom packaged in flashy soul. 'You' had been written for Ronnie Spector in 1971 but was now recast as a love song to Olivia for bringing him back from Peyton Place. One line in particular, showing the simple sweetness of which he was capable, sounds horribly sad in hindsight: 'Would you stay with me till I'm eighty?'

GEORGE BOUNCES BACK was the *Melody Maker's* headline and so it seemed when *Extra Texture* reached number 8 in *Billboard* and 16 in Britain, earning him another Gold Disc, and 'You' made number 20 on *Billboard's* singles chart.

But the hostile press he'd acquired with *Dark Horse* seemed implacable. In the *New Musical Express*, Neil Spencer derided 'the customary doom-laden Harrison we've come to know and fear', forgetful of that other soaringly upbeat Harrison millions had come to know and admire.

Rolling Stone seemed to have settled into a chilly dislike that rendered it deaf and blind to all the first-rate musicians George had used on the album. 'He is no longer a Beatle as he has reminded us more times than we have asked,' wrote its critic, Dave Marsh. 'But if he learned nothing else from his experience in that organization, it ought to have been that a good guitar-player isn't worth much without a band.'

If meditation was George's solace at such moments, so at the uttermost opposite extreme was *Monty Python's Flying Circus*.

First broadcast on BBC television in 1969, the show was in a hallowed British tradition dating back to *Alice in Wonderland*, Gilbert and Sullivan and the Goons of clever people being incredibly silly. Its writer/performers John Cleese, Michael Palin, Eric Idle, Terry Jones and Graham Chapman broke every rule of television comedy with sketches that flowed into each other, petered out without resolution – very like the Beatles' much-panned *Magical Mystery Tour* two years earlier – or segued into vaguely indecent Victorian-style graphics by the American-born animator Terry Gilliam.

George had loved that first series and could quote its maddest moments, the Ministry of Silly Walks, the Dead Parrot Sketch or the 'Lumberjack Song' word for word. He often said they'd saved his sanity during the bleakest days of the Beatles' breakup.

For all Monty Python's seemingly incomprehensible Britishness, it had been a huge hit in America, first on public service television, then in live shows that turned its performers almost into posher comedic Beatles.

George was a Python fan in the way that other people were George fans. He'd taken tapes of his favourite episodes with him on the Dark Horse tour, often turning to them at moments when *Rolling Stone* was being particularly horrid. At every venue, he had the 'Lumberjack Song' played during the count-down to showtime and registered at hotels as 'Jack Lumber'.

In 1975, the Python team released their first feature film, *Monty Python and the Holy Grail*, a send-up of the Arthurian leg-ends with a touch of sacrilege that seemed to bother no one. At an advance screening in Los Angeles, Eric Idle was told George Harrison was in the audience and wanted to meet him. Idle had recently contributed a sketch to the television show about an actor having drugs planted on him by the police which George believed to be based on his own deeply suspect bust in 1969.

'Who could resist his opening line?' Idle would recall. '"We can't talk here. Let's go and have a reefer in the projection-room."'

There followed one of his rare invitations to hang out with him, so Idle spent the rest of the night at A&M studios where Tom Scott was working on final overdubs for *Extra Texture* and Joni Mitchell, who was having an affair with Scott's drummer, happened to drop by.

George was soon on the friendliest of terms with Idle's

fellow 'Pythons', the anarchic Terry Gilliam, the long-shanked John Cleese, a genius in both verbal and physical comedy, and the affable Michael Palin, who portrayed the cross-dressing lumberjack.

Palin had been a besotted Beatles fan since his earliest days as a comedy writer in partnership with Terry Jones, 'when we'd creep out of our tiny flat in Waterloo to queue up for their latest album'. Now George proved an equal fan of his and Jones's post-Python television series *Ripping Yarns*, satirising boys' adventure stories from the innocent 1920s and '30s.

Palin was amused to discover the truth about the Beatles' so-called Quiet One. 'That must have meant just with John and Paul. When he was around us, you could hardly get him to shut up.'

He became closest to Eric Idle, the most hyperactive of the troupe, who was exactly his age and a competent guitarist and, moreover, had to fight Cleese and Palin for screen time just as he used to John and Paul for album time.

'George became kind of a guru to me,' Idle recalls. 'He was a pal, we got drunk together, we did all kind of naughty, wicked things, we had a ball. He'd been one of the most famous people in the world but by then his attitude was "Fame, what does it give you? You're still going to die like everyone else. Just make sure you live life to the fullest every moment."

'He was always saying: "Don't forget you're going to die." From about the time I knew him, he was preparing to die.'

He became an ex-officio Python that October when the Charisma label proposed issuing the 'Lumberjack Song' as a Christmas single. George produced the session at London's Work House studio, then mixed it at Friar Park in company with Michael Palin, for whom this introduction to the rock star's all-night working hours came as a severe shock.

Eric Idle altered the public image of someone who'd always seemed to take himself far too seriously. For his first TV project after *Monty Python*, Idle had teamed with Neil Innes from the Bonzo Dog Band, a group of brilliant musical pasticheurs whose drummer 'Legs' Larry Smith had inspired a track on *Extra Texture*.

The Idle–Innes show was titled *Rutland Weekend Television* – a pun on real-life London Weekend Television – and purported to chronicle Britain's smallest TV station, transmitting from Rutland, its real-life smallest county.

Rutland Weekend Television's 1975 Christmas special featured George as 'Pirate Bob' with a peg-leg, a crutch and an artificial parrot clamped to one shoulder. The finale showed him with a band, wearing a guitar and a Concert For Bangladesh-style white suit, but when the musicians struck up the intro to 'My Sweet Lord', he only uttered a stream of 'Jolly Roger-yo-ho-ho' gibberish.

His screen-credit, after the regular cast's, said: 'And introducing George Harrison.'

Another farce in which he played a walk-on role wasn't such a laughing matter.

Five years after being launched, the lawsuit alleging his three-note 'My Sweet Lord' riff had plagiarised the Chiffons' 'He's So Fine' finally came before the United States District Court in Manhattan in February 1976.

George's lawyers had tried to settle with the Bright Tunes Music Corporation for $148,000 and 10 per cent of the composer's and publishers' royalties on 'My Sweet Lord' in the US, in return for which he would retain its copyright. But Bright Tunes insisted on 75 per cent of its worldwide earnings and its transference to their catalogue.

The case brought him back into unwelcome contact with Allen Klein, who'd been lurking in the wings throughout its long preamble, initially as his manager, trying to settle the matter as quickly and cheaply as possible, then as his disaffected ex-manager, on the lookout for any way of screwing him.

Klein was now negotiating to purchase Bright Tunes as a means to this end and, meanwhile, urging the publishers not to accept any out-of-court settlement and feeding them financial information about 'My Sweet Lord' from his old Apple files, hence the punitive compensation claim that George was never likely to accept.

The three-day court hearing was more like a seminar in music theory, with outsize charts comparing the notations of 'My Sweet Lord' and 'He's So Fine' and testimony from a string of experts. On the stand, George admitted having been familiar with the Chiffons' song but said what had always been uppermost in his mind was the Edwin Hawkins Singers' 'Oh Happy Day'.

At one point, he was made to get up with a guitar and 'demonstrate his songwriting process' as clerks and ushers from neighbouring courtrooms crowded in to listen, which he afterwards called 'the worst experience of my life', surpassing even school.

Judge Richard Owen – a composer himself, according to the *New York Times* – ruled that 'My Sweet Lord' was 'the very same song as "He's So Fine"' so George was guilty of plagiarism, albeit unwittingly so. 'His subconscious mind knew the combination of sounds would work because it had already worked in a song his conscious mind did not remember.'

The damages due to Bright Tunes and songwriter Johnny Mack's estate were set at 50 per cent of the royalties not just from 'My Sweet Lord' but from its parent album, *All Things Must Pass*, estimated to be just over $1.5 million. However, George's lawyers successfully pleaded that Allen Klein's intervention in the case had been improper, payment of the damages was put on hold and the suit dragged on subterraneously, not to return to court for another five years.

A few weeks later, when the Monty Python troupe appeared onstage at New York's City Center auditorium, George joined the chorus of dubious Mounties in the 'Lumberjack Song', preserving his incognito by tipping his hat over his face and leaving the ensemble before the curtain call. Michael Palin remembers thinking that he looked 'tired and ill'.

Nonetheless, he returned to his Friar Park studio in May to make the first of the four albums Dark Horse Records were contracted to supply to A&M. Tom Scott, the only collaborator he could tolerate, came from California to co-produce, bringing along a top-notch engineer named Hank Acelo.

Progress was slow for, after his experience in court, George agonised over every note and word of his new songs in case he might be subconsciously plagiarising someone, and continually quizzed Scott and the other musicians as to whether they'd heard anything similar before.

He was also losing weight at an alarming rate and his skin had taken on a yellowish tinge. The basic tracks were barely complete when he was diagnosed with hepatitis B, a liver disorder generally caused by excessive alcohol use and, in those days before AIDS, the most dangerous sexually transmitted disease.

At first, he believed he could cure himself with chanting, as prescribed in Paramahansa Yogananda's book *Scientific Healing Affirmations*. But it had no effect and after several weeks' inactivity Tom Scott and engineer Hank Acelo had to return to the US to fulfil other recording commitments.

His life could well have been saved by Olivia for the first time when she persuaded him to seek help from conventional medicine. This proving ineffectual, she researched natural remedies and got him to an acupuncturist in California named Zion Yu. His treatment combined with a regimen of herbal supplements programmed by Olivia quickly restored him to health.

'I needed the hepatitis to quit drinking,' he joked afterwards, although this abstinence would be far from permanent.

He spent a brief convalescence with Olivia in the United States Virgin Islands, for part of which Eric Idle came out to join them. The two men were strumming their guitars in the Harrisons' suite late one night when an embarrassed young woman knocked at the door and told them they were disturbing an American TV producer named Norman Lear in the room below. But, as Idle recalls, no rock-star bolshiness followed: '"Oh, sorry love," George said, "We'll stop."'

He'd intended to call his new album *Second Resurrection*, implying a creative rebirth after the Dark Horse tour like the one after he left the Beatles, but changed it to the more light-hearted *Thirty Three & ⅓*. That was his age (and Idle's) and also the number of times per minute a vinyl album revolved on a turntable.

Thanks to the plagiarism case, then the hepatitis, it missed its contracted delivery-date to A&M in July. Having chosen the company for its seeming musician-friendliness, George now found it suing him for $10 million and demanding the termination of his Dark Horse label's five-year recording deal and the return of his $1 million advance against royalties. The missed deadline was merely an excuse, for despite the large sums spent by George on producing and promoting Dark Horse's handful of signings, only the duo Splinter had enjoyed any real success.

Here, the bad luck that had dogged him for months finally seemed to let up. An immediate alternative offer came from Mo Ostin, CEO of the Warner/Elektra/Asylum corporation, the much-enlarged descendant of the Warner Brothers label which long ago had released the soundtrack albums of *A Hard Day's Night* and *Help!*.

At WEA, Ostin presided over an array of talent including Neil Young, Joni Mitchell, Fleetwood Mac, the Grateful Dead, Randy Newman and Van Morrison, to all of whom his dedication was absolute. Whereas A&M's seeming cosiness concealed flintiness, he gave his corporate milieu in arid Burbank, as one colleague said, 'the atmosphere of a for-profit arts commune'. To seal the deal in George's mind, WEA were now employing Apple's former press officer and his old ally, Derek Taylor, as Head of Special Projects in its London office.

He was therefore thankful to settle out of court with A&M for $4 million, keep Dark Horse alive and take *Thirty Three & ⅓* as a finished product to Mo Ostin, with whom he would become close friends and remain so for the rest of his recording career.

Considering the stresses that had surrounded it, the album released in September 1976 was astonishingly mellow. Its fourth track, 'This Song', even managed to see a funny side to the plagiarism trial and George's terror of subconsciously copying someone else: 'This tune has nothing bright about it ... my expert tells me it's okay ...' The video showed him being hauled into court handcuffed to a helmeted cop, then singing in the witness box as a red-robed judge beat time with his gavel.

As a single, it reached number 25 in America; with the earnings from 'My Sweet Lord' held in escrow pending the resolution of the case, that was about the only income George had yet seen from it.

'Dear One' had a faint electronic whisper of the Indian ragas he was thought to have left far behind, while 'Pure Smokey' was a thanksgiving to God for the lead singer of Motown's Miracles 'who's really got a hold on me'. 'Learning How To Love You' had originally been written for A&M's co-founder Herb Alpert as one of the Tijuana Brass man's rare vocals, before his company showed how little it had learned to love Dark Horse Records. Bizarrely, there was a cover-version of Cole Porter's 'True Love' from the 1956 Bing Crosby/Grace Kelly film *High Society*.

Even now, George was still using up material dating back to the Lennon–McCartney album blockade. 'See Yourself' was from 1967, after Paul had confessed to taking LSD, and pointedly aimed at those 'who stand around and crucify while you do your best' (i.e., in the recording studio). 'Woman Don't You Cry For Me' was a memento of Gothenberg, Sweden, on the 1969 Delaney & Bonnie tour when Delaney Bramlett had first handed him a bottleneck slide guitar. 'Beautiful Girl', also written in '69 and held over from *All Things Must Pass*, was readdressed to Olivia.

As payback for 'Pirate Bob', Eric Idle contributed some of the lines in 'This Song' and directed the videos for 'Crackerbox

PHILIP NORMAN

Palace' and 'True Love' like miniature *Monty Python* sketches. Both were shot in Friar Park's grounds with George popping out of an antique baby-carriage in the first; togged up in an Edwardian blazer, straw hat and moustachio, punting on his lake and falling into the water in the second.

The album meant enough for him to agree to a demanding promotional campaign and endure it with a good grace, even when interviewers asked about the plagiarism trial. He blamed only himself for failing to notice the similarity between 'My Sweet Lord' and 'He's So Fine' when 'it would have been easy to change a note here or there without affecting the feel of the song. But as far as I'm concerned [its] effect has far exceeded any clash caused by greed and envy.'

One personal appearance in New York he positively relished was on *Saturday Night Live*, a new television comedy show with more than a touch of *Monty Python* that refused to treat its rock-star guests with the usual fawning reverence. In the wake of zillion-dollar offers to the ex-Beatles for a single reunion con-cert, *SNL* regularly invited them onto the show to play three songs for a $3,000 fee.

George appeared in a guitar duet with Paul Simon, first per-forming 'Here Comes The Sun', then Simon and Garfunkel's 'Homeward Bound'. No longer bearded or moustached, his hair lifted off his forehead, he looked younger than for years and his elusive charm was turned up to the maximum.

In America, *Thirty Three & ⅓* was greeted as a triumphant return to form. It far surpassed *Dark Horse* or *Extra Texture*, reaching 16 on the *Billboard* chart and selling 800,000 copies, despite EMI's spoiler release of a compilation album, *The Best of George Harrison*.

Billboard called it 'a sunny, upbeat collection of love songs and cheerful jokes that is his happiest and most commercial package with least high-flown posturing for perhaps his entire solo career.' The *Village Voice* went so far as to rank it with Bob Dylan's *Blood On The Tracks*. Here and there, praise was tempered with condescension. 'If the new record label, new girlfriend .... Olivia Arias ... and new disc have put him in a more secure place in the material world,' opined *Swank* magazine, 'he could well regain his spot as the Beatle to watch.'

But in Britain, 'love songs and cheerful jokes' made little headway against the Punk New Wave and in the charts *Thirty Three & ⅓* failed to match its title numerically, stalling at 38.

That partial Second Resurrection would once have made George hungry for more but instead it marked his transition to adulthood. For the first time ever, he questioned the all-consuming priority of 'going round the world, trying to be a rock star' and realised that, with Olivia now in his life, it needn't and shouldn't be.

So in 1977 he slipped the choke-chain of songwriting and recording and set about following his own advice to Eric Idle to make the most of every moment because you never knew when you were going to die.

It extended even to putting aside his essential prop, almost like an extra limb, since he was twelve years old. For the whole of that year, he didn't so much as pick up a guitar and, he would claim, 'never missed it for a moment'. Several months were spent travelling with Olivia, mostly in semi-anonymity and the blessed knowledge that each day didn't have to end with a performance. They went to India for the wedding of

Ravi Shankar's nephew, Kumar, and around Europe, taking in Hamburg for a look at the Grosse Freiheit (a quick one as George was wary of bumping into his old Indra Club girlfriend, Monika Pricken), then to meet Olivia's family in Los Angeles.

She'd rather dreaded showing him the simple house in which she'd grown up, but he told her it was 'a mansion' compared with 12 Arnold Grove, Wavertree, with its tin bath hanging on the wall and its outside toilet.

Herself a long-time convert to meditation, Olivia encouraged him to reconnect with his old teacher, Bhaktivedanta Swami, and the house he'd bought for the International Society for Krishna Consciousness. He even had a nice word to say about the Beatles' former guru, Maharishi Mahesh Yogi, for whom he'd coined the nickname 'Sexy Sadie' for John's lampoon on the White Album. Now he called the Maharishi 'fantastic' for having weathered all such mockery and still being in business, attracting converts by the thousand.

Without the guilt-making call of his recording-studio, he could spend as long as he liked in Friar Park's gardens with Olivia shielding him from phone calls by lawyers and accountants. Gardening, for him, became much the same as meditating: 'You can get everything [bad] out of your head in the same way,' he said. 'You can watch the seasons come and go; whatever you do can affect it, but the flowers don't answer back.'

With Olivia's further encouragement, he got to know his fellow Henley-dwellers as never before. They took to frequenting the Row Barge, a pub in the centre of town run by a married couple named Norman and Dot who, refreshingly, treated them no differently from any other customers.

George's Hare Krishna friend Shyamsundar Das had lately returned from India, bringing him a quantity of rubies, not worth very much but impressive to the eye. George would take a pocketful with him to the Row Barge and usually give one to anybody with whom he and Olivia fell into conversation. Reports of an ex-Beatle handing out rubies as casually as cherry lozenges there increased the pub's business about a thousandfold.

One evening when George came in with a visitor from America, it happened to be landlord Norman's birthday. 'He closed the bar early and had a party for his special friends,' the visitor recalls. 'After a few rounds, someone produced a guitar and George played every Beatles song he could remember.'

Before getting involved with the *Monty Python* gang, he'd always had as many celebrity friends outside music as in it. The most notable was Peter Sellers, his boyhood *Goon Show* hero, now an international film star with whom he shared a business manager, Denis O'Brien.

Sellers had been among the visitors to the Twickenham Studios film set while the Beatles were struggling with their *Get Back* album and had even briefly joined George's Dark Horse tour. He was always unpredictable company, at some moments breaking into the voice of Bluebottle from *The Goons* or Inspector Clouseau from *The Pink Panther*, at others just sitting silently with a superior smile. Yet he and George got along well enough to start a property company together (soon wound up when its profits failed to materialise quickly enough for Sellers).

Like all George's friends, he could drop by Friar Park at any time without warning and the huge ornamental front gates were always left open wide. 'I was there once when he came round,'

Klaus Voormann recalls. 'We watched a movie, Mel Brooks's *The Producers*. George knew almost every line by heart.'

At the opposite extreme from tranquil, timeless gardens, his other great non-musical passion was speed, the kind that didn't come in pill form. He'd been a fan of motor racing since his schooldays in the mid-Fifties when the cars had romantic double-barrelled names like Cooper Bristol and Talbot Lago, British drivers were gentlemanly types like Stirling Moss and Mike Hawthorn, and he'd seen the Argentinian ace Juan Manuel Fangio in action when the British Grand Prix took place at Merseyside's Aintree circuit.

The 1977 Formula One season was the longest and most crowded in its history and, accompanied by a now pregnant Olivia, George followed it for much of its progress around the world. Granted an 'access all areas' pass at every circuit, he socialised with all the leading drivers of the day – Mario Andretti, Jody Scheckter and Emerson Fittipaldi, and in particular three times world champion Jackie Stewart, aka 'the Flying Scot' – and hosted lavish pre- and post-race parties for them at Friar Park.

The sport, he said, was 'noisy rock 'n' roll really. The drivers are like rock 'n' roll musicians. They live for now and don't really care too much about everything else that's happening in the world, they just want to have fun. Except I think more rock 'n' roll people die than racing drivers.'

This was untrue: fatalities regularly occurred, often the result of inadequate safety measures at even the most prestigious events. Jackie Stewart was currently putting his career in jeopardy by campaigning for their improvement. George never ceased to be impressed by the stoicism with which Stewart's fellow contestants faced such hazards on top of the mad jostle of their cars on the track and their iron resolve to be first past the chequered flag, whatever the cost.

The Austrian Niki Lauda for instance had suffered horrific burns in a crash during the previous year's German Grand Prix but six weeks later was back competing in the Italian Grand Prix, his injuries still unhealed, to lose the championship title by only one point to Britain's James Hunt.

Lauda turned out to be a devotee of George's music – something he'd never expected to find in the pits at a motorsport meeting – and was upset to hear about his sabbatical from songwriting. That restarted the motor in his head and he began tuning up a lyric prompted by Jackie Stewart's recent autobiography, *Faster: A Racer's Diary*.

On 19 June, his divorce from Pattie was made absolute by their having lived apart for two years. She could legitimately claim to have been a major benefit to his career by inspiring 'Something', his highest-grossing song, as well as first pointing him towards meditation, and therefore entitled to a substantial part of his fortune. Nonetheless she accepted his lawyers' offer of £120,000.

Her own solicitor, Paddy Grafton-Green, having handled many other such high-profile divorces, was surprised by the lack of greed on her part. Hardly less surprising was the lack of generosity on George's.

25

'THE MOST EXPENSIVE CINEMA TICKET IN HISTORY'

Olivia's baby was due in midsummer 1978 and for her sake George had agreed to do things by the book and get married in May. This had to be rethought when his father, Harold, died on 3 May from respiratory failure due to emphysema and chronic bronchitis, aged sixty-eight.

Latterly, Harold had relocated from Friar Park to Seven Oaks, the house in Appleton, Lancashire, that George bought his parents but his mother, Louise, hadn't had enough time to enjoy. Harold died in his own bed with his eldest son, Harry, beside him. His funeral, like Louise's, was a private family one at St Wilfrid's Church in nearby Grappenhall, and he, too, was cremated at Walton Lea Crematorium and buried beside her in its garden of remembrance.

The sadness was lightened by the birth of a healthy baby boy to Olivia at HRH Princess Christian's Hospital, Windsor, on 1 August. Like George from Harold, the baby received only one forename, although nothing like so straightforward as his. It was Dhani, a fusion of 'dah' and 'ni', the sixth and seventh notes in the Indian musical scale. A month later, the parents were unobtrusively married at Henley-on-Thames Register Office.

This new arrival at Friar Park was followed by a significant departure: Terry Doran left George's employ, and his life, after ten years as his personal assistant and latterly his estate manager. Doran had always seemed an indispensable part of the place, Pattie recalls, 'striding around with his long coat flapping, followed by his two dogs'. They had stayed in touch since her own departure and when he phoned to tell her the news, 'he was in tears.'

Olivia was a natural and capable mother, but George played his part with the tiny presence in his Gothic pile that was more powerful than all the memorials and mottoes of Sir Frank Crisp added together. For the rest of 1978, what little free time Dhani allowed him was mainly occupied with Eric Idle and the Pythons.

Considering George's touchiness on the subject of the Beatles, Idle's next extra-Python project after *Rutland Weekend Television* might have been expected to put their friendship in extreme peril. This was a spoof documentary entitled *All You Need Is Cash* about the rise and fall of a band named the Rutles, aka 'The Prefab Four', each one clearly based on an actual Beatle aside from being a total moron.

A production inconceivable to the modern BBC, its cast included talents imported from *Saturday Night Live* like John Belushi and Dan Aykroyd and real-life music names Mick Jagger, Ronnie Wood and Paul Simon playing themselves. Idle's collaborator, Neil Innes, supplied brilliant pastiches of the Beatles' landmark hits, close enough for their models to be instantly recognisable yet without infringing the world's most sensitive copyrights.

All You Need Is Cash so touched George's unpredictable funny bone that he became actively involved in it, raiding Apple's film archives for genuine footage to be spliced into the spoofery. He even played a cameo role as a television reporter earnestly interviewing Michael Palin as the Rutles' press agent, Eric Manchester, about rumoured thefts from their 'Rutles Corps' house while figures in the background made off with typewriters, photocopiers and finally the microphone in the reporter's hand.

One day he was watching the filming of a scene between Idle as the 'Paul' character and Neil Innes as the 'John' character at the famous zebra crossing from the *Abbey Road* album cover. A fan pushed roughly past him, not recognising a genuine Beatle in her eagerness to get to two ersatz ones. His feeling that the Rutles had liberated him from the Beatles was never truer than at that moment.

In his turn, he was to bring liberation in the economic sense to Idle, Palin and Co. That autumn, they were far advanced with their second feature film, *Monty Python's Life of Brian*, whose content was pretty much wall-to-wall blasphemy. It was about a young man named Brian Cohen, born 'in the stable next-door' to Jesus Christ's, who gets mistaken for the Messiah and also suffers crucifixion. On the strength of its mildly sacrilegious, hugely profitable predecessor, *Monty Python and the Holy Grail*, EMI Films were putting up the Hollywood-size budget of $4 million.

Then, with shooting about to start in Tunisia, EMI's chairman, Lord Bernard Delfont, happened belatedly to read the script – ending with a mass crucifixion and Eric Idle hanging from a cross singing 'Always Look on the Bright Side of Life' – and pulled the plug forthwith.

That C-word seemed to wipe out the Pythons' previous bankability. No Hollywood studio would take over the production and Idle drew a similar blank with potential investors in New York. 'I told George we were looking for this money and he kept saying, "Don't worry, I'll get it." I didn't believe him because I didn't think you could just pick up a film like that for four million.'

If you were George Harrison, still with a Beatle's whim of iron, you could. Within a few days, his business manager, Denis O'Brien, had found most of the four million by borrowing £400,000 privately and negotiating a bank loan, secured by O'Brien's Cadogan Square office building and Friar Park.

Staking the house he loved more than anything else in his life on the riskiest of all gambles was an act of incredible, foolhardy generosity to his Python friends (and a glaring contrast to fobbing off his first wife and incontrovertible creative muse with £120,000). 'I just wanted to see the film' was his throwaway explanation, prompting the quip to which various Pythons would claim authorship, that he'd bought 'the most expensive cinema ticket in history'.

Friendship and philanthropy weren't quite the whole story. His investment allowed him a hefty tax write-off at a time when he was paying the hated Taxman under James Callaghan's Labour government around 95 per cent. And O'Brien expected the Pythons to show their gratitude by engaging him as their financial adviser, too, both as a group and individually.

Once the *Life of Brian* film-cameras were safely turning over in Tunisia, George paid a visit to the location and was given a tiny role as Mr Papadopoulos, the owner of The Mount, briefly glimpsed in a tumultuous crowd scene shaking hands with Graham Chapman's Messianic Brian. His single line of dialogue, 'Hello', was later thought to sound too Liverpudlian and revoiced by Michael Palin.

'I think the shock of finding himself in a crowd mobbing someone else was too much,' Palin commented.

26

'MAYBE HE THOUGHT GOD WOULD JUST SORT OF LET HIM OFF'

Monty Python's Life of Brian was released in August 1979, amid storms of protest from the extreme Righteous.

In Britain, it was banned by twenty-nine local authorities (many of which didn't have cinemas within their boundaries or feel a need to view it first) and denounced by the clean-up-TV campaigner, Mary Whitehouse; its New York opening was picketed by both rabbis and nuns. The freethinking Swedes advertised it with a dig at their po-faced neighbour as 'so funny, it was banned in Norway.'

All of which added up to a promotional campaign that seemed almost Heaven-sent. *Life of Brian* became the year's fourth highest-grossing film in Britain and the highest-grossing British one in America, eventually raking in almost $20 million, five times George's investment.

He was hardly a newcomer to producing or, indeed, financing films, having done both with *Little Malcolm and His Struggle Against the Eunuchs* (admittedly using Beatles money) and *Raga*, the Ravi Shankar documentary, coming up with around £1 million of his own to enable its completion. But initially he regarded the Pythons' epic as just a one-off gamble that had miraculously paid off.

Soon afterwards, Eric Idle was approached by Bob Hoskins, an actor previously best known for Cockney tough-guy roles on television. 'Do you want to buy a film?' Hoskins asked – a question clearly not aimed at Idle but at his close friend, George.

The Long Good Friday, co-starring Hoskins and the young Helen Mirren, was a story mixing London's gangland with the Mafia and the IRA. It had been destined for ATV television until the company's chairman, Lord Lew Grade, had watched it with the same horror his brother, EMI's Lord Delfont, had read the *Life of Brian* script, only this time because of the violence involved. Lord Grade refused to transmit it without heavy cuts, which the filmmakers and Hoskins refused to consider.

George and O'Brien were thus able to acquire it ready-made for around £200,000, less than its production costs. It was to raise the gangster genre to a new level of wit and sophistication, not to mention bloodshed, at many moments foreshadowing Martin Scorsese's *Goodfellas*. 'George never saw it before they bought it,' Hoskins recalled. 'He told me he never would have if he'd known how violent it was.'

O'Brien had previously handled George's finances through his company, EuroAtlantic, but now, as the moviemakers they'd inadvertently become, he decreed they should form a separate business partnership, registered in early 1980 as HandMade Films. The name came from an advertisement George had seen for 'British hand-made paper'; he liked its suggestion of individual craftsmanship rather than the conventional studio conveyor-belt and was sorry he couldn't throw in the 'British' as well.

He left the business side completely to O'Brien operating out of HandMade (and EuroAtlantic's and Dark Horse Records') Cadogan Square offices with a much-expanded team of in-house lawyers and accountants and also living in a top-floor apartment in between flying around the world on numerous portentous errands seemingly all for George's good.

George had never had patience enough to read even paperwork as crucial as the Beatles' dissolution documents and, as on that historic occasion, would sign agreements without understanding a word of them. HandMade staff later recalled how he would lie on a couch in O'Brien's sumptuous office, never asking questions as the soft American voice through the rigid ventriloquist-doll lips assured him this or that piece of paper was designed only to save him from the clutches of the detested Taxman.

He had not lacked early warnings of his role as the ventriloquist's unwitting dummy. His ex-wife Pattie had never like or trusted O'Brien, though this was mostly down to instinct: 'There was just something about him.' Even when the couple were breaking up, she'd been less concerned about her own paltry divorce settlement than how O'Brien might be using and misusing George's earnings. 'I said to him, "I'll open a bank-account in my name and you can pay a sum of money into it that you'll know will always be safe." But he'd never hear a word against Denis.'

He kept a small office and permanent assistant at HandMade but seldom put in an appearance there, relying on two trusted friends to keep him abreast of events. The first was Derek Taylor, the Beatles' former press officer, now George's ghost-writer and spokesperson where necessary. Despite all Taylor's high-powered jobs in music, he had ended up with few financial resources and George, as ever generous over big things, had helped him buy a mill house in Suffolk.

A newer but no less stalwart ally was the percussionist Ray Cooper, who lent his colossal stage presence to various mega-performers, notably Elton John, but pursued a parallel career as a composer and actor, in both of which roles he would also serve HandMade.

The week that *Monty Python's Life of Brian* was released, a young accountant named Steve Abbott, who'd previously been with the prestigious Price Waterhouse company, entered O'Brien's employ. His first task was to look into the tax-saving arrangements in place for George with a view to doing the same for the Python troupe when, as O'Brien, anticipated, they also became his clients.

Abbott found a tangled web of companies in tax havens like Panama and the Dutch Antilles and Swiss bank accounts – in those days, immune from inspection by the British or US tax authorities – over which George had no control and sometimes no knowledge of. 'With the resources he had all over the world, he could easily have financed *Life of Brian* without putting his house on the line. But that would have meant repatriating the money to Britain, something Denis was totally against.'

Abbott further discovered that O'Brien owned an Atlantic island called Fisher's Island and a yacht he kept in the Caribbean when his client could boast neither such luxury. 'It looked to me that arrangements supposedly set up to benefit George were benefiting Denis.'

George's 1979 album was to have been called *Faster* after Jackie Stewart's autobiography and in recognition of the fascinating times he'd spent on the Grand Prix circuit, when Stewart, Nicki

Lauda and other drivers would often ask when he was going to write a song about them.

In the end, the album was titled *George Harrison* but on it he gave them a song called 'Faster', also released separately as a picture disc whose vinyl showed moving images of Formula One cars as it revolved and whose label bore crossed chequered flags and headshots of Stewart, Lauda and Co.

The accompanying video had film footage shot by George at the Brazilian Grand Prix, intercut with himself and a guitar in the back of a limo being driven around the Monaco Grand Prix circuit the weekend after it had taken place. His uniformed chauffeur, visible only long enough to give a conspiratorial wink, was Jackie Stewart, the lyric's 'master at going faster'.

To Formula One with its frequent tragedies George brought some of the charitable spirit of the Concerts For Bangladesh. The proceeds from 'Faster' were donated to the cancer research fund set up by the brilliant young Swedish driver Gunnar Nilsson before his death from testicular cancer and to aid the family of Nilsson's fellow countryman and friend, Ronnie Peterson, who'd died after a crash in the 1978 Italian Grand Prix.

As a gesture of appreciation, George got to take part in an actual race, completing eleven laps of the Donington Park track during a benefit for the Gunnar Nilsson cancer fund, anonymous in his goggled helmet, watched by the cream of the profession including the great Juan Manuel Fangio.

In the TV interview with Jackie Stewart and himself that followed, the reporter spoke first to Stewart, as was right and proper, after which George admitted that, test-driving the Lotus in the rain, he'd 'spun out a couple of times ... The car was a bit old but then again, so am I.'

'I think a racing driver was what he'd really have liked to be,' Michael Palin says. 'I remember once he took me and Ray Cooper in one of his Maseratis from Friar Park to lunch in Marlow, which is about eight miles away, We seemed to do it in a few seconds, overtaking when there was no sightline of oncoming traffic, terrifying every other driver on the road.'

In March 1979, Eric Clapton married the former Pattie Harrison without his friendship with George suffering the smallest damage. Quite the opposite: it was practically an arranged marriage, mooted during the early days of Pattie's relationship with Clapton in a cold-blooded manner that robbed it of any romance.

As she recalls, she and Clapton were sitting with George in the great hall at Friar Park, her former home, she as usual feeling shut out by the two guitar demigods' blokeish bond.

'I suppose I'd better divorce her,' George said to Clapton as if she wasn't there.

'Well, if you do,' Clapton answered, in the same vein, 'I suppose that means I've got to marry her.'

The wedding reception at Clapton's Surrey mansion, Hurtwood Edge, was a mass turnout of his superstar friends, including George, Paul and Ringo. It was only three weeks since Ringo had undergone major intestinal surgery, the legacy of childhood peritonitis, and narrowly escaped becoming the first deceased ex-Beatle.

After Paul's arrest for drug possession at Tokyo airport the previous January, George had sent him a supportive message, so the two were on speaking terms again and readily joined in the mass jam that was the highlight of the afternoon. Earlier,

John had phoned from New York to wish the new newlyweds luck and said he would have attended the party if he'd known about it. The chance of a full Beatles reunion came that close, but never would again.

It was wholly in keeping with George's endless self-contradictions that, in the summer of 1980, this most obsessively private ex-Beatle should be the first to put out an autobiography. However, *I Me Mine*, titled after one of his least memorable songs, was in no sense a revelatory document.

Published by the specialist Genesis imprint, it was a large-format, opulently bound hardback in a slipcase, more suited to a coffee table than serious reading. Its autobiographical sections, based on interviews with Derek Taylor, were brief and random, supplemented by a few photographs. Mainly it was a vehicle for colour reproductions of his song lyrics handwritten on hotel and airline stationery, pages torn from diaries or scrap paper – one with a cigarette burn meticulously reproduced, another with the ring from a wet glass – accompanied by brief descriptions of why and where he'd written them.

I Me Mine was marketed like an artwork in a limited edition of 2,000 numbered copies at the astounding price of £150: from the most unassuming of songwriters, speciality publishing at its most naked.

Yet nothing could have seemed more unlike the George whom Michael Palin would often visit with his wife, Helen, and their three small children. 'It was always very relaxed and easy-going,' Palin recalls. 'He loved showing us whatever he was doing in the garden – "I've got eight new trees on their way by truck," he'd say. Funnily enough, though, I never remember him showing us around the house. We'd always be in the kitchen, which was just like any kitchen except for a rather good jukebox.'

That summer, with his fortieth birthday looming, John ended his retirement from music as impulsively as he'd begun it by going into New York's Hit Factory studio to make his first album for five years, half consisting of his own songs, the other half his accompaniments to Yoko's. Called *Double Fantasy*, after his favourite freesia bloom, it seemed to portray a completely new John, purged of his old demons and obsessions, cured of his rock-star egomania by raising his son, Sean, and content for the first time in his life.

With the album's release in November came an intense round of media interviews dispelling the long-standing rumours of a Howard Hughes–style hermit who'd gone completely bald, the ultimate Beatle tragedy, and snorted so much cocaine that it had destroyed the septum between his nostrils.

He was suntanned and fit, yet still as funny and bluntly honest as ever. Beside him at every moment still sat Yoko, proclaiming the durability of a relationship on which the whole world had once poured scorn.

This tranquil, optimistic John, singing almost McCartneyesque love letters to his wife and child, came as rather too much of a surprise to his old public and neither *Double Fantasy* nor its single, '(Just Like) Starting Over', initially made much headway in the international charts.

Early in the morning of 9 December, Olivia Harrison answered a phone call from George's sister, Louise, in Illinois, five hours behind Britain. She'd just heard a news report from New York that as John returned home from the recording studio to the Dakota Building with Yoko late the previous evening, he'd been shot five times in the back and died in the emergency room at St Luke's–Roosevelt Hospital.

George's first public reaction displayed his tactless gene at its worst. He said that when Olivia had woken him with the news, he'd turned over and gone back to sleep. 'And when I woke up, it was still true.' Some allowance must, of course be made for shock; even the usually pitch-perfect Paul told a television reporter it was 'a drag'.

At Derek Taylor's prompting, George released a more considered statement that still sounded oddly impersonal. 'After all that we went through together, I had and still have great love and respect for [John]. I am shocked and stunned. To rob life is the ultimate robbery in life. The perpetual encroachment on other people's space is taken to the limit with the use of a gun. It is an outrage that people can take other people's lives when they obviously haven't got their own lives in order.'

That Christmas and for long afterwards, ('Just Like) Starting Over' and other 'John' tracks from *Double Fantasy* topped charts around the world. And the knowledge that now the Beatles could never come back unleashed a second wave of Beatlemania which was never to recede.

For George, the mourning had a sting in the tale. The January 1981 issue of *Playboy* magazine contained a long interview John had given the previous September with several references to him that ranged from the slighting to the patronising. *All Things Must Pass*, his acknowledged masterpiece, had been 'all right', John opined, 'it just went on too long.' He added what George had already acknowledged: that the 'My Sweet Lord' plagiarism suit could easily have been avoided by changing a couple of notes [but] 'maybe he thought God would just sort of let him off.'

The reason for the broadside was soon revealed as *I Me Mine*. 'He put a book out privately on his life that by glaring omission says that my influence on him was zilch and nil ... George's relationship with me was of young follower to older guy ... and I think he bears resentment to me for being the daddy who left home ... I am just cut out as if I didn't exist.'

Actually, John was mentioned ten times (and appeared in seven of the photographs) but mere namechecks couldn't assuage his sense of hurtful ingratitude. He went on to cite an occasion when George sought his help with the lyric to 'Taxman' – 'one of his better songs' – and he had obliged 'because it had been John and Paul for so long' (i.e., monopolising the Beatles' songwriting). He'd also felt guilty because George had been so much kept down as a lead vocalist, usually 'doing songs I chose for him from my repertoire in the dance-halls ... the easier ones to sing.'

'[John] was annoyed with me because I didn't say he wrote one line of "Taxman",' George would respond (although not until long afterwards.) 'But I also didn't say how I wrote two lines of "Come Together" or three lines of "Eleanor Rigby." I think ... I would have more things to be niggled with him about than he would have had with me.'

Wronged as George felt, his 1981 album *Somewhere In England* tried to make amends with a tribute to John titled 'All Those Years Ago'. Speaking directly to its subject, it said all the right things like 'I always looked up to you' (almost John's very words in the *Playboy* interview), 'They treated you like a dog' (meaning the press for his Sixties peace campaigns) and 'You *imagined* it all but not many had ears.'

The song's glaring flaw – perhaps indicative of his mixed emotions in writing it – was a perkily upbeat tempo suggesting an aerobics class more than a eulogy. It still gave him his first hit single in years, a number 2 in America and 13 in Britain, which John may have added to his list of gripes in the Hereafter.

From this moment on, assassination ceased to be a hazard confined to royalty and politicians or an expression of comprehensible hatred. John's killer, Mark David Chapman, was an obsessive Beatles fan for whom he'd autographed an album earlier that day and who felt obscurely 'betrayed' by the life led since leaving Beatledom behind. Such feelings of ownership were common among hardcore Beatlemaniacs, though never carried to such a hideous extreme.

It might well not have stopped there. In the immediate aftermath, a death threat reached George from another such individual in America who claimed to have bought a gun for the purpose. A man was later detained by police in Baltimore, Maryland, but no charges resulted.

As a result. the gates of Friar Park ceased to stand open wide, regulars at the Row Barge received no further visitations from a former Beatle handing out rubies and Sir Frank Crisp's whimsical domain was overlaid with a veneer of fear. George was reported to have spent £1 million on electronic gates, infra-red sensors, CCTV cameras with a room of monitors linked to the town's police station and, by a special dispensation from the local authority, razor-wire protecting its entire perimeter.

After an appeals process lasting five years, 1981 finally brought a resolution of the lawsuit by the Bright Tunes Corporation, now owned by George's portly nemesis, Allen Klein, for 'My Sweet Lord's' 'unconscious plagiarism' of 'He's So Fine'.

While Klein had been pursuing George, the US Internal Revenue Service had been pursuing him for suspected financial chicanery dating back to the early Sixties. In 1979, the IRS had finally nailed him for failing to declare income from promotional copies of his clients' albums that he'd been selling for pin-money. He received a two-month prison sentence and was fined $5,000.

Klein's victory over George in the appeal court did little to restore his morale. The judge ruled that he was entitled to damages but his attempted manipulation of the case had been such that 'he should not be allowed to profit from them.' He was therefore awarded just $587,000, the sum he'd paid to acquire Bright Tunes. In a final bizarre twist, the copyright of 'He's So Fine' was transferred to George, leaving him free to plagiarise it to his heart's content if he so wished.

HandMade Films' 1981 release was *Time Bandits*, which transformed Terry Gilliam from Monty Python's animator and occasional bit part-player to the decade's most original – and profligate – director. A kind of *Wizard of Oz* plus animation and violence, it was about an eleven-year-old boy abducted by a gang of dwarfs who travel through the ages, stealing treasure of different kinds from each one. Its only major star was Sean Connery, the first James Bond and a former golfing buddy of Denis O'Brien's, resisting typecasting in the role of King Agamemnon from ancient Greek history.

George had been supposed to write a soundtrack album but then refused O'Brien's demand to fill it with cheery 'Hi-Ho' numbers like Disney's *Snow White and the Seven Dwarfs*, so his only musical contribution was a single song, 'Dream Away', heard over the closing credits.

Although Terry Gilliam brought in *Time Bandits* inside its $5 million budget– a directorial feat he would seldom repeat – he was a truculently independent spirit who resisted all attempts at interference from his executive producers and at one point threatened to destroy the film's only negative if he didn't get his way. George said this 'bolshiness' reminded him of John Lennon, which Gilliam took as the greatest compliment he'd ever been paid.

Rather than pull rank, however, George added a reproach-ful note to the 'Dream Away' lyric, suggesting Gilliam should remember who'd given him his big break with *Life of Brian* and that coming in under budget wasn't everything: 'Lucky you got so far/All you owe is apologies.'

Time Bandits did even better box office than *Monty Python's Life of Brian*, grossing $36 million. In contrast, George's 1980 album, *Somewhere In England*, had been his first not to reach the Top 20 in Britain or America, despite containing the John tribute 'All Those Years Ago'; from here on, HandMade Films would seem a more dependable source of hits.

His 1982 album felt undersold in advance by the obscure title *Gone Troppo*, an Australian phrase meaning gone crazy as if from tropical heat. It had several serviceable tracks, notably 'Wake Up My Love' and *Time Bandits*' 'Dream Away', but such was the conflicting pull of HandMade that he refused to promote it or even make a video. His old persecutor *Rolling Stone* took the opportunity to say it showed him to be 'a better movie financier than musician'. *Gone Troppo* reached only number 108 in the US and got nowhere in England. Apart from soundtrack appearances, it would be his last album for five years.

He always described his main purpose at HandMade as to 'help' people like the Monty Python troupe realise their projects, somewhat in the spirit of the Beatles' doomed Apple Corps. Denis O'Brien's main purpose, on the other hand, would ultimately be revealed as to help himself to George's money in every possible way.

His young in-house accountant, Steve Abbott, already suspected as much from the labyrinth of offshore companies and bank accounts allegedly set up to shield George from the Taxman, which he wanted the Pythons to utilise once they, too, became his clients.

But unfortunately for O'Brien, Palin, Idle and Co. were not as instantly captivated as George had been. 'Denis got us to go out to Fisher's Island in New York and used a blackboard to show us all the places where he wanted to put our money,' Michael Palin remembers. 'Afterwards, we all asked each other, "Did you understand a word of what he was saying?" and none of us had. The real trouble was that none of us had the same objection to paying tax that George did.'

For Steve Abbott, the final eye-opener was a weekend jaunt O'Brien organised to Guernsey in the Channel Islands, the nearest of his tax shelters, to thank the directors and board members of the offshore companies he'd set up for their 'work'. 'One of them was Peter Sellers's ex-chauffeur whose only qualification was having an Irish passport. Another one was a former Apple Scruff named Lucy Rigo who had an Italian passport and had ended up running the payroll at Friar Park, signing cheques for hundreds of thousands of pounds.'

Abbott by now regarded the Pythons as friends more than clients, so applied himself to prising them from O'Brien's clutches, in the process getting himself fired and earning his ex-employer's undying hatred.

'At one point, Eric Idle came to me and said, "Can you get George out as well?"' he recalls 'But I had to tell him, "I've already got my hands full with you guys."'

On the surface, the Harrison/O'Brien partnership seemed an ideal mix of megastar and money man. For HandMade was to become integral to the 1980s' renaissance in British independent filmmaking, a name spoken in the same breath as the mighty Goldcrest company with its cinematic power-brokers David Puttnam and Sir Richard Attenborough.

The two organisations were seldom direct competitors. Goldcrest went in for big productions on international themes such as *Gandhi*, *The Killing Fields* and *The Mission* while HandMade specialised in smaller and very British subjects often pushing the bounds of censorship: *A Private Function*, *Privates on Parade*, *Nuns on the Run*, *Withnail and I*. It drew first-class work from an impressive array of actors like Maggie Smith , Michael Caine, Denholm Elliott and Sir Ralph Richardson, writers like Alan Bennett, Dennis Potter, Dick Clement and Ian La Frenais, and directors like Bruce Robinson, Neil Jordan, Nicolas Roeg and Jack Clayton.

While always insisting that the company was only a sideline and he 'already had a job', George was the executive producer for twenty-three of its films including the Oscar-nominated *Mona Lisa*.

Filmmaking brought out a self-restraint and diplomacy that would have astonished anyone who'd known him in the Beatles.

He never tried to make HandMade merely a reflection of his own taste, and would green-light films he personally didn't like but that had obvious artistic merit. As an executive producer, he paid conscientious visits to sets and locations, never failing to boost the morale of actors and crews alike.

By now entering his forties, he had cast off all hippieness and adopted the Eighties' new male silhouette: hair shaped and heaped with an overhanging 'mullet' at the rear, big-shouldered jackets with sleeves pushed up to the elbows, trousers ballooning like the ones he'd detested at school. Unnoticed by the media, he'd undergone radical dentistry that replaced his former toothy grin with a more discreet, quirky smile, sometimes below a small moustache, sometimes not.

Like many others whose Sixties sensibilities had survived the Seventies, he was deeply unhappy to be living under Margaret Thatcher's Conservative government and appalled by its two defining adventures, the Falklands 'conflict' (no one liked to say 'war') and the miners' strike in which the police were converted into a paramilitary force to crush the strikers.

But also like many a former beard-and-sandal wearer, he found nothing to complain of in the booming stock market, the encouragement of private enterprise (which brought significant financial benefits to HandMade), and the reduction of income tax at his level by rapid stages from 95 to 60 per cent.

The Dark Horse tour still cast its long shadow in George's refusal to go on the road again or even perform live. When Bob Dylan had returned to Britain in the summer of 1981, he'd sent an invitation to George to revive their Concert For Bangladesh partnership onstage at Wembley Arena, but received an apologetic but steadfast refusal.

Yet the impulse to play music remained as strong as ever. The Henley area was home to several top-echelon musicians such as Ten Years After guitarist Alvin Lee, Deep Purple's keyboard player Jon Lord, ex-Thin Lizzy guitarist Gary Moore and bass-virtuoso Herbie Flowers. All were invited to jam with George so often that they practically became Friar Park's house band.

At other times, he'd use his ballroom-sized recording studio with its enormous mixing-desk and fine old English wood-work purely for his own amusement. After seeing the Everly Brothers' reunion concert at the Royal Albert Hall in 1983, he went home and spent the rest of the night taping and mixing a private tribute to Don and Phil.

The other musicians were just mates, but in Joe Brown he discovered a boon companion. During the pre–Beatles dark age, Brown had been Britain's leading electric guitarist; the early Beatles had appeared with him, far down the bill, at venues like Southport's Floral Hall, and his song 'A Picture of You' had been one of the few that John and Paul considered within George's vocal range.

Now, learning that Brown had moved to the Henley area, George invited him over to view Friar Park and initially play guitars, but soon switching to a smaller, less solemn stringed instrument.

Both were passionate about ukuleles and equally about George Formby, a hugely popular star of the 1930s and '40s whose songs of faux-innocent double-entendre, like 'Me Little Stick of Blackpool Rock' and 'Fanlight Fanny the Frowsy Nightclub Queen' were accompanied by lightning flurries on a banjo-ukulele, or banjolele.

Although George possessed a huge collection of ukes, Brown

PHILIP NORMAN

discovered 'he wasn't that proficient', so the Cockney taught the Merseysider George Formby's 'scissors' strumming-action – and took him back on the road in a wholly unexpected way. 'Every now and then he'd phone me up and say, "What are you doing, Joe? Come to the house tomorrow and bring a suitcase." And we'd go all over the world. He'd say, "I brought the ukuleles" and we'd play all over.'

As a Beatle he'd lived a life in which every day was different but with a small son, every day had to be predictable with its fixed mealtimes, bathtimes and bedtimes. Photographers now tended to catch him at airports with Dhani in his arms or carrying childcare equipment that, from any angle, was incapable of looking cool.

John's assassination had made him fearful for Dhani's and Olivia's safety even more than his own and he began searching for a bolthole outside Britain offering security as well as the privacy and peace he craved.

He found it on the Hawaiian island of Maui, buying a sixty-three-acre plot in Nahiku on its remote south-east corner on a bluff overlooking the Pacific, building a house and starting a new garden in which every flower and plant grew at about seven times the rate of those at Friar Park.

An added attraction was the ukulele being Hawaii's national instrument, the rhythm for hula-dancing generations before George Formby's little stick of Blackpool rock. George quickly discovered the Rolls-Royce of Hawaiian ukes, the traditionally made Kamaka; with his new expertise he played both its six- and eight-string 'concert' models and would buy up a music store's entire stock as gifts for friends back home.

*

In 1985, HandMade released *Water*, a rather old-fashioned comedy about a Caribbean island and British colonial possession named Cascara whose water supply is found to be both as naturally fizzy as Perrier and to contain a powerful laxative (the latter always guaranteed to have the Brits rolling in the aisles).

George played a cameo role but as a musician rather than actor, fronting 'the Singing Rebels Band' whose superstar line-up, including Ringo, Eric Clapton and Ray Cooper as well as the comedian Billy Connolly, was a foretaste of another pseudonymous band soon to come. The scene in which they played a reggae song called 'Freedom' to the United Nations General Assembly had an obvious resonance of the Concert For Bangladesh.

Ironically, while he was pastiching this climactic moment in his career, its spirit was being revived with total seriousness on a hugely expanded scale.

The previous year, a catastrophic famine in Ethiopia had moved what was now recognisably a British rock community just as Bangladesh's famine and genocide had moved George thirteen years earlier. Following his example, the Boomtown Rats' Bob Geldof and Ultravox's Midge Ure mobilised friends such as Phil Collins, Spandau Ballet, Boy George, Duran Duran, Sting and U2's Bono, collectively known as Band Aid, to record a seasonal charity single, 'Do They Know It's Christmas?' which went straight to number one and raised $24 million. The formula was repeated in America a few weeks later with a single called 'We Are The World' and an ensemble led by Michael Jackson, Bruce Springsteen, Stevie Wonder, Tina Turner, Dionne Warwick, Ray Charles and Bob Dylan.

The two initiatives coalesced on 13 July 1985 in Live Aid,

a marathon concert televised simultaneously from London's Wembley Stadium and the John F. Kennedy Stadium in Philadelphia, with an added layer of talents such as Queen, David Bowie, U2, the Who, Madonna, Elton John and George Michael. It was watched by an estimated 1.8 billion people in 150 countries or 40 per cent of the world's population.

Despite all George's experience of juggling superstar egos with the Concert For Bangladesh, he'd played no part in organising Live Aid, Bob Geldof merely asking if he had any advice to offer. 'Get yourselves a good accountant,' he cautioned, still bitter about the wrangling over tax that had soured his great endeavour in 1971.

Nor was he offered a solo spot in the massive rock 'n' roll-out, just an appearance with Paul, singing 'Let It Be' in company with Geldof, Alison Moyet and Pete Townshend. His response, somewhat lacking in charitable spirit, was that Paul 'didn't want me to sing on it ten [sic] years ago, so why does he want me now?'

'Let It Be' would hardly have been appropriate in any case since he and Ringo were currently suing Paul for $6.5 million. In 1979, Paul had re-signed with EMI at a higher royalty rate than theirs, a fact that had only recently come to light. In addition, George suspected that, out there in front of that global audience, Ringo might suddenly walk onstage and he'd find himself trapped in a three-quarter Beatles reunion.

But an invitation onto a smaller stage, before a much smaller audience, was impossible for him to turn down. In January 1986, British television's new Channel 4 showed *Blue Suede Shoes: A Rockabilly Special*, celebrating his great idol Carl Perkins whose career he'd done so much to revitalise.

Perkins was barely recognisable as the performer with the odd, prancing step and unstable hairline he'd first seen in the film *Disc Jockey Jamboree* in 1957, now resplendent in a curly wig and outsize designer spectacles, but with a touch as light and playful as ever.

George joined a group of his devotees including Ringo, Eric Clapton and Johnny Cash's daughter, Roseanne, seated in a row rather like a school class to play along with Perkins classics like 'Honey Don't', 'Matchbox' and his early signature track with the Beatles, 'Everybody's Tryin' To Be My Baby'.

Discounting the spoof concert in *Water*, it was his first stage performance for more than ten years and, far from just going through the motions as in the film, he plainly loved every moment.

27

'HE WAS LOOKING AT POTENTIAL DEBTS OF AROUND £32 MILLION'

In March 1986, a surreal moment was caught on television screens on both sides of the Atlantic. George Harrison, still after all this time one of the world's most famous male pop stars, was acting as a minder to the world's most famous female pop star and looking horribly uncomfortable about it.

Madonna Louise Ciccone went by her first name only, but there the aura of saintliness evaporated. A dancer and choreographer as much as a singer, she had brought a bold new sexuality to the rock stage that belied an independent and calculating mind in appealing to women as well as men. It was not for male titillation but as an expression of feminist freewill that Madonna dyed her hair 18-carat blonde, reprinted her lips as a scarlet cupid's bow and adopted the persona of an urchin Marilyn Monroe.

At this time, she was just married to the emergent Hollywood star and tearaway Sean Penn, so creating a glamour couple of the same order as Elizabeth Taylor and Richard Burton in the Sixties and David and Victoria Beckham in the next century.

Since the Beatles and *A Hard Day's Night*, the next step for any high-grossing pop act had been to make a movie. This one had already co-starred in the critically acclaimed *Desperately Seeking Susan*, playing a screen version of herself, and now wished to broaden her range as well as play opposite her new spouse. Amid huge industry astonishment and envy, they decided to go with HandMade.

The company had never before dealt in celebrity at such a level but Denis O'Brien saw it as a transition from oddball little British films to Hollywood. The vehicle was to be *Shanghai Surprise*, a screwball comedy set in the 1930s in that traditionally raffish Chinese seaport. By his usual miraculous-seeming sleight of hand, O'Brien raised $17 million to finance it, HandMade's biggest budget ever.

The decisive factor in securing the two stars had been George's reluctant magic as a Beatle; he therefore became *Shanghai Surprise*'s executive producer, in addition writing and recording five songs for the soundtrack and playing a cameo role as a nightclub singer.

Permission to film in the real Shanghai was refused by the Chinese government because of Madonna's raunchy stage shows (although in the film she played a Christian missionary, decorously clothed throughout), so the location had to be switched to Hong Kong, then in its final days as a British colonial possession.

There, the shoot quickly descended into chaos. Every exterior set-up was plagued by paparazzi, the British as always much the worst. The director, Jim Goddard, lost any control of his two star players on the first day and never managed to regain it. Sean Penn was repeatedly involved in fisticuffs with photographers, on one occasion ordering his bodyguard to douse a group of them with a firehose. Husband and wife became so disliked by the British film crew, they were nicknamed 'the Poison Penns'.

Eventually, under pressure from Denis O'Brien, George had to fly out to Hong Kong and use his Beatleness to make peace on the set. He bitterly resented being exploited by O'Brien in this way, never dreaming the full scale of the exploitation.

With the cast back in London to film interiors at Shepperton Studios, he called a press conference to try to stem the unremittingly bad publicity that had filled the British papers. Unfortunately, this only succeeded in intensifying it: true to her Marilyn persona, Madonna arrived an hour late while Penn didn't show at all.

George was the picture of unease throughout, rather showily chewing gum as a sign of his disdain for the assembled hacks. He said he'd expected the press to create 'a certain amount of commotion' in Hong Kong but that he'd 'overestimated their intelligence'.

He was clearly on uncomfortable terms with his star, who later complained he'd prevented her from answering the journalists' questions while mishandling them himself. 'He kept saying the wrong things to try to calm people down,' she said, 'putting his foot in his mouth and in my mouth, too.' Never had a minder been so much in need of a minder.

Shanghai Surprise, unsurprisingly, was a total flop. The sexual chemistry between Madonna and Penn, all too audible from their trailer between takes, failed utterly to transfer to the screen. Nor had there been any attempt to woo her huge public into the movie theatres by extracting a song or two from the cupid's-bow mouth she had maintained even as a missionary. Even the soundtrack album George had been working on was aborted. 'The nice thing about *Shanghai Surprise*,' commented the *New York Times*, 'is that one can watch it [at cinemas] in near total privacy.'

It wasn't a financial disaster for HandMade since Denis O'Brien had pre-sold it in sufficient overseas territories to recoup its budget, which meant his final unmasking would be postponed a little longer.

But for George, it could be said to have amounted to a death sentence. The project came along just when he'd managed to give up the chain-smoking habit he'd acquired as a schoolboy at the Inny. Amid the unfamiliar stresses of coping with rather than exercising a superstar ego, it took hold again, this time unbreakably.

The sixty-one-acre estate in Maui's remotest south-east corner was less secluded than it had first seemed. Through its garden, only ten metres from the house George and Olivia had built, ran a path that turned out to be a public right of way and the only access to the most popular fishing spot on the island.

The people passing by at these horrifically close quarters, invariably in holiday mood, shattered the perfect silence, trampled on George's flowers, sometimes even detoured to peer in through his bedroom window. His fear of falling victim to another Mark David Chapman (who had travelled from Hawaii to murder John) was augmented by his childhood phobia about 'nosy neighbours'.

He had the long-standing access blocked by a metal barrier adorned with two characteristically blunt notices, one saying KEEP OUT, the other NO TRESPASSING. The neighbours were outraged and a legal battle began that would end up in court; meanwhile, his hunt for the perfect hideaway was on again.

His friend Jackie Stewart came up with a suggestion while they were both at the Australian Grand Prix amid the roaring crowds and reek of gasoline George also couldn't live without. The world-travelled Stewart told him about Hamilton Island in the Whitsunday archipelago, off the central Queensland coast, that forms part of the Great Barrier Reef.

It was some time before he and Olivia managed to visit the island, but they were both instantly captivated. In its 1.9 square mile, there was then only a single bungalow; the rest might have been a ready-made tropical garden but for the monitor lizards, kookaburras and wallabies that abounded (especially the wallabies). George purchased a six-acre plot on a bluff overlooking the ocean, where they began building another hoped-for haven.

In 1987, he made time away from HandMade for his first album in five years, with a co-producer who couldn't have been more of a contrast to the Poison Penns.

Jeff Lynne was as much of an all-rounder as himself but of longer standing: a guitarist, singer, songwriter and producer, first with the Move in the late Sixties, then the quasi-classical Electric Light Orchestra (ELO), often called 'the Beatles of the Seventies'. He came from Birmingham, whose accent is as salty as Liverpool's; this would be the first time a Scouser and a 'Brummie' had attempted such a high-profile artistic merger.

Lynne recalls his first visit to Friar Park, intimidated by its Gothic splendours, even more so by the prospect of meeting one of his greatest heroes. 'Olivia greeted me at the door and said, "George is waiting for you down by the lake. He's got a boat ready for you to go for a ride."

'He was real friendly and as I got in, he said, "When we start off, don't put your hands outside the boat. You have to grip with your bum." And that was it . . . I knew he was my kind of guy.'

So it also was with George for, on top of polymathic musicianship, Lynne turned out to be as big a Formula One fan as he was, and totally up for being taught the ukulele.

The album was titled *Cloud Nine*, the same as one by the Temptations in 1969 but this time no legal nightmare over copyright resulted. George's usual star back-up including Ringo and Eric Clapton was augmented by a pianist whose session days might have seemed far behind him. This was Elton John, lately recovered from what had seemed like terminal throat cancer and currently the target of a vicious homophobic onslaught by the *Sun* newspaper. George wasn't the only one for whom the Friar Park studio seemed like a rest-cure.

Jeff Lynne's lightening-up influence was pervasive, nowhere more than in 'When We Was Fab,' a song he co-wrote with George actually making fun of the Beatle years and their chief curse, 'back when income tax was all we had'. At the end there was even a brief burst on a long-neglected sitar.

Elton was both the personification of music with a conscience and a pet of the royal family, especially the then Prince of Wales and pop-savvy Princess Diana. As part of the promotion for *Cloud Nine*, he persuaded George to appear with Ringo in a gala in aid of the Prince's Trust charity for disadvantaged young people, topping a bill that included Eric Clapton, Bryan Adams and Dave Edmunds. 'Without them,' Elton reminded the company when he announced the ex-Beatle duo, 'there wouldn't be us.'

Cloud Nine was hailed as George's best work since *All Things Must Pass* and gave him a surprise hit single: his cover of James Ray's 'Got My Mind Set On You' from 1962 reached number one in the US and two in Britain and contained an irony which only a couple of accountants picked up, the line about needing 'a whole lotta spending money'.

It was to be the last solo studio album he would see through to the end.

Despite the monumental dissolution document signed by the ex-Beatles in 1974, there still remained numerous issues between them that a summit meeting at London's Dorchester Hotel in 1983, with Yoko now representing John, still hadn't settled.

Nonetheless, George's enmity towards Paul seemed to have subsided, doubtless helped by HandMade's success compared with Paul's disastrous foray into filmmaking,1984's *Give My Regards to Broad Street*. Just after *Cloud Nine* came out, they'd had dinner together and got along better than for years.

In January 1988, somewhat belatedly, the Beatles were inducted into the Rock & Roll Hall of Fame. Paul declined to attend the ceremony, citing 'business differences'. Watched by Yoko and John's two sons, Julian and Sean, George for once hit exactly the right note in making light of Paul's no-show, unfazed by interruptions from a helplessly plastered Ringo:

'I don't have much to say because I'm the quiet Beatle. It's unfortunate Paul's not here because he's the one who had the speech in his pocket. We all know why John can't be here because I'm sure he would be, and it's hard really to stand here representing the Beatles ... it's what's left I'm afraid. We all loved him so much and we all love Paul very much.'

During the *Cloud Nine* sessions, he and Jeff Lynne had played a game of naming the one person each would most like to be in a band with. George had picked Bob Dylan; Lynne had picked Roy Orbison, with whom the Beatles had toured Britain in

1963, displacing him from the top of the bill when Beatlemania took hold.

In the spring of '88, George was in Los Angeles on business connected with a new HandMade production, *Checking Out*. One of his first pleasure calls was on guitarist/singer/songwriter Tom Petty, an occasional touring partner of Bob Dylan with his band, the Heartbreakers, and the blondest man in country rock.

Petty had been another Harrison convert to the ukulele. 'I remember George showing up at my house with two of them and saying, "We may need more." He opened the trunk of his car and it was like *full* of ukuleles.'

George needed a B-side for his third *Cloud Nine* single, 'This Is Love', another collaboration with Jeff Lynne. As it happened, Lynne was also in town, preparing in his usual multi-tasking mode to produce albums both for Tom Petty and the very Roy Orbison who'd featured in his and George's studio name-game.

Naturally Lynne wasn't too busy to help George come up with the B-side, whereupon Orbison, with whom they were having dinner – and who proved nothing like the frigid statue on that 1963 British package-tour – said he'd like to come and watch. Later, when George dropped by Tom Petty's house for a guitar he'd left there, Petty decided to tag along also.

Finding a studio at such short notice looked impossible, but then George recalled that Bob Dylan had a small one in the garage of his house in Malibu. Dylan could be unreachable by phone there for months on end, but this time he picked up first ring, said they were welcome to use the studio and that he'd make them a barbecue.

The next day, George and Lynne began working on a song that had some pleasing chords but no clear theme until, glancing around the tiny utilitarian space, George saw a cardboard carton inscribed HANDLE WITH CARE, an accidentally perfect encapsulation of his own fragile ego.

Only then did he fully appreciate that Roy Orbison and Tom Petty were also in the room, and Bob Dylan outside, firing up the barbecue, and impulsively decided they, too, must be in on it.

When George took the five-handed 'Handle With Care' to Mo Ostin at Warner Brothers records, Ostin's first reaction was that it was brilliant, his second that it would be criminally wasted as the B-side of a single and the five must make an album together.

The other four were happy to involve themselves in what seemed like an enjoyable sideline to their real careers. The problem was that Bob Dylan had a tour starting nine days later and didn't know when he'd be available again. George therefore set them to write and record nine further songs at the breakneck speed of one per day in the home studio of an LA-based British musician, Dave Stewart from the Eurythmics.

Despite the pressure, it hardly seemed like work since they were all *Monty Python* fans – the inscrutable-seeming Roy Orbison especially – more competitive in quoting from the show than in their collective writing or taping. And their guitars' baby brothers were always on hand to keep up their spirits; Tom Petty would recall how, even after the longest day in the studio, 'it was ukuleles till dawn.'

They were the ultimate supergroup, yet with none of the pressures George had seen almost destroy Eric Clapton in Cream.

Most importantly to him, they were a true democracy, sharing songwriting credits and vocals equally as the Beatles never had.

Casting around for a folksy, gospel-y, 1930s-y collective name, they decided on the Traveling Wilburys after an expression of George's: if a taping turned out to have a mistake, he'd say, 'We'll bury it in the mix.'

Recording under an alias was not just a superstar conceit. Between them, they represented several different record labels and George wanted none of the same wrangling over contracts as had followed the Concert For Bangladesh. So they extended the masquerade by pretending to be members of a real family, George becoming 'Nelson Wilbury', Orbison 'Lefty Wilbury', Dylan 'Lucky Wilbury', Petty 'Charlie T. Wilbury Junior' and Lynne 'Otis Wilbury'. Mo Ostin joined in the joke, and the precaution, by issuing their album, *The Traveling Wilburys Vol. 1* on a dedicated Wilbury label.

The moment couldn't have been better. The Sixties' pop audience now in their late thirties had for years felt left behind, variously battered by Punk and baffled by Disco. Male and female alike embraced the Wilburys' unchallenging, strummy sound with George in unprecedentedly relaxed mode, augmented by the occasional muted snarl from Dylan or seam of velvety anguish from Orbison. People with long enough memories dubbed it 'Skiffle for the Eighties'.

The album sold two million in six months, going Triple Platinum, winning a Grammy and giving a fillip to the careers of Dylan, Orbison and Petty. Orbison, alas, had little time to enjoy it, for two months after the album's release he died from a heart attack aged fifty-two. The Wilburys' second single, 'End Of The Line', featured his vocal but the video, shot some time after the recording, showed only his photograph and a guitar sitting in a rocking-chair.

It was sad for a Wilbury to reach the end of the line so soon and only in his fifties, nor would he be the last.

In September 1988, HandMade Films' tenth anniversary was celebrated by a lavish dinner in a marquee at Shepperton film studios to which all the great and good of the British film industry were bidden.

It was a night of triumph for Denis O'Brien, so much so that the 120 guests magnanimously included members of the *Monty Python* team who'd sidestepped his management nine years earlier and even Steve Abbott, the then HandMade staff accountant who'd helped them slip from O'Brien's grasp.

The after-dinner speeches included one by Michael Palin, paying tongue-in-cheek tribute to the company's inadvertent founder, EMI's Lord Delfont, who'd pulled the plug on *Monty Python's Life Of Brian* for its 'blasphemous' script, and to its 'unexpected saviour in the shape of George Harrison'.

Palin even worked in a light-hearted reference to the Python team's ditching of O'Brien after Steve Abbott had raised concerns about his proposed dispersal of their money among 'a great many [supposedly tax-sheltering] islands whose names I hadn't heard since stamp-collecting days'.

The evening saw the first cracks appear in George's relationship with O'Brien, which had nothing to do with Palin's gentle digs. There had already been discord over his involvement with the Traveling Wilburys, whose breakthrough hadn't yet happened and whom O'Brien, deaf to their quality, considered a needless distraction from HandMade business.

Now the £85,000 O'Brien had spent on the party seemed absurdly extravagant, like a breath of Apple Corps at its most profligate. George's own brief speech began: 'Thank you for coming, now all fuck off,' which his glittery audience mistook for droll Liverpool humour and so laughed dutifully.

Even the fact that Carl Perkins had come specially from America to provide the after-dinner entertainment failed to placate him, for without his knowledge O'Brien had arranged for what was supposedly a private occasion to be filmed by Granada Television.

'I remember him going ballistic at Denis,' Steve Abbott says, 'shouting "Televise this, you cunt."' 'George wasn't happy that night,' Michael Palin concurs. Yet he still had no inkling of what the big glasses and ventriloquist-doll mouth were concealing from him.

During the Thatcher economic boom of the mid-Eighties, banks had been happy to lend the capital sums necessary to finance HandMade films, enjoying the kudos of dealing with a former Beatle and confident that, should repayment be necessary, George had all the money in the world. But after a recent spate of box-office failures, they were starting to request tangible proof.

To this end, O'Brien hired as a consultant John Reiss, previously finance director at Thorn/EMI with whom he'd often dealt over HandMade video releases. Reiss's immediate task was to prepare a George Harrison balance sheet, which required a more detailed examination of O'Brien's files than Steve Abbott had been given nine years earlier.

Reiss had expected drawing up a balance sheet for George would involve lengthy conferences with its subject. However, the two of them were tête-à-tête only twice and both times O'Brien soon arrived and stayed for the rest of the meeting. 'I soon realised that George had no idea about his finances and was totally reliant on Denis.'

Puzzlingly, too, he showed few external signs of the wealth a former Beatle might be expected to possess. All his day-to-day expenses were paid by O'Brien's EuroAtlantic company much as Apple Corps and Brian Epstein's NEMS company before that used to do. 'Sometimes,' Reiss recalls, 'he'd drive into the office all the way from Oxfordshire to pick up £50 in cash to pay one of his gardeners.'

In so many ways the consummate swindler, O'Brien had nonetheless failed to follow rule number one in the swindlers' handbook: take care to destroy every incriminating document as you go. 'Like the Nazis, Denis had kept every single piece of paper,' Reiss says. 'The evidence against him was all there in his own office.'

The files revealed there to be 'no single legal entity for George's activity; everything was spread across a network of companies and partnerships based in different jurisdictions. [Denis] told George that this was for tax purposes. but in reality it was to create obscurity.'

After all these decades of Beatledom and post-Beatledom, the value of his assets was 'paltry' next to that of his manager. Besides Friar Park, there were only his house on Maui and his half-built one on Australia's Great Barrier Reef, both of them recently damaged by hurricanes. Yet O'Brien, in addition to his yacht and private island, now owned a house in Switzerland and another he was building in New York, seemingly at George's expense.

A recent hit solo album and another with the Traveling Wilburys did little to tip the balance in his favour. The flow of royalties was irregular and variable and impossible to quantify on paper. When they did come in, O'Brien or one of his many satellite companies would deduct up to 50 per cent in management-fees, even those relating to the era before he took George over.

While much of the foregoing might be classified merely as sharp practice, Reiss uncovered one serial instance of bald-headed, bespectacled, rigid-mouthed, cold-hearted deception. Whenever HandMade borrowed money from a bank, George had guaranteed the loan, as he thought, in equal partnership with O'Brien. 'I found all these guarantees with George's signature which Denis said he'd co-signed, but hadn't. If all the loans were to be called in, he was looking at potential debts of around £32 million.'

Reiss took his findings to Ray Cooper, George's chief ally in the office who'd long harboured his own suspicions about O'Brien, and they decided to go to Friar Park together and break the news. 'Olivia was out and little Dhani was running around in his pyjamas. When he'd gone to bed, we had pasta and salad made for us by a Beatle.

'Then George took us into his music room, with all the guitars given to him by people like Elvis and Clapton, and said, "What do you want to see me about?" I told him what had come to light and advised him to seek independent financial advice if he didn't want to see a newspaper headline saying Bankrupt Beatle.

'With that, he threw both of us out. I believe he was a bit of an ostrich. He didn't like to hear bad news and hoped it would go away.'

As the two whistleblowers expected, George's immediate reaction was to phone Denis O'Brien, who moved swiftly to silence any further incriminating. blasts. Reiss arrived at the EuroAtlantic office the next morning to learn that a letter from O'Brien terminating his consultancy was already on its way. Soon afterwards, O'Brien fired Ray Cooper by telephone without a word of thanks for his nine years' service.

George's head was to remain deeply buried in the sand for some time yet. No creditors were actually pounding on HandMade's door at that moment and O'Brien managed to ventriloquise away the network of dodgy offshore companies as being all in the sacred cause of saving him tax. Even when creditors did start pounding on the door, in ever-increasing numbers, he was kept completely unaware of them.

HandMade was to release one more film under his and O'Brien's joint aegis, the comedy *Nuns on the Run* starring Eric Idle in 1990. It was a sizeable hit, grossing almost $11 million in the US and £3.5 million in the UK, yet according to Idle 'not a single penny' found its way into his pocket. 'Two of the distributors had been screwed by Denis on another deal so they refused to hand over any money.'

Not even this mistreatment of his favourite Python could shake the sand out of George's hair.

His final decade began with a powerful reminder of his apotheosis both as a musician and human being in 1971 – and, as before, he had to be steered to it.

The collapse of Communism throughout Eastern Europe laid bare the inner workings of many repellent totalitarian regimes, none more chillingly than that of Romania's dictator, Nicolae

Ceauşescu and his equally brutal and corrupt wife, Elena. Along with a ruined economy and a plundered national exchequer, the Ceauşescus' legacy was a network of state orphanages where around 100,000 children had literally been left to die.

George at the time was in LA, making the Traveling Wilburys' second album, so Olivia Harrison was by herself at Friar Park when the first television reports came through of suffering and misery with which the usual international relief agencies could barely cope. Olivia was moved to the same horror and pity George had been by the famine and genocide in Bangladesh.

She was a woman of action – as she would later demonstrate spectacularly in her own home – and, rather than simply donate to the existing relief funds, she flew to Romania's capital to see what the situation was and how she might help, without letting George know in advance. The next time they spoke on the phone, she told him, 'I'm in Bucharest.'

In the following week, she saw for herself the hellish nether-worlds where children had been left malnourished and in rags without washing facilities or sanitation, often physically and sexually abused, in many cases permanently tethered to their filthy beds and infected with HIV from unsterilised needles.

Her response was to set up a private foundation to aid them whose name, the Romanian Angels Appeal, pronounced an end to their cruel anonymity. With the diplomatic skill she showed throughout, she even managed to bypass the former Beatles' always tricky internal politics and persuade Yoko Ono Lennon, Linda McCartney and Ringo's second wife, the American actress Barbara Bach, to take an active role in it.

George still being in the studio with the Traveling Wilburys,

Olivia asked him if they'd contribute a track as a fundraiser in the spirit of Band Aid and Live Aid. They immediately paused what they'd been doing and, at Bob Dylan's suggestion, recorded the old country song 'Nobody's Child' whose many previous cover-versions included one by the Beatles as Tony Sheridan's backing band in Hamburg. George wrote an additional verse specifically referring to Romania's disowned children.

The single begat a Concert For Bangladesh-style charity album, this one consisting of ready-recorded tracks donated by, among others, Ringo, Stevie Wonder, Elton John, Eric Clapton, the Bee Gees, Guns N' Roses and Paul Simon. George was its compiler rather than producer, keeping a low profile so as not to distract from the importance of the cause.

The proceeds from the album and the Traveling Wilburys' single enabled ten truckloads of food and medical supplies to be sent to Romania, their 'administration charges' prepaid to ensure they went directly to the children. It was to be only the start of a relief programme Olivia would later continue in George's memory, supporting new, humane orphanages, clinics and schools.

The now four-strong Wilbury 'brothers' released their second album, jokily named *Traveling Wilburys Vol. 3*, under a new set of aliases, George now billed as Spike, Dylan as Boo, Jeff Lynne as Clayton and Tom Petty as Muddy. It didn't repeat the huge success of Vol. 1, but still appeared in the US and UK Top 20 and went single Platinum.

In early March 1991, George attended the first in a series of Eric Clapton concerts at the Royal Albert Hall. Backstage, Clapton suggested he should do some real travelling in the form of a tour if he wanted to stay in touch with his record-buying public. He seemed tempted, but the memory of the 'dark hoarse' tour in 1974 was still too raw.

Clapton and George's first wife, Pattie, had divorced in 1988 after nine years in which his alcoholism and increasingly blatant infidelities made her view life with George, for all its meditational misanthropy, as easy by comparison.

Since then, Clapton had tardily begun the growing-up process, first by getting permanently sober, then having a child with the Italian film actress Lory Del Santo. Though the relationship with Del Santo was transitory, he took fatherhood with utter seriousness, thereby becoming a person in his own right rather than a bundle of impersonations of musicians he admired, George foremost among them.

A couple of weeks after Clapton's Albert Hall season, he went to New York to see his adored son, Conor, now four years old. As he was preparing to collect Conor from the high-rise apartment where Del Santo was staying, the boy strayed, unsupervised, to an open window and fell fifty-three storeys to his death.

It was a dark time for someone who, in his ex-wife's words, had 'never bumped into life before'. It saw Clapton, in an abyss of sorrow and guilt, write 'Tears In Heaven', a requiem for Conor that, paradoxically, became his bestselling single ever and won a clutch of awards bringing him no more joy than so many coffin nails. And the friends to whom he turned most often, and who never failed him, were George and Olivia.

That December, Clapton was to give twelve concerts in Japan. Although these were primarily therapy for himself, he saw them as a way to thank George for his supportiveness by easing him back onto the road, just as he had once before, with the Delaney & Bonnie tour in 1969.

George, it so happened, needed an escape from a new media furore, one which made his old antagonists in the music press seem paragons of accuracy and sobriety by comparison. An American supermarket tabloid, *The Globe*, purveying fantastical fiction as fact, had recently accused him of being 'a fan of Hitler... given to strutting around in Nazi uniform'.

The sensible thing would have been to ignore *The Globe*'s story, letting its patent absurdity speak for itself and thereby limiting its readership to prurient food-shoppers; instead, George had retained the celebrated LA attorney Bert Fields to hit the tabloid with a $200 million lawsuit, so ensuring its garbage would truly go global.

'Eric told him, "You can have my band and my whole set-up,"' Clapton's then assistant Vivien Griffin recalls. 'Even so, George took a long time to make up his mind. First it was on, then it was off, then he said he didn't want [Clapton's manager] Roger Forrester there, though Roger did go in the end.'

In the end, he was to dominate the tour, performing most of the twenty-four-title setlist with Clapton merely backing him apart from in a block of four songs mid-show.

This remarkable gesture of friendship actually drove a wedge between the long-time best friends that was no less damaging for its smallness and lightness. George brought along a couple of ukuleles for the kind of strum-athons he so enjoyed with the Wilburys only to discover Clapton was totally indifferent to the instrument and not in the least amenable to being converted.

As ever, George was the soul of inconsistency, first treating Clapton with such sensitivity after Conor's death, then showing no awareness of his situation as a recovering alcoholic on a tour whose other members still partied unchecked. On the contrary, there was a resurgence of what Pattie had termed George 'minxiness' on the road with the Delaney & Bonnie tour, before she'd been aware of Clapton's obsession with her, when he tried to pair the two of them off so he could attempt to seduce her sister Paula.

'Eric didn't hang out with the band,' Vivien Griffin recalls, 'but George was always inviting them to his room to drink and listen to him play the ukulele. He kind of seduced them away and split the camp.'

The minxiness may have gone still further. When the tour reached Hiroshima, Clapton learned that Conor's mother, Lory Del Santo – who by now had another boyfriend with whom she'd had another son – was on her way from Milan to see him for what threatened to be a kind of emotional post-mortem. 'When Lory arrived, Eric talked to her, saying it was completely inappropriate and he didn't want her there', says Vivien Griffin. 'But George was very sweet to her and she ended up staying a few days.'

In 2007, when George was no longer around, Del Santo would allege they'd had a brief affair which for her had been 'sweet revenge' on Clapton for leaving her after Conor was born and, for George, his friend's belated punishment for wooing away Pattie.

The revenge motive on George's part scarcely holds up and at this remove the affair cannot possibly be verified. Yet Vivien Griffin recalls it being the talk of the show's female backing singers, always the first to know about such goings-on.

28

'Do you want to go on a yacht to the South Pacific and run away for ever?

George had never quite got Liverpool Institute High School out of his system. In 1967, at the height of his hippie/meditation phase, he told a journalist that if he ever had children, he'd never send them to any such repository of pointless rules and traditions, but have them taught 'privately by gurus'.

Now that he finally had a son to educate, the guru option might have seemed irresistible given all the distinguished holy men he counted as friends and the weight of knowledge they'd already imparted to him. However, it was difficult to ignore the several excellent private schools in the Henley area, or the thirst for book-learning Dhani had shown in his kindergarten, so unlike his father at that age.

George therefore allowed the boy to be encased in the same kind of school caps and blazers he'd detested at the Inny, but remained watchful for any signs of the same confinement and oppression he'd once felt. 'You don't have to go to school today,' Dahni would recall him saying almost every morning in term-time, followed by some wildly alluring alternative like 'Do you want to go on a yacht to the South Pacific and run away for ever?'

After a brief spell at a Montessori free expression school, Dhani was enrolled at Henley's thoroughly conventional Shiplake College where he shone from the beginning, especially in the science and technical subjects that had always been a mystery to George.

Least of all did Dhani resemble the Liverpool Institute boy of the 1950s whose end-of-term reports always complained that he'd 'taken no part in school activities whatsoever'. Dhani was into every sport, especially competitive rowing. He even joined the school's Combined Cadet Force, which prepared pupils for possible military careers, shocking his one-time flower power dad by wearing a blue-grey Royal Air Force uniform one day each week.

However, with Olivia's help, George had defied convention as surely as if Dhani had spent years in study of ancient texts with saffron-robed monks. For he'd grown up a normal, if privileged, boy, rather than a spoiled, neglected and mixed-up rock star's brat.

As he turned into a near-facsimile of the young George, covetous eyes were trained on him by a record industry which already had already got hold of John's elder son, Julian, and could hardly wait for his younger son, Sean, to grow up.

With Dhani, all the necessary ingredients seemed to be in place. Ringo had given him his first drumkit when he was six; three years later, George had started him on guitar by showing him how to play Buddy Holly's 'Words of Love' with the rippling riffs that had been an early triumph for a much-treasured Höfner President.

Dhani enjoyed spending time in the Friar Park studio, watching George 'push buttons' as he expressed it, sometimes even pushing a few himself. But the vari-curved silhouettes of his father's guitar collection attracted him less than those of the cars he saw at close quarters during their privileged backstage access at Grand Prix races.

It was almost a replay in reverse of when George's father had given him a set of screwdrivers in hopes they might be the first step towards his starting a garage with his two brothers, an occupation so much wiser than the guitar. And like Harold then, he never tried to bend Dhani to his wishes.

The steadfastness with which George could hold a grudge – as against his old school not to mention his old schoolfellow, Paul – was seen most positively in his pastimes. For his was not the usual rock-star's minuscule attention-span: when something engaged his interest, it would be for his lifetime.

The most obvious example were Friar Park's grounds which he'd come to regard as a vocation far surpassing music. He once told Olivia he hoped to be remembered as a gardener who'd had a few record hits on the side. Dhani – the one person on earth allowed to tease him – nicknamed him Capability George after the eighteenth-century garden designer Capability Brown who called the potential of any landscape put in his charge its 'capabilities'.

Despite the many more exclusive gurus at whose feet George had sat, he'd stayed loyal to the Maharishi Mahesh Yogi's Transcendental Meditation as the launchpad for his spiritual journey in 1967 – seeing no inconsistency with having helped John lampoon the Maharishi as 'Sexy Sadie'.

Far from fading into obscurity as expected after being dumped by the Beatles, the Transcendental Meditation movement had purchased Mentmore House in Buckinghamshire, former country seat of the Rothschild family, a Victorian mansion as extravagant in its mock-Elizabethan and -Jacobean flourishes as Friar Park in its Gothic ones. Here, the Maharishi's followers were now taught so-called 'yogic flying', reportedly with mattresses nailed to the walls to soften collisions with chandeliers and cornices – though the 'flying' consisted only of assuming the Lotus position and bouncing energetically up and down.

Transcendental Meditation (TM) had also produced a political wing, the Natural Law Party, aimed at applying its philosophy to international governance and active in seventy-three countries. For the British General Election of April 1992, it was to field 310 candidates to contest parliamentary seats and invited George to stand for one of them.

Predictably he declined but, instead, headlined a fundraising concert in aid of the party at the Royal Albert Hall with friends including Ringo, his drummer son Zak, Joe Brown, two of the Beach Boys and the Irish guitarist Gary Moore who'd become an auxiliary Traveling Wilbury. It was George's first full-length show in London since the Beatles' rooftop concert in 1969, his first solo one there – and would be his last anywhere.

Afterwards, he affirmed his support for the National Law Party and, implicitly, TM: 'For a couple of hundred years, we've had these parties who haven't done anything because they don't know who they are themselves. What we need is a party of people who are involved with consciousness because that's where everything begins ... people who can just go beyond this bickering.'

This unheard-of political pronouncement from 'the Quiet

One' was to have negligible effect. The election three days later put not a single National Law Party MP into Parliament, all its candidates polled so few votes that they lost their deposits and the Conservatives regained power for the fourth time in a row.

What would be his final stage appearance took place that October at Madison Square Garden, the scene of his zenith as a musician and humanitarian, the Concerts For Bangladesh. To mark Bob Dylan's thirtieth year in the business, George joined a constellation of performers who'd covered Dylan songs, often in adventurous new ways, like Stevie Wonder, Lou Reed and Tracy Chapman. One of George's two choices expressed the shared feeling of indebtedness to his unpredictable, often cantankerous but still firm friend: 'If Not For You'.

His love of the ukulele remained as obsessive as ever, matched by his devotion to the half-namesake who'd enjoyed superstardom in the grey 1940s with risqué little ditties about honeymooning couples and peeping Tom window-cleaners that were the antithesis of all things rock.

Britain had, and still has, a George Formby Appreciation Society staging regular conventions at which members compete to simulate Formby's squeaky Lancashire tones, melon-slice grin, and 'scissors' strumming action. George joined the society during the early Nineties, became a regular attendee at conventions (while always refusing to go near similar events organised by Beatles fans) and took part in the soundalikes competition, often finding himself totally outclassed.

'I once saw him at Blackpool Winter Gardens, up against a nine-year-old lad,' recalls Mal Jefferson, a fellow Liverpool musician and uke-enthusiast. 'The lad slaughtered him, with Olivia and Dhani looking on.'

The society's president, John Croft, had managed to acquire Formby's own gold-plated and engraved Ludwig banjolele, then spent years restoring it to pristine condition. With uke-players, as with guitarists, there was no higher compliment than to give a fellow enthusiast one's favourite instrument; hence the Formby banjolele became the *pièce-de-résistance* of George's vast collection. 'He was like a kid at Christmas,' Croft recalls.

Monogamy had not been easy for someone who'd considered himself almost a born-again Krishna, entitled to take his pick of the women who constantly threw themselves at him. On his vast home turf, his devotion to Olivia was undivided but for many years when he went travelling on his own, an old Beatle rule came back into play: 'sex on the road doesn't count.'

In New York he would pay incognito visits to clubs like Max's Kansas City carrying in his pocket three rubies from his Indian hoard. Any woman who caught his eye would have a ruby tossed in front of her, either on her table or at the bar, as if he was betting on a roulette wheel (the difference being that his number was always guaranteed to come up).

Latterly, such escapades had featured a surprising musical element. A Los Angeles sex worker identified only as 'Tiffany' claimed that when she kept her appointment with George, he'd been playing a ukulele and singing a George Formby song. She then performed a sexual service for him, during which, she recollected, 'he was not one for small talk ... the entire time, he kept strumming that damn' ukulele.'

The encounter concluded with what, falling into uke-parlance herself, Tiffany described as a 'grand strum', following it with an innocent double-entendre rivalling any of Formby's calculated ones: 'Then, without missing a lick, he started in on another song.'

'He did like the women,' Olivia would concede many years later. 'He was pursued and ... he was a very sensual person. During our marriage there was a lot of flirtation, [and] there were some bumps in the road.'

A friend of the couple recalls that Olivia knew the name of every 'bump' and resolutely looked the other way on the principle that all things must pass. Thus when a British tabloid alleged that George had had an affair with Madonna, she knew for certain it had never happened.

And with 'patience and time', to quote his last hit single. that trap door in his marriage finally closed for good. 'He wanted the normal life,' Olivia said, 'and that's what I gave him.'

It took George a long time to accept that Denis O'Brien had for years been using him like a credit card with no limit – and longer still to bestir himself to any action.

His previous manager, Allen Klein, had been such an obvious crook that he'd always been to a degree forewarned and forearmed. O'Brien by contrast was so smooth, so reassuring, so apparently tireless in shielding his one trophy client from the cursed Taxman. Ordinarily the least trusting of mortals, George had had absolute faith in that studious bald cranium, those gleaming spectacles, that fixed ventriloquial smile.

Even when their business partnership came to an end in 1993, there still had been no showdown with O'Brien. Haunted by memories of the Beatles' numerous incomprehensible dissolution documents, George insisted on there being a single piece of paper for him to sign.

Only at this point did he belatedly heed the separate urgings of O'Brien's two honest in-house accountants, Steve Abbott and John Reiss, seek independent financial advice and discover the awesome size of the financial hole in which O'Brien had left him.

His state of denial ended with the writing of a song entitled 'Lying O'Brien' which he previewed to his friend Eric Idle, the recent victim of a different O'Brien rip-off over the *Nuns on the Run* film. 'Every time I let someone in, they let me down,' its lyric said, which seemed hardly fair to Olivia or Dhani.

In 1994, HandMade Films was sold to the Canadian Paragon entertainment group for a knockdown $8.5 million, an ignominious end for a company that had galvanised the British film industry. George's share did little to mitigate the bank debts in respect of several past productions for which O'Brien had secretly made him personally responsible.

One of the few outsiders to whom he revealed his predicament was Mal Jefferson when they met at the George Formby convention. 'After he'd played, I offered to buy his uke off him and to my amazement he agreed. "But I paid two grand for it," he said. "I need every penny at the moment; I've just lost my shirt with HandMade."

'I wrote him a cheque for £2001, just as a joke, but he said, "Thanks very much" and stuffed it into his pocket.'

In mid-Nineties Britain, the Sixties were back, in style if not spirit, its fashionable young once again sporting high-buttoned suits, Paisley shirts, elastic-sided boots, Mary Quant bobs, miniskirts and glossy PVC, its national flag back as a Pop Art icon on plastic shopping bags, Swinging London homogenised into

'Cool Britannia' – and barely a detail anywhere not suggestive in some way of the Beatles.

George's comments about the music he heard on the radio and acts he saw on *Top Of The Pops* remained as scathing as ever, only now, very often, they would be mimicking or pastiching him. For this was the brief season of so-called Britpop when bands without a definite article between them, like Blur, Suede or Pulp, rejected the Eighties' electronic fripperies for good old-fashioned guitars and drums and – like the Beatles – sang in their native accents, not gum-chewing American ones.

The biggest by far were Oasis from Manchester, fronted by two brothers, songwriter Noel and vocalist Liam Gallagher, virtually a Beatles tribute band who'd even named one of their mega-selling singles 'Wonderwall' after George's first solo album, *Wonderwall Music*.

Reverence turned to rudeness, however, when he dismissed Oasis's guitar-heavy sound as 'not very interesting' and advised them to drop singer Liam Gallagher, whom he described as 'the silly one'. Gallagher retaliated with Lennon-like overkill, calling him 'a fucking nipple' ... Anyway, John and Ringo were the Beatles ... Isn't it a pity? [quoting the Harrisong] It will be when I meet George Harrison, I'm gonna stand on his head and play golf.'

By now, Paul was over the ex-Beatles' collective denial and had begun to perform some of his and John's songs onstage, provoking yet another barb from George. 'He's decided *he's* the Beatles. I'm not interested. For me it's the past ... "Be here now" is my motto.'

Since the breakup, their former roadie and still trusted friend Neil Aspinall had managed the tiny remnant of their Apple organisation, his principal – and seemingly endless – task the compilation of a film documentary from the vast store of footage in their archives, to be titled *The Long And Winding Road.*

Amid the resurgent Beatlemania of the Nineties, the project widened in scope to a documentary, three double albums of rarities and out-takes put together by their nonpareil producer, George Martin, and an 'in their own words' book.

A few years earlier, George probably would have wanted no part of any of this. But as he was now faced with the real threat of bankruptcy thanks to Denis O'Brien, it came as a lifeline. His only objection was to naming the project after a song wholly identified with Paul, so an absolutely neutral and impartial title was substituted: *The Beatles Anthology.*

He even went along with the idea that, as a bonus to the compilation albums, Paul, Ringo and himself should record some new music, even though it would be seen as the reunion he'd evaded for so many years – and fraudulent, too, in delivering only 'the Threetles'.

There was, of course, someone else whose agreement to the *Anthology* was just as essential and even more uncertain. In the years since John's death, Yoko had maintained diplomatic relations with her fellow Apple directors – 'the in-laws', as she called them – but many old resentments on both sides had still simmered behind their camera-ready smiles.

As the one currently on best terms with Yoko, Paul was deputed to ask her approval of the project but received much more. She gave him a cassette tape on which John had recorded four demos during his supposed retirement from 'the game', when in reality he'd never stopped watching and competing with his old songwriting partner.

The others were given licence to overdub their accompaniment to these home recordings without Yoko being present or any creative input from her. Thus the woman universally accused of breaking up the Beatles was to be responsible for bringing them back together, musically if not corporeally.

The song chosen to be worked into a single to launch the *Anthology* was 'Free As A Bird', a wistful ballad John had laid down in 1977, in a faraway voice barely recognisable as him. It was so short that Paul and George had to bulk it out by singing an extra bridge in turn, a format the old-time Beatles had never used, which left no scope for their matchless three-part harmony.

It was recorded in March 1994, not – to George's annoyance – at Friar Park but in the studio Paul had built in his Sussex mill. The original plan had been for George Martin to co-produce the session, like so many classic ones of yore. But Martin had begun to suffer hearing problems, the result of decades of exposure to high-decibel rock, so regretfully declined the job while still continuing to oversee the albums of archive material. Instead, George proposed his Traveling Wilburys collaborator, Jeff Lynne, making clear that if Lynne were not brought in, he was out.

After that, the atmosphere was friendly enough. Paul made no attempt to influence George's slide-guitar motif (very close to that contentious one in 'My Sweet Lord') and George didn't complain about Paul's solo verse being three lines longer than his.

He even succumbed to a little covert nostalgia. The song ended with a brief burst on his banjolele, followed by John's voice mimicking George Formby's chirpy catchphrase about the weather, 'Turned out nice again.'

Which indeed it had.

*

In January 1995, George's long-delayed lawsuit against Denis O'Brien came before Los Angeles County Superior Court. An eighteen-page complaint charged O'Brien with 'tortuous misconduct' in that 'pretending to serve the interests of his musician client, he misused his position and his client's credit to finance secret profit and a lavish international lifestyle while subjecting his trusting client to massive risks and losses.'

He was accused of 'drastically reorganising' George's finances and business holdings into 'a complicated Byzantine structure involving multiple offshore corporations and other related entities all under his direct or indirect control', and secondly of 'improper and inept management' during their joint ownership of HandMade Films. To keep HandMade going, he'd said it was necessary to borrow 'vast amounts of money' but by tricking George into being sole signatory of the repayment guarantees, had been taking half the company's profits while sharing none of the risk.

O'Brien, who'd since returned to America without a stain on his character to resume his former career in banking, denied any wrongdoing and a vastly expensive hearing loomed whose costs George would struggle to meet.

His anxiety over the lawsuit inevitably had an effect on the frail creative spark struck by working with Paul and Ringo on 'Free As A Bird.' The second *Anthology* double album was also to include a spruced-up John demo, 'Real Love', dating from 1979–80, but nothing else on Yoko's tape felt right for the third album. George and Paul began working on a song called 'All For Love', which might have revived a joint credit in abeyance since 'In Spite Of All The Danger' in 1958, but was never recorded.

There was even so an unscheduled reappearance of the group mind – three-quarters of it anyway – on a night when Paul and Ringo visited the Friar Park studio and he found himself jamming and positively enjoying a set of their earliest material including 'Raunchy', his audition piece for John at the Morgue club when he was fourteen.

The Beatles Anthology was to begin its staggered release in November 1995, a quarter of a century after a breakup the world had never really accepted. The news brought a media furore like none since those which used to rage around 3 Savile Row in 1969–70. George's old ally Derek Taylor was brought back as press officer, meaning that not all the attention would be given to Paul and to John's memory.

However, on 20 November, the headlines were stolen by the BBC television interview with Diana Princess of Wales in which she revealed that her husband, the heir to the throne, had had a mistress since the ink was barely dry on their supposedly 'fairytale' marriage. Different days indeed when Beatles could be bumped from the front pages by royalty.

George at the outset had expressed disdain for the whole project in words that would come back to haunt everyone else involved with it. 'I hope someone does this to all my crap demos when I'm dead and makes them into hit songs.' To be sure, 'Free As A Bird' scarcely lived up to its advance billing; John's wispy vocal seemed little more than a ghost on vinyl, though there was a deep poignancy in Paul and George each singing, 'Whatever happened to/the love that we once knew?' from segregated sound-chambers. It still went to number 2 in Britain, was a worldwide hit and won a Grammy award for Best Performance by Group or Duo with Vocal.

The first of the double albums, released with the television documentary and large- (indeed, massive-) format book, sold

450,000 on its first day, more than any previous Beatles album or any other one. *Anthology 2*, early in 1996, including John's 'Real Love', was number 4 in the UK and 11 in the US, and went gold. *Anthology 3*, despite having no overdubbed John track, went triple Platinum.

The royalties, going directly to George rather than into Denis O'Brien's offshore archipelago, restored his financial equilibrium. How much these amounted to was never revealed. But even for Pete Best, the drummer sacked on the threshold of the Beatles' breakthrough who'd played on a handful of *Anthology* tracks, the payout ran into millions.

Quoted at length in the *Anthology* book, George was warm and often endearing as he talked about his family and the Beatles' early misadventures in Hamburg and at the Cavern. In the television documentary, by contrast, he struck a churlish note with his comment on their MBE awards in 1965: 'After all we did for Great Britain, selling all that corduroy and making it swing, they gave us that bloody old leather medal with a wooden string [sic] through it.'

By the 1990s, he had done appreciably more. What had become known as the George Harrison Fund for UNICEF was estimated to have raised around $45 million for aid work in Bangladesh and other humanitarian ends. It was philanthropy far exceeding that of his two fellow Beatles (both of whom were to receive knighthoods) and would seem to have cried out for further recognition in the royal honours which had created him a Member of the Most Excellent Order of the British Empire just for shaking his hair and going 'Oooh!'

But that was never to come, not even posthumously.

*

In January 1996 the court in Los Angeles upheld George's claim against Denis O'Brien, awarding him $11 million in compensatory damages. Despite having been represented by the lethal Bert Fields, it was only half what he had asked and didn't cover even the bank loan for *Cold Dog Soup*, one of HandMade's misses, for which he was personally liable. O'Brien promptly lodged an appeal both against the verdict and on grounds that the case ought to have been heard in Britain rather than the US. So there was no question of damages until the California Court of Appeal's decision, months or even years hence.

Terry Gilliam from the Monty Pythons – currently looking for another saviour to bankroll a *Time Bandits 2* movie – bumped into George around this time and thought the lawsuit had 'aged him by about ten years'.

Fortunately, he had the *Beatles Anthology* to do much more than cover his bank debts. That year, he was able to announce a seven-figure donation to Olivia's Romanian Angels foundation for its work on behalf of the country's forgotten orphans.

Mixing the flash and the sacred as ever, he also could pay £540,000 for one of a series of only twenty road cars produced by the McLaren racing company, customised in a unique shade of purple with black satin wheels and a top speed of 230 mph. McLaren's chief designer, Gordon Murray, allowed him to oversee every stage of the car's evolution including the painting of fourteen different religious symbols and quotations on various parts of its bodywork.

Dhani by now was at America's Brown University in Rhode Island, studying for a bachelor's degree in physics and industrial design and as crazy about racing cars as ever. Through his father's friendship with Murray and other McLaren executives, he was to join the company's aerodynamics department straight after graduation.

George had reached the end of his five-year deal with Warner, but at fifty-three still had a more than viable recording career. But he was in no hurry to make another album; he told Olivia the only ambition he had left was to have no more ambition.

In these months before multiple blows began to fall, India was uppermost in his thoughts. At the beginning of 1997, he, Olivia and his friend Shyamsundar Das travelled to Vrindavan in Uttar Pradesh, where Krishna is said to have grown up, and toured the numerous temples and shrines to both Krishna and Radha.

He also produced a new album for his surrogate father, Ravi Shankar, on which not a single sitar could be heard. *Chants of India* was a collection of Vedic and other sacred prayers set to music on the theme of peace and harmony among all creatures. Shankar thought it the supreme achievement of his sixty-year career.

George threw himself into promoting *Chants of India* and in May taped a television special with Shankar entitled *George and Ravi, Yin and Yang* for the American cable channel VH1. His beard now flecked with grey, as dishevelled as if he'd come straight from his garden, he reflected on the album's themes of mortality and eternity with what would seem almost second sight. 'Bob Dylan said, "He not busy being born is busy dying." Nobody tries to find out what is the cause of death, what happens when we die, and to me that is the only thing of any importance.'

The interviewer, John Fugelsang, daringly offered him an acoustic guitar and, although not what he was there for, he took it and began to strum and sing 'All Things Must Pass'. Embalmed on YouTube for ever, it's no longer a generalised observation on the transience of earthly life but a chilling prophecy about himself.

29

'I'M BEING MURDERED IN
MY OWN HOUSE'

In July 1997, while gardening at Friar Park, George noticed a lump in his neck that turned out to be cancerous. He went into the Princess Margaret Hospital in Windsor (under the alias of 'Sid Smith') for surgery to remove the lump, followed by two courses of radiation treatment at Britain's foremost cancer hospital, the Royal Marsden in south-west London. The following January, he travelled to America for a check-up at the Mayo Clinic in Rochester, Minnesota, and was pronounced to be in the clear.

The media knew nothing of his diagnosis or treatment until he was spotted leaving the Mayo Clinic. On returning home, he took the uncharacteristic step of going out to the reporters gathered at his front gate and admitting to the cancer. 'I got it purely from smoking,' he said. 'I gave up cigarettes many years ago, but started again for a while [under the stress of producing *Shanghai Surprise*] and then stopped. Luckily for me, they found this nodule [which] was more a warning than anything.'

Others in the Beatles' extended family didn't share his seeming good luck. His old friend and supporter, Derek Taylor, also a heavy smoker, died from throat cancer that same year as did

Paul's wife, Linda, after a long fight against breast cancer a year later.

In 1998, too, his greatest musical hero, Carl Perkins, outwardly the most tranquil of men, suffered a series of strokes of which the last proved fatal. George attended the funeral in Jackson, Tennessee, and by way of a eulogy played a snatch of Perkins's song 'Your True Love'. It was to be his last public performance.

On the West Coast, meanwhile, the California Court of Appeal upheld his award of $11 million in damages two years earlier for Denis O'Brien's mismanagement and fraudulence at HandMade films.

The basis of O'Brien's appeal was that California hadn't been a proper place to try a case involving a British company turning out preponderantly British films. The appeal judge dismissed this claim when it emerged that O'Brien spent one day per month in the States, held a California driving licence and owned a house in Encino apparently built with George's money. But he'd continue to find ways not to pay out damages to the point where George would have no further need of them.

At the same time, George found himself back in the British High Court where the Beatles' partnership had been dissolved, but this time in a united front with Paul, Ringo and Yoko. At issue was a live recording of the band onstage at the Hamburg Star-Club in December 1962, their last stint among the strippers and mud-wrestlers before fame picked them up like a cyclone. As captured by a fellow Liverpool musician, Adrian Barber, on a cheap tape-recorder with a single microphone, they were barely audible above the German hubbub, with one song, Ray Charles's 'Hallelujah, I Love Her So', ceded to the club's chief bouncer, Horst Fascher, as a reward for watching their backs.

Put out as an album by a company named Lingasong, it had been in circulation since the early Seventies, finding a ready market among hardcore Beatle obscurists. Apple had already made one unsuccessful attempt to suppress it; now, with its reappearance as a two-CD set on Sony, they were bringing out their heaviest artillery.

George was especially keen to acquire, then pulp this 'crummiest ever' recording by the band. Giving evidence at the hearing, he struck all the right notes in responding to the defendants' claim that it hadn't been unauthorised and illicit because John had given Barber verbal permission beforehand.

'One drunken person recording another bunch of drunks doesn't constitute business deals,' he said. 'The only person who allegedly knew anything about it is the person who's dead ... who can say it's a load of rubbish.' The judge, Mr Justice Neuberger, said he accepted all the plaintiffs' arguments, 'with particular reference to Mr George Harrison'.

The success of the *Beatles Anthology* had changed George's focus on the present tense only. The approaching new millennium would mark the thirtieth anniversary of his first, triumphant solo album *All Things Must Pass* and, although it still sold in huge quantities, he began planning a revised and remastered version.

With health and money worries both seemingly allayed, only one cloud remained hanging over him. It was that both the refuges he'd found at what felt like the far ends of the earth no longer offered their former peace and privacy.

On Maui, his blockage of the public right of way through his garden had soured relations with the islanders beyond repair, no matter how many local hand-crafted ukuleles he bought. And during one of his long absences from the house, a local woman had broken in, stolen a pizza from the freezer, cooked and eaten it on the premises, then gone on to use the washing machine to do her laundry.

Even his estate on Hamilton Island on the edge of Australia's Great Barrier Reef, almost deserted when he'd bought it, was now attracting tourists in increasing numbers, hoping for a glimpse of him.

Friar Park itself had ceased to be sacrosanct when thieves raided its garden and stole two bronze busts of friars valued at £50,000, then slipped away undetected. But infinitely worse was to follow.

In the early hours of 30 December 1999 an intruder broke through the perimeter fence at a blind spot for the CCTV cameras and found his way to the house, pausing en route to wrench a small stone statue of St George and the Dragon from its plinth.

George and Olivia had only just gone to bed, but he was already asleep when she heard a sound of breaking glass which at first she thought was a falling chandelier. Realising somebody was in the house, she roused George, who put on a jacket over his pyjamas, slipped on a pair of boots and went to investigate while Olivia phoned the police.

In the kitchen, he smelled cigarette smoke and saw part of a stone wing from the St George and the Dragon statue lying on the floor, having been used to smash one of the glass patio doors.

He shouted a warning to Olivia and was on his way back along the gallery to their bedroom when he saw a man below in the great hall, holding the stone sword from the statue in one hand and a kitchen knife in the other.

'Get down here!' the man screamed at him. Remembering how a previous would-be burglar had fled on being challenged by his then wife, Pattie, he shouted back the first thing that came into his head: 'Hare Krishna!'

With that, the man ran up the sweeping staircase to the gallery with evidently murderous intent. As if transformed suddenly into St George, thinking only of Olivia and her mother, who was with them for New Year, George faced up to this inexplicable dragon and tried to grab the knife.

After a brief struggle, they both fell onto a heap of meditation cushions, his assailant on top of him and stabbing him repeatedly in the upper body. He would remember thinking with the strange detachment that can come at moments of mortal danger, 'I'm being murdered in my own house.'

When Olivia appeared, it seemed she might become the second Beatle wife to see her husband assassinated in front of her. Like Yoko after five shots had been pumped into John, she noticed a 'horrible confused look' on the victim's face. 'He was very pale,' she would later testify, 'and staring at me in a really bizarre manner.'

Woman of action that she was, she picked up the nearest weapon to hand, a brass-handled poker, and laid into George's attacker with it. When that had no effect, she grabbed a standard-lamp, inverted it, and bludgeoned their assailant with its heavy base.

Thanks to the direct phone-line to Henley police station installed after John's murder, officers were at the scene in twelve minutes. They were ahead of Dhani, now twenty-two, who had his own quarters in one of the outlying lodges and was awoken by Rachel, the housekeeper, to be told 'something' had happened over at the house. 'I asked her, "Are my parents all right?" he would recall. 'But she said nothing.'

He reached the great hall to find its gallery alive with uniformed constables and his mother lying at the bottom of the staircase, the poker with which she'd tried to defend George still beside her. She had herself sustained a nasty head wound, but she waved Dhani on almost impatiently: 'Daddy's upstairs. He's badly hurt. *Go.*'

In the gallery, the intruder was prone on the ground with two officers standing over him. He made eye-contact with Dhani for a long moment, but that was all.

George was lying just inside the half-open bedroom door, bleeding profusely from multiple stab wounds, a mixture of blood and air bubbling from the gashes in his chest, his very lips and teeth bloody. There was blood on the walls and all over the floor, mixed with scarlet fragments from the lamp-base Olivia had used as a club; they were some of the ruby chips his friend Shyamsundara Das had brought from India that he'd been so fond of distributing at the Row Barge pub.

With no paramedics there yet, Dhani tried to staunch his wounds with paper tissues and a towel, but it was a hopeless task. Indeed, George seemed beyond help. 'He was drifting, he looked even paler in the face. He kept murmuring, "Hare Krishna" and saying, "I'm going out."'

Dhani supported his head and held one of his hands, a policeman held the other and between them they tried to keep him in the world. 'I kept flicking my fingers and saying, "Dad, stay with me,"' Dhani would recollect. '"This is the worst it gets. From now on, it only gets better."'

In the minutes before the paramedics arrived and took over,

George nearly died four times but was pulled back from the brink by the sound of his son's voice.

George's assailant was thirty-four-year-old Liverpudlian Michael Abram, a paranoid schizophrenic who, six weeks earlier, had been denied treatment by the psychiatric unit at Whiston Hospital after doctors there concluded he wasn't suffering from any mental illness. Like John's killer, Mark Chapman, Abram was an obsessive Beatles fan whose worship had curdled into hatred and envy and who believed his homicidal mission to be 'doing God's will'.

George had received forty stab wounds which had punctured one lung and only just missed his heart. Olivia, the heroine of the night, needed stitches for the gash in her forehead and was badly cut and bruised.

As soon as he was able, he issued a statement of suitable Beatle jokiness, saying that Abram 'wasn't a burglar and certainly wasn't auditioning for the Traveling Wilburys', and quoting the Vedic scholar Adi Shankara: 'life is fragile like a raindrop on a lotus-leaf.'

Messages of sympathy poured in, from Paul, Ringo, fellow Wilbury Tom Petty (who quipped 'Aren't you glad you married a Mexican girl?') and thousands of his fans across three generations.

There was also an ugly manifestation of the different country Britain had become since the sunny, peace-loving Sixties. The author and playwright John Mortimer, who lived near Friar Park, recalled seeing a carload of people drive past its front gate, shouting their support for Michael Abram. Others sent flowers to Abram while he was in the hospital being treated for the battering Olivia had given him.

George's special *Monty Python* friend Eric Idle heard the news in California and rushed straight to Friar Park with his wife Tania, arriving in time to join in the *puja*, or thanksgiving, to Shiva that the assassin had been foiled. For Idle, George couldn't resist adding a Pythonesque detail to the bloody scene: that he'd been stretchered out to the ambulance in front of two house-keepers who'd just joined his staff, and asked them: 'What do you think of the job so far?'

His realisation of how much worse things would have been without the police's prompt arrival and bravery in facing the knife-wielding Abram unarmed still couldn't overcome his obsession with his personal privacy. The officer who'd held his hand and helped Dhani, Police Constable Matt Morgans, subsequently gave an interview to the *Henley Standard*, which hardly counted as broadcasting it to the world. Nonetheless, George was furious and had to be dissuaded by Olivia from making an official complaint.

It took eleven months for Abram to be tried at Oxford Crown Court on two counts of attempted murder. During that time there was severe criticism of Whiston Hospital, which had failed to properly assess his mental state while he was a patient there and so bore direct responsibility for his being at large to try to murder George. The chief executive of the hospital's governing body, Knowsley and St Helens NHS Trust, acknowledged its failings and made a public apology.

Abram himself had written a letter of apology to George and Olivia, pleading that he'd had no idea he was schizophrenic, so couldn't be held accountable for his crime. 'I thought my delusions were real,' it read in part, 'and everything I was experiencing was some kind of witchcraft.'

Olivia and Dhani attended the trial with heavy police and private security protection but George, still too weak from his wounds and traumatised by the experience to appear in person, was allowed to give written evidence.

The jury took two days to return a verdict. Abram was found not guilty by reason of insanity and ordered to be detained indefinitely at the Scott Clinic, a secure psychiatric unit at Rainhill, near Liverpool. The Harrisons' counsel, Geoffrey Robertson, asked that when he was released, the family should be given advance warning, but the judge said he had no powers to make such an order.

The family's response was given to the press by Dhani, making his first appearance in the public spotlight. 'It's tragic that anyone should suffer such a mental breakdown [but] we can never forget he was full of violence and hatred when he came into our home. Naturally the prospect of him being released back into society is abhorrent to us.'

'Indefinitely' in this case was to prove highly elastic. In July 2002 – by which time George was far beyond his reach – Abram was deemed fit to be released back 'into the community'. Three years later, he was reportedly training to become a volunteer adviser for the Citizens Advice Bureau.

That summer of 2000, George and Olivia had decided to brave the autograph-hunters and gawping tourists and spend some time at their house – or, rather, compound – on Hamilton Island. He'd taken a close interest in its construction, insisting that only local stone and wood be used and that his favourite tropical plants always took precedence over its stunning views of the Great Barrier Reef.

He gave it the ironic name 'Letsbeavenue', pronounced 'Let's be 'avin' you', a northern expression roughly translated as 'Come on in everyone. The more the merrier.' It's hard to imagine a more un-Georgian sentiment.

Like the Hollywood home of Burt Lancaster he'd visited with the Beatles in 1964, its swimming pool came right into the living room. And, like the lake at Friar Park, it had stepping stones so that he could enjoy the home-like sensation of walking on water.

'That was the last of our big journeys together,' Olivia was to say, 'and the start of a bigger one for George.'

The remastered *All Things Must Pass* was released in January 2001, a double rather than triple album this time, with several bonus tracks that had been left off the 1970 version. The particular bonus was George's re-recording of 'My Sweet Lord', its original Eric Clapton ensemble replaced by Joe Brown's daughter Sam on vocals, Ray Cooper on mega-percussion and Dhani on guitar and vocals, a first indication that his future might lie in music rather than racing car aerodynamics.

Twenty years on, the charge of plagiarising the Chiffons' 'He's So Fine' still rankled with George and he made a point of changing the three notes that had been the basis of the Bright Tunes lawsuit even though he now owned the copyright to 'He's So Fine', so was free to plagiarise it as he chose.

The new *All Things Must Pass* bore the label Gnome Records after the circle of garden gnomes that had surrounded his rubber-booted figure on its former black-and-white cover and still did on this colourised one. But the former bucolic view beyond Friar Park's lawns had changed to an urban wasteland of office buildings, a gasworks and a traffic flyover, symbolising the despoliation of the whole planet during the intervening years. The re-release was to become an even greater success than its predecessor, ultimately going seven times Platinum.

George's promotional round included a radio interview with Chris Carter for Los Angeles' Channel 103.1 in which he mentioned he now intended to remaster his entire back catalogue, 'to have everything nice and crisp and clean and fresh'. He'd just turned fifty-eight and clearly was still very far from his ambition 'to have no ambition'.

In March, he was due to go back into the studio with Jeff Lynne to begin work on a new album but, before it could happen, a check-up at the Mayo Clinic showed the cancer had returned, this time to his lungs. There was no provable medical connection but his wife and son had both sensed a new vulnerability in him since almost dying under Michael Abram's knife.

In contrast with the secrecy surrounding the first bout, the media were told he'd had part of one lung removed but had made 'an excellent recovery'; he was said to be 'in the best of spirits and on top form, the most relaxed since the attack on him in 1999' and with unexpected benevolence wished 'everyone all the very best, God bless and not to worry'.

But many suspected otherwise, among them his first wife, Pattie, when, after years of non-communication, George telephoned her at her cottage in West Sussex. 'He said, "I'm in the area visiting Ringo and Barbara and if you're home, I'll drop in and see you."'

That day, all the sweetness she remembered in him seemed to come flooding back. 'He brought me flowers and little presents, like a figure of the Indian monkey god, Hanuman. We walked in the field behind the cottage, he looked very fragile and somehow I knew it was the last time I'd ever see him.'

Of all the miseries George's illness would bring him, one of the worst was being separated from his beloved house and twice-beloved garden and turned into a nomad in search of a cure.

It took him first to Switzerland's Italian quarter to consult one of Europe's top cancer specialists, Professor Franco Cavalli at his San Giovanni clinic in Bellanzona. But Cavalli could only confirm an even grimmer diagnosis: the cancer had now spread to his brain.

Business worries showed no mercy, in particular his efforts to collect the $11 million in damages from Denis O'Brien that the California Court of Appeals had ratified three years earlier. In August, the ever-slippery O'Brien tried to get out of it by filing for bankruptcy in St Louis, where he'd settled.

George's attempt to prevent the filing via local lawyers was rejected by the judge because he hadn't given a personal deposition as Missouri law required. His lawyers' plea that he was too ill to do so was dismissed because not long previously he'd travelled to Rhode Island for Dhani's graduation from Brown. The judge described the non-appearance of a plaintiff suffering from cancer as 'wilful'.

His treatment by Professor Cavalli was to last several months, so he paid £7 million for a house just outside Bellanzona, a Palladian-style villa named Collina d'Oro, perched high above Lake Lugano that had once belonged to the writer and Nobel Laureate Hermann Hesse. He also got himself on a fast track to Swiss residency that would deny millions to the British Taxman.

At Collina d'Oro he began songwriting and recording demos

with Dhani under the name Swiss Army Studios after the multi-blade Swiss Army clasp knife. With gallows humour, he used one of his cancers to title their album-in-progress *Brainwashed* and credited the songs to 'R.I.P. Music Ltd'.

A steady stream of visitors came from Britain to see him, among them Michael Palin, who was distressed to see George's once-luxuriant hair all burned away by the chemotherapy he'd been having. 'One evening, I remember, George spent the whole time playing Hoagy Carmichael songs. The next evening, we watched a documentary on Swiss TV about Hitler. It's strange to think of my last moments with him being spent like that.'

The British press had already discovered where he was, and guessed why. 'When I walked past a window, Dhani warned me not to show myself,' Palin recalls. 'Someone from the *Mail* or the *Mail On Sunday* had been spotted that day in the village.'

Ringo also came, by which time 'George was very ill . . . he could only lay down. I had to leave and go to Boston where my daughter, Lee, was also having treatment for a brain tumour. The last words I heard him say were: "Do you want me to come with you?" That was the incredible side of George.'

When no cure was to be found in Switzerland's clear mountain air, the nomad moved on, or was moved on, to the more questionable air of Staten Island in New York City.

His last hope was a new technique for treating brain tumours called fractionated stereotactic radiosurgery, developed at Staten Island University Hospital, in which a frame attached to the patient's skull focused the radiation beams on the tumour more accurately but in smaller doses, so causing less damage to surrounding tissue.

He, Olivia and Dhani stayed in a small – by his standards – rented house near the hospital, where visitors could come and go without restriction. One of the first was Paul: the long antagonism between them instantly evaporated, they hugged and agreed how silly all those disputes about guitar solos had been.

His sister Louise came from Benton, Illinois, where she still lived, far from affluently. Latterly, George had given her a monthly pension of $2,000, but had broken off contact after she became involved in turning the house where he'd stayed with her in 1962 into a 'Beatle bed-and breakfast' called the Hard Day's Nite.

She found the baby brother she'd once adored propped in a chair, looking desperately frail. Olivia left them alone together and they spent an hour and a half holding hands and reminiscing about their childhood in the Harrison family's tiny house in Wavertree; how she'd loved to bath and dress him, taught him the alphabet, and calmed his fear of going to the dark outdoor privy.

Like all of George's visitors, she found the bombardments of radiation hadn't killed off her brother's sense of humour. As a child, he'd been teased for his protruding ears: now he indicated the oxygen tube looped over them and said they'd come in useful for something at last.

In his case, the fractionated stereotactic radiosurgery proved ineffectual, and was to have a sour sequel when he was no longer around.

In 2004, his estate filed a $10 million lawsuit against the hospital and its director of radiation oncology, Dr Gilbert Lederman, alleging that only two weeks before George's death Dr Lederman had taken advantage of his enfeebled condition by making him listen to Lederman's young son, Ariel, play the guitar, then autograph the guitar and sign autographs for his two daughters while a photograph was being taken.

According to the suit, a 'weak and exhausted' George had protested, 'I don't even know if I know how to sign my name any more' but the doctor had guided the pen in his hand, urging: 'Come on, you can do this.' The photograph of himself with Ariel and the guitar had afterwards appeared in the *National Enquirer* in hopes of increasing its value.

Lederman denied exploiting his patient, claiming they had had 'a close personal relationship', and the case was settled by Ariel surrendering the autographed guitar and receiving a new one in exchange.

George's final problem, putting it brutally, was where to die. It should have been Friar Park among the shades of Sir Frank Crisp, with his garden horizonless outside the window, but he couldn't bear the thought of the reporters waiting for the news like birds of prey at the front gate.

The same applied to the houses in Switzerland and on Maui and Hamilton Island, the existence of all of which had become well known. The end of his life found him still seeking the absolute privacy he'd so seldom found throughout it.

The answer came from the fellow Beatle who'd never felt any such obsession. Paul had recently bought a house in Beverly Hills, Los Angeles, of which the media were still unaware and which he offered to George as a token of their rekindled friendship.

There he spent his last days under palliative care provided by the University of California Los Angeles Medical Center and guarded by the security consultant Gavin de Becker whose celebrity clients included Dolly Parton, Jane Fonda, Tina Turner and John Travolta.

One of his last visitors was Eric Idle. 'Even his death was filled with laughter,' Idle would write. 'In the hospital, he asked the nurses to put fish and chips into his intravenous feeding-tube. The doctor, thinking he was delusional, told Dhani, "Don't worry, we have a medical name for this condition."

'"Yes," Dhani said. "Humour."'

George died on 29 November 2001, just after 1.30 p.m. Pacific time with Olivia and Dhani at his side, his favourite Hari Krishnas Shyamsundara and Mukunda softly chanting, pictures of Krishna and Rama on the walls and sweet-smouldering incense – completing the circle begun one wartime Liverpool night when he'd been born in the same bed as his three older siblings and his mother, Louise, had prophesied this one would be 'special'.

Olivia was to recall his passing as a moment of 'profound beauty', the room seeming momentarily to light up as the soul left the body.

He had asked to be cremated according to Hindu custom, which meant immediately after death. Within twenty minutes, a team from the Hollywood Forever funeral home collected his body, placed it in a cardboard coffin, transported it in an unmarked van to the UCLA Medical Center for the official paperwork, then to the nearest Hindu temple for the simplest of ceremonies costing the equivalent of £350. His ashes were then turned over to Olivia to be taken to India and scattered onto the River Ganges.

To keep the secret of Paul's house, the media were initially told George had passed away at the home of his security consultant, Gavin de Becker; then Olivia entered on his death certificate that he'd died at 1971 Coldwater Canyon, a fictitious address using the year of the Concert For Bangladesh.

Hinduism allowed a maximum of thirteen days between a person's demise and the casting of his or her ashes into the Ganges. Accordingly, large crowds gathered at the customary spot in Varanasi to witness this ceremony for George but when the thirteenth day ended without anything happening, the police ordered them to disperse.

By then, the ceremony had already been performed in two different places: Brindavan, where Krishna allegedly spent his boyhood, and Allahabad, the confluence of the Ganges with two other sacred rivers, the Yamuna and the Saraswati.

How like him to remain elusive to the last – and beyond.

Epilogue: Plaudit from a Prince

In 2004, ten years after John and five after Paul, in their eternal pecking-order, George is inducted into the Rock & Roll Hall of Fame as a solo performer. The subsequent musical tribute features his co-inductors Tom Petty and Jeff Lynne (*still* wearing that annoying hat) with a stage full of musicians including Dhani and Steve Winwood in a by-the-book rendition of 'While My Guitar Gently Weeps'.

The book gets comprehensively rewritten, however, when a slight figure walks onstage unannounced, wearing a pink trilby hat, an explosion of pink shirtfront and a charcoal grey frock coat, thigh-length on one side, knee-length on the other. It's the artist who, despite his change of name to an unpronounceable hieroglyphic, will always be known as Prince.

On a caramel-coloured guitar that looks a size too big, he plunges into a solo instantly eclipsing every legendary picker there ever was – Scotty Moore, Keith Richards, James Burton, even Eric Clapton, even Jimi Hendrix – much of it seemingly produced by a single oscillating finger at the very edge of his fretboard. It is a display to convince the sourest sceptic that rock can be high art. It goes on and on surpassing itself, making even this author forget about rendering music as prose and simply watch and marvel and wish it would never end.

When at last it does, he sinks to his knees in front of Dhani, whose look of amazed delight suggests none of it was rehearsed. He unstraps his guitar, hurls it to the ground and strolls away, a secretive smile his only response to the wild applause behind him.

Thus the final and most meaningful requiem for George: to be saluted by genius.

ACKNOWLEDGEMENTS

I must first acknowledge a serious mistake. When George died, the London *Sunday Times* asked me to write an obituary for the front of its Review section. At that time, almost everything I knew about him had gone into *Shout!*, my Beatles biography, first published twenty years earlier, which had ended with the band's breakup and barely mentioned their respective solo careers. Having no time for further research or reflection, I judged George solely on his years with Ringo in an obvious second division where he so often radiated impatience and discontentment.

My article ran to more than 3,000 words and was unremittingly negative, in places crudely insulting. It was meant to counteract the gush of his other obituarists but went much too far the other way and gave great offence to many people, among them several professional colleagues whose opinions I respected. It has been on the Internet ever since, a troubling blot on my record given seemingly everlasting life.

While writing the individual biographies of John and Paul, then one of George's best friends, Eric Clapton, I began to see how wrong I had been. Even so, I was unprepared for the many discoveries and surprises in this journey through George's fifty-eight years. They have something in common with the labyrinth underneath Friar Park's garden where one side-cave might display a jewel, the next a skeleton.

My abiding regret is not having spoken to his second wife, Olivia, and their son, Dhani, who have done so much to keep his memory alive. After my *Sunday Times* obituary, I could hardly expect Olivia to see me, as I told her in a private letter of apology. I can only hope she – and his fans – feel I've now redeemed myself.

My heartfelt thanks go to George's first wife, the former Pattie Boyd, whose memories of their life together, often bizarre or hilarious, are untainted by the slightest bitterness; to my research associate, Peter Trollope, for the same brilliant work he put into five of my nine previous music biographies; to Bill Harry, that incomparable fount of Beatle knowledge for advice and guidance; to the erudite Alan Clayson, author of his own George biography, who magnanimously fact-checked my manuscript (as did Bill Harry); to Steve Abbott and John Reiss, who helped me piece together the massive financial fraud perpetrated on George which added to the burden of his cruel final illness.

I'm grateful all over again to the leading players in the Beatles' saga I interviewed for *Shout!* and the Lennon and McCartney biographies, whose testimony has proved relevant here. Some of them turned from 'sources' into friends and many are no longer with us: Neil Aspinall, Mona Best, Mal Evans, Clive Epstein, Queenie Epstein, Joe Flannery, Bill Graham, Bert Kaempfert, Bruno Koschmider, Astrid Kirchherr, Cynthia Lennon, Ray McFall, Gerry Marsden, Sir George Martin, Larry Parnes, Tony

Sheridan, Mimi Smith, Millie Sutcliffe, Pauline Sutcliffe, Derek Taylor, Allan Williams and Bob Wooler.

Thanks also for help past and present to Arthur Ballard. Carol Bedford, Pete Best, Tony Bramwell, Peter Brown, Bernadette Byrne, the former Iris Caldwell, Royston Ellis, Quentin Falk, Horst Fascher, Ray Foulk, Johnny Gentle, Debbie Greenberg, Jim Gretty, John Gustafson, Colin Hanton, Johnny Hutchinson, Peter Kavanagh, Arthur Kelly, Frieda Kelly, Yoko Ono Lennon, Richard Lester, Michael Lindsay-Hogg, Sir Paul McCartney, Ray McFall, Sir George Martin, Chas Newby, Chris O'Dell, Sir Michael Palin, Paul Saltzman, Tom Scott, Walter Shenson, Iain Taylor, Jürgen Vollmer and Klaus Voormann.

A final word of sincere appreciation to my American agent and dear friend, Peter Matson and Christopher Combemale at Sterling Lord Literistic, to my ever supportive UK agent, Fiona Petheram, and Lucy Barry and Laurie Robertson at Peters, Fraser & Dunlop, to Rick Horgan, Brian Belfiglio and Sophie Guimaraes at Scribner, and Suzanne Baboneau and Sophia Akhtar at Simon & Schuster UK.

This book is dedicated to my wife, Sue, and daughter, Jessica, always my first and most influential readers.

Philip Norman
London, 2023

SOURCE NOTES

1. 'TAKE CARE OF HIM BECAUSE HE'S GOING TO
BE SPECIAL'

Shout!: The Beatles in their Generation by Philip Norman,
   Fireside, 1981.
The Beatles Anthology, Chronicle Books, 2000.
I Me Mine by George Harrison, Harrisongs Ltd, 2017.
Interviews with Iain Taylor, Arthur Kelly, Bert Weedon, Iris
   Caldwell, Tony Bramwell and Jim Gretty.

2. 'HE WAS SO MUCH IN THE BACKGROUND HE WAS LIKE
THE INVISIBLE MAN'

Shout! by Philip Norman.
John Lennon: The Life by Philip Norman, Ecco, 2008.
Paul McCartney: The Biography by Philip Norman, Weidenfeld &
   Nicolson, 2016.
The Beatles Anthology.
Rave On: The Biography of Buddy Holly by Philip Norman, Simon

& Schuster, 1996. *Pre: Fab* by Colin Hanton, The Book Guild, 2018.

Interviews with Arthur Kelly, Colin Hanton, Mimi Smith, Arthur Ballard, Cynthia Lennon, Tony Bramwell and Bill Harry.

3. 'PLAYING JUST CHORDS WAS BETTER THAN NOT PLAYING AT ALL'

The Beatles Anthology.

I Me Mine by George Harrison.

Shout! by Philip Norman.

Paul McCartney: The Biography by Philip Norman.

Rave On: The Biography of Buddy Holly by Philip Norman.

George Harrison: Living in the Material World, documentary, dir. Martin Scorsese, 2011.

Interviews with Mimi Smith, Carl Perkins. Arthur Kelly, Pete Best, Mona Best, Millie Sutcliffe and Bill Harry.

4. 'FROM THEN, NINE-TO-FIVE NEVER CAME BACK INTO MY THINKING'

Shout! by Philip Norman.

The Beatles Anthology.

Paul McCartney: The Biography by Philip Norman.

Interviews with Mona Best, Rod Murray, Bill Harry, Arthur Kelly, Cynthia Lennon, Millie Sutcliffe, Allan Williams, Larry Parnes, Johnny Gentle, Tommy Moore and Johnny Hutchinson.

5. 'WE WERE LIKE ORPHANS'

Shout! by Philip Norman.
Paul McCartney: The Biography by Philip Norman.
John Lennon: The Life by Philip Norman.
The Beatles Anthology.
Interviews with Ray Ennis, Bill Harry, Mona Best, Rod Murray, Millie Sutcliffe, Allan Williams, Larry Parnes, Johnny Gentle, Tommy Moore and Royston Ellis.

6. 'MY FIRST SHAG ... WITH JOHN AND PAUL AND PETE BEST ALL WATCHING'

Shout! by Philip Norman.
John Lennon: The Life by Philip Norman.
Paul McCartney: The Biography by Philip Norman.
The Beatles Anthology.
Interviews with Allan Williams, Pete Best, Mona Best, Bruno Koschmider, Klaus Voormann, Astrid Kirchherr, Jürgen Vollmer and Millie Sutcliffe.

7. 'THE FIRST ROCK 'N' DOLE GROUP'

Shout! by Philip Norman.
John Lennon: The Life by Philip Norman.
Paul McCartney: The Biography by Philip Norman.
The Beatles Anthology.
Cavern Club, The Inside Story by Debbie Greenberg, Jorvik Press, 2016.
Interviews with Tony Bramwell, Chas Newby, Bob Wooler, Brian

Kelly, Mimi Smith, Tony Sheridan, Brian Kelly, Neil Aspinall, Ray McFall, Debbie Greenberg, Cynthia Lennon, Frieda Kelly and Bert Kaempfert.

8. 'IT WAS THE BEST BUZZ OF ALL TIME'

Shout! by Philip Norman.
John Lennon: The Life by Philip Norman.
Paul McCartney: The Biography by Philip Norman.
The Beatles Anthology.
Magical Mystery Tours: My Life With The Beatles by Tony Bramwell, Robson Books, 2005.
Interviews with Queenie Epstein, Clive Epstein, Joe Flannery, Bill Harry, Bob Wooler, Alistair Taylor, Dick Rowe, Bernardette Farrell, Iris Caldwell, Mimi Smith, Sir George Martin, Millie Sutcliffe, Astrid Kirchherr, Jürgen Vollmer, Klaus Voormann and Horst Fascher.

9. 'I WAS ALWAYS RATHER BEASTLY TO GEORGE'

Shout! by Philip Norman.
The Beatles Anthology.
John Lennon: The Life by Philip Norman.
Paul McCartney: The Biography by Philip Norman.
Forever Young, A Memoir by Hayley Mills, Orion, 2021.
George Harrison: Living in the Material World (documentary).
Interviews with Sir George Martin, Neil Aspinall, Derek Taylor, Dick Rowe and Bernardette O'Farrell.

10. 'I HAD TO LEARN TO THINK LIKE A SPY, LEAVING NO TRACE'

Shout! by Philip Norman.

The Beatles Anthology.

John Lennon: The Life by Philip Norman.

Paul McCartney: The Biography by Philip Norman.

Wonderful Tonight: George Harrison, Eric Clapton and Me by Pattie Boyd, Crown, 2003.

A Hard Day's Night souvenir booklet.

Interviews with Pattie Boyd, Sir George Martin, Neil Aspinall, Derek Taylor, Richard Lester and Walter Shenson.

11. 'THE ONLY BEATLE GLARE EVER CAUGHT ON CAMERA'

Shout! by Philip Norman.

The Beatles Anthology.

Paul McCartney: The Biography by Philip Norman.

John Lennon: The Life by Philip Norman.

George Harrison: Living in the Material World (documentary).

Wonderful Tonight by Pattie Boyd.

Interviews with Pattie Boyd, Sir George Martin, Neil Aspinall, Cynthia Lennon, Derek Taylor, Larry Kane, Richard Lester and Arthur Kelly.

12. 'WELL, THAT'S IT. I'M NOT A BEATLE ANY MORE'

Shout! by Philip Norman.

The Beatles Anthology.

John Lennon: The Life by Philip Norman.

Paul McCartney: The Biography by Philip Norman.

Wonderful Tonight by Pattie Boyd.

Eight Days A Week, film, dir. Ron Howard, 2016.

Interviews with Neil Aspinall, Pattie Boyd and Cynthia Lennon.

13. 'The meditation buzz'

Shout! by Philip Norman.

John Lennon: The Life by Philip Norman.

Paul McCartney: The Biography by Philip Norman.

Slowhand: The Life and Music of Eric Clapton by Philip Norman, Weidenfeld & Nicolson, 2018.

Karma and Rebirth by Christmas Humphreys, Chapman Press, 1948. Interviews with Sir George Martin, Klaus Voormann, Keith Richards, Marianne Faithfull, Pattie Boyd, Derek Taylor, Joan Taylor, Jenny Boyd and Paul Saltzman.

14. 'Please don't think I've gone off my rocker'

Shout! by Philip Norman.

John Lennon: The Life by Philip Norman.

Paul McCartney: The Biography by Philip Norman.

Slowhand: The Life and Music of Eric Clapton by Philip Norman, Weidenfeld & Nicolson, 2018.

Karma and Rebirth by Christmas Humphreys, Chapman Press, 1948.

Interviews with Sir George Martin, Klaus Voormann, Keith Richards, Marianne Faithfull, Pattie Boyd, Derek Taylor, Joan Taylor, Jenny Boyd and Paul Saltzman.

15. 'DON'T UPSET THE HELL'S ANGELS'

Shout! by Philip Norman.
The BeatlesAnthology.
John Lennon: The Life by Philip Norman.
Paul McCartney: The Biography by Philip Norman.
Slowhand by Philip Norman.
Wonderful Tonight by Pattie Boyd.
The Longest Cocktail Party by Richard DiLello, Playboy Press, 1973.
Interviews with Sir George Martin, Pattie Boyd, Neil Aspinall,
    Yoko Ono Lennon, Derek Taylor and Philippe Mora. Author's
    eyewitness observations.

16. 'HE WANTED SO MUCH TO BE A SPIRITUAL BEING'

Shout! by Philip Norman.
Paul McCartney: The Biography by Philip Norman.
Slowhand by Philip Norman.
Wonderful Tonight by Pattie Boyd.
Get Back documentaries dir. Peter Jackson, 2022.
Interviews with Pattie Boyd, Sir George Martin, Yoko Ono
    Lennon, Neil Aspinall, Allen Klein, Derek Taylor, John
    Eastman, Charlotte Martin and Michael Lindsay-Hogg. Author's
    eyewitness observations.

17. 'THAT WAS MINXY OF GEORGE. HE COULD BE VERY MINXY'

Shout! by Philip Norman.
Paul McCartney: The Biography by Philip Norman.

John Lennon: The Life by Philip Norman.

Slowhand by Philip Norman.

Wonderful Tonight by Pattie Boyd.

Get Back documentaries dir. Peter Jackson.

Interviews with Yoko Ono Lennon, Sir George Martin, Pattie Boyd, Neil Aspinall, Derek Taylor, Allen Klein, John Eastman, Bonnie Bramlett and Ray Foulk. Author's eyewitness observations.

18. 'Beatle George's new pad – turrets and all'

Shout! by Philip Norman.

I Me Mine by George Harrison.

John Lennon: The Life by Philip Norman.

Paul McCartney: The Biography by Philip Norman.

Wonderful Tonight by Pattie Boyd.

Waiting for The Beatles: An Apple Scruff's Story by Carol Bedford, Blandford Press, 1984.

Auctioneers' prospectus for Friar Park, 1920s.

Interviews with Sir George Martin, Yoko Ono Lennon, Pattie Boyd, Neil Aspinall, Allen Klein, Tony Bramwell and Carol Bedford.

19. 'Garbo speaks – Harrison is free'

Shout! by Philip Norman.

John Lennon: The Life by Philip Norman.

Paul McCartney: The Biography by Philip Norman.

Miss O'Dell: Hard Days and Long Nights with the Beatles, the Stones, Bob Dylan and Eric Clapton by Chris O'Dell, Touchstone. 2009.

Waiting for The Beatles by Carol Bedford.

The Times Law Report.
Interviews with Chris O'Dell, Pattie Boyd, Carol Bedford and
    John Eastman.

20. 'I SUPPOSE HE IS STILL A PERSON OF CONSIDERABLE
MEANS'

Shout! by Philip Norman.
John Lennon: The Life by Philip Norman.
Paul McCartney: The Biography by Philip Norman.
*Miss O'Dell: Hard Days and Long Nights with the Beatles, the Stones,
    Bob Dylan and Eric Clapton* by Chris O'Dell, Touchstone. 2009.
Waiting for The Beatles by Carol Bedford.
The Times Law Report.
Interviews with Chris O'Dell, Pattie Boyd, Carol Bedford and
    John Eastman.

21. 'I HAVE TO TELL YOU, MAN, I'M IN LOVE WITH
YOUR WIFE'

Slowhand by Philip Norman.
Miss O'Dell by Chris O'Dell.
Wonderful Tonight by Pattie Boyd.
Waiting for The Beatles by Carol Bedford.
Once Were Brothers: Robbie Robertson and The Band, documentary
    dir. Daniel Roher, 2019.
Interviews with Pattie Boyd, Chris O'Dell, Carol Bedford.

22. 'BY THE GRACE OF KRISHNA, YOU ARE ONE OF THE GREAT MEN'

John Lennon: The Life by Philip Norman.
Ronnie, The Autobiography of Ronnie Wood, St Martin's Press 2007.
Slowhand by Philip Norman.
Waiting for The Beatles by Carol Bedford.
Miss O'Dell by Chris O'Dell.
Wonderful Tonight by Pattie Boyd.
Interviews with Pattie Boyd, Chris O'Dell, Carol Bedford.

23. 'IF PEOPLE WANT THEIR MONEY BACK, THEY CAN HAVE IT'

The Stones by Philip Norman, Penguin, 1984.
Wonderful Tonight by Pattie Boyd.
John Lennon: The Life by Philip Norman.
Miss O'Dell by Chris O'Dell.
Slowhand by Philip Norman.
Interviews with Yoko Ono Lennon, Pattie Boyd, Chris O'Dell,
    Tom Scott, Bill Graham.

24. 'INTRODUCING GEORGE HARRISON'

John Lennon: The Life by Philip Norman.
Paul McCartney: The Biography by Philip Norman.
Wonderful Tonight by Pattie Boyd.
Always Look on the Bright Side of Life: A Sortabiography by Eric Idle,
    Weidenfeld & Nicolson, 2018.
Interviews with Sir Michael Palin, Pattie Boyd, Chris O'Dell.

25. 'THE MOST EXPENSIVE CINEMA TICKET IN HISTORY'

John Lennon: The Life by Philip Norman.

Paul McCartney: The Biography by Philip Norman.

Wonderful Tonight by Pattie Boyd.

Always Look on the Bright Side of Life: A Sortabiography by Eric Idle, Weidenfeld & Nicolson, 2018.

Interviews with Sir Michael Palin, Pattie Boyd, Chris O'Dell.

26. 'MAYBE HE THOUGHT GOD WOULD JUST SORT OF LET HIM OFF'

John Lennon: The Life by Philip Norman.

Paul McCartney: The Biography by Philip Norman.

Slowhand by Philip Norman.

George Harrison: Living in the Material World, (documentary).

Wonderful Tonight by Pattie Boyd.

Faster: A Racer's Diary by Jackie Stewart, Farrar, Straus and Giroux, 1972.

Very Naughty Boys: The Amazing True Story of HandMade Films by Robert Sellers, Titan, 2003.

Interviews with Sir Michael Palin, Steve Abbott, Pattie Boyd.

27. 'HE WAS LOOKING AT POTENTIAL DEBTS OF AROUND £32 MILLION'

Elton: The Biography of Elton John by Philip Norman, Hutchinson,1990.

Slowhand by Philip Norman.

Paul McCartney: The Biography by Philip Norman.

Very Naughty Boys by Robert Sellers.

Always Look on the Bright Side of Life by Eric Idle.
Interviews with Sir Michael Palin, Steve Abbott, John Reiss,
  Vivien Griffin.

28. 'DO YOU WANT TO GO ON A YACHT TO THE SOUTH PACIFIC AND RUN AWAY FOR EVER?'

John Lennon: The Life by Philip Norman.
Paul McCartney: The Biography by Philip Norman.
Very Naughty Boys by Robert Sellers.
Always Look on the Bright Side of Life by Eric Idle.
Olivia Harrison interview, *Sunday Times*, 2022. Interviews with
  Yoko Ono Lennon, Sir George Martin, Sir Michael Palin, Neil
  Aspinall, Derek Taylor, Mal Jeffries.

29. 'I'M BEING MURDERED IN MY OWN HOUSE'

Press reports of Michael Abram's trial and rehabilitation.
Interviews with Pattie Boyd, Kingsize Taylor, Sir Michael Palin.

INDEX